International Social Work

PROFESSIONAL ACTION IN AN INTERDEPENDENT WORLD

Second Edition

Lynne M. Healy

OXFORD

UNIVERSITY PRESS

2008

OXFORD
UNIVERSITY PRESS

Oxford University Press, Inc., publishes works that further
Oxford University's objective of excellence
in research, scholarship, and education.

Oxford   New York
Auckland   Cape Town   Dar es Salaam   Hong Kong   Karachi
Kuala Lumpur   Madrid   Melbourne   Mexico City   Nairobi
New Delhi   Shanghai   Taipei   Toronto

With offices in
Argentina   Austria   Brazil   Chile   Czech Republic   France   Greece
Guatemala   Hungary   Italy   Japan   Poland   Portugal   Singapore
South Korea   Switzerland   Thailand   Turkey   Ukraine   Vietnam

Published by Oxford University Press, Inc.
198 Madison Avenue, New York, New York 10016
www.oup.com

Oxford is a registered trademark of Oxford University Press

The Library of Congress has cataloged the first edition as follows:
Healy, Lynne M.
International social work : professional action in an interdependent world /
Lynne M. Healy.
p. cm.
Includes bibliographic references and index.
ISBN 978-0-19-512445-3; 978-0-19-512446-0 (pbk.)
1. Social work—International cooperation.   2. Social workers—vocational guidance.
I. Title.
HV40.35. H43 2001
361.3'2—dc21   00-058875
ISBN 9780195301670

Photographs by Lynne M. Healy or Henry S. Healy unless otherwise credited.

9 8 7 6 5 4 3 2 1

Printed in the United States of America
on acid-free paper

To my husband, Henry,
and son, Michael,
for their love and support,
and to my colleagues
in the International Association of Schools
of Social Work
for all that I have learned from them

Foreword

Lynne Healy, in the first edition of this scholarly book, presented to all concerned with individual well-being and social justice the challenge of global interdependence and how to meet it. This second edition responds to the book's highly favorable reception by social work educators and other readers in the United States and around the world. What was already an impressive volume now provides significant additional content with coverage even more comprehensive than before of the many facets of international social work. Expanded and updated content on globalization brings into sharp focus its impact, positive and negative, on social policies and programs, the economy, cultural traditions, and the environment. Along with development and human rights, globalization is placed at the core of international social work.

The social work profession has begun to recognize the impact of globalization on almost every problem with which its practitioners are involved. Universal everyday problems, such as poverty, hunger, women's issues, aging populations, family breakdowns, drug addiction, and child abuse and neglect, persist while massive new problems have emerged. The worldwide spread of AIDS has established a new category of abandoned and orphaned children while civil strife has led to the mustering of children as soldiers. Increasingly negative approaches to immigration policy along with denial of basic rights and services to migrants have created a host of national and transnational problems. Armed conflict and ethnic cleansing have given rise to new waves of refugees and displaced persons, exacerbating an already critical problem.

In this new edition, Dr. Healy clearly demonstrates how the nature and substance of social problems such as those noted above are affected by globalization. While giving full recognition to its negative impact on human welfare and the social environment, she directs attention not only to its real and potential benefits but also to its continued presence as an "irrefutable fact of life." The many ways in which global interdependence affects social work practice are described initially in a new Chapter 2 on globalization and spelled out in further detail in additional new chapters. Even the most skeptical of critics will find convincing evidence that globalization as presented by Healy does indeed set the context for the practice of international social work in the twenty-first century.

Several completely new chapters provide a wealth of information within that context for use by social work educators and practitioners. To the question of what makes a social problem global, Healy identifies and discusses in clarifying detail in Chapter 4 a series of issues and problems that will sound familiar to social workers but take on new meaning when seen within an international frame of reference. Pervasive worldwide poverty, the root of most of the problems with which social workers deal, is properly characterized as the most fundamental of all global problems. Addressing poverty and related problems on a global scale is the subject of Chapter 3 in which development and human rights are put forward as concepts central to international social work.

The reduction of poverty and the miseries it fosters is a major goal of development, whether seen as a process or end result. As in the case of globalization, critics within the social work profession have raised many questions about the success or failure of development strategies and programs in achieving that goal. In Chapter 3, Dr. Healy analyzes the complex relationship between development and poverty and provides sufficient background information to encourage careful and reasoned assessment of the outcomes of a variety of different approaches to improving the conditions of the poor. Social development, a subject of special interest for social work, has for a number of decades been discussed but not fully accepted as an area of professional education and practice.

There was a missed opportunity in the turbulent 1960s and early 1970s for more active involvement in development when changing the social system became a burning issue for many social work educators and students. At the same time, educators in the developing countries were voicing discontent with the Western-oriented model of social work education. A possible breakthrough did in fact come for the developing countries when the historic United Nations Conference of Ministers of Social Welfare, held in 1968, challenged the profession to find a new approach to social welfare through emphasis on a development function. International and regional seminars on developmental social welfare figured prominently in Africa and Asia as sources of help and encouragement as schools of social work sought to reorient their educational programs. What emerged was a stronger emphasis on community work, an important avenue for social development, but considerably short of what would be needed for full participation in national development programs. In the Western world, development was often discussed but, as noted by Healy, it is still not a widely understood concept.

Although developmental social welfare was often overshadowed by economic development, a number of international social work scholars continued to document the need for a recognized contribution of the profession to the achievement of social development goals. Their perseverance and production of excellent material on the positive results of social development along with a growing interest in international social work have created a new and welcoming audience. Dr. Healy's portrayal of development appears at an opportune time for serious consideration of the relevance of its theories and principles to the practice of international social work.

Beginning with a sound overview in Chapter 3, human rights is introduced as a companion priority of the global community and a particularly relevant framework for international social work. Although social work may indeed be a human rights profession in terms of its values and philosophy, explicit emphasis on human rights is much more recent. The information and analysis presented in Chapter 3 and elaborated in later chapters brings the Universal Declaration of Human Rights, shepherded through the then-new United Nations by Eleanor Roosevelt, to life for social work practice and ethical theory.

For over a century, social work has demonstrated some ambivalence about its role as a global profession. The United States in particular has had an off-and-on engagement with international movements and professional activities and, until recently, neglected international content in social work curricula. Neglect of international content in the social work curriculum is perhaps due not so much to lack of interest on the part of faculty members, but rather to lack of knowledge, particularly knowledge drawn from first-hand experience in other lands. This has not always been the case. In fact, the importance of international communication can been seen as far back as the later years of the nineteenth century and the early twentieth century.

The historical record of the profession contains many descriptions of the way in which the problems and remedial programs associated with poverty devised in Britain traveled across the Atlantic. Stephen Gurteen spent a summer in London observing the work of the Charity Organization Society, adapted what he saw to the needs of Buffalo, New York, and founded a nationwide movement. Mary Richmond visited London and looked to Britain's friendly visiting for guidance on what became American social casework. After an eye-opening visit to Toynbee Hall in London, Jane Addams established Hull House in Chicago. Edith Abbott studied at the London School of Economics; and for decades, every issue of the *Social Service Review* contained significant material on social movements and professional developments in other countries.

Organizations, as well as individuals, fostered an international exchange of ideas and experience. An International Conference of Charities, Correction and Philanthropy held in Chicago in 1893 at the time of the World's Fair brought together a considerable number of charity workers and philanthropists from a variety of countries to remodel charity work as scientific philanthropy. Although the need to replicate this gathering was often discussed in charity circles, it was not until 1928 that some 3,000 delegates from 42 countries met in Paris to search again for a new and improved approach to humanitarian work. At that meeting, under the leadership of Dr. René Sand of Belgium, two significant professional organizations were founded: the International Conference of Social Work (now the International Council on Social Welfare) and the International Committee of Schools of Social Work (now the International Association of Schools of Social Work). The attention paid to the enduring influence of pioneers like Dr. Sand and to the international professional social work organizations is an important feature of Dr. Healy's book.

World War II and its aftermath engaged U.S. social workers and educators in international efforts. With the advent of the United Nations in 1945, the entire profession, as represented by the national employing agencies, the professional associations of social workers, and schools of social work, recognized the need for U.S. social workers to contribute to humanitarian efforts to deal with the massive social problems caused by World War II and its aftermath. The time was ripe for an international awakening. Educational exchange and advisory services, originally authorized by the U.S. Congress in 1939 to foster good neighbor relations with Latin America, had already involved schools of social work and individual faculty members in consultation assignments and work with colleagues from other countries. Many educators and practitioners had also served in the relief and welfare activities of UN Relief and Rehabilitation Administration (UNRRA) as explained by Healy. All the major voluntary social work organizations together with key governmental agencies came together to work with the United Nations and promote continuing international cooperation in the field of social welfare through a permanent Committee on International Organization for Social Work. This Committee continued to operate for many years within the National Social Welfare Assembly.

The United Nations undoubtedly exerted the major energizing influence on social work to embrace international activities and was largely responsible for the rapid spread of programs of social work education throughout the developing world. The Social Commission, now the Commission for Social Development, assumed broad responsibility for humanitarian programs, leading to emphasis on social welfare programs and services. U.S. social workers, particularly social work educators, were much in demand for assignments in other countries as consultants and as mentors to colleagues from abroad in social welfare exchange programs. Firsthand international experience inevitably influenced the educators in their teaching; at the same time, scores of social welfare personnel, in all categories from the highest government officials to the untrained aspiring social workers, flocked to the United States for programs of observation and professional education. Whether from granting or receiving countries, social workers who were involved at the time in international or bilateral exchange programs and advisory services remember, with wistful appreciation, the exciting and rewarding experience of sharing with colleagues from around the world. And only those who participated perhaps understand the hunger expressed for help in reconstructing social work education in the war-torn countries and in developing services and training of personnel in the new nations.

At a later date, the result of this intensive international involvement was excoriated as social work imperialism. Instances of inappropriate imposition of educational structures and content may indeed have existed, but again, this was probably due to insufficient knowledge of other cultures and their social and economic forces. This book—especially Chapter 8 on similarities and differences in social work around the world, Chapter 9 on values and ethics, and the new Chapter 13 on international exchange—provides the essential knowledge for productive collegial interaction in international work. The expression of discontent with the borrowing of foreign models of social work mentioned earlier coincided with preoccupation with domestic problems in the United States in the 1960s and early 1970s, pretty much eliminating the flourishing internationalism of the immediate postwar period. Social work schools and practitioners focused on student unrest, domestic poverty, and civil rights movements; and a general malaise related to the Vietnam War turned many against international involvement. With the end of the cold war and emergence of requests from countries of the former Soviet block for assistance in establishing social work education, interest in international social work reemerged.

As this comprehensive book thoroughly demonstrates, social work must be international to be relevant in the twenty-first century. The social problems and conditions arising out of globalization create for the social work profession significant areas of international responsibility and demands for expanded knowledge and competencies. This, combined with the far-reaching opportunities offered by the technological revolution in communication, makes international involvement inevitable.

In her closing chapter, Healy sums up the challenges of the twenty-first century and outlines the opportunities for social work, if it finds its true mission as a global profession, to make a stronger positive impact on poverty and its related problems. She charts ambitious goals for international social work. Inevitably, a question arises as to the possibility of their achievement. Dr. Healy makes it clear that the place to start is in preparation for the profession. Certainly it is hard to imagine a social work career in the twenty-first century that does not involve practice or problem situations with a global dimension. In 1945, Gordon Hamilton, better known in the United States and abroad as a theorist and teacher of casework, underlined the importance of a world view in social work education. She wrote: "An international or world view should be the natural heritage of students of social work . . . courses which promote international and interracial understanding are as significant for social welfare as those that teach standard of living, social security, personality, and family relationships" (Hamilton, 1945, pp. 142–143). Today, not only is a world view essential but also social workers must equip themselves with knowledge of globalization, development, human rights, and global dimensions of social problems and must acquire skills for international action. This thoroughly researched and scholarly presentation of international social work in its every aspect—policy, practice, theory, history, education, ethics, and values—should become required reading for social work faculty and students in North America and elsewhere, and for all professionals facing the challenge of improving human well-being in the twenty-first century.

Katherine A. Kendall, Ph.D., ACSW
Honorary President, IASSW

REFERENCE

Hamilton, G. (1945). Education for social work. In R. Kurtz (Ed.), *Social Work Year Book 1945* (pp. 137–145). New York: Russell Sage Foundation.

Preface

International Social Work: Professional Action in an Interdependent World was written to encourage social workers to think beyond national borders and to become active on global issues. It is now more obvious than ever that globalization affects social work wherever it is practiced and that solutions to social as well as economic and political problems require cross-national collaboration. In everyday practice situations and in broader professional responsibilities, social workers need international knowledge to be competent professionals in the twenty-first century.

Since the publication of the first edition in 2001, there have been significant changes in the social work profession and in the global environment. This second edition responds to these developments by extensively updating the material in the first edition and by enhancing the content of the original book to incorporate new knowledge.

First, there has been considerable growth of interest in international social work in the last 7 years. One indicator is the increased scholarship in this area, with several important new books and publication of many articles on international topics. Increased interest is evident in many different parts of the world. Specialized courses of study in international social work are under way in Europe, Canada, and the United States, books on the topic have been published in diverse countries, including Australia, Germany, and Denmark, and important critical scholarship on globalization and social work by writers in Asia, Africa, and Latin America add to a diverse global dialogue.

Social work has also continued to advance as a global profession. Most notably, in 2004 the International Association of Schools of Social Work (IASSW) and the International Federation of Social Workers (IFSW) adopted the first ever *Global Standards for Social Work Education and Training* and continued their collaboration on international ethics by agreeing to a new global document. These documents extend the work that had just begun at the time of the first publication, as IFSW and IASSW had agreed on a global definition of social work shortly before the book's publication.

Many significant global events and changes have occurred in the period between 2000 and 2007. Social work's attention is drawn to new and old but reemerging themes. Six months after the first edition was released, terrorist attacks on New York and Washington, D.C., in September of 2001 shook U.S. complacency about security in the global era. For the United States, and perhaps for some other countries, the attacks changed worldviews and resulted in policy shifts. The official and personal reactions to terrorism have introduced new threats to security and to human rights. War was declared on Afghanistan and then on Iraq, a devastating conflict that is ongoing and has renewed fears about regional wars. Social workers now cope with returning soldiers with life-altering injuries and severe post-traumatic stress, and with families torn apart by loss, separation, and disability. Measures introduced in the "war on terrorism" have undermined the emerging global consensus about human rights and tarnished the U.S.'s reputation as a defender of civil liberties. Ripple effects of fears and insecurity have renewed hostility to immigrants across much of the industrialized world.

A series of devastating natural disasters—the Asian tsunami, Hurricane Katrina, Hurricane Ivan, and the great earthquake in Pakistan, for example—brought renewed social work attention to disaster mitigation, relief, and recovery. Human trafficking, an issue addressed by social work through the League of Nations early in the last century, has reemerged as a major social concern, quite likely fueled by Internet pornography and communication. These are just a few examples of the changing global context of social work addressed in *International Social Work*.

CONTENT AND AREAS OF EMPHASIS

The aim of this book is to provide comprehensive treatment of international social work. Two themes are emphasized throughout: globalization (and the resulting interdependence) and professional action. Social work is an applied profession that uses knowledge to effect change at all levels from individual to institutional and community to societal. Therefore, the definition of *international social work* used in this book is a dynamic and action-oriented conceptualization. Knowledge of globalization and international issues is presented for social workers to use in their practice and professional advocacy roles.

Reflecting the growing scholarship and sophistication in international social work, I have introduced a section on theories and concepts underlying international social work. Beginning with a sharper focus on globalization, the text identifies development, human rights, and transnationalism as foundation concepts for international social work. A new chapter has also been added on global social issues or problems, recognizing that social workers' interest in knowledge and action on global issues has grown. The book is divided into sections to aid the reader. The first part defines international social work, the underlying concepts of globalization, development, and human rights and concludes with two chapters: one that discusses selected global problems and one that describes international organizations that address these problems. Part II focuses on the profession of social work, its history around the world, the history of the profession's international presence, and examples of social work as it is defined and practiced in seven very different countries. Part III includes chapters on global ethics and values, relief and development practice, international aspects of "domestic practice," and global policy. The final part has a largely new chapter on international exchange, and a concluding chapter.

Other significant additions are a section on transnationalism in the discussion of practice with immigrants and refugees, discussion of natural disasters as a social problem and an area of practice, new case examples, and addition of Ethiopia as an example in the chapter on social work around the world. Ethiopia is a least developing country and is also one where there are exciting new developments in social work education. Adding Ethiopia enhances the geographic and socioeconomic range of the countries selected for comparison.

AUDIENCE

The book is intended for all social workers who want to increase their knowledge of the international dimensions of social work. I have worked to write a book that is useful to graduate and undergraduate students, faculty, and practitioners. Although the primary market remains North America, the first edition is being used in many different countries. Therefore, I have tried to enhance the global relevance of the text, while providing some anchoring in the North American practice and policy context to strengthen global professional responsibility among social workers in the United States and Canada.

APOLOGIES

As noted earlier, I make an effort to be comprehensive to introduce students and practitioners to the arena of international social work and its context. Comprehensiveness, of course, is impossible, especially when tackling such a vast topic area, and therefore comprehensiveness is a strength and a weakness of the book. There are many omissions and other areas that deserve much more depth. I have tried to respond to helpful comments from readers of the first edition in deciding on areas to expand and have been gratified that educators from many parts of the world have let me know that they are using the text. Hopefully readers will use the information provided in the book as a base from which to research additional topics of interest.

The global environment is constantly changing. Within days after sending the manuscript to the publisher, accounts of tainted products imported from China hit the news. These accounts make my comment on the impossibility of protecting one's environment through unilateral action rather meek. Undoubtedly, by the time of publication, there will be other examples of change and new developments.

I have tried to maintain a tone that allows the reader to make his or her own judgments and to avoid preaching. When speaking to a class at another university that was using this text, the instructor and students said to me, "You are a lot more radical than you write." This is indeed intentional, as international social work is an extremely vast and complex area for study and reflection. It is easy to react without adequate knowledge and understanding. Yet it is critically important for social work to ensure that its mission and values are introduced into global deliberations.

ACKNOWLEDGMENTS

It has been my own good fortune to meet many outstanding pioneers, leaders, and current scholars and activists in international social work. To many, I owe considerable debt for ideas and inspiration. Katherine Kendall deserves special mention. Her unflagging dedication and enormous contributions to international social work are an inspiration and a rich source of knowledge. I am grateful that she agreed to write the foreword for the second edition, as well as for the original book.

Through serving on the Board of the IASSW, and through international partnerships through my work at the University of Connecticut School of Social Work, I have met, interacted with, learned from, and become friends with wonderful colleagues from around the world. Many of them helped me with this project, especially Helle Strauss (Denmark), John Maxwell and Peta-anne Baker (Jamaica), Abye Tasse (Ethiopia), Tatsuru Akimoto (Japan), Satinder Ragobur (Mauritius), and Ludmila Haroutunian (Armenia). I would also like to thank Aya Kuroda, Irene Queiro-Tajalli, Nancy Humphreys, Kasumi Hirayama, and Alice Johnson for assisting with information about social work around the world. Several former students contributed cases for the book: Vichhyka Ngy Shelto, Amanda Mihaly, David Bourns, and Ada Sanchez. David Bourns of Save the Children deserves special thanks for providing guest speakers and hosting our international development class several times. Through these visits to Save the Children a number of cases for the book were developed. Former student and colleague Thomas Felke graciously allowed me to include several of his photographs from Armenia. Lara Herscovitch, MSW graduate of the University of Connecticut and formerly of Save the Children, wrote the chapter on international relief and development practice for the first edition. Although I have modified and added content, much of the chapter remains Lara's work.

I would also like to thank Lori Caswell, University of Connecticut MSW student, for her research assistance, and colleagues Barbara Pine (University of Connecticut) and Lorrie Greenhouse Gardella (Saint Joseph College) who read and critiqued chapters as I drafted them.

Finally, I want to thank Oxford University Press and Maura Roessner and Mallory Jensen. It has been a pleasure to work with Maura throughout the entire process of preparing the second edition, from conceptualization to realization.

Contents

International Social Work

CHAPTER 1

INTERNATIONAL SOCIAL WORK
Why Is It Important and What Is It?

> I imagine centuries in which in the higher minds in the States a noble
> sense of world duty, a world consciousness, will struggle with mass
> mentality and gradually pervade it.
>
> Jane Addams, 1930, p. 8, quoting George Russell

Social workers around the world have numerous opportunities for international action:

- A social worker administering a shelter for battered women in Massachusetts is asked to admit an undocumented immigrant from El Salvador whose husband has threatened to kill her.
- Social workers from Mexico and Texas meet to work out policies to deal with parents who move their children back and forth across the border to evade child abuse and neglect investigations.
- A social worker serving in the Peace Corps helps a community in Equatorial Guinea determine its priorities for involvement in a rural health project.
- Members of the International Federation of Social Workers (IFSW) and the International Association of Schools of Social Work (IASSW) prepare position statements as nongovernmental organization (NGO) representatives at the United Nations (UN).
- Institutional social workers and social pedagogues from Denmark and Germany introduce child-care institutions in New York to a professional model of child care.
- Social workers in Jamaica organize a coalition on the Rights of the Child and prepare an alternative report on their country's progress to submit to the UN Center for Human Rights in Geneva.
- Social workers from Barbados and Trinidad provide disaster relief services in Grenada after the island is devastated by Hurricane Ivan.

In each brief vignette above, social workers, individually or through their agencies and organizations, have engaged in international action, action that requires knowledge about international relations, about the realities of other nations, and about the profession of social work as it is practiced throughout the world. The range of action is broad—from full-time professional overseas practice to domestic practice in which an occasional case with international dimensions is encountered. Still other actions call on the advocacy responsibilities of the profession and its members and are often carried out in addition to regular employment duties.

This book is based on a number of assumptions about the importance of international learning in social work and about the nature of the social work environment. Globalization has grown enormously over the past several decades to the point that its general acceptance has become almost a cliché. But in spite of Jane Addams's early embrace of globalmindedness (as shown in part by her selection of "Growing World Consciousness" as the subtitle of her second autobiographical book) social work has not fully recognized the extent to which its practice and professional environment are shaped by interdependence, nor has the profession seized available opportunities for increasing its impact internationally. This text will provide knowledge of the international dimension of social work—to strengthen the ability of social workers to contribute to and benefit from international developments in the profession and to improve social workers' competence in their everyday practice in the context of global interdependence. Globalization, therefore, is an overarching theme in the pages that follow.

Another theme is international professional action. Considerable emphasis is put on the responsibilities of the social work profession as a whole and of individual social workers for action related to global injustice, global social problems, and practice challenges. For many this is a new idea. What is meant by *international responsibilities* is explained briefly below and in depth in the chapters that follow.

GLOBALIZATION: WHY INTERNATIONAL SOCIAL WORK?

As expressed by Walter Lorenz (1997), " 'Going beyond the national level' in social work cannot be the personal hobby of a few specialists who are dealing with migrant and refugee groups or with ethnic minorities . . . or of a few idealists who want to promote international exchanges to widen their horizon and to learn more about methods and practices in other countries. On the contrary, all social work is enmeshed in global processes of change" (p. 2). Globalization has created significant areas of international responsibility as well as new opportunities for social work impact by reshaping the social work environment in four important ways.

1. International social forces and events, most dramatically the movement of populations, have changed the makeup of social agency caseloads and

affected domestic practice in many countries, including the United States. Competent social work practice in most countries now demands new knowledge and competencies to cope with the social problems and conditions emerging from interdependence.

2. Social problems are now shared by more and less economically developed countries far more often than in previous decades, making mutual work and exchange more desirable. Increasingly, it is as likely that practice innovations and potential problem solutions will be generated in places previously labeled less developed, as in the industrialized nations. This aspect of globalization has led to a growing shared agenda for social work action. Most nations are currently struggling with homelessness and street children, growing numbers of aged, changes in family patterns leading to less available family care, unemployment and underemployment, and many other social problems. In addition, as Lyons (1999) pointed out, an understanding of global problems "can contribute to a refocusing on the core values of social work, as concerned with human rights and social justice" (p. 163).

3. The actions of one country—politically, economically, and socially—now directly and indirectly affect other countries' social and economic well-being and the overall social health of the planet. As U.S. President Clinton (1993) noted in his first inaugural address, it is difficult to identify a purely domestic problem: "There is no longer a clear division between what is foreign and what is domestic. The world economy, the world environment, the world AIDS crisis, the world arms race—they affect us all" (p. A15). Thus nations increasingly share social problems, and the actions that any nation takes can directly affect the well-being of the population of other nations. The nuclear accident at Chernobyl in the Ukraine in 1986, which spread radioactive material over much of Europe, was a dramatic, but by no means isolated, example of this fact. Similarly the 2001 terrorist attacks on New York and Washington, D.C., led to deepening poverty across the Caribbean as tourists stayed home; the "fallout" included wars in Iraq and Afghanistan. Logically, then, no single nation or the professional groups within it can solve these problems by acting alone.

4. Finally, there are enhanced opportunities for international sharing and exchanging made possible by rapidly advancing technological developments in areas such as communications. Computer and video linkages, for example, have dramatically changed global communications (Asamoah, Healy, & Mayadas, 1997). The dimensions of globalization will be explored in more depth in Chapter 2.

Appropriate goals for the social work profession and individual social workers across the globe grow out of these trends. Thus it is important that social workers be prepared to (a) address internationally related case and community problems that arise in their domestic practice, (b) contribute to mutual problem solving on global social problems, and (c) monitor the impact of their own nation's policies on other countries' and peoples' well-being. In addition, they need to develop the capacity to benefit from and contribute to international dialogue and exchange to support the achievement of the three main goals cited above (Asamoah et al., 1997). Each of these goals moves beyond awareness to professional action—professional action that will require new knowledge and attitudes.

What Every Social Worker Needs to Know

Awareness may well be the starting point for international action. Noted experts in the field of higher education have long argued that a general worldview achieved through education in the history, literature, art, religions, and cultures of the world is an essential part of being an "educated person." Successive reform efforts in higher education in the United States have sought to ensure that students receive some baseline level of world knowledge. Recognizing serious gaps in graduates' knowledge of the world, many U.S. colleges and universities have adopted requirements that students take at least one course in "non-Western" studies. In spite of these efforts, education for global awareness seems to have been less successful in the United States than in many other countries. A study of university professors in 14 countries (England, Russia, Germany, Japan, South Korea, Chile, Israel, Australia, Brazil, Mexico, Sweden, Hong Kong, the Netherlands, and the United States) found that "with the exception of the United States, international mindedness in the surveyed countries is quite high" (Lewis & Altbach, 1996, p. 33). More than 90% of American professors surveyed expressed no need to read books or journals published outside their own country to keep up in their fields—a quite astounding finding of disinterest in their professions beyond national borders, and possibly indicative of ethnocentrism.

Social work is an applied profession, and the emphasis of its baccalaureate- and masters-level educational programs is on preparing students for effective practice. For this reason, the majority of social work students, practitioners, and faculty do not define acquisition of a worldview as a priority educational outcome. Although it is hoped that students and practitioners will in fact gain a worldview from reading this book, its emphasis will be on the international knowledge that is specifically focused on social work and that prepares the reader for professional action. Readers will gain the following essential professional knowledge from the chapters that follow:

- familiarity with the history, scope, and functions of social work around the world, including a discussion of its similarities and differences
- knowledge of ways the profession is organized for international action through the major professional organizations
- knowledge of the major agencies involved in international social work and social welfare and their functions, including the social welfare responsibilities of the UN

- key theories and concepts including globalization, development, human rights, and transnationalism
- awareness of practice roles and opportunities for social work in international relief and development
- awareness of aspects of global interdependence that affect domestic social welfare issues and related knowledge to improve international aspects of domestic social work practice
- knowledge of the role of the UN in setting standards for international social welfare policy
- awareness of the impact of national policies on social welfare conditions in other countries and the reciprocal impact of other countries' policies
- appreciation of the international aspects of cultural diversity to facilitate enhanced service to international populations
- knowledge of the major sources of global and cross-national data on social work
- examination of value dilemmas in international work

Throughout the book, applicability of these knowledge areas to practice and other forms of professional action will be discussed.

WHAT IS INTERNATIONAL SOCIAL WORK?

The definition of the term *international social work* has been the subject of much debate. First, there may be confusion over the use of the terms *international, global,* and *cross-national.* Beginning with the *Random House Webster's College Dictionary* (1995) definitions, *global* means pertaining to or involving the whole world, whereas *international* can mean any of the following: between or among two or more nations, of or pertaining to two or more nations or their citizens, pertaining to the relations between nations, having members or activities in several nations, or transcending national boundaries or viewpoints. Stein (1990) agrees with this distinction, noting that though the terms are often used interchangeably, the more technical usage of *global* "signified phenomena affecting the entire planet" (p. 13). *Cross-national,* too, is sometimes used interchangeably with *international.* When it is differentiated, cross-national has a more limited meaning and is used to apply to comparisons or transactions of or between several or a limited number of nations (Estes, 1984).

   Beyond these simple definitions, international social work remains a complex concept, actually comprising a number of component concepts. It is used to refer to comparative social welfare, international practice, cross-cultural knowledge and understanding, intergovernmental work on social welfare, concern and action on global social problems, a worldwide collegiality among social workers, professional exchange activities, and a general worldview. At least one author has argued that the concept is so complex and amorphous that there may be no such thing as international social work (Akimoto, 1995). Is he correct? Or is international social work any one of the above-listed concepts, a combination of several, or perhaps an umbrella concept that can encompass all these ideas?

Evolution of the Concept

In 1956, the Council on Social Work Education (CSWE) in the United States formed a working committee to develop a definition of international social work. Committee members wrestled with the question of narrow versus broad interpretation and examined at least six different usages of the term *international social work*, "ranging from social workers working in other countries to refugee services to common professional concerns with social workers in other parts of the world" (Healy, 1995, p. 423). The committee opted for a narrow definition, thus ruling out most of the aspects of international work noted above.

> It was the consensus of our sub-committee that the term "international social work" should properly be confined to programs of social work of international scope, such as those carried on by intergovernmental agencies, chiefly those of the U.N.; governmental; or non-governmental agencies with international programs. (Stein, 1957, p. 3)

Others, earlier and more recently, have favored a broad definition. Kimberly (1984) argued that international social work, as a relatively new field, should be left open for broad interpretation rather than prematurely limiting its scope. Sanders and Pederson (1984), too, used a broad definition: "International social work means those social work activities and concerns that transcend national and cultural boundaries" (p. xiv).

Many recent writers have assumed that international social work is a new term and have neglected historical sources. In fact, in a paper delivered at the First International Conference of Social Work in 1928, Jebb (1929), from London, used the term and discussed the conditions needed for such work to be practical. Articles titled "International Social Work" appeared in the *Social Work Yearbook* beginning in 1937. Selecting a broad view of the international field, Warren defined international social work as follows in his 1939 article in the *Social Work Yearbook*:

> International Social Work includes four main types of activities: a) international social case work; b) international assistance, public and private, to disaster or war sufferers and distressed minority groups; c) international conferences on social work; and d) international cooperation by governments and private bodies through the medium of the League of Nations, the International Labour Organization and the Health Organization of the League, in combatting disease and securing social and political peace and harmony throughout the world. (p. 192)

It is interesting to note that this early definition includes the exchanges of ideas by social workers at international meetings as well as intercountry work, intergovernmental work, and relief work.

International social case work was defined in the same article as "the application of case work methods to the problems of families and individuals whose social adjustments require cooperative action in two or more countries" (Warren, 1939, p. 192).

In a survey of member schools of the International Association of Schools of Social Work (IASSW) in 1989/90, educators were asked to identify the component concepts they considered essential to the definition of international social work. Respondents from over 200 member schools from all five regions of the world (Africa, Asia and the Pacific, Europe, North America, and Latin America) selected the following concepts as essential, in descending order: cross-cultural understanding, comparative social policy, concern with global problems, a general worldview, knowledge of a common profession worldwide, international practice, intergovernmental social welfare, and a sense of collegiality with social workers in other countries (Healy, 1990). The number of educators selecting the concepts ranged from a high of 59% identifying cross-cultural understanding as key to only 15% selecting a sense of worldwide professional collegiality. This indicates that no concept was viewed as essential by all.

Critical of the often apolitical conceptualization of international social work, Haug (2005) advocated clear emphasis on social justice and human rights. Her definition, which expands beyond the recognized profession, is, "International social work includes any social work activity anywhere in the world, directed toward global social justice and human rights, in which local practice is dialectically linked to the global context" (p. 133). In what is perhaps the most recent definition, Cox and Pawar (2006) reinforce my emphasis on action and introduce significant core concepts:

International social work is the promotion of social work education and practice globally and locally, with the purpose of building a truly integrated international profession that reflects social work's capacity to respond appropriately and effectively, in education and practice terms, to the various global challenges that are having a significant impact on the well-being of large sections of the world's population. This global and local promotion of social work education and practice is based on an integrated-perspectives approach that synthesizes global, human rights, ecological, and social development perspectives of international situations and responses to them. (p. 20)

Their inclusion of profession building is in keeping with recent developments in the IFSW and IASSW.

Akimoto (1995) raised challenging questions about the concept of international social work. Because most definitions of international social work include a social worker working in another country or a social work researcher collecting data in another country, he asked whether it is appropriate to call it *domestic social work* if a Japanese person does something in Japan while labeling the same activity international social work if it is performed in Japan by a Kenyan or an American. At the end of the book, an answer to this question will be attempted, although the issues raised by Akimoto remain thorny ones for those concerned with definition.

What is clear from a review of recent and historical literature and research is that the concept of international social work is complex and can be defined either narrowly or broadly. It is not a new idea, having been explored in some detail for at least 70 years, yet it remains open to further work and interpretation.

Author's Definition of International Social Work

In this book, *international social work* is defined as international professional action and the capacity for international action by the social work profession and its members. International action has four dimensions: internationally related domestic practice and advocacy, professional exchange, international practice, and international policy development and advocacy. Each is explained below and illustrated in an accompanying case example.

Internationally Related Domestic Practice and Advocacy. The first dimension is social work competence in internationally related aspects of domestic social work practice and professional advocacy. Social workers are increasingly called on to deal with problems that have an international dimension, meaning that two or more countries are involved in some way in the case or policy issue. There are many examples of internationally related domestic practice problems, including refugee resettlement, work with other international populations, international adoption work, and social work in border areas. Although some social workers specialize in these areas, all social workers may encounter international issues in carrying out their professional responsibilities.

Case 1.1 shows an example of internationally related domestic practice. The vignette describes the challenges faced by a young refugee boy in an urban, Western school system and those of the social worker assigned to help him.

To assist this student—who could be encountered in the United States, Canada, Denmark, or many other places—the social worker needs knowledge about life in Somalia, Somali family patterns, and the migration experience of Somali refugees including transit camps and their resettlement challenges. In such circumstances, international knowledge is necessary to provide competent social work services to cases in the domestic caseload.

A related "domestic" professional responsibility requires the capacity and willingness of the profession to develop and promulgate positions on social aspects of their own country's foreign policy and aspects of national policy that affect peoples in other countries, such as legislation on immigration. It is logical that as part of accepted advocacy responsibilities of the profession, social workers have an obligation to monitor such legislation as it is being proposed, to follow impending votes at the UN and foreign policy

---

CASE 1.1: WORKING WITH INTERNATIONAL POPULATIONS:
MUSSA—A SOMALI BANTU BOY IN AN AMERICAN
MIDDLE SCHOOL

A social worker at the Family Assistance Center (FAC) at a middle school in a northeastern U.S. city was assigned to work with a 12-year-old Somali Bantu refugee boy, Mussa. He was referred to the FAC by his English for Speakers of Other Languages (ESOL) teacher, as she felt participation in the New Arrivals support group would be helpful. His ESOL and special education teachers agreed that Mussa wasn't understanding much English and that he was getting nothing out of school. Yet the school seemed to be doing little to remedy his situation; the other students in the ESOL class and the teacher were Spanish speakers.

The social worker began with individual work; she discovered that although Mussa's English was limited, he was able to communicate better in a one-on-one situation. She also recognized that it was important to gain some understanding of the history and experiences of Somali Bantu refugees and began her own research. Mussa had come to the United States with his mother and older siblings and lived in the third floor of an apartment in the city. In Somalia, the Bantu were targets of severe violence. Thus, "for his entire life in Somalia, Mussa had been surrounded by war, violence, destruction, starvation and disease." When Mussa talked about Somalia with the social worker, he usually looked down and said sadly, "It's bad." What he remembers most about living in Somalia was running—running from animals, and running from people with weapons. He had seen a number of people killed before he and his family decided to leave and seek refugee status in Kenya. Although safer, resettlement in the United States has also been difficult. The Somali Bantu were completely unprepared for life in an American city, having never experienced electricity, appliances, traffic, or school. Resettlement workers recount having to teach the refugees not to build fires in their ovens.

As the social worker recounted, "the school system was grossly underprepared for Mussa and his needs.... Teachers are overwhelmed and frustrated by his presence" as he had never been to school and could not follow the bilingual classes (not surprisingly, as they were conducted in English and Spanish). In addition, teachers and other staff seemed to have no appreciation of the trauma and loss that Mussa had experienced.

> Working as Mussa's caseworker has involved many different practice approaches. The first step was self-education. I needed to gather information and teach myself about Somalia and about the collective experience of Somali Bantu refugees. Without an understanding of his background and his life, I was unable to comprehend Mussa's struggles. I would have risked retraumatizing Mussa.

(continued)

With self-education an ongoing process, the caseworker engaged in advocacy on Mussa's behalf. She educated his teachers and organized meetings with his teachers to brainstorm ways to meet his needs. She held one-on-one sessions with Mussa in which she used drawing and looking at pictures in books and on the Internet to engage him and get him to express some of his feelings. At one point, they came across a photo in a refugee magazine, and he began to shout, "Kakuma, Kakuma" in an agitated voice. She thought perhaps this was a word in his language that meant some dreadful thing. Research after the session revealed that *Kakuma* was the name of the refugee camp where he had stayed in Kenya; it was evident that his memories were not happy ones. She realized that it was difficult to engage Mussa in learning English using the standard ESOL textbooks, as the pictures did not interest him. She suggested using some alternative materials, and Mussa began to make progress with the language.

Although Mussa has a long road ahead, the advocacy efforts of the social worker, along with involvement in a New Arrivals support group at the middle school, provides some hope for the future. Indeed, an administrator at the Central Office of the school district commented, "without that young social worker, no one was showing any interest in helping this young refugee."

Adapted from a case contributed by Amanda Mihaly (2005).

directives and to ensure that social work's voice is heard on relevant issues. Case 1.2 discusses an example of advocacy following World War II.

Case 1.2 demonstrates that the social workers who attended the 1947 delegate meeting of their professional organization engaged in discussions of important international issues of their day. They were sufficiently educated on the issues and on their potential impact to take a policy position for the profession and to advocate for their position with national decision makers.

Professional Exchange. The second dimension of international action is the capacity to exchange social work information and experiences internationally and to use the knowledge and experience to improve social work practice and social welfare policy at home. This includes a range of actions, such as reading foreign periodicals and books in one's field, corresponding with professionals in other countries or hosting visitors, participating in professional interchange at international meetings, and identifying and adapting social welfare innovations in other countries to one's own setting. Increasingly, professional exchange is facilitated by technological advances in computer-assisted communications and teleconferencing.

Case 1.3 describes borrowing and adapting an innovation to address extreme poverty: the well-known Grameen Bank concept. The importance

CASE 1.2: INFLUENCING FOREIGN SOCIAL POLICY

In 1947, a number of important policy issues before the U.S. Congress were matters concerned with international social welfare. One of the most urgent was a requested appropriation for continued postwar relief. Others included matters relating to immigration—especially the relaxation of U.S. immigration limits to permit resettlement of displaced persons—and to U.S. participation in the emerging international organizations being organized under the UN umbrella.

The pending appropriations bill was to approve $350 million for relief to Austria, Greece, Hungary, Italy, Poland, and China. The issue was brought to the 1947 Delegate Conference of the American Association of Social Workers (AASW), one of the predecessor organizations to the National Association of Social Workers (NASW). The delegates passed a resolution urging Congress to appropriate the money at once to continue to provide basic supplies of food, clothing, shelter, and medicines to Europe and China. The resolution continued:

> Be it further resolved that this and any other funds appropriated be made available to countries in proportion to their need as appraised by competent international instrumentalities such as the Technical Committee of the United Nations, and regardless of political or other considerations. (American Association of Social Workers, 1947)

The resolution indicates that social workers in 1947 advocated sound principles for foreign aid. They were concerned that need take precedence over politics and that aid be fairly distributed. "This government should spare no effort to assure fair and non-discriminatory administration not only between groups within a given country but also between one country and another" (Howard, 1947, p. 5). They also recognized the advantages of multilateral aid rather than aid given specifically from one country to another. "The U.S. government . . . should do all in its power to strengthen and make more effective all international agencies responsible for social welfare services, thus speeding the day when unilateral approaches to world needs may be abandoned in favor of world cooperation" (Howard, 1947, p. 4).

The AASW resolution was sent to the secretary of state, the chair of the Foreign Relations Committee of the Senate, and the chair of the Foreign Affairs Committee of the House of Representatives.

---

of the microcredit approach popularized by the Grameen Bank was underscored when its founder Muhammad Yunus and the Bank won the 2006 Nobel Peace Prize.

The ability to transfer international human service innovations to one's own setting first requires knowledge of social welfare developments in other

CASE 1.3: INTERNATIONAL EXCHANGE AND BORROWING

International exchange among social workers can yield many benefits. Perhaps the highest order of exchange is what is called *international technology transfer*—the identification, adaptation, and transplantation of innovations from one country to another. This case discusses transfer of innovations in microlending from Bangladesh to the United States.

Case

The Grameen Bank is world renowned for its success in encouraging small enterprise development among impoverished and powerless women in Bangladesh. Founded in 1976, the Grameen Bank (*Grameen* means "rural" in Bengali) introduced a "peer-lending banking approach geared to improving the human rights of mainly poor women" (Jansen & Pippard, 1998, p. 104). Through provision of very small loans without collateral and through collective "savings clubs," poor women have been able to start small businesses, gain at least minimal financial security, and, as a result, improve their status in the community.

The impact has been widespread. As Banerjee (1998) noted: "The Grameen Bank's phenomenal success with micro-lending . . . reverberates throughout much of the globe" (p. 64). A number of microenterprise projects for the poor in the United States are now being introduced using the Grameen model. Although controversial among U.S. social workers, many of whom object to encouraging people living below the poverty level to save some of their meager grants, the adaptation of an international innovation is yielding some promising results. Jansen and Pippard (1998) mentioned two such projects: the Women's Self Employment Project, "Full Circle Fund," in urban Chicago and the "Good Faith Fund" in rural Pine Bluff, Arkansas. Evaluations of the U.S. efforts show "not only is economic success evident but studies indicate women gained a sense of autonomy, as well as improved family relationships as part of these economic opportunities, findings not unlike those documented about women participants of the Grameen Bank" (Jansen & Pippard, 1998, p. 118).

countries. Successful transfer also requires sophisticated understanding of the similarities and differences between the "exporting" and "importing" countries to determine needed adaptations. Indeed, "borrowers" of the Grameen concept in the United States and other industrialized countries realized that among the conditions making microlending successful in Bangladesh were "unregulated market conditions that thrive on low-skilled enterprises; absence of income maintenance programs; availability of free health care; and a lower cost of living" (Banerjee, 1998, p. 79). But other cultural and structural differences favored successful adaptation such as the relatively better social position for women and acceptance of their free movement in society. Increasingly, potential innovations can be found in industrialized and developing countries alike, making knowledge of other systems more valuable for its potential for domestic applicability.

International Practice. The third dimension of international action is the preparation of some professional social workers to contribute directly to international development work through employment or volunteer work in international development agencies. Success in this sphere depends on the extent to which international knowledge can be blended with social work skills. Case 1.4 briefly describes an intervention designed and carried out by an interdisciplinary team at a nongovernmental development agency with several social workers as members. The social workers in this case used their knowledge of human behavior, skill in community organizing, and practice skills in planning, management, and evaluation to contribute to the development project in war-torn Bosnia.

Thus social workers in international relief and development work utilize many of the skills learned in their professional training. They combine these with a commitment to development, knowledge of the international context, and well-honed sensitivity and communication skills for cross-cultural work.

International Policy Development and Advocacy. Finally, the capacity of the social work profession as a worldwide movement to formulate and promulgate positions on important social issues and make a contribution to the resolution of important global problems related to its sphere of expertise is the fourth component of international professional action. Case 1.5 describes an educational activity carried out by a group under the auspices of the IASSW at the UN Conference on Women in Beijing, China, in 1995. The goal of the educational effort was to influence UN policy deliberations.

This effort required more than knowledge of domestic violence in each organizer's country. Knowledge about women's status around the world, about political constraints in various countries that make some types of social action impossible, and skill in cross-cultural communication were necessary. Real change and action on global problems are possible when professionals engage in mutual work across national and cultural boundaries.

To summarize, the definition of international social work to be used in this book encompasses four areas for action: internationally informed domestic practice and related policy advocacy, participation in and utilization of international exchange, international practice, and international policy formulation and advocacy. The first two potentially involve all social workers; the third will involve only a small percentage; and the fourth, though involving all social workers indirectly as part of the profession, may directly involve relatively few. This four-pronged definition will serve as the theme for the book—international action for the profession—along with globalization, which makes it timely. The themes, issues, and examples addressed

---

CASE 1.4: INTERNATIONAL DEVELOPMENT PRACTICE WITH CHILDREN IN ESPECIALLY DIFFICULT CIRCUMSTANCES
David Bourns

An emergency education program initiated in the then war-torn country of Bosnia demonstrates the usefulness of social work skills in overseas work with international relief and development organizations. This program sought to provide support to preschool-age children who had been exposed to the violence of war and to begin to normalize their chaotic existence amid the destruction. The program, a neighborhood preschool, needed to meet local educational standards but also had to address the specific needs of war-affected children. Many skills were demanded of the international staff working on the program. They worked closely with Bosnian educators, establishing constructive cross-cultural communication to develop a mutually acceptable curriculum. The staff's experience with abused and traumatized children and knowledge of child development were essential to program success. Although individual counseling could not be provided within the scope of the project, staff did refer children in need of special services wherever possible.

Community involvement was key to ensuring that the program could be sustained. A safe structure had to be located, and community members had to be mobilized to help clean war debris from bombed-out buildings. Teachers had to be identified among the local population; if trained teachers were not available, then other adults who were willing to volunteer and be trained had to be found. Motivating people suffering from the effects of a protracted conflict required solid community organizing skills. The task of the international staff, as in most development projects, was to help build local capacity, not to do the job. There were also many administrative and logistical support tasks. From the delivery of material supplies to the monitoring of project funding in each location and to enhancing and monitoring the personal security of all staff working in the field, constant vigilance of well-designed administrative systems meant the difference not only between success and failure but also between life and death.

---

in the book also make it clear that international social work is value-driven action aimed at promoting human rights and human well-being globally.

KNOWLEDGE BASE FOR INTERNATIONAL SOCIAL WORK—MAJOR CONCEPTS

International social work can also be defined as a composite of the major concepts that inform its practice. Along with the body of social work theories and

---

CASE 1.5: INFLUENCING POLICY THROUGH DIALOGUE

Through the IASSW, social workers organized a symposium on violence against women for the nongovernmental organization (NGO) forum held in conjunction with the UN Fourth World Conference on Women held in Beijing, China, in 1995. Building on an area of social work expertise, a 4-hour workshop was organized to share knowledge about domestic violence and, more importantly, to develop action strategies for antiviolence work in participants' home settings. Social workers from 27 nations heard panel presentations and joined working discussion groups. The participants developed and adopted a resolution for presentation to the official UN delegates conference the next day. This resolution, offered by IASSW through its consultative status with the UN, contained 10 recommendations for reducing gender-based violence and enhancing personal, social, and economic development (Wetzel, 1995).

This venture incorporated key elements of mutual work on policy development. Social workers from many nations met, exchanged information, and worked together to develop policy recommendations on a key world social problem. Then they used mechanisms available through an established social work professional organization to advance the recommendations to the relevant UN policy body. Although social workers have participated in other UN meetings, it was noted that this may have been the first organized social work presence at a UN conference on women.

---

practice skills, concepts central to international social work are globalization, development, human rights, and transnationalism.

Globalization provides the context for twenty-first-century practice. Understandings of theories and manifestations of globalization are essential components of understanding the social environment. Increasingly, the forces of globalization affect human well-being and influence human behavior.

Development and human rights are the two major thrusts of international social and humanitarian action in the late twentieth and early twenty-first centuries. Both are compatible with social work values, mission, and practice. Development, as most commonly understood, is a major focus of international practice roles for social workers, directed at poverty alleviation and improving human social and economic well-being. Human rights work and perspectives provide international standards and goals that can be applied internationally and domestically. Theories of development and human rights are elements of the core of international social work.

For those social workers who emphasize practice and policy with international populations, transnationalism provides a new lens for understanding current migration patterns and relationships. In the chapters that follow, globalization, development, human rights, and transnationalism will be examined in more depth.

TERMINOLOGY

Terminology in international social work can be confusing and, at times, controversial. Throughout the almost 50 years of the development movement, terms used to classify nations have changed several times, and there is still no agreement on optimal terms.

The terms *first world*, *second world*, and *third world* were common descriptors in the 1960s. Describing the mostly Western industrialized nations; the Soviet Union and its satellite nations; and the newly independent and nonaligned nations of Asia, Africa, and Latin America; respectively, these terms had some relevance during the cold war era. The term *third world* increasingly was viewed as a negative term, implying to some the idea of third rate or last in consideration; the actual derivation of the term is from a phrase describing the Third Estate in the French Revolution.

Developed and *developing* are the most commonly used replacement terms for first and third world, respectively. The labels *North* and *South* are also used. These terms refer loosely to geography, as generally more of the developed nations are in the Northern Hemisphere and more of the developing nations are in the Southern Hemisphere. Where used, *North* and *South* should be viewed more as political terms than geographic ones; Australia, for example, is in the North.

In this book, I will use the UN Development Programme (UNDP) and UNICEF terms *industrialized* and *developing* to refer to nations where broad classifications are needed. This choice has been made for several reasons. The use of *industrialized* improves on *developed-developing* by avoiding the implication that the development process has been completed in some nations. *North* and *South* will be used sparingly because the terms may be confusing to readers. Most importantly, using terms currently accepted by UNDP and UNICEF is in harmony with one of the purposes of the book, which is to introduce social workers to the international arena, including the work of major global organizations.

Many statistics are cited in the book. Readers are cautioned that international statistics are often only approximations and estimates. Methods used to collect statistics are imprecise. Recently, for example, some experts are questioning whether rates of infection for HIV/AIDS have been overstated, especially for the most severely affected African countries.

COUNTRIES SELECTED AS SPECIAL EXAMPLES FOR THE TEXT

Studying international social work requires examination of individual countries as well as the global picture to understand and assess the global profession. Although the book will refer to many different countries, seven have been selected for special purposes of comparison: Argentina, Armenia, Denmark, Ethiopia, Jamaica, Japan, and Mauritius. As explained in the preface, the countries were selected for their diversity and because the author had access to needed data. These countries' experiences in social work will be discussed in Chapter 8 to aid the reader's understanding of international social work. In many places, comparisons with U.S. and Canadian examples will also be provided to accommodate the readership.

The countries selected vary along many dimensions, including factors related to their state of development and their experiences in the establishment and current status of the social work profession. Table 1.1 compares the countries on a number of dimensions. Readers are encouraged to refer to the table periodically to relate social work comparisons to levels of human well-being and population characteristics of the example countries.

One way of comparing countries is to use rankings of well-being developed by the international intergovernmental agencies of the UN or the World Bank. For example, the countries selected range in their rank (of 177 countries) on the UNDP's Human Development Index (HDI)—an index of progress on well-being—from a high of 7th for Japan to 170th for Ethiopia, putting Ethiopia near the bottom of the group of low-human-development countries (UNDP, 2006). The low-human-development group are those countries that have the worst performance on the index comprising measures of per capita gross national product (GNP), life expectancy, and literacy and school enrollment. UNICEF uses a single measure for assessing a country's progress in meeting human needs—the under-5 (U-5) mortality rate. On this measure, Japan leads the way with a rate of only 4 per 1,000 live births; this compares to 7 for the United States. There are a few countries, Singapore and Iceland, that have U-5 mortality rates of 3, the best in the world. Among our example countries, Ethiopia's U-5 mortality is 166, Jamaica's is 20, measuring an increase over the past 8 years, while the rate in Mauritius has fallen from 23 to 15 since UNICEF's 1997 measures. Summary statistics for the seven countries plus the United States are given in Table 1.1.

Population statistics give only a limited picture of national differences. National aggregate data are limited by being just that, national aggregates. They fail to express the range of experiences within a country and cannot capture important dimensions of culture and history. Within-country differences among the population in levels of well-being can be great. Denmark is characterized by fairly equitable distribution of social benefits, and only a small percentage of the population lives in poverty. In the United States, income disparity is great, as it is in Jamaica and Argentina. The majority of Ethiopia's population are not only poor but also food insecure (70%) meaning that any misfortune can tip a family into hunger. Thus though overall levels of health and educational attainment may be satisfactory, sectors of the population live in severe poverty.

The countries selected represent many geographic regions—Asia, South America, Africa, the Caribbean, and Europe. Each has had a unique history, which has shaped its national culture and population, including experiences with colonization, mass immigration, and struggles for independence. Jamaica was colonized by Great Britain and experienced many years of slavery and colonial rule prior to the independence movement that was finally

TABLE 1.1

	Popu-lation (in Millions) UNDP 2006	GDP per Capita UNDP 2006	Infant Mortality UNICEF 2006	Under 5 Mortality UNICEF 2006	UNDP Life Expec-tancy	UNDP % Popu-lation over 65	UNDP % Popu-lation Under 15	% Living in Poverty UNDP 2006	Human Devel-opment Index rank	Date of National Indepen-dence	Date of First Social Work	Social Work Professional Organization
Argentina	38.4	$13,298	16	18	75	10.1	26.7	23.0^1	36	1816	1936	Association of Social Workers
Armenia	3.0	$4,101	29	32	72	11.9	21.7	N/A	80	1991	1990	Armenian National Association of the Social Services, Social Work Section 1998
Denmark	5.4	$31,914	4	5	77	14.9	18.8	8.0^3	15	N/A	1937	Association of Social Workers
Ethiopia	75.6	$756	110	166	48	2.9	44.8	77.8^1	170	N/A	1959	
Jamaica	2.6	$4,163	17	20	71	7.6	31.7	13.3^1	104	1962	1961	Jamaica Association of Social Workers
Japan	127.9	$29,251	3	4	82	19.2	14.1	11.8	7	N/A	1921	Japan Association of Social Workers 1960
Mauritius	1.2	$12,027	14	15	72	6.5	24.9	11.0^3	63	1968	N/A	Mauritius Association of Social Workers 1964
United States	295.4	$39,676	7	8	78	12.3	20.9	17.0^2	8	1776	1898	National Association of Social Workers 1955

Sources: UNICEF (2006); UNDP (2006).
Note: UNDP = UN Development Program; GDP = gross domestic product.
1. Less than $2 per day.
2. Below 50% of median income.
3. Figures from 1998. No recent data.

successful in 1962. Argentina was colonized by Spain, with near annihilation of the indigenous population; independence was secured in 1816, only a generation after the United States' war for independence. Mauritius was colonized first by the French and then by the British and experienced the importation and enslavement of Africans followed by the slavery-like period of indentured servitude of peoples from India. As a result, Mauritius is a highly diverse society, ethnically, religiously, and linguistically, and diversity is a major policy issue. Although never colonized, Ethiopia was squeezed between the Italian colonies in Somalia and Eritrea and was invaded and occupied by Italy from 1935 to 1941. The United States, having experienced many waves of large-scale immigration from many parts of the world, also has a highly diverse population. Denmark and Japan, on the other hand, have had considerable homogeneity within their populations, although migration to Denmark has increased.

Among the countries included, religious traditions vary widely, with a Hindu majority and sizable Christian and Muslim groups in Mauritius, Buddhism and Shintoism practiced by most of the population in Japan, almost equal numbers of followers of Islam and Ethiopian Orthodox Christianity in Ethiopia, and large majority religions in Argentina (90% Roman Catholic) and Denmark (91% Lutheran). Although Armenia is considered 94% Armenian Orthodox, Armenia was subsumed into the Soviet Union from 1921 to 1991 and endured 70 years of religious suppression.

These brief comments on history and population diversity only suggest the richness of differences in national experiences of the countries highlighted. The important lesson is that the variety of national characteristics and histories of the countries discussed will assist in examining social work in its international context. Through gaining an understanding of social work's development, current definitions and practice, and future challenges in these national contexts, comprehension of the profession in its global reality can be approached.

REFERENCES

Addams, J. (1930). *The second twenty years at Hull House: September 1909 to September 1929 with a record of a growing world consciousness.* New York: MacMillan.

Akimoto, T. (1995). *Towards the establishment of an international social work/welfare concept.* Unpublished paper. Japan Women's University, Kanagawa Japan.

American Association of Social Workers. (1947, May). Resolutions on international social welfare. *The Compass,* as reprinted in "From the Archives," *Journal of Progressive Human Services, 9*(1), 72–73.

Asamoah, Y. A., Healy, L. M., & Mayadas, N. S. (1997). Ending the international-domestic dichotomy: New approaches to a global curriculum for the millennium. *Journal of Social Work Education, 33*(2), 389–401.

Banerjee, M. M. (1998). Micro-enterprise development: A response to poverty. *Journal of Community Practice, 5*(1/2), 63–83.

Clinton, W. J. (1993, January 21). Inaugural address. *The New York Times,* p. A15.

Cox, D., & Pawar, M. (2006). *International social work: Issues, strategies and programs.* Thousand Oaks, CA: Sage.

Estes, R. J. (1984). Education for International social welfare research. In D. S. Sanders & P. Pederson (Eds.), *Education for international social welfare* (pp. 56–86). Manoa: University of Hawaii School of Social Work.

Haug, E. (2005). Critical reflections on the emerging discourse of international social work. *International Social Work 48*(2), 126–135.

Healy, L. M. (1990). [International content in social work educational programs worldwide]. Unpublished raw data.

Healy, L. M. (1995). Comparative and international overview. In T. D. Watts, D. Elliott, & N. S. Mayadas (Eds.), *International handbook on social work education* (pp. 421–439). Westport, CT: Greenwood Press.

Howard, D. S. (1947, May). Urgent international welfare measures—Our responsibility. *The Compass*, reprinted in "From the Archives," (1998). *Journal of Progressive Human Services, 9*(1), 65–72.

Jansen, G. G., & Pippard, J. L. (1998). The Grameen Bank in Bangladesh: Helping poor women with credit for self-employment. *Journal of Community Practice, 5*(1/2), 103–123.

Jebb, E. (1929). International social service. In *International Conference of Social Work* [Proceedings] (Vol. I, pp. 637–655). First Conference, Paris, July 8–13, 1928.

Kimberly, M. D. (Ed.). (1984). *Beyond national boundaries: Canadian contributions to international social work and social welfare.* Ottawa: Canadian Association of Schools of Social Work.

Lewis, L. S., & Altbach, P. G. (1996). The professoriate in international perspective. *Academe, Bulletin of the AAUP, 82*(3), 29–33.

Lorenz, W. (1997, August 24). *Social work in a changing Europe.* Paper presented to the Joint European Regional Seminar of IFSW and EASSW on Culture and Identity, Dublin, Ireland.

Lyons, K. (1999). *International social work: Themes and perspectives.* Aldershot, England: Ashgate Publishing.

Mihaly, A. (2005). *Mussa: A Somali Bantu refugee in Hartford.* Unpublished paper, University of Connecticut School of Social Work, West Hartford.

Sanders, D. S., & Pederson, P. (Eds.). (1984). *Education for international social welfare.* Manoa: University of Hawaii School of Social Work.

Stein, H. (1957, January). *An international perspective in the social work curriculum.* Paper presented at the Annual Meeting of the Council on Social Work Education, Los Angeles, CA.

Stein, H. (1990). The international and the global in education for the future. In K. Kendall (Ed.), *The international in American education* (pp. 11–16). New York: Hunter College School of Social Work.

UNICEF. (2006). *The state of the world's children 2006.* New York: Author.

UNDP. (2006). *Human development report 2006.* New York: Palgrave Macmillan for UNDP.

Warren, G. (1939). International social work. In R. Kurtz (Ed.), *Social work yearbook* (pp. 192–196). New York: Russell Sage Foundation.

Wetzel, J. W. (1995). "IASSW woman's caucus in China," *IASSW Newsletter.* Issue 3, International Association of Schools of Social Work.

PART I

THE CONTEXT OF INTERNATIONAL SOCIAL WORK: CONCEPTS, ISSUES, AND ORGANIZATIONS

CHAPTER 2

THEORIES AND CONCEPTS UNDERPINNING INTERNATIONAL SOCIAL WORK
Globalization

> There is no point to a globalization that reduces the price of a child's
> shoes, but costs the father his job.
>
> Philippine citizen, cited in World Commission
> on the Social Dimension of Globalization, 2004, p. 13

International social work requires understanding of theories and concepts of globalization, development, and human rights. Although other concepts such as human security and social inclusion/exclusion are important, globalization, development, and human rights are at the core of international social work. When added to more traditional social work theories of human behavior and the social environment, these redefine "social environment" for the twenty-first century. This chapter will address globalization and global interdependence as the context of international social work. The impact of globalization will be illustrated through selected examples.

GLOBALIZATION

Globalization sets the context for present-day international social work. Most writers agree that forces of globalization have intensified and that globalization has transformed economic and social institutions at global, national, and, sometimes, local levels. The forces of globalization have an impact on many aspects of daily life, although sectors of the global population may be outside its reach.

The debate over globalization is often a polarized one. Globalization is portrayed either as the avenue to improved living standards throughout the world, or as the intrusion of aggressive capitalism and cultural homogenization into all corners of the world. It is important not to either glorify or vilify globalization. Social workers must instead understand the forces of globalization and gain sufficient knowledge to be able to separate widely accepted myth from verifiable impacts.

Definition: What is Globalization?

Although the term *global interdependence* was widely used in the 1980s and early 1990s, the current discourse emphasizes globalization. "Globalization is a package of transnational flows of people, production, investment, information, ideas and authority" (Brysk, 2002, p. 1). Globalization also reflects "the growing interpenetration of states, markets, communications and ideas across borders" (p. 1). "A more globalized world is simultaneously more connected, cosmopolitan, commodified, and influenced by communication" (p. 6). Although Brysk discusses three arenas or streams of globalization— the interstate realm, global markets, and global civil society—the theme of commodification suggests that global markets and emphasis on consumption are dominant.

Brysk (2002), as well as other authors, suggests that globalization is not a new phenomenon, but what is new is that its forces are now "stronger and faster" (p. 1). We are reminded of earlier eras of globalization by the comments made in a speech to the First International Conference of Social Work:

> In the last hundred years, the technical application of human invention has wrought nothing short of a revolution in international relations. . . . Ships, railways, aeroplanes, telephones, wireless telegraphy, broadcasting—all these have made the world smaller, have brought us into close contact with one another for better or for worse. (Jebb, 1929, p. 637)

In the social work literature, *globalization* has been described as "a process of global integration in which diverse peoples, economies, cultures and political processes are increasingly subjected to international influences" (Midgley, 1997, p. xi). Additionally, and quite positively, Midgley suggests that globalization indicates "the emergence of an inclusive worldwide culture, a global economy, and above all, a shared awareness of the world as a single place" (p. 21). Social work literature has paid considerable attention to the negative impacts of globalization. According to Rowlands and Tan (2004), the negative social effects of globalization include harm or destruction to indigenous communities; trafficking, prostitution, and other violent and labor abuses of women and children; discrimination against or exploitation of migrants; "reductions in national budget allocations to health, education and social services; privatization of services" and "dominance of consumerism and materialism culture; increase of fundamentalist and fanatic religious groups"; and increases in crime (p. 115). The International Council on Social Welfare (ICSW; 2007) concurs that "the benefits of globalization have been unequally distributed within and between countries" (p. 15). As globalization has opened markets and sometimes increased productivity, it has failed at job creation and often resulted in job loss and deteriorating conditions for workers. Temporary work without benefits and informal sector employment have replaced full-time work for many (ICSW, 2007).

The World Commission on the Social Dimension of Globalization (2004) in their report, *A Fair Globalization*, identified winners and losers in globalization to date. Simply put, those "with capital, entrepreneurial ability, and education and skills" have benefited, while "the poor, the assetless, illiterate and unskilled workers, and indigenous people" have lost out (p. 46). The report further states that overall women have fared worse than men as a result of globalization, as freer trade has often displaced farming and market women; according to a 2003 Food and Agriculture Organization of the UN (FAO) report, women still "own less than 2% of the land worldwide and receive less than 10% of the credit" (World Commission on the Social Dimension of Globalization, 2004, p. 48). However, the report also points out that globalization has brought more women into wage employment and that this has improved their degree of independence and status in a number of societies (see the discussion of Mauritius in Chapter 8).

Even given the above statement about "losers" in globalization, the report suggests that the impact of globalization on poverty levels is ambiguous and somewhat contradictory. The authors indicate that globalization has probably hastened a decline in poverty in India and China but may have contributed to its rise, along with many other factors, in Latin America, the former East Bloc countries, and Africa. The report also cautions: "it is important to avoid the common error of attributing all observed outcomes, positive or negative, entirely to globalization" (World Commission on the Social Dimension of Globalization, 2004, p. 45). It acknowledges, however, that "globalization has developed in an ethical vacuum, where market success and failure have tended to become the ultimate standard of behaviour" and the "winner take all" approach dominates (p. 7).

Sub-Saharan Africa has fared particularly poorly since 1990, with worsening poverty and social and health indicators in many countries. Africans consulted in preparation of the fair globalization report (World Commission on the Social Dimension of Globalization, 2004) referred to globalization as "the recolonialization of our countries" (p. 15). Others from the dialogue held in Senegal said the impact of globalization on African business is "an unequal combat which would lead to certain death" and feared that Africa is being reduced to a "beggar economy" (p. 15). A contributor from the Philippines expressed what is often felt across developed and developing countries alike: "there is no point to a globalization that reduces the price of a child's shoes, but costs the father his job" (p. 13).

The fair globalization report also identified the real and potential benefits that can be reaped from globalization. Among them are increased productive capacity and the ability to distribute goods throughout the global market; "interconnectivity" among people that enhances the sense of interdependence and hopefully community; encouragement of democracy through sharing of information globally; and the growing capacity of civil society to act on the global or at least cross-national level.

To minimize the negative effects of globalization, *A Fair Globalization* called for a number of reforms. Key among them is the need to establish a minimum set of global labor standards and a minimum level of social protections for all. In addition, the report identified the need for reform of the world trade and investment systems toward increased fairness for poorer countries, increased aid, and reforms in governance to ensure meeting the Millennium Development Goals (discussed in the next chapter).

THE IMPACT OF GLOBALIZATION AND GLOBAL INTERDEPENDENCE ON VARIOUS SECTORS

Over two decades ago, Interaction's Joint Working Group on Development Education (1984) stated that "global interdependence needs to be recognized as "an irrefutable fact of life on which action must be based" (pp. 3–4). Yet, although the impact of globalization and global interdependence have been widely recognized in economic and environmental matters, the impact has been less well understood as a force affecting social work practice and professional action. This gap in comprehension is particularly acute in Western nations. Social workers in less economically powerful nations and former colonies have lived with the impact of global interdependence for many years. Borrowing of social work curriculum from the industrialized nations, presence of foreign experts in social and educational programs, and involvement with the social services initiatives of UNICEF (UN Children's Fund), the World Health Organization (WHO), UN Development Programme (UNDP), and other organizations have all contributed to a more global perspective for social work in the developing world. In the 1980s and 1990s, the impact of global economic interdependence has been acutely felt as social workers in Africa and the Caribbean have coped with structural adjustment, bringing them into personal and professional contact with International Monetary Fund (IMF) policies.

Only more recently has globalization been recognized as a force affecting social work in the industrialized countries of Europe, North America, and Japan. Yet does globalization truly matter to the individual social worker in North America? Yes, in at least the following ways: *(1)* as citizens and as social workers, personal health, security, and well-being and that of clients are directly affected by globalization and interdependence; *(2)* the impacts of globalization on economy, culture, environment, and security have social aspects; *(3)* the forces of globalization have led to increased similarities in the social problems experienced in the countries of the world, creating a large shared agenda for knowledge and action; and *(4)* countries can no longer "solve" their social problems (or protect their environments or economies) in isolation but must take other nations into account. Social workers in most if not all nations must be cognizant of global matters to understand the problems they face in working with clients and communities and in contributing to problem resolutions.

The dimensions of globalization/global interdependence and their indicators will be discussed first. Then, two issues—migration and AIDS—will be briefly presented as manifestations of global interdependence in the social welfare sphere. The impact of national policies on other nations, an important but less recognized dimension of interdependence, will be illustrated through a discussion of ways in which nations model social welfare policies after those adopted elsewhere.

Dimensions of Globalization and Interdependence

John Maxwell Hamilton, author of *Entangling Alliances* and *Main Street America and the Third World*, defined *interdependence* simply as "a nation's increased sensitivity to external forces" (p. 21). As suggested in Midgley's (1997) definition of globalization included earlier in this chapter, there are many areas affected by global interdependence: the environment, including biodiversity, pollution, and natural resources; trade; international investments and banking; use of foreign labor; dependence on resources from other countries; the range and reach of military weapons and terrorist movements; information and knowledge flows; travel and human migration; and more. Interdependence is aided by fast, cheap means of travel, by networks of telephone and computer communications, and by viewing television programs that reach far beyond the originating nation (Hamilton, 1990).

The environmental, cultural, and economic arenas of this interdependence have been widely recognized and awareness of security interdependence— the threat of nuclear war and, increasingly, terrorism, and other assaults on physical security—is acute. In this chapter, social welfare interdependence is added to the list of dimensions to be explored and is given special emphasis.

Environmental Interdependence

Environmental problems in one country are truly the problems of neighboring countries and, quite possibly, the globe. There are two main categories of environmental problems: pollution and resource depletion. Air pollution and ocean pollution do not respect national boundaries. Pollution of the ocean in any part of the world can wash onto the shores of other nations or taint fish eaten throughout the world. Pollution from industrialized cities in the northern United States affects air quality in Canada, and towns on the southern U.S. border are increasingly worried about the environmental hazards of industrial development in northern Mexico. Particulate matter collected in monitoring sites in California and Oregon has been traced to China and other Asian countries; "the U.S. Environmental Protection Agency estimates that on certain days nearly 25 percent of the particulate matter in the skies above Los Angeles can be traced to China" (Chea, 2006, p. E3). Thus, continued industrial development in China will affect the air quality of many other nations—even those thousands of miles away.

Possibly no event catalyzed world realization that environmental damage crosses borders as much as the nuclear meltdown at the factory in Chernobyl in the Ukraine in 1986. Dangerously high radiation levels were detected in Finland, Poland, Sweden, and many other nations, shocking policy makers into the realization that whatever environmental safeguards may be adopted at home are not sufficient to protect their populations.

Air pollution is linked to increases in lung cancer, asthma, bronchitis, and pneumonia. These ailments are particularly serious in crowded cities and in areas of rapid and relatively unregulated industrial development, such as China. Pollution also contributes to global warming; scientists are predicting significant climate change and rises in sea level. All nations need to be concerned about these predictions; some are more immediately imperiled. Tiny Maldives, a nation of islands in the Indian Ocean, would lose 80% of its land if sea level rises one meter ("Maldives: On the Beach," 1999). Maldives cannot address this problem alone or even make a significant contribution to its resolution; instead, it must depend on policies and actions of the rest of the nations of the world to prevent the sea from swallowing it up. Already, a small community of 100 in Vanuatu was moved to higher ground in the interior of Tegua island in August 2005 "after their coastal homes were repeatedly swamped by storm surges and aggressive waves linked with climate change" (UN Environment Program [UNEP], 2005). The increased number of natural disasters—especially hurricanes and cyclones—in the first years of the twenty-first century are blamed at least in part on climate change attributed to pollution.

The use of pesticide provides another example. Pesticides banned for use in some nations are still being exported to countries with fewer regulations. These pesticides then reenter other countries' food supplies on imported fruits and vegetables. Still other pesticides, such as DDT, travel in rain and wind to affect areas where their use has been banned (Hamilton, 1986).

According to the UN Division for the Advancement of Women (2005), 2.4 billion people lack essential sanitation—a number that has remained static or increased slightly for a decade. Through globalization, unsanitary conditions in one part of the world can be spread by affected food imported by another or can lead to infections being passed through international travel and migration. Tuberculosis is prevalent in crowded and unsanitary conditions; it then fans out to other places with migrants. "Tuberculosis travels across the border between El Paso, Texas, and Ciudad Juarez, Mexico, as does malaria, cysticerosis, typhoid, leprosy, schistosomiasis, viral hepatitis and Chagas' disease" (Keigher & Lowery, 1998, p. 155). Once again, the conditions of sanitation and pollution become everyone's concern. Thus, a suburban businessman may be sitting next to an undocumented immigrant with drug-resistant tuberculosis on the New York subway. The conditions in the immigrant's homeland and the policy of denying health care to undocumented immigrants may cost the businessman his health or even his life. The need for new policies was demonstrated in mid-2007 when a lawyer from the United States with drug-resistant TB made several trans-Atlantic flights and crossed several borders in spite of instructions not to do so and an order to the border control agents not to let him reenter the United States. In many ways, environmental interdependence can be devastating even at the personal level.

Depletion is the second dimension in environmental degradation. Depletion of the world's resources through overuse and carelessness includes mineral resources, forests, water, and soil. As of 1997, there were 26 countries classified as water scarce (Hoff, 1997). Soil loss and desertification (the loss of agricultural land to encroaching desert) contribute to food shortages and push rural people into already crowded cities. Deforestation contributes to increased erosion, pollution, and global warming, and to the extinction of species. It has been estimated that deforestation in the tropics may cost the world 15% to 20% of its species (Hoff, 1997, p. 31). Efforts or lack of efforts in various countries affect all of our futures, yet conservation is feared as an undue burden in poorer nations. Hamilton (1990) quoted a small farmer in Costa Rica, "I know I can destroy the future of the forest and the people, but I have to eat today" (p. 91). Costa Rica was 75% natural forest in 1950, and by 1977 only 33%. Since 2000, Costa Rica has reversed the loss of forest and has seen a very modest gain in forestation (Food and Agriculture Organization of the UN [FAO], 2007). Globally, however, forest loss continues.

More than one billion people live without access to improved sources of drinking water. UNDP further notes that 1.4 billion people live in areas where "water use exceeds sustainable levels" (UNDP, 2006, p. 26) setting up conditions for future, if not present, crisis. This water stress is projected to grow considerably over the next 15 to 20 years. According to UNDP (2006), " 'not having access' to water and sanitation is a polite euphemism for a form of deprivation that threatens life, destroys opportunity and undermines human dignity" (p. 14).

Environmental interdependence affects all peoples of the world and is a major challenge to world policy processes and goals. The loss of biodiversity and the increase in deforestation and desertification are causing immediate severe hardships for people in the affected areas. Famine and regular food shortages, displacement of communities, and increasingly harsh daily routines of water and fuel gathering for women and children are among the social effects. Environmental challenges complicate development efforts and have led to demands for development models that emphasize sustainability—the preservation of the future capacity for development.

Cultural Interdependence

Advancements in communications technologies, cheap world travel, and movements of populations internationally bring cultures into frequent contact with each other. Speaking of the Caribbean region, Robotham (1996) said that transnational culture has invaded even the masses: "Able to access relatively cheap travel, to exploit the wide extension of modern digital international telephone linkages in the region, and to receive substantial remittances from relatives in North America and Britain, a whole informal transnational culture has been generated among this group" (pp. 23–24). Exchange of cultural influences and consumer goods is spread by legions of women in the Caribbean who travel throughout the region to the Cayman islands, Martinique, Panama, and even New York and Miami, buying and selling produce, crafts, and other consumer goods; their activities are so extensive that they have earned the title of informal commercial importers—ICIs.

The influences of cultures on other cultures are seen in changes in food, entertainment, and lifestyles. These changes can be seen as enriching, homogenizing, or evil. Hokenstad and Midgley (1997) discussed the importance of "international roots" of culture in countries that are increasingly diverse. Celebrating diversity expresses the enrichment view of cross-cultural influence.

Cross-cultural influence can, however, have a homogenizing effect on mass culture. Rock, rap, and reggae music can be heard in Boston, Bucharest, Bujumbura, and Bogotá. Teens wear jeans and U.S. sports team T-shirts from Uruguay to Uganda. The spread of franchised fast-food chains means one can eat the same food in most countries of the world. Cross-cultural influence is at once welcomed and rejected. In Kenya, the popularity of Western rock music led a television critic to comment: "Kenyan culture suffers as the nation is bombarded by foreign styles of music and dance—as though Kenyans are incapable of making their own" (Amboka Andere of *The Standard*, cited in Hamilton, 1990, p. 128). Diffusion of culture, although linked with Westernization, can also be South to North, as suggested by the worldwide spread and popularity of reggae music from its origins in Jamaica. Although much of this cultural impact is superficial, it causes concern that deeper cultural traditions and values may be lost if the homogenizing influence of mass culture expands.

Globalization as an evil cultural influence is expressed in a book *Social Strains of Globalization in India* (Taber & Batra, 1995). "Globalization is first of all, a threat to accustomed ways of living and solving problems.... While globalization means more consumer goods and better incomes for many, it also means, for example, increased materialism with higher dowry demands and more degradation for female infants" (Taber & Batra, p. 24). Thus, global influences are seen as attacks on positive aspects of traditional cultures, resulting either in loss of tradition or in strange mutations, such as dowry demands for television sets, VCRs, and cars.

The UNDP (1998) concurs that consumption is having negative effects on culture, as well as on health and environment. Particularly noted are "the pressure of competitive spending and rising social standards of consumption, with worrying trends showing the consumption of 'luxuries' rising faster than the consumption of 'necessities' " (p. 65). These developments mean that consumption becomes a force for social exclusion rather than inclusion.

Tourism—"the quintessential transnational industry"—brings other forms of cultural influence, in some cases changing the way a nation portrays

Figure 2.1 Tourists are warned of the dangers of leaving hotel property in Barbados, 2007.

itself to the world (Robotham, 1996). There are real and potential benefits to tourism. Tourism provides a means for countries without an industrial base to use their natural assets, such as beaches, forests, and animal and bird life to generate jobs and earn income. In a number of countries, tourism is a leading source of foreign exchange. Tourism also provides opportunities for cultural enrichment and intercultural exchange. Visitors may learn about new places, explore historical sites and museums, experience different natural environments, learn about cultures, and have opportunities to meet people from cultures very different from their own. These experiences can affect tourists' attitudes and build global mindedness. Still other tourist locations, such as the Disney theme parks, New York, and Paris, are potential meeting places for visitors from many parts of the world.

But there are darker sides to this "quintessential transnational industry." Sex tourism is perhaps the darkest. In Thailand, for example, rural poverty and unemployment drive women into cities to seek work, where "sex tourism has created a great demand for women in the 'service sector' " (Mensendiek, 1997, p. 173). Traditional family and religious ideologies are upset when poor women become prostitutes to support their families. Although the cost to society is high, the cost to the women themselves is higher, as AIDS and other sexually transmitted diseases are rampant. And, "for those who profit from the sex industry, women are commodities easily replaced if they become ill or die" (Mensendiek, p. 173). In other parts of the world, young boys are also lured into prostitution as part of the sex tourist industry and face early death from AIDS, ostracism from societies hostile to homosexual activity, and the typical risks to prostitutes of exploitation and physical abuse. International human trafficking has joined trafficking in drugs and weapons as lucrative forms of international organized crime. Sex trafficking has been furthered by the Internet, which permits "shopping" for opportunities to sexually exploit others.

When tourism is not respectful of local peoples and traditions, the potentials for positive cross-cultural contact are violated. Tourists may remain in opulent fortresses, whereas local residents are banned from entering the premises and using their own beaches. Or tourists may venture out to snap pictures of residents as if they were oddities or mere parts of the scenery. Environmental damage also results from tourism, whether from the chemicals used on newly constructed golf courses or from careless destruction of coral reefs.

The impact of tourism and cultural homogenization on indigenous cultures may be particularly severe. Even efforts to preserve indigenous culture through showcasing them for tourists are controversial. Promotion of Maori villages in New Zealand as tourist sites earns income for Maori residents and encourages preservation of indigenous practices and arts. Yet there is a thin line between exploitation and preservation and learning.

Security Interdependence

During the many years of the cold war, people in the United States and the Soviet Union knew that their security depended on a stand-off and restraint between the two nuclear superpowers. The euphoria that greeted the breakup of the Soviet empire and the turn of the newly independent parts of that nation toward democracy was short lived. What replaced the stand-off of superpowers was the potential decentralization of conflict and lessened control in ensuring nuclear restraint. With nuclear weapons held in various parts of the former Soviet Union—new and relatively politically unstable countries—and in Pakistan and India—neighboring countries with a history of hostility toward each other—nuclear insecurity has increased. Still other countries, notably Iran and North Korea, are developing nuclear capacities. Global interdependence is obvious in the face of the nuclear threat, in terms of the inability to contain the effects of a nuclear explosion and the likely spread of regional conflicts into wider attacks.

International Terrorism. International terrorism is a newer threat to security, although terrorism has long been used in domestic situations. A tool often used by groups who are oppressed and feel powerless in the larger world system, terrorist attacks have been carried out against military bases, commercial airliners, a cruise ship, department stores, embassies, night clubs, trains, buses, and crowded market areas of city streets. The international dimension of terrorism was widely publicized after the September 2001 attacks by the al-Qaida network on the World Trade Center in New York City and the Pentagon in Washington, D.C. The extensive global nature of the network was evident, as the perpetrators came from and trained in various countries in the

IMPACT OF SEPTEMBER 11, 2001, ATTACKS ON WORLD TRADE CENTER: A LOCAL EVENT/A GLOBAL IMPACT	
Number of additional people pushed into poverty	10,000,000 estimated (World Bank, 2001)
Reduction in remittances sent	Various estimates
% of Caribbean vacations for 2001–2002 cancelled	65%
Number of countries of origin of people killed	91 (Hirschkorn, 2003)
Number of jobs lost in travel and tourism	10.5 million (ICSW, 2007)

Middle East; planned the attacks during stays in various European cities; and then carried out the attacks in the United States. Financing for the complex plot surely involved even more countries. The list of victims of the 2001 attacks further demonstrates globalization; an estimated 500 foreign nationals from 91 countries are believed to have been killed at the World Trade Center alone (Hirschkorn, 2003). Attacks have followed around the world, in Spain, Bali, England, and other places. Although assigning motives for terrorism is complex, it appears that they include complex issues of globalization, global politics, and fears of cultural imperialism. The rise of fundamentalism in Islam, Hinduism, and Christianity has been linked to cultural and political hegemonies as well as fear of the changing world. International cooperation is needed to not only improve security and detection but also to work on resolutions to persistent situations of deprivation and conflict, such as those in Palestine and in Northern Ireland.

Regional and Internal Conflicts. Other challenges to the hope for an era of peace have been two wars in Iraq and numerous internal and regional conflicts. Often internal conflicts spread into other countries. Chad is increasingly threatened by the civil conflict in Darfur, Sudan, and the conflicts that gave rise to genocide in Rwanda involved Burundi and the Democratic Republic of Congo as well. Severe and persistent tensions in the Middle East have generated periodic bombings in Lebanon and Palestinian refugee camps and terrorist attacks in Israel. The cost in human suffering and destruction resulting from local and regional conflicts is staggering.

Economic Interdependence

The global economy is the most recognized dimension of globalization. Its impacts are of particular importance to social workers and their clients. The flaws of the global economy, including long-term unemployment, labor in-security, debt, and low incomes continue to have negative impacts on human welfare around the world. In countries where the impact is severe, social cohesion is being affected (Wagner, 1997). Countries are economically inter-dependent in many ways, including through world trade, investments, cur-rency regulations, aid, and lending. Multinational corporations produce products through complex arrangements in many countries, blurring the concept of domestic and foreign production. Cumulatively these corporations have a significant global impact because of their size.

Countries have long recognized their dependence on other nations for access to raw materials that could not be produced domestically, and for markets to sell products produced in abundance and to generate income. Countries that have few mineral resources, or have limited land for agricul-tural production, or short growing seasons are highly dependent on inter-national trade to obtain goods for survival. Some countries continue to grow or produce only one or two major commodities for export, leaving them highly vulnerable to the global market forces that determine the price of their products and their imports. At independence in 1968, for example, Mauritius received nearly all of its foreign exchange earnings from sugar, which con-stituted 93% of annual exports (Bowman, 1991). In a table labeled "desperate dependence," UN Conference on Trade and Development (UNCTAD) sta-tistics showed that in 1989 Burundi earned 84% of foreign exchange from coffee; Zambia 88% from copper; Ghana 66% from cocoa; and the Nether-lands Antilles 92% from oil products (UN, 1990). Presently, the more than 40 developing countries that depend on a single agricultural product such as coffee or bananas for more than 20% of their export earnings are suffering from declining agricultural prices (Global Policy Forum, 2005). As prices fall, such countries experience a major drop in income and diminished well-being for the population.

The growth of multinational companies and the globalization of the economy means that jobs can be moved from country to country in search of lower costs and higher profits. Industrialized countries and some of the more successful newly industrializing countries have experienced plant closings and loss of jobs to other countries, resulting in high unemployment and severe dislocation for workers in affected industries. These trends affect many, thus social workers need to understand that "even in the most individual casework efforts, the international economy has an effect" (Day, 1989, p. 232).

Oil and Debt: Economic Interdependence at the Crisis Level. Two world crises of the last quarter of the twentieth century underscore the impact of global economic interdependence and the interaction between global economic forces and social welfare. These are the "oil crisis" of the early 1970s and the debt crisis, which began shortly thereafter and continues to the present. Ac-cording to Isbister (2003), the oil crisis and the debt crisis demonstrate the extent to which economies of poor countries are "enmeshed in an increasingly globalized economy" (p. 183).

Oil is recognized as one of the world's crucial and essentially nonrenewable resources. Although oil reserves are concentrated in the Middle East, multinational oil companies controlled production and pricing until the early 1970s, with oil prices fixed at about US$3.00 per barrel. In 1973, Saudi Arabia and its allies, angered by U.S. support of Israel, realized that oil was a potent political weapon. They joined together in the Organization of Petroleum Exporting Countries (OPEC) and instituted first a boycott of sales to the United States and then a large oil price increase to $13 a barrel. These actions touched off shortages (Isbister, 2003). By 1979, the price had risen to $30 per barrel, a tenfold increase in just 6 years. According to Isbister, "the price increase was easily the biggest shock the international economy had sustained since the Second World War" (p. 177). In the industrialized countries, recession, inflation, and a scramble for conservation resulted. There were human casualties, as well. Sharp increases in utility costs for home heating, cooking, and lighting produced a new class of homeless people—those forced out of their homes by astronomical utility bills that led to inability to pay rents or mortgages. Still others were sheltered in apartments or homes without heat or lights, after utilities were turned off for nonpayment. A demand for new social services resulted, spurring development of fuel banks and utility assistance programs across the United States.

In poorer countries, the impact was and is much greater. Non-OPEC countries began to borrow money to pay for greatly increased costs of imported oil. Their options were limited, as most oil in developing countries was used for industry, not personal home or transportation consumption. Thus, consumption could not be curtailed without harming productivity. Indeed, "the origin of the third world debt crisis was the OPEC price increases of the 1970's . . . the price increases produced a tidal wave of change in international monetary relations" (Isbister, 2003, p. 180).

The urgent need for money to buy oil in poorer countries coincided with the availability of money for loans, as OPEC countries were investing in Western banks the huge sums of cash they had earned from oil sales. Soon, a new crisis, the international debt crisis, eclipsed the oil crisis. National governments took on big loans, and these debts were increased by rising interest rates; falling commodities prices impaired ability to repay. Many countries in Latin America and Africa were soon faced with debt repayments that were so large that they were impossible to pay. This, in turn, was a threat to banks in industrialized countries and, potentially, to the world banking system because the loans were so large that for a time they exceeded the net worth of the banks. Interdependence was painfully obvious to officials in borrowing and lending countries alike, and it was having an impact on ordinary people through appeals for bank bailouts, cuts in production in the North, and through rapidly falling standards of living in the South. The heaviest burden fell on the poorer countries: "for the developed countries, the debt crisis was only a potential danger (of bank collapse), but for the third world it was a monumental present disaster" (Isbister, 2003, p. 181).

As the amount of principal and interest that a country was expected to pay back each year reached or even exceeded half the total value of their exports in any one year, it was clear that these countries were in deep trouble. To address such negative debt ratios, imports had to be cut, government spending for services was reduced, and as a result standards of living fell— often dramatically. In Mexico, for example, real wages fell by 40% from 1982 to 1988 and poverty increased. More shocking was the decrease in per-capita annual income in Nigeria, an oil-exporting country that borrowed to expand projects and was devastated by falling oil prices and poor management of funds, from $800 to $380 in just the 2-year period from 1985 to 1987 (Isbister, 2003). The numbers do not begin to express the human misery that resulted from debt and its "remedy."

Structural Adjustment. The remedy for the debt crisis was structural adjustment, a set of reform policies designed by the international financial institutions and imposed on indebted countries as a condition of eligibility for future loans and/or for refinancing of existing debt to permit lower payments. As defined by Hoy (1998), structural adjustment is a cluster of policies that "demand that governments spend within their means, keep exchange rates competitive, let markets determine prices, withdraw from regulation and subsidy, and privatize industries that had previously been nationalized" (p. 163). Thus, governments were required to spend less on health and education, to remove subsidies on food and transportation, and to devalue their currencies—a move that resulted in drastic declines in purchasing power for wage earners. The structural adjustment cure has been as painful as the disease of debt for the people in many countries.

In Jamaica between 1977/78 and 1988/89, the percentage of public expenditures on debt payments rose from 17.7% to almost 40%, while the percentage spent on education dropped from 16% to 12% (Anderson & Witter, 1994, p. 20). In discussing the impact of structural adjustment in Jamaica:

> The losers were clear. They were seen in the increased numbers of homeless and mentally ill searching routinely through garbage containers, they were absorbed among the numbers of youth recruited into criminal posses, they were included among the fixed income pensioners whose private poverty could not be relieved by food stamps, they were numbered among those who stood grimly in visa lines, and they were to be found among those whose incomes were increasingly inadequate for the purchase of basic food requirements. (Anderson & Witter, 1994, p. 52)

The impact of cutbacks in education included increased teacher–pupil ratio, lower attendance, declines in performance on standardized tests, and crumbling facilities. Although major health indicators do not easily show short-term changes, statistics showed an increase of certain infectious diseases, and the children's hospital reported rate of admissions of children for malnutrition changed from 3.5 per 1000 admissions in 1975 to 8.3 in 1985 (Fox, cited in Anderson & Witter, 1994, p. 49).

These results were not confined to Jamaica. Indeed, throughout the "structurally adjusted world," researchers and field staff from UNICEF and nongovernmental organizations (NGOs) found increased poverty, rising rates of infant mortality in countries such as Ghana and Brazil, reappearances of diseases thought to be eliminated, including yellow fever in Ghana and malaria in Peru, and falling school enrollments (Hoy, 1998, p. 54). The economic policies imposed on poorer countries by the international financial institutions continue to have a demonstrable affect on the social well-being of people and the social welfare services of the affected countries. Increased poverty, lower access to health care and education, and resulting rises in infant mortality, infectious disease, and illiteracy resulted. Additional social problems arose as secondary results, including increases in homelessness, street children, child labor, youth unemployment, and youth violence.

Structural adjustment has had an impact beyond the economic ones and has created what Anderson and Witter (1994) call a new and dangerous "belief system."

> Structural adjustment was viewed as a set of externally-imposed measures designed to swing the balance further in favour of the propertied classes, and to extract resources from the country through increasing foreign penetration and international indebtedness. The prevailing ethos at all levels of society was consequently one of negativism and futility. What needs to be explored is the extent to which this ethos becomes entrenched and unsurmountable. (p. 54)

Why did countries agree to adjust their economies in such damaging ways? Most likely, they had no choice if they were to remain within the international economic system at all.

> As first Mexico and then Venezuela discovered and now South Africa is discovering, within the space of a day, a state whose finances loses the confidence of transnational finance capital faces the immediate collapse of its currency. It has little choice but to adopt the fiscal austerity measures demanded by the global market or to face financial ruin and the collapse of its ability to rule. (Robotham, 1996, p. 15)

Although the crisis has eased somewhat—especially from the perspective of Northern financial institutions which no longer face collapse because of debt—many countries remain heavily indebted, and debt continues to weigh down prospects for development. There are currently 30 countries with foreign debt of over 100% of gross domestic product (GDP) and another 9 are dangerously close. Jamaica has an external debt of US$6.9 billion, which is 133% of its GDP, earning it the distinction of being a SILIC—one of 45 severely indebted low-income countries. Tiny Mauritius owes $2.5 billion, 46% of its GDP, and though Argentina paid its debts to the IMF, it still owes a staggering $109 billion in external debt (Central Intelligence Agency [CIA], 2007). In addition, in 2007, oil prices climbed rapidly to new highs, topping out at almost $100 a barrel. The cost of energy continues to present a serious barrier to development in poorer, energy-importing countries.

The IMF and the World Bank have recognized that the structural adjustment measures of the 1980s had serious unintended consequences and have modified the conditions for lending. Although the world financial institutions have softened demands for cutbacks in government spending, the financial pressures on poor countries, including energy costs, constrain their ability to devote significant new resources to basic human needs.

Trade. World trade relationships are a significant element of globalization and have more impact on poor countries than international aid: "trade-facilitated globalization has profound human effect" (International Federation for Human Rights, 2005, p. 3). The opening up of markets to permit free movement of goods and services has been the goal of recent trade negotiations. In 1994, the World Trade Organization (WTO) was established to negotiate trade agreements. The round of trade negotiations held in 1994 in Uruguay (therefore called the "Uruguay Round") resulted in new agreements on trade in services in addition to earlier agreements on goods and tariffs. Under the General Agreement on Trade in Services (GATS), "national governments may not regulate the entry of firms from such sectors as financial services, insurance, telecommunications, transport, advertising and professional services which operate in other member states" (Prigoff, 2000, p. 134). Social services may well be covered under this set of agreements. Of more concern is that GATS permits foreign competition in essential services, such as water supplies.

With less political and economic power, poorer nations have been disadvantaged in trade negotiations and therefore in the outcomes of international trade (Prigoff, 2000). Their inability to protect their weaker agricultural sectors has led to economic ruin for some developing country farmers, such as banana growers in the Caribbean.

> For many of the world's poorer countries, rapid globalization and trade liberalization without appropriate changes in the international trading system, such as reforming agricultural subsidies in developed countries and better access to developed country markets, have led to unfair competition, adverse terms of trade, job displacements, and worsening employment prospects. (ICSW, 2007, p. 15)

Social Issues and Globalization: Two Examples

The dimensions of globalization discussed above—environment, culture, security, and economics—have significant implications for social work. Globalization is also directly evident in the social welfare issues that are the focus of social work professional responsibility. Migration and the AIDS crisis will be discussed as two examples of interdependence in the social welfare arena; both show the interplay of various dimensions of globalization.

Migration. The international movement of peoples is undoubtedly the most dramatic social indicator of globalization, especially to the people-focused profession of social work. "Globalisation causes increased interdependency between nations and increased migration over borders" (Hessle, 2007, p. 240). Among these international populations are refugees, forced from their countries by war or by various forms of political and religious oppression. Others flee famine, internal strife, and severe economic deprivation, including that caused by structural adjustment. Still others migrate, temporarily or permanently, to seek better opportunities in education or employment. According to Moreno (2006), 175 million people are currently living outside their country of origin.

Refugees are a special class of migrants with particularly severe needs; they are dependent on international organizations to arrange temporary and permanent settlement—a status sometimes difficult to achieve. The total population of concern to the UN High Commission for Refugees (UNHCR; 2005) in 2004 was 19.2 million, 9.2 million of them classified officially as refugees. Figures for FY 2004 show that the United States admitted 52,875 refugees (down from 112,000 in 1997), and Canada admitted 32,686 in 2004 (Martin, 2005; Ray, 2005). There were particularly sharp drop-offs in resettlement of refugees after the 2001 terrorist attacks on the United States; numbers for FY 2002 and 2003 were below 29,000 per year, extending the stay in overcrowded refugee camps for many (Martin, 2005).

Although the United States, Canada, and European countries accept significant numbers of refugees for resettlement, it is important to understand that "the large majority of refugees from the developing nations have fled to other developing countries" (Mupedziswa, 1997, p. 112). The impact of refugee influx on the world's poorest countries is significant. Although the international community provides assistance, the burden on the countries hosting the refugees is often hard to manage. Mupedziswa (1997) cites the case of the Mozambican refugees who fled into Malawi at such a rate that at one point there was one Mozambican refugee to every nine Malawians; the sending and receiving countries are among the world's poorest. Pakistan, ranked 134th on the Human Development Index and therefore struggling to meet its own development needs, has had to cope with Afghan refugees for many years. As of 1998, Pakistan was providing asylum to 1,202,700 refugees (UNDP, 1998), and numbers remain at almost a million, although an estimated 1.8 million Afghans had returned home as of 2004 (UNHCR, 2005). The influx of Rwandan refugees into the former Zaire (now Democratic Republic of the Congo) was a destabilizing force, contributing to that country's 1997 coup. In 1996, 1,700,000 refugees from tiny Rwanda were in neighboring Burundi, Tanzania, Uganda, and Zaire (UNDP, 1996). The war in Iraq caused four million refugees to flee during the period from the invasion in 2003 to mid-2007. More than a million went to Syria and 750,000 to Jordan (Kuykendall, 2007).

Even in wealthy countries, providing refugee asylum or resettlement is difficult and costly. The practice implications of resettlement will be discussed further in Chapter 11.

A far larger number of international migrants are legal and illegal immigrants. Although they migrate voluntarily, many do so only because opportunities are severely limited in their own countries or because they are enduring oppressions and persecutions not officially recognized by the UN or by receiving countries. The number of legal "conventional" immigrants admitted into the United States in 2005, for example, was a little over one million, excluding refugees. About 650,000 of these came under family-sponsored, reunification, and preferences categories, with another 246,000 admitted as employment preferences (U.S. Office of Immigration Statistics, 2006). Temporary migrants—guest workers—are prevalent in Europe and the Middle East. In times of labor shortage in northern Europe, laborers from Greece, Turkey, and other countries were recruited to work in such countries as Germany and Sweden. Although some guest workers returned to their home countries, others stayed on and became targets of resentment and discrimination as economic conditions worsened in the host countries. Workers from developing countries, including Mauritius, the Philippines, and others have been recruited to work in the Gulf States as work opportunities there expanded rapidly because of oil prosperity. Migration is becoming increasingly a female phenomenon in some areas; for example, temporary migrants in Spain from the Dominican Republic are mostly women, according to a recent study by Institute for Research and Training for the Advancement of Women (INSTRAW) (Moreno, 2006).

Figure 2.2 Immigrant workers from Burkina Faso work as launderers in Côte d'Ivoire, 1981.

In addition to legal immigrants, there are a large number of illegal immigrants. Although numbers cannot be accurately determined, the number of undocumented immigrants in the United States was estimated at over 10 million in 2005 (Capp & Fix, 2005). Although most come from Mexico, there are also significant numbers who enter from Europe and Asia and overstay tourist visas. A final group making up "international populations" are visitors, students, diplomats, and employees of foreign companies and their families residing temporarily in another country.

Together, these various groups are the willing and unwilling ambassadors of global interdependence. Their presence demonstrates that political and economic conditions in one country affect the very population makeup of other countries. Increases in international population movements in the 1980s, 1990s, and the early twenty-first century have turned formerly homogeneous countries such as Denmark and Sweden into multicultural ones and have further diversified already diverse populations, such as those in Canada and the United States. A welcoming refugee policy resulted in more than a million refugees resettled in Sweden in just 30 years; today, 20% of Swedish residents were born in another country (Hessle, 2007). The 2001 census of Canada revealed that 17.7% of the population was foreign born, whereas in 2006 12.5% of the population of the United States was foreign born (Ray, 2005; U.S. Census Bureau, 2007). This was an increase in the United States from 7.9% in 1990 and from a low of 4.8% in 1970 (*World Almanac*, 1999). The contribution to diversity can be seen by review of the top ten countries of origin of the foreign born in the United States: Mexico, China, Philippines, India, Cuba, Vietnam, El Salvador, Korea, Dominican Republic, and Canada (U.S. Census Bureau, 2001). Such population transformations are a direct result of globalization that, to use Hessle's (2007) words, is "relentlessly" drawing nations "into an increasing interdependency with the rest of the world" (p. 231).

Often, only part of a family migrates, creating transnational families. The interactions of these families create new sets of interdependencies, at micro- and macrolevels. Within the family, phone calls and visits are made, plans may be made for other family members to migrate, and money and gifts are sent home. Cumulatively, these activities have an impact at the macrolevel. Remittances—payments sent to family members in other countries from their kin and friends—totaled $126 billion in 2004 (Moreno, 2006). Remittances make up the second largest source of foreign exchange for many developing countries, including Jamaica. Modifications in immigration policy in the United States, Canada, or Great Britain can therefore have a direct impact on Jamaica's balance of payments. In addition to money, there are "social remittances"—the "constant bidirectional flow of resources, discourses, ideas and images" between family members (Moreno, 2006). These exchanges symbolize and strengthen globalization.

Immigration policies in one country often dictate social conditions in other countries in other ways. Officials in Jamaica believe that the stricter provisions adopted in 1996 for deportation of immigrants who commit criminal offenses in the United States has led to a measurable increase in violent crime in Jamaica—crime committed by "drug-dealing 'posse' members deported home to Jamaica from the U.S." (J. Maxwell, personal communication, April 25, 1997). In 2006, 3,004 offenders were deported to Jamaica from various countries; of these, 1,005 had committed drug offenses; 55 murder or manslaughter; and 58 rape (Planning Institute of Jamaica, 2007). The burden on a small country with a population of fewer than 3 million is considerable. The volume and changing patterns of migration make transnationalism a new and potent reality and one of critical importance to social work.

AIDS. The rapid spread of HIV/AIDS to every country in the world has been another stunning health and social indicator demonstrating that no country is a fortress. According to Peter Piot, executive director of Joint UN Programme on HIV/AIDS (UNAIDS), AIDS is the ultimate disease of globalization and interdependence, as each person with HIV is connected to all the others around the world with the virus. HIV can only be transmitted through the "most intimate of contacts"—sexual relations, sharing blood, or mother's milk—yet it spread rapidly to every country of the world (Piot, 2004). Today, HIV infection has been acknowledged around the world, and AIDS is recognized as a major global problem with health, economic, and social dimensions. AIDS has crossed borders with ease, moving along routes of international transport and travel. A writer for *The Economist* described its spread across Africa this way: "it marched with rebel armies through the continent's numerous war zones, rode with truckers from one rest-stop brothel to the next, and eventually flew, perhaps with an air steward, to America" ("AIDS in the Third World," 1999, p. 42). Even if this dramatic scenario is not completely accurate, it is clear that globalization—in transport of goods, the impact of armed conflict, and air travel—was and is a force in the spread of AIDS.

Although universally present, AIDS, like poverty, is differentially affecting the countries of the world. More than 47 million people have been infected, and approximately 25 million have died since identification of the virus (UNAIDS, 2005). In 2005, there were 4.9 million new infections, bringing the estimated number of persons living with HIV to over 40 million (UNAIDS, 2005). Although India has the largest number of people living with HIV (estimated at 3–5 million), the countries of southern and eastern Africa have the highest proportion of infection; in Botswana, for example, 37.3% of people between the ages of 15 and 49 are HIV positive (UNAIDS, 2005). Of the more than 3 million deaths from AIDS in 2005, 2.4 million were in Sub-Saharan Africa, showing the unequal toll of this epidemic. High rates of infection mean that life expectancies have been dramatically lowered for Botswana, Zambia, Kenya, Zimbabwe, Guyana, Honduras, and other countries. By 2010, life expectancy in Guyana is projected to fall from 60 today to 50; without AIDS, the projected life span would be 68. The numbers for Botswana are even worse. Infants in 1998 could only expect to live 40 years; without AIDS, the

Figure 2.3 AIDS prevention is urged in a rusting sign in Addis Ababa where little treatment is available, 2005.

life expectancy would have been 62. In 1998, UNDP predicted that by 2010 an infant born in Botswana would face a life span in the 30s (p. 35); by 2005, actual life expectancy at birth in Botswana was 37 years (UNAIDS, 2005). Between 1990 and 2003, life expectancies fell by 15 or more years in five countries and from 6–15 years in an additional 10 (UNICEF, 2004).

Social workers are particularly concerned about the number of AIDS orphans. By 2003, 15 million children had lost one or both parents to AIDS, with many more living in households with ill and dying parents (UNICEF, 2004). Especially in Africa, child-headed households are a growing concern, as adolescents or younger children assume care for their dying parents or for siblings when parents die. Child mortality has also increased. Children die directly from AIDS and indirectly from the effects of the disease because of malnutrition and lack of care either because of the death of parents or from impoverishment of families and communities when breadwinners die.

The economic impact of AIDS affects families, businesses, and even national economies. The death of large numbers of workers in their prime productive years means shortages of skilled labor, wasted investments in training, and expenses of rehiring and training. Absenteeism for illness and funeral attendance impairs productivity; in Zambia, one cement plant experienced a 15-fold increase in absenteeism caused by funeral attendance between 1992 and 1995 (McNeil, 1998). When life expectancies are significantly lowered, it becomes economically inefficient to train highly skilled professionals, such as doctors and teachers. Some countries are finding it impossible to replace teachers or nurses who die from the disease. AIDS-related health care costs strain national budgets, even though most in poor countries have no access to life-prolonging drugs. The cost of the AIDS drug "cocktail" for just one patient could provide primary health care or schooling for many children for one year in Africa. Health systems thus have to make harsh choices, meaning that those infected die sooner than they would in richer countries. Even burial expenses are a burden for families and for those industries that pay for them as employee benefits. A recent report suggests that as a result of the costs of deaths, absenteeism, and care giving, Kenya's GDP is 15% lower than it would have been without AIDS and per capita income is 10% less (Thumbi, 2005). It is obvious, then, that HIV/AIDS is a global problem of such magnitude that it is reversing development progress in some countries and impeding it in many others.

There are some success stories in HIV education and prevention, suggesting ways for social work to contribute locally and globally. Many of the factors fueling the rapid spread of AIDS exist in all countries, rich and poor alike: taboos on talking about sex, myths and misinformation about the disease and how it is spread, stigma associated with HIV infection, and sexism that forces women to submit to men's sexual demands. Unless and until a cure or vaccine is developed, education and prevention along with expanding life-prolonging drug treatment remain the key strategies for fighting AIDS. The UNAIDS documented the success of education in Uganda, a poor country with low levels of literacy. One of the first African countries to admit the threat posed by AIDS, the government commissioned low-cost but useful surveys of sexual behavior and mounted an anti-AIDS public information campaign. A key ingredient was to give "free rein to scores of non-governmental organizations, usually foreign-financed, to do whatever it took to educate people about risky sex" ("Aids in the Third World," 1999, p. 44). As a result, the "potholed streets of Kampala are lined with signs promoting fidelity and condoms" ("Aids in the Third World," p. 44), frank information is widely distributed, and schools use role-playing to teach adolescents how to deal with risky situations. Surveys show that Ugandans are delaying sexual activity, using condoms more frequently, and having fewer sexual partners. The results were impressive; HIV rates among women tested at prenatal clinics fell from about 30% to 15% in just 5 years ("Aids in the Third World," 1999).

Social work is among the active professions in the Ugandan struggle against AIDS; indeed, no human service profession in Uganda has been able to ignore AIDS (Ankrah, 1992). Social workers have taken on a variety of roles, including provision of supportive counseling to AIDS sufferers and their families, development of community support networks to assist those with AIDS, health education, and research (Ankrah, 1992). Health education activities have been extensive. Social workers have worked through the Red Cross, through churches, and with the AIDS Information Center to prepare educational materials, conduct supportive studies, and train groups including local leaders, religious leaders, teachers, police, women's groups, and agricultural extension staff on AIDS prevention. Training of trainers is another social work role. The Department of Social Work and Social Administration at Makerere University has conducted research into "social, cultural and behavioral aspects of AIDS" (Ankrah, 1992, p. 58); students have been involved in this field research, resulting in a number being employed full time as AIDS researchers at graduation. The Department's work was recognized; the government granted the department a seat on the National Committee for the Prevention of AIDS (Ankrah, 1992).

There have also been significant improvements in provision of antiretroviral drugs to severely affected countries. Here again, globalization is demonstrated through the coalitions of international aid organizations including the UN, industrialized country governments, and private foundations, such as the Bill and Melinda Gates Foundation. Although falling short of targets, there have been impressive increases in the numbers of Africans with HIV receiving life-sustaining drug treatments. Prevention advocates realize that prevention strategies work best when coupled with efforts to increase availability of treatment, as combined strategies overcome the fatalism common in areas with high prevalence and severe poverty. Antiretrovirals also play an important role in "orphan prevention" if lives of parents can be sustained and their child-raising capabilities preserved.

Although international migration and AIDS have been highlighted, there are other examples of global interdependence in the social arena, for example, drug and human trafficking. The desperate situation of farmers in Bolivia and the addictions of city dwellers throughout the world are linked through a profitable and often-violent international trade in drugs. Human trafficking has grown in volume and profitability with globalization and international use of the Internet. In addition to the problems whose very nature and substance are shaped by globalization, there are many social problems that can be classified as global in nature in that they are shared by many or all nations and require multinational action. These will be explored further in Chapter 4.

Social Policy Emulation

The final aspect of global social welfare interdependence to be considered here is the phenomenon of social policy emulation. Globalization can be seen in the extent to which policies adopted in one country affect other countries. In some cases, the effect is due to the conditions caused by provisions of a policy; in other cases, the effect is felt when one nation models its social welfare policies on those of another nation.

Nations around the world shape and reshape their own social policies to fit with trends elsewhere. In some places, this homogenization has been encouraged or even pressured by regional economic groups (such as the European Union) or required by the IMF, as described earlier in this chapter. Other instances of emulation have been voluntary, as countries look to others as models. Until the early 1980s, the modern welfare state was regarded as the model toward which developing countries aspired; the Scandinavian and northern European welfare state provisions were seen as standards of excellence in social welfare, against which other systems would be measured. In the 1980s, privatization and austerity grew in popularity. Initiated in the United Kingdom under Margaret Thatcher and in the United States under Ronald Reagan, privatization and reductions in entitlements and subsidies for the poor increasingly became the policies emulated by other nations and institutionalized as part of the IMF's structural adjustment plan. More recently, policies of managed care in the health sector have been exported.

Social policy homogenization has been a concern among social welfare experts throughout the strengthening of the European Community and European Union. As mobility between states has become free, there are strong forces encouraging adoption of social policy modifications. Although these would likely improve provisions in the countries with the least developed social welfare, states with generous and comprehensive benefits would be pressured to reduce them. It is increasingly likely, therefore, that innovations, advances, or retrenchments in social welfare in one nation will reverberate through this process of policy emulation to create similar changes in other nations' policies. Although the process itself is neutral, forces of global economic competition tend to support conservative trends toward less welfare. It is particularly true that policies of powerful nations send signals to other nations about acceptable policies. Curtailments of rights to abortion and family planning in the United States from 2000 on led Peru to severely restrict women's access to contraception (Cardenas, 2003). Antiterrorist curtailments of civil liberties in the United States and United Kingdom may well send signals to regimes eager to restrict human rights that their actions will be tolerated. As suggested in Chapter 1, then, the policies of one nation increasingly affect the well-being of people in other nations. This occurs not only from direct impact but also from the influence of policies as models for other countries' policies.

PROSPECTS FOR ACTION: OPPORTUNITIES IN GLOBALIZATION

Globalization does offer increased opportunities for exchange and mutual problem solving, in addition to presenting an agenda of shared problems. Advances in technology have eased international communication through telephone, computer links, and video conferences. It is now easier than ever before to exchange information and ideas and to work with colleagues around the world—without leaving one's home or office. The challenge is to prepare for seizing these opportunities by accepting globalization and interdependence as "irrefutable facts" and to overcome tendencies toward isolationism that prevent this recognition. In later chapters, strategies for professional action to use the opportunities for mutual problem solving and to promote development and human rights through active participation in global civil society will be discussed in more depth.

REFERENCES

Aids in the third world: A global disaster. (1999, January 2), *Economist*, 43–44.

Anderson, P., & Witter, M. (1994). Crisis, adjustment and social change: A case study of Jamaica. In E. LeFranc (Ed.), *Consequences of structural adjustment: A review of the Jamaican experience* (pp. 1–55). Kingston, Jamaica: Canoe Press, University of the West Indies.

Ankrah, E. M. (1992). AIDS in Uganda: Initial social work responses. *Journal of Social Development in Africa, 7*(2), 53–61.

Bowman, L. W. (1991). *Mauritius: Democracy and development in the Indian Ocean.* Boulder, CO: Westview Press.

Brysk, A. (Ed.). (2002). *Globalization and human rights.* Berkeley and Los Angeles: University of California Press

Capp, R., & Fix, M. E. (2005). *Undocumented immigrants: Myths and reality.* Washington, DC: The Urban Institute.

Cardenas, C. (2003, April 8). *Human rights and health.* Presentation to the University of Connecticut School of Social Work Annual International Day, West Hartford.

Central Intelligence Agency. (2007). *The world factbook.* Accessed June 14, 2007, at www.cia.gov.library/publications/the-world-factbook/index.html

Chea, T. (2006, August 1). China's pollution reaching U.S. *The Hartford Courant*, p. E3.

Day, P. J. (1989). The new poor in America: Isolationism in an international political economy. *Social Work, 34*(3), 227–233.

Food and Agriculture Organization of the United Nations. (2007). *The state of the world's forests.* Accessed April 26, 2007, at www.fao.org

Global Policy Forum. (2005, February 15). Agricultural prices decline, devastating countries that export single product—UN report. *UN News.* Accessed April 26, 2007, at www.globalpolicy.org/socecon/trade/2005/0215fao.htm

Hamilton, J. M. (1986). *Main street America and the third world.* Cabin John, MD: Seven Locks Press.

Hamilton, J. M. (1990). *Entangling alliances: How the third world shapes our lives.* Cabin John, MD: Seven Locks Press.

Hessle, S. (2007). Globalisation: Implications for international development work, social work and the integration of immigrants in Sweden. In L. Dominelli (Ed.), *Revitalising communities in a globalizing world* (pp. 231–241). Aldershot, UK: Ashgate Publishing.

Hirshkorn, P. (2003, October 29). New York reduces 9/11 death toll by 40. *CNN News.* Accessed October 15, 2006, at www.cnn.com

Hoff, M. D. (1997). Social work, the environment, and sustainable growth. In M. C. Hokenstad & J. Midgley (Eds.), *Issues in international social work* (pp. 27–44.). Washington, DC: NASW Press.

Hokenstad, M. C., & Midgley, J. (Eds.). (1997). *Issues in international social work.* Washington, DC: NASW Press.

Hoy, P. (1998). *Players and issues in international aid.* West Hartford, CT: Kumarian Press.

International Council on Social Welfare. (2007). *Promoting full employment and decent work for all.* Unabridged version of the Statement to United Nations Commission for Social Development, 45th Session. 7–16 February 2007. Utrecht, The Nether-lands: Author.

International Federation for Human Rights. (2005). *Understanding global trade & human rights: Report & resource guide for national human rights NGOs in view of the 2005 WTO ministerial conference, Hong Kong.* Paris, France: Author.

Isbister, J. (2003). *Promises not kept: The betrayal of social change in the third world* (6th ed.). Bloomfield, CT: Kumarian Press.

Jebb, E. (1929). International social service. In *International Conference of Social Work [Proceedings]* (Vol. I, pp. 637–655). First Conference, Paris, July 8–13, 1928.

Joint UN Programme on HIV/AIDS. (2005). *AIDS epidemic update December 2005.* Geneva, Switzerland: Joint UN Programme on HIV/AIDS and World Health Organization.

Joint Working Group on Development Education. (1984). *A framework for development education in the United States.* Westport, CT: Save the Children for InterAction.

Keigher, S. M., & Lowery, C. T. (1998). The sickening implications of globalization. *Health and Social Work, 23*(2), 153–158.

Kuykendall, J. (2007, June 4). Refugee crisis in the Middle East. *The Hartford Courant,* p. A2.

Maldives: On the beach. (1999, January 9). *Economist,* p. 39.

Martin, D. (2005). *The U.S. Refugee Program in transition. Migration Information Service.* Accessed March 16, 2006, at www.migrationinformation.org

Maxwell, J. A. (1990, September 2–8). *Development of social welfare services and the field of social work in Jamaica.* Paper presented at the Caribbean Conference for Social Workers, Paramaribo, Surinam.

McNeil, D. G., Jr. (1998, November 15). AIDS stalking Africa's struggling economies. *New York Times,* pp. 1, 20.

Mensendiek, M. (1997). Women, migration and prostitution in Thailand. *International Social Work, 40,* 163–176.

Midgley, J. (1997). *Social welfare in global context.* Thousand Oaks, CA: Sage Publications.

Moreno, C. (2006, February 28). *Gender, remittances and development.* INSTRSAW. Paper presented at the United Nations Commission on Women, New York, NY.

Mupedziswa, R. (1997). Social work with refugees: The growing international crisis. In M. C. Hokenstad & J. Midgley (Eds.), *Issues in international social work* (pp. 110–124). Washington, DC: NASW Press.

Piot, P. (2004, April 23). *The global AIDS pandemic: Keynote presentation.* Presented at Provoking Hope: A Brown University HIV/AIDS Symposium, Providence, RI.

Planning Institute of Jamaica. (2007). *Economic and social survey Jamaica 2006.* Kingston, Jamaica: Author.

Prigoff, A. (2000). *Economics for social workers: Social outcomes of economic globalization with strategies for community action.* Belmont, CA: Wadsworth/Thomson Learning.

Ray, B. (2005). *Canada: Policy changes and integration challenges in an increasingly diverse society. Migration Information Service.* Accessed June 16, 2006, at www.migrationinformation.org/Profiles/display.cfm?ID=348

Robotham, D. (1996, April 20). *Transnationalism in the Caribbean: Formal and informal.* AES Distinguished Lecture, Spring Meeting, San Juan, PR.

Rowlands, A., & Tan, N.-T. (2004). International survey on globalization and social work. In N.-T. Tan & A. Rowlands (Eds.), *Social work around the world III* (pp. 113–129). Berne, Switzerland: International Federation of Social Workers.

Taber, M. A., & Batra, S. (1995). *Social strains of globalization in India*. New Delhi, India: New Concepts International Publishers.

Thumbi, P. W. (2005). *Kenya country report on reproductive health and reproductive rights: Emphasis on HIV/AIDS*. Accessed April 25, 2007, at www.uneca.org/po pia/Peda/Kenya.doc

UN Division for the Advancement of Women. (2005). *Women and water*. New York: Author.

UN Environment Program. (2005, December 6). Pacific islanders move to escape global warming. *The Environment in the News*: 2005. Accessed June 30, 2007, at www.unep.org/cpi/briefs/2005Dec06.doc

UN High Commissioner for Refugees. (2005). *2004 global refugee trends*. Geneva, Switzerland: Author.

UNICEF. (2004). *The state of the world's children 2005*. New York: Author.

United Nations. (1990). *The world economy: A global challenge*. New York: U.N. Department of Public Information.

United Nations Development Programme. (1996). *Human development report 1996*. New York: Oxford University Press for UNDP.

United Nations Development Programme. (1998). *Human development report 1998*. New York: Oxford University Press for UNDP.

United Nations Development Programme. (2006). *Summary human development report 2006. Beyond scarcity: Power, poverty and the global water crisis*. New York: Palgrave Macmillan.

U.S. Census Bureau. (2001). *Profile of the foreign born population of the United States—2000*. Washington, DC: Author.

U.S. Census Bureau. (2007). Percent of people who are foreign born, Table R0501. *2006 American Community Survey*. Accessed December 22, 2007, at www.census.gov

U.S. Office of Immigration Statistics. (2006). *Yearbook of immigration statistics 2005*. Accessed August 10, 2006, at www.uscis.gov

Wagner, A. (1997). Social work and the global economy. In M. C. Hokenstad. & J. Midgley (Eds.), *Issues in international social work* (pp. 45–56). Washington, DC: NASW Press.

World almanac and book of facts. (1999). Mahwah, NJ: World Almanac Books, Primedia Reference Inc.

World Bank. (2001). Poverty to rise in wake of terrorist attacks in U.S. Statement issued Otober 1, 2001. Accessed June 10, 2007, at http://go.worldbank.org/A2OYNNQ320

World Commission on the Social Dimension of Globalization. (2004). *A fair globalization: Creating opportunities for all*. Geneva, Switzerland: International Labour Organisation.

CHAPTER 3

THEORIES AND CONCEPTS UNDERPINNING INTERNATIONAL SOCIAL WORK

Development and Human Rights

> The objective of development is to create an enabling environment for people to enjoy long, healthy and creative lives.
>
> ul Haq, 1990, p. 9

The overriding concerns of international social work are to promote development and enhance and protect human rights. Development is the major thrust of international organizations and many national and local organizations to address poverty and its many associated problems. Human rights are an orientation to practice and a philosophy of overarching human dignity. This chapter will address theories and important principles of development and human rights.

DEVELOPMENT

Development, whether a process or end result, is seen as the avenue to alleviation of poverty and its associated ills. Although discussions of development have appeared in the social work literature for 30 years or more, with early works by Paiva (1977), Omer (1979), and Sanders (1982), it is still not a widely understood concept among Western (or Northern) social workers. Commitment to development requires an understanding of theories of development and "underdevelopment," the history of development efforts, and models or concepts underlying development initiatives. The need for development is still acute. As expressed by Brundtland, chair of the World Commission for Environment and Development (1987), "After a century of unprecedented growth, marked by scientific and technological triumphs that would have been unthinkable a century ago, there have never been so many poor, illiterate and unemployed people in the world and their number is growing" (p. 13). More recently, UN Development Programme (UNDP; 2003) reported that "more than 1.2 billion people—one in every five on Earth—survive on less than $1 a day" (p. 5).

Why have the world and individual nations and communities been unable to make more significant headway in poverty reduction? There are no easy answers, although much development theory, strategy, and effort have been devoted to the search for solutions.

Definition

Definitions of development have evolved over more than four decades as understanding of its complexities has increased. Early definitions and development strategies emphasized economic growth: development was seen as the process of strengthening the capacity of the economies of relatively undeveloped countries to enable them to more adequately address people's needs. Additional emphases were soon added to the concept of development. The importance of institution building was recognized and reflected in the definition of *development* emerging from the UN Symposium on Social Policy and Planning held in 1970: development is "a process of improving the capability of a nation's institutions and value system to meet increasing and different demands, whether they are social, political or economic" (Omer, 1979, p. 12). The Society for International Development, a nongovernmental organization (NGO) comprising professionals and others interested in development, defined *development* in 1984 as: "a sustainable process geared to the satisfaction of the needs of the majority of peoples, and not merely to the growth of things or to the benefit of a minority" (Mattis, 1984). This clearly indicates concerns with equitable distribution and with development as more than material progress or accumulation.

Twenty years ago, a social work scholar from Zimbabwe wrote that development is "the development of an individual as a social being, aiming as his [sic] liberation and at his fulfillment. Development should be geared to the satisfaction of needs beginning with the eradication of poverty, ignorance and disease" (Agere, 1986, p. 95). Agere's emphasis on liberation and human potential are embedded in more current definitions, such as that by Bryant and Kappaz (2005) who see development as "the rights of people to develop their capabilities to affect their own futures" (p. 32). Economist Amartya Sen (1999) expressed similar ideas in his book *Development as Freedom.*

Social work has particular interest in the social dimensions of development in addition to the empowerment and liberation concepts reflected above. Social development will be discussed further later in this chapter.

Theories of Development

Most definitions of development clearly identify development as a process. However, to early development theorists, development was sometimes regarded as an end result. At the launch of the First UN Development Decade in 1961, the process was guided by classic capitalist development theory or modernization theory. Walt Rostow, using the analogy of an airplane moving from a parked position to gather speed on the runway toward takeoff, identified five stages of development that he believed characterized the necessary process: tradition, preconditions, takeoff, maturation, and mass consumption (Isbister, 2003). Traditional societies were defined as somewhat static and supporting life largely at a subsistence level. The critical takeoff phase "is the interval when the old blocks and resistances to steady growth are finally overcome" (Rostow quoted in Isbister, 2003, p. 37). This occurs "when political power accrues to a group that regards economic growth as its main business; when the country's savings rate, as a proportion of national income, doubles; and when modern technology is applied to a few leading sectors, both agricultural and industrial" (Isbister, 2003, pp. 37–38). This classic modernization theory predicted that development would occur along similar trajectories in all societies, that what had been successful in moving European nations out of their feudal patterns would be similarly successful in Asia and Africa. Economic growth was seen as the solution to underdevelopment and the severe poverty evident in many of the newly independent nations. Such growth must be initiated through a process of "transformation of traditional societies" (Isbister, 2003, p. 39). It was further posited that economic growth as measured by increased Gross National Product (GNP) would lead to better conditions for all, as the benefits of growth "trickle down" to the masses. For development to occur, what is needed according to modernists are "better policies, more technology, more aid, freer markets, sounder planning"—not revolutionary changes in political or economic relationships (Isbister, 2003, p. 41).

Although contested as not sufficiently explanatory, modernization theory lives on. As stated in a recent book on Latin America, "neoliberal economists, who see the world through modernization-theoretical and transnational-homogenizing lenses, presume that the world is increasingly following a Western developmental course and also that such a path is normatively preferred" (Eckstein & Wickham-Crowley, 2003, p. 5). Thus, as noted in the preceding chapter, these economists push reforms emphasizing the market and "encourage" countries to reduce governmental programs and end trade restrictions.

Dependency theory contests the essential assumptions of modernization theory. Rather than blaming failure to develop on traditional ways, dependency theory posits that development is essentially a struggle between the "have" and "have-not" countries of the world. The richer countries play an active "underdeveloping" role in the poorer countries and contribute to their continued impoverishment. Thus, "the poverty of the Third World is not traditional and it is not accidental. It is the necessary companion to the richness of the developed countries" (Isbister, 2003, p. 43). The preconditions for underdevelopment were set in the era of colonialism, when the institutions, infrastructures, and productive capacities of colonized countries were designed solely to meet the needs of the colonial powers. In Equatorial Guinea, for example, at independence there were only two roads leading from the interior to the coast and no connecting roads between them. The roads were developed solely to transport timber from the forests to the coast for export and provided no useful infrastructure for unifying the country. Under-development continues to be fed today by neo-colonialist forces. The main barriers to development are seen as dependence of poorer countries on the industrialized countries for markets, imports, technology, and information, all within a global economy in which poor countries exert very little power. They suffer from lack of infrastructure and lack of control over prices, trade conditions, and currency valuation. Development, according to dependency theory, depends on a radical restructuring of the relationships between rich and poor nations—especially the forces of global capitalism. From the call for a New International Economic Order in the 1970s to the more recent rounds of trade talks, poorer countries have been demanding this restructuring. Many who subscribe to dependency theory believe that global capitalism can never deliver on its promise of universal development.

Marxist theories of development contain some elements of modernization and dependency theory; however, they place more emphasis on the clash of interests and classes within developing societies and between rich and poor nations. Class issues are increasingly "traced to relations of production or to global market forces" including the "unequal benefits that accrue to different social classes under global neoliberal restructuring" (Eckstein & Wickham-Crowley, 2003, p. 5).

Brief History of Development Efforts

Beginning with the independence of Ghana in 1957, the colonized areas of Africa, the Caribbean, and Asia began to achieve their independence and emerge as new nations at a rapid rate. Many South American countries achieved independence in the nineteenth century, and India became independent in 1947. Nonetheless, it was the emergence of so many newly independent countries and their increased influence at the UN that led to increased focus on the challenges of "underdevelopment" in the 1960s by the international body. The UN launched the first Development Decade in 1961. At that time, development clearly meant economic growth and the UN program emphasized support for industry, infrastructure for a modern economy, and mechanization of agriculture. Following the modernist prescription, it was believed that the benefits of these approaches would trickle down and improve the standard of living for all.

Even as soon as the late 1960s, however, it began to be evident that benefits of growth often did not trickle down. Countries that experienced high growth rates did not necessarily see improvements in human well-being. In fact, there was often little connection between increased GNP and improved well-being of the people. Between 1965 and 1986, for example, Brazil's GNP per capita grew at an average annual rate of 4.3%, compared to a rate of only

1.6% in Costa Rica. Yet, during the same time period, Costa Rica reduced its illiteracy rate by almost twice as much per year as Brazil (5% compared to 2.9%, respectively) and reduced its under-age-5 mortality by an average annual rate of 6.8% compared to 2.3% for Brazil—three times the rate of reduction (UNICEF, 1990). This is but one example among many that suggested that linear notions about growth and development were faulty and that economic growth could not be reliably linked to improvements in social or health well-being.

These realizations led to recognition that development is complex and requires more than economic strategies. From the late 1970s to the present, a stream of additional concepts has contended with economics for centrality in development theory and initiatives. Among these are the basic needs approach, social development or integrated development, sustainable development, gendered development/women in development, and an emphasis on measures and targets.

Basic Needs Approach. Concern over the failure of trickle down to address poverty led to a call for the basic needs approach. This requires a conscious effort by governments to ensure that basic needs of the population are met through whatever development strategies are undertaken. Emphasis is given to ensuring availability of essential food, sanitation, shelter, primary education, and primary health care (Streeten & Burki, 1978). There are important examples of success in following the basic needs approach. Costa Rica and the state of Kerala in India are often cited for their attention to basic needs and success in improved indicators of well-being as a result. Other countries professed a basic needs approach but did not follow it, as large infrastructure projects were often more attractive to aid givers and governments (that is, building of large urban hospitals rather than immunization programs in rural areas). The basic needs approach often entailed government subsidies for food and essential services, swelling the percentage of gross domestic product (GDP) devoted to government expenditures. The structural adjustment programs of the 1980s and 1990s curtailed successful basic needs efforts, as discussed in Chapter 2. More recently, however, renewed basic needs strategies are showing success. Kenya, Malawi, Uganda, and Tanzania abolished school fees and have seen increased primary school enrolment as a result; other countries, such as Zambia and Burundi have eliminated fees for rural health services and/or health care for women and children (Annan, 2006).

Social Development. Among the many development concepts, social development is particularly important to social work. Social development acknowledges the importance of social factors in ensuring that development improves human well-being, arguing that development should be a holistic process. It aims to integrate social with economic factors. As Midgley (1995) explains: *social development* "is a process of planned social change designed to promote the well-being of the population as a whole in conjunction with a dynamic process of economic development" (p. 25).

Social development also gives emphasis to outcomes of improving well-being of the poor and processes that emphasize participation. Paiva's (1977) early definition of social development is a useful one:

> The goal and substance of social development is the welfare of the people, as determined by the people themselves, and the consequent creation or alteration of institutions so as to create a capacity for meeting human needs at all levels (especially those at the lower levels) and for improving the quality of human relationships and relationships between people and societal institutions. (p. 329)

It includes the ideas of participation, institution building, and distributive justice, key component concepts in social development. Another social work author Salima Omer (1979) wrote, "social development can be defined as a goal and a process that aims to achieve an integrated, balanced and unified (social and economic) development of society" (p. 15). She noted further that social development addresses qualitative aspects of relationships of people and their environment as well as "structural and institutional reforms to bring about changes in the distribution of income, wealth and services" (p. 16).

These elements of early social work authored definitions of social development are repeated in more current UN definitions. The International Forum for Social Development, an initiative of the UN Secretariat, characterized social development as a set of objectives, a process, and a prospective. Advances in social development mean advances in

> the well-being of the person and to the harmonious functioning of society. It includes improvements in individual and family well-being through the enjoyment of human rights, the provision of economic opportunities, the reduction of poverty, and access to social security, social protection and social services. It includes also the building or maintenance of social relations, structures and institutions through which individuals and groups constitute a viable society. (UN, 2002, p. 3)

The Forum's definition continues, indicating that as a process, "social development implies various forms of redistribution of opportunities, income, assets and power" and as a perspective, it includes a value-based approach or a "moral perspective on development" (UN, 2002, p. 3). The core ideas are social development as a value-driven, integrative effort with the dual emphases of enhancement of individual well-being and strengthening of social institutions.

In some parts of the world, social work redefined itself as social development to align the profession more closely with national objectives. This was particularly true in Africa and parts of Asia. Midgley (1999) recommends human capital development, social capital development, and productive employment projects as social development intervention strategies relevant for social work.

Because social development theorists and practitioners do not reject economic considerations, the approach is sometimes labeled integrated development or an integrated approach to development.

Sustainable Development. The concept of sustainable development reflects concern with stresses on the physical environment and recognition that economic development puts strains on resources. At various times in history, there have been dire predictions that the world will collapse from overpopulation, that massive famines will result from exhausted land, and that mineral resources will be depleted. In 1972, *Limits to Growth* was published and received considerable attention (Meadows, Randers, & Meadows, 1972); the book declared development unsustainable. Its predictions of exponential and exhaustive growth proved wrong; nonetheless, the main argument that resource-depleting growth could not be sustained has been accepted (Stoesz, Guzzetta, & Lusk, 1999). The experience of the former Soviet bloc countries and China, countries that rapidly industrialized without safeguards for the environment or for workers, has underscored the dangers and costs of aggressive growth. Severe pollution, contaminated soil, and worker health destroyed by hazardous working conditions are some of the legacies of unrestrained development. More recently concerns have grown about climate change and global warming, processes linked to human activity.

Sustainable development—a "path of human progress which meet the needs and aspirations of the present generation without compromising the ability of future generations to meet their needs" (World Commission on Environment and Development, 1987, p. 43)—arose as the alternative way. New emphasis was put on appropriate technology, renewable energy, and care of the environment in designing development initiatives. The movement for sustainable development grew through the 1970s and 1980s as recognition of the environmental impacts of globalization, described in Chapter 2, increased. Publication of the report *Our Common Future* by the UN World Commission on Environment and Development in 1987 was an important milestone in defining the sustainable development approach. The impact of globalization, especially world production and trade, is recognized as a force intensifying the threat to sustainability (UNESCO, 2005).

The UN identifies three "interlinked" areas as key to sustainable development: society, environment, and economy. Cross-cutting themes are culture—the recognition that "practice, identity, and values" play a big role in prospects for sustainable development—and concern with poverty eradication (UNESCO, 2005). Thus sustainability is not only about resources and the physical environment and the economic pressures toward growth but also about social institutions and human development. A holistic approach is essential if progress is to be made.

Enhancing sustainability is complex and intertwined with the politics of international relations. The sustainability movement was fueled by recognition that if poorer countries emulate the consumption patterns of rich nations, global resources will be depleted. Poverty and wealth put strains on the world's resources. The poor are forced by their circumstances to use firewood and water in ways that harm the environment and its capacity to renew itself; the rich consume energy and other resources at rates many times those of the

Figure 3.1 The Armenia Tree Project encourages sustainable development. (Photo by Thomas Felke)

world's poor. Adopting policies to preserve the environment are often seen as actions by the wealthier sectors to deny equal opportunities for development to poorer countries. However, "degradation of ecosystem services is exacerbating the problems of poverty and food insecurity in the developing world, particularly in the poorest countries" (Food and Agriculture Organization, International Fund for Agricultural Development, UN Centre for Human Settlements, World Food Programme, 2006). What is needed is "a twofold response in both industrialized and developing countries: responsible patterns of production and consumption, and pro-active stewardship of resources of all kinds" (UNESCO, 2005, p. 10).

The concept of sustainability remains important in all levels of development, from community-based initiatives to global goal setting. The Earth Charter (see Box) represents a global civil society contribution to the understanding of sustainable development and suggests far-reaching actions to ensure ecological and human harmony.

Women in Development: The Importance of a Gender Lens. Women were largely left out of the early development models and interventions. As one author put it, "the goal of all of this Development Decade activity, planned and carried out by men, was to increase the productivity of the male worker" (Boulding &

THE EARTH CHARTER

The Earth Charter was agreed on in 2000 after a number of years of negotiation. Work on the present charter began after a draft UN Earth Charter failed to gain support at the 1992 Earth Summit in Rio de Janeiro. Civil society organizations came together under the leadership of Maurice Strong (who had been secretary general of the Rio Summit) and Mikhail Gorbachev to develop the document. It is widely recognized as "a global consensus statement on the meaning of sustainability, the challenge and vision of sustainable development, and the principles by which sustainable development is to be achieved" (Earth Charter, 2000). As stated in the Charter, "We must join together to bring forth a sustainable global society founded on respect for nature, universal human rights, economic justice, and a culture of peace." The Charter includes a set of principles organized into four themes: Respect and Care for the Community of Life; Ecological Integrity; Social and Economic Justice; and Nonviolence and Peace. This comprehensive perspective on interdependence defines all spheres of the physical and human environment holistically. The Charter is based not only on global interdependence but also on the concept of universal responsibility. It calls on everyone to "imaginatively develop and apply the vision of a sustainable way of life locally, nationally, regionally, and globally" (Earth Charter, 2000). The Charter has been endorsed by several thousand organizations and had an important influence on the United Nations Educational, Scientific and Cultural Organization's Decade for Education on Sustainable Development.

Dye, 2002, p. 182). Research by Ester Boserup, a Danish female economist, revealed a significant reason for the failure of development approaches—that they ignored women, the population that was actually responsible for the majority of food production in Africa and elsewhere. "The majority of food producers were women, not men, but all agricultural aid, including credit and tools was given to men. This aid not only failed to reach the women but encouraged men to grow cash crops (which needed irrigation) for export" (Boulding & Dye, 2002, p. 183). In the third world, then, "gender-based dualism (was) linked to an economic dualism that trapped women in the subsistence sector" (p. 187).

Through the work of Boserup and many others, the importance of including women in development was recognized. Ignoring women not only impeded progress for women but also had a serious negative impact on families, children, and on development progress overall. Women's literacy and involvement in income generation are highly correlated with child survival and family well-being. Therefore, approaches that specifically target women have been added to the development mix, and many organizations encourage a gender screen to ensure that some attention is paid to women. Amartya Sen (1999), Nobel Prize–winning economist, emphasizes the idea of women's agency—women as "active agents of change" (p. 189). Women's empowerment, he says,

> is one of the central issues in the process of development for many countries in the world today. The factors involved include women's education, their ownership pattern, their employment opportunities and the workings of the labor market. But . . . they include also the nature of the employment arrangements, attitudes of the family and of the society at large toward women's economic activities, and the economic and social circumstances that encourage or resist change in these attitudes. (p. 202)

He concludes "Nothing, arguably, is as important today in the political economy of development as an adequate recognition of political, economic and social participation and leadership of women. This is indeed a crucial aspect of 'development as freedom' " (p. 203).

As of 2007, development approaches encompass elements of all the ideas outlined here, including economic and social development, sustainability considerations, and attention to women and those in need of basic provisions.

Measures and Targets. Various measures have been used to assess the level of development of various countries. A key one is the Human Development Index (HDI) used by the UNDP to assess country progress on several indicators and to rank countries according to the measure. The HDI comprises indicators of adult literacy; enrollment in primary, secondary, and tertiary school; life expectancy at birth; and GDP per capita (in purchasing power parity U.S. dollars) (UNDP, 2006). UNDP believes that the HDI is a satisfactory summary measure of human development. It is expressed as an index; scores for 2006 ranged from a low of .311 for Niger to a high of .965 for Norway. As the HDI has been in existence since 1990, trend data are available. The Index is widely used and often expressed in terms of rank ordering of countries; HDI ranks are cited for countries used as examples in this text. An innovation by the UNDP in 2005 was to calculate HDIs for the poorest 20% of the population of selected countries, as the HDI itself reflects average development achievements—achievements often not shared by the very poor.

A much more comprehensive measure was developed by social work scholar Richard Estes. His Index of Social Progress (ISP) comprises 45 indicators that express a country's status in 10 sectors: education, health, women, defense effort, economic, demographic, geographic (such as incidence of major natural disasters), cultural diversity, political chaos, and welfare effort (Estes, 2005). The ISP's inclusion of such a broad range of indicators underscores the complexity of social development and of the factors that influence human well-being. It mixes outcome with effort measures, including, for example, a country's enactment of provisions for social security (a positive contributor) and military spending (a drain on capacity to improve human well-being). A particularly important idea underscored by the ISP is that development is an open-ended process and that all countries in many respects are "developing" or in need of development.

The Millennium Development Goals (MDGs) (development goals and targets for the early twenty-first century) represent an effort to spur development by setting measurable targets for development outcomes (see Appendix C). In 2000, the UN held its millennium summit and set forth eight goals, identified at the time as reasonable and achievable targets for making progress in development by the year 2015. The Millennium Summit followed the Summit on Social Development held in 1995 that issued the 10 Commitments for Development. Although the 10 Commitments were broadly stated—for example, Commitment 2 is to eradicate poverty in the world—the MDGs translate these Commitments into specific and measurable goals. Briefly, the eight goals are

- Goal 1: Eradicate extreme poverty and hunger. Target: halve between 1990 and 2015 the proportion of people living on less than $1 a day.
- Goal 2: Achieve universal primary education by 2015.
- Goal 3: Promote gender equality and empower women. Target: Eliminate gender disparity in primary and secondary education, preferably by 2005, and in all levels of education no later than 2015.
- Goal 4: Reduce child mortality. Target: Reduce by two-thirds between 1990 and 2015 the under-five mortality rate.
- Goal 5: Improve maternal health. Target: Reduce by three-fourths between 1990 and 2015 the maternal mortality ratio.
- Goal 6: Combat HIV/AIDS, malaria, and other diseases. Target: Halt and begin to reverse the spread of HIV/AIDS by 2015.
- Goal 7: Ensure environmental sustainability. Target: Integrate the principles of sustainable development into country policies and programs and reverse the loss of environmental resources. Halve the proportion of people without access to safe drinking water and sanitation.
- Goal 8: Develop a global partnership for development. Targets: *(1)* Address the special needs of the least-developed countries; *(2)* Develop an open, rule-based, predictable, nondiscriminatory trading and financial system; *(3)* Deal comprehensively with developing countries' debt; *(4)* In cooperation with developing countries, develop and implement strategies for decent and productive work for youth; *(5)* In cooperation with pharmaceutical companies, provide access to affordable essential drugs in developing countries; *(6)* In cooperation with the private sector, make available the new technologies, especially information and communi-

cations. (UN Department of Public Information [UNDPI], 2005; UNDP, 2003).

In the early twenty-first century, the MDGs are dominating UN discussions on development and are influencing much of the work of development NGOs as well. Progress toward the goals is tracked by country, region, and for overall achievement, and the UN issues periodic reports. To date, only a few countries are on track to fully meet the goals. One of the targets for Goal 3, for example, was to eliminate gender disparity in primary and secondary education by 2005. Many countries fell short of meeting this intermediate target.

Summary on Development

Development continues to undergo refinement as a concept as work proceeds on new strategies for implementing development projects. Bryant and Kappaz (2005) argued that development should be reconceptualized as poverty reduction, globally and locally. Their emphasis "makes fewer distinctions between 'developing' and 'developed' countries and simply focuses on reducing poverty" (p. 59). This is consistent with Estes' ISP approach to measuring national progress on development. Coupled with the Copenhagen Declaration principle that people must be at the center of development, a principle repeated in the 2006 UN secretary-general's report, a people-centered poverty reduction focus for development would fit with the social work mission (Annan, 2006). As the following chapters will indicate, much work remains to make development progress a reality for many of the world's people.

HUMAN RIGHTS

A second major global thrust is the campaign for human rights. Human rights are also increasingly at the core of international social work. Human rights are at one and the same time the simple and extraordinarily powerful idea that all people have rights simply because they are human and are an extensive and complex system of international laws and procedures. This section will discuss the idea of human rights and delineate the major international human rights treaties that make up international human rights law. A brief description of the UN human rights machinery will also be included, as well as discussion of unresolved issues in human rights. The chapter will conclude with comments on the social work role in human rights, a theme emphasized in several other chapters.

Human Rights Philosophy

The Universal Declaration of Human Rights (UDHR) clearly states that the philosophy underlying human rights is that "All human beings are born free and equal in dignity and rights" (UN, 1948, article 1). As noted by Jack Donnelly (1993), human rights scholar,

The very term *human rights* indicates both their nature and their source: they are rights that one has simply because one is human. They are held by all human beings, irrespective of any rights or duties one may have (or not have) as citizens, members of families, workers, or parts of any public or private organization or association. (p. 19)

Thus, human rights are not something to be earned. Nor are they to be withheld from certain groups. Article 2 of the UDHR states, "everyone is entitled to all the rights and freedoms set forth in this Declaration, without distinction of any kind, such as race, colour, sex, language, religion, political or other opinion, national or social origin, property, birth or other status."

Although the adoption of the UDHR by the newly organized UN in 1948 is the watershed of modern human rights, the document did not arise in a vacuum. Philosophic ideas about human rights are imbedded in many if not

---

HUMAN RIGHTS GLOSSARY

- Accession: "An act whereby a state that has not signed a treaty expresses its consent to become a party to that treaty by depositing an 'instrument of accession' with the Secretary-General of the United Nations. Accession has the same legal effect as ratification" (United Nations Office of the High Commissioner for Human Rights [UNOHCHR], 2005b).
- Convention: A legally binding international treaty.
- Covenant: A legally binding international agreement.
- Declaration: A statement of international intent or "agreed upon principles and standards" but not a legally binding document (United Nations Development Programme [UNDP], 2000, p. 17).
- Reservation: A statement that a state party reserves the right not to uphold a particular provision of a treaty. In so doing, the state indicates that "while it consents to be bound by most of the provisions, it does not agree to be bound by certain specific provisions. However, a reservation may not defeat the object and purpose of the treaty" (UNOHCHR, 2004).
- Ratification: Ratification of a treaty by a country creates a legal obligation to uphold the treaty and the ratifying country becomes a state party to the treaty. Only countries that have previously signed treaties can ratify them. Otherwise, they must accede to the treaty (see Accession, above).
- Signature: A first step that indicates the intentions of the state to comply but does not create a legal obligation to do so.
- States Parties: Those countries that have ratified the treaty.
- Treaty Bodies: "the committees formally established through the principal international human rights treaties to monitor states parties' compliance with the treaties" (UNDP, 2000, p. 17).

all of the major world religions. Antecedents in the political realm stretch back at least to the Magna Carta (1215), the French Declaration of the Rights of Man and Citizen, and the U.S. Constitution's Bill of Rights. Activists during the French revolution wrote declarations on women's rights.

In the twentieth century, the Covenant of the League of Nations and many of the initiatives of the League and of the International Labour Organization expressed at least some minimal human rights ideals, although there was no comprehensive definition of these rights. As will be described in Chapter 7 on the history of international social work action, a Declaration on the Rights of the Child was drafted in the early 1920s and adopted by the League of Nations. The League maintained committees on human rights matters, such as a Committee Against Trafficking (chaired by social work pioneer Grace Abbott), and sponsored many initiatives to address child labor and penal reform. The League Covenant also called for special protections for certain civil and religious liberties of those still in colonized areas.

Specific impetus to codify human rights in international law came from reactions to the horrors of World War II, especially the Holocaust and other Nazi atrocities. Perhaps guilt also played a role as the major Western powers had gathered several times in the 1930s to discuss Germany's aggression and human rights violations but had decided that national sovereignty precluded action (Wronka, 2003). Thus, the preamble includes the phrase "whereas disregard and contempt for human rights have resulted in barbarous acts which have outraged the conscience of mankind" (UN, 1948).

At the urging of some delegates and a number of NGOs, the newly formed UN organization set up a Commission on Human Rights in 1947, with Eleanor Roosevelt as chair. Some scholars believe that the appointment of a woman was an intentional move to downplay the importance of the issue (Wronka, 2003). Nonetheless, by the summer of 1948, the Commission had produced a draft human rights document, and the General Assembly began debate (Morsink, cited in Reichert, 2003) (as contrasted to a 10-year process for the drafting of the Convention on the Rights of the Child). The document was adopted with no opposing votes; however, the Soviet bloc, Saudi Arabia, and South Africa abstained. A sobering, but perhaps little noticed affront to the impact of the treaty was that 1948 also marked the official full implementation of apartheid law in South Africa.

At the time of the adoption of the UDHR, there were 56 member nations in the UN, with very few African members. Although this is often stated as an indication of the Western bias of the document, among the members of the Commission on Human Rights were the USSR, Chile, China, Egypt, India, Iran, Lebanon, Panama, the Philippine Republic, and Uruguay, in addition to the United States and European countries (Reichert, 2003).

Human Rights as a Regime of International Law

Beginning with the UDHR, the UN has approved more than 200 human rights documents (Snarr, 2002), and still others have been promulgated by regional bodies—thus the extensive and complex side of the human rights discussion. Since 1948, the field of human rights has been defined by the provisions of the UDHR, adopted by the UN on December 10, 1948. This watershed document is stunningly comprehensive. Three "generations" of rights are delineated (Wronka, 1995). The first set of rights is civil and political rights. Articles 3 through 21 set forth these rights such as right to life and liberty; freedom from torture or cruel, inhuman punishment; freedom from arbitrary arrest or detention; freedom of assembly; freedom of expression and opinion; and so forth. The document also seems to promise the right to democratic governance, as Article 21 states, "Everyone has the right to take part in the government of his country, directly or through freely chosen representatives" and continues, "The will of the people shall be the basis of the authority of government; this will shall be expressed in periodic and genuine elections which shall be by universal and equal suffrage and shall be held by secret vote or by equivalent free voting procedures" (UN, 1948). These first-generation rights are sometimes referred to as "negative rights," as they require governments to refrain from negative actions or refrain from constraining human civil and political liberties.

Articles 22 through 27 spell out the second-generation rights of economic, social, and cultural entitlements. These include the right to social security, decent employment, to rest and leisure, food, clothing, housing, medical care, education, and participation in cultural life. Article 25, section 1, is of particular interest to social work. It reads,

> Everyone has the right to a standard of living adequate for the health and well-being of himself and of his family, including food, clothing, housing and medical care and necessary social services, and the right to security in the event of unemployment, sickness, disability, widowhood, old age or other lack of livelihood in circumstances beyond his control.

The economic and social rights are labeled "positive rights," as they require countries to take specific actions to provide for its citizens.

Article 28 very briefly introduces the ideas of third-generation rights—those rights that can only be guaranteed through international action and cooperation. It states, "everyone is entitled to a social and international order in which the rights and freedoms set forth in this Declaration can be fully realized." That statement, coupled with the phrase in Article 22 that states, "Everyone, as a member of society, has the right to social security and is entitled to realization, through national effort and *international cooperation* . . . of the economic, social and cultural rights indispensable for his dignity [italics added for emphasis]" is interpreted to bestow rights to such things as peace, fair trade, and a just international economic order. According to Ife (2001), "third generation rights include the right to economic development, the right to belong to a stable, cohesive society, and environmental rights, namely rights to clean and uncontaminated air, water and food, and a physical environment that allows humans to reach their full human potential" (p. 39).

The International Covenants. The far-reaching UDHR is a declaration. In international law, this means that it is a statement of good intentions but has no force of law. The UDHR is translated into two covenants that create obligations on the part of ratifying countries: the International Covenant on Civil and Political Rights (ICCPR) and the International Covenant on Economic, Social, and Cultural Rights (ICESCR). Both were adopted by the General Assembly in 1966. These two important documents further detail the relevant provisions of the UDHR. The ICCPR entered into force on March 23, 1976, after the needed 35 countries had ratified the treaty (UNOHCHR, 2005a); currently, a total of 155 countries have ratified and become states parties to the treaty (UNOHCHR, 2006). The ICESCR entered into force on January 3, 1976, and there are 152 countries that have ratified or acceded to the treaty; the United States has not ratified this treaty and has remained largely unsupportive of the concept of social and, especially, economic rights (UNOHCHR, 2006).

Treaties Protecting Special Populations. In spite of the fact that the language of the UDHR and the covenants guarantee protections for all people, the continuing oppression and denial of rights for certain groups have led to drafting and adoption of many additional declarations and conventions. Among these the three most important for social work are the International Convention on the Elimination of all Forms of Racial Discrimination, the Convention on the Elimination of All Forms of Discrimination Against Women (CEDAW), and the Convention on the Rights of the Child (CRC). The two covenants, the three treaties described here, and two additional treaties, The Convention Against Torture and Other Cruel, Inhuman or Degrading Treatment or Punishment (1984) and the International Convention on the Protection of the Rights of All Migrant Workers and Their Families (1990), make up the seven "core international human rights treaties" (UNOHCHR, 2005b). Each of these is governed by its own human rights committee that receives reports and oversees progress made by states parties in implementing the treaty provisions. Of the seven core treaties, the United States has ratified only the convention on racial discrimination, the Covenant on Civil and Political Rights, and the Convention Against Torture. The CRC, guaranteeing children the rights to survival, protection, and development is the most widely ratified human rights treaty; only the United States and Somalia have not ratified this document. CEDAW, also signed but not ratified by the United States, is discussed in more detail in Chapter 9. Canada has ratified all the core treaties except the treaty on migrant workers. This treaty entered into force in 2003 and has only 34 states parties to date (UNOHCHR, 2006).

To take effect (or come into force, in human rights language), a human rights treaty must be ratified or acceded to by a designated number of countries. As noted in the definitions given above, ratifying or acceding to a treaty means that a country has agreed to comply with its provisions and to take part in treaty implementation. Countries may also simply sign a treaty to indicate their general support of the principles; treaties do not take on the force of law in countries that only sign a treaty.

In addition to the many declarations and treaties promulgated by the UN, there are also regional human rights treaties. One example is the European Social Charter, originally issued in 1961 and updated in expanded form.

Ife (2001) cautions that we should be open to new and changing views on human rights:

> the Universal Declaration of Human Rights, though representing perhaps one of the more remarkable human achievements of the twentieth century, should not therefore be reified and seen as expressing a universal and unchanging truth....It is an impressive and inspirational statement, with significant radical implications...but it is not holy writ, and it can and should be subject to challenge in different times, as different voices are heard and different issues are given priority. (p. 6)

He adds that this is not an argument against universalism, but rather an openness to improving the concept of human rights.

Principle of Indivisibility. An important component of the concept of human rights is the principle of indivisibility of rights. This is a holistic view of human rights that holds that human dignity cannot be assured unless all generations of rights are protected and provided, including economic, social, civil, cultural, and political rights, and the global context in which these are possible. Political freedoms cannot be meaningful to starving people; well-fed people without civil freedoms are denied an essential component of human dignity; and ultimately, without a world order of peace and fairness, none of these rights can be guaranteed.

THE EUROPEAN SOCIAL CHARTER

The European Social Charter was issued by the Council of Europe in 1961; its aim is to achieve maintenance and further realization of human rights and fundamental freedoms in the member-states. It proposes that social and economic rights should be secured without discrimination "on grounds of race, colour, sex, religion, political opinion, national extraction or social origin" (Council of Europe, 1961). The Charter was revised in 1996 to preserve gains made and to "give it fresh impetus" (Council of Europe, 1996, p. 1). The 1996 version attempts to address the social changes that have occurred since the Charter's original adoption. The original Charter laid out as its goal the attainment of basic rights and principles, including the rights of workers, women, children, and people with disabilities. The 1996 version expands these principles, particularly in the area of workers' rights. In addition, it emphasizes rights to social welfare services, medical assistance, protection against poverty and social exclusion, housing, and social protection of the elderly.

Indivisibility is a marvelous principle, but one that has often been ignored throughout the history of human rights. During the cold war, struggles on the international scene were often struggles of the Soviet bloc rejecting civil and political rights, and the United States and sometimes its allies rejecting or qualifying the ideas of economic and social rights. The social work profession may have a special claim to truly comprehending the idea of indivisibility of rights in its simultaneous emphasis on individual self-determination and development and on social and economic justice.

Universalism. In general, international human rights law is written to be universally applicable. Yet the process does allow states to enter reservations to certain provisions of treaties, suggesting some qualification of the idea of universalism. Entered reservations are not supposed to challenge or undermine the essential purposes of the treaty. Charges of Western bias have been leveled at the human rights "regime," and others fear that human rights are used as a tool to challenge the sovereignty of weaker countries, especially poorer developing countries. Indeed, in 1948, the American Anthropological Association issued a statement "rejecting the universality of human rights norms," indicating that the UDHR "enumerated rights and freedoms which were culturally, ideologically and politically nonuniversal" (Fox, 1998). Debates on universalism versus cultural relativism have raged since that time. Applied to areas close to social work practice—rights of children, women, other oppressed groups, and the family—the debate is particularly contentious and challenging.

Among the regional treaties, the *African Charter of Human and Peoples' Rights* adopted by the Organization of African Unity in 1981 is particularly interesting as a treaty that attempts to put human rights into a cultural context. The Charter incorporates the idea of duties and responsibilities as well as rights (Mutua, 2000). As explained by Mutua (2000), the Charter "takes the view that individual rights cannot make sense in a social and political vacuum, unless they are coupled with duties on individuals. . . . Thus it seeks to balance the rights of the individual with those of the community and political society through the imposition of duties on the individual" (p. 8). For example, Article 21 states that an individual "has a duty to 'preserve the harmonious development of the family and to work for the cohesion and respect of the family; to respect his parents at all times, to maintain them in case of need'" (Mutua, 2000, p. 8).

Discussion of universalism and cultural relativism is continued in Chapter 9.

The Human Rights Machinery

Human rights as defined and managed through the UN is implemented through the Office of the High Commissioner for Human Rights (a department of the UN Secretariat), a set of treaty committees, the Human Rights Council, special rapporteurs, and more, in a complex bureaucracy. In 1946, the Economic and Social Council (ECOSOC) formed a Commission on Human

Rights, a body comprising 56 member-states that met yearly to address human rights issues. Dissatisfactions with the Commission—including the fact that some of its members were gross human rights–violating states—led recently to its abolishment and replacement with a new body, the Human Rights Council. Approved in 2006, it remains to be seen whether the Council will prove less controversial.

The high commissioner position serves as an important focal point for setting the global moral tone on human rights. Mary Robinson of Ireland, who served from 1997–2002, was particularly outspoken on the issue of poverty, which she labeled the world's worst violation of human rights. The term of her successor, Sergio Vieira de Mello of Brazil, was cut short by his tragic death in Iraq in 2003 while on special assignment for the secretary-general. Louise Arbour of Canada was appointed high commissioner in 2004.

Implementation of the treaties of special interest to social work is carried out under a variety of human rights committees, including the Committee on Economic, Social, and Cultural Rights; the Committee on the Elimination of Racial Discrimination; the Committee on the Elimination of Discrimination Against Women; and the Committee on the Rights of the Child. These committees review and comment on the states parties' reports on their implementation and compliance with the provisions of the respective treaties. Ratifying countries contribute to the maintenance of the human rights committees and their staffs and must periodically report to the Committee on progress. The states parties' reports are self-studies of compliance with a particular covenant or convention. At each of its scheduled Committee sessions, the Committee considers a number of states' reports and has a dialogue with the representatives of the government. Readers will find the states parties' reports, the comments by the respective human rights Committee, and the response by the presenting government on the website of the Office of the High Commissioner for Human Rights: www.ohchr.org

Ensuring Compliance: Roles of the UN and Human Rights Advocacy NGOs

This global human rights machinery is far from perfect in its ability to ensure compliance. In fact, some wonder what purpose these international laws serve if they can't be enforced; after all, the genocides in Rwanda, Darfur, Cambodia, and Bosnia all postdate the UN UDHR and the Covenants, the Taliban was able to grossly oppress women in spite of CEDAW, and so forth.

The UN human rights system works best as a repository of global standards and as a set of institutions that can encourage and facilitate the actions of willing states. There is little the UN can do to force the unwilling to respect the human rights of their citizens. Therefore, countries that have ratified treaties are found among some of the worst violators of the human rights they have committed their governments to uphold. Robert Drinan (2001) recommended increased use of shaming as a tactic to encourage human rights compliance, as explicated in his book *The Mobilization of Shame*. A successful use of "shaming" is discussed in Chapter 12. Unfortunately, not all countries can be shamed.

How should the world community intervene when violations of the human rights of citizens are evident? Even in situations of genocide, the UN has been slow and reluctant to act. The overriding principle of international relations is state sovereignty, a principle that encompasses noninterference in a state's domestic affairs and protection from armed intervention by other states. The adoption of global human rights standards and the machinery to oversee compliance does constrain sovereignty to some extent. According to one analysis, "In the post-Cold War era, there is an emerging sense that when states engage in gross, systemic, or large-scale human rights abuses, they thereby forfeit or suspend their status as sovereign equals in the interstate society" (Sandholtz, 2002, p. 208). In several instances, including Bosnia and Somalia in the 1990s, the international community approved military intervention for largely human rights or humanitarian concerns. In other cases, economic sanctions have been tried, although Donnelly (2002) notes that these have usually increased the suffering of the people—the victims—rather than their leaders. Sovereignty is usually seriously challenged only in extreme cases.

In 2002, the International Criminal Court (ICC) came into force after its initial approval by the world community in 1998. As described on the ICC Web page (2007), the court is "an independent, permanent court that tries

Figure 3.2 Social workers engage families of the disappeared in Chile in memorial projects to aid healing, 2006.

persons accused of the most serious crimes of international concern, namely genocide, crimes against humanity and war crimes" (n.p.). The ICC is intended to be a last resort and becomes involved only in the most serious cases and only if national courts fail to act. The ICC has initiated investigations in four situations: Uganda, the Democratic Republic of the Congo, the Central African Republic, and Darfur, Sudan; the last case was referred by the UN Security Council, as Sudan is not a current party to the ICC (ICC, 2007). To date, 104 countries have become parties to the treaty; the United States pulled out of the agreement before the ICC became operational in 2002, citing fears that U.S. citizens would be targets for political reasons, in spite of the many protections provided in the treaty and court procedures ("International Criminal Court: Let the Child Live," 2007). Although the court is an important step forward in ending impunity for heinous violations of human rights, means for effective enforcement of human rights standards—especially nonmilitary means—remain underdeveloped.

Nongovernmental Human Rights Advocates. Nongovernmental advocacy groups play an important role in the human rights movement. For the most part, they base their work on the standards established through the UN treaties. They offer a voice independent of governments and can advocate more vigorously against specific abuses. Amnesty International is one of the best known of the human rights NGOs. Founded in 1961 as a "permanent international movement in defense of freedom of opinion and religion," the organization pressures abusive governments by highlighting cases of human rights abuse and describes itself as "a worldwide movement of people who campaign for internationally recognized human rights" (Amnesty International [AI], 2006). AI advocacy has undoubtedly saved the lives of a number of detainees and has successfully brought the human face of abuse to the public. The main focus of AI has been on civil and political rights. Although expressing a belief that human rights are indivisible, the organization "concentrates on ending grave abuses of the rights to physical and mental integrity, freedom of conscience and expression, and freedom from discrimination" (AI, 2006).

In 1996, AI issued a Declaration calling for health professionals to take special responsibility for reporting human rights abuses. "Amnesty International believes that the skills which health professionals can contribute to the investigation of human rights violations in general, and torture in particular, should be used in defense of human rights" (AI, 1996). Although aimed at doctors and nurses, social workers are also health professionals and should be aware of these responsibilities. In addition, the Declaration "calls on international professional associations and the United Nations and its relevant agencies to publicize the ethical responsibility of health professionals to report human rights violations inflicted on their patients," suggesting important roles for the IFSW and IASSW (AI, 1996).

Human Rights Watch (HRW) is the largest human rights organization based in the United States and has a worldwide scope to its work. Predecessor groups began in 1978 and became solidified as Human Rights Watch in 1988. Its primary tools to promote human rights are research and publicity, with some direct advocacy for change. The HRW website identifies one of its goals as to "embarrass abusive governments" (Human Rights Watch, 2006a). HRW addresses a wide range of human rights issues, including armed conflict, treatment of street children, trials of abusive leaders, detainee abuse, immigration laws, lesbian/gay issues, and more.

Emerging and Unresolved Areas of International Human Rights Protection

There are several groups that have remained largely unprotected in international human rights law, except for the protections implied in the UDHR and covenants or provisions of other specialized treaties. A new treaty, not yet in force at the time of writing, will extend specific protections to persons with disabilities. There are no special treaty protections for sexual minorities and protections for violations by nonstate actors remain weak at best.

Persons with Disabilities. In December 2006, a new Convention on the Rights of Persons with Disabilities was adopted by the General Assembly of the UN by consensus. On March 30, 2007, the Convention on the Rights of Persons with Disabilities and its Optional Protocol were opened for signature and ratification. By May of 2007, 81 countries and the European Community (EC) had signed the Convention, and 44 countries signed the Optional Protocol. Jamaica became the first country to ratify the treaty in March, and six more countries ratified by the end of 2007 (UNOHCHR, 2007). Once ratified by 20 countries, the treaty will become international law and extend important human rights to more of the world's citizens.

The treaty has taken many years to come to life. A Declaration on the Rights of Disabled Persons was adopted by the General Assembly of the UN in 1975. Like all declarations, this established moral principles but did not have the force of law. In 2001, the General Assembly established a committee to consider developing an international convention on persons with disabilities. In the interim, a study commissioned by the UN and published in 2002—Human Rights and Disability: The Current Use and Future Potential of United Nations Human Rights Instruments in the Context of Disability—emphasized use of then-current human rights instruments to promote the rights of persons with disabilities. The drafting and agreement of the actual treaty was relatively quick. In June 2003, the Ad Hoc Committee on a Comprehensive and Integral International Convention on the Protection and Promotion of the Rights and Dignity of Persons with Disabilities established a Working Group to prepare a draft text of a proposed convention. This action was endorsed by the General Assembly. When passed, Secretary-General Kofi Annan hailed the treaty as "the most rapidly negotiated human rights treaty in the history of international law and the first to emerge from lobbying conducted extensively through the internet" (UN News Centre, December 13, 2006).

The Convention calls for states parties to abolish any discriminatory laws or customs that targeted persons with disabilities and to pass new laws to protect disability rights. As stated in the treaty, "the purpose of the present Convention is to promote, protect and ensure the full and equal enjoyment of all human rights and fundamental freedoms by all persons with disabilities, and to promote respect for their inherent dignity" (UNOHCHR, 2007, Article 1). Persons with disabilities are defined as "those who have long-term physical, mental, intellectual or sensory impairments which in interaction with various barriers may hinder their full and effective participation in society on an equal basis with others" (Article 1). Among the major provisions of the treaty, states parties must ensure that persons with disabilities "enjoy their inherent right to life on an equal basis with others." It also states that disabled persons should be able to live independently and to make their own choices about their living arrangements.

Sexual Orientation. Much less has been done at the global level on sexual orientation rights or rights of sexual minorities. Indeed, the website for the Office of the High Commissioner for Human Rights does not list sexual orientation as a subject area. More than 80 countries have laws that make consensual sex between same-sex persons a criminal offense; in seven, the death penalty can be applied in such cases (Fleshman, 2007). Gay men and lesbians remain at serious risk of harassment and physical attack in many parts of the world (Carr, 2003; Fleshman, 2007).

Nonetheless, the treaty bodies have raised issues of discrimination and violence against gays in their review of country reports for existing treaties. Brazil sponsored a draft resolution on human rights and sexual orientation for consideration at the 59th session of the Commission on Human Rights. There was strong opposition and so much resistance that no action was taken. (UN Economics and Social Council, 2003). NGOs are more active in advocating for gay rights. A recent HRW initiative pressed for recognition of same sex partners in immigration law (Human Rights Watch, 2006b). Many U.S. citizens are forced into exile in countries where their relationships are recognized. At least 19 nations worldwide provide some form of immigration benefits to the same-sex partners of citizens and permanent residents, while the United States still refuses to do so. These include Canada as well as 13 European countries (Belgium, Denmark, Finland, France, Germany, Iceland, the Netherlands, Norway, Portugal, Spain, Sweden, Switzerland, and the United Kingdom). On other continents, this list includes Brazil, Israel, South Africa, Australia, and New Zealand (Human Rights Watch, 2006b).

Although discrimination on the grounds of sexual orientation continues to be a serious violation of human rights in many countries, there are signs of progress. The South African Constitution includes protection from discrimination on the basis of sexual orientation. Ecuador, Portugal, and Fiji also have constitutional provisions outlawing discrimination on the basis of sexual orientation ("Gay Rights: Until Death Do Us Part," 2006). Brazil has established a procedure to receive complaints of antigay discrimination and has done some education on the issue with police. Civil unions of same-sex partners were recognized by Denmark beginning in 1989, and Netherlands and Belgium have removed all references to gender in their marriage laws (Sterling, 2004). At the time of writing, marriage of same-sex couples was legal in five countries (Belgium, Canada, the Netherlands, South Africa, and Spain) and one U.S. state (Massachusetts). Civil unions or partnerships were recognized in 10 European countries, New Zealand, and Hong Kong and one state in Argentina ("Gay Rights," 2006).

Notwithstanding the progress made, in many parts of the world, homosexuality remains criminalized, and gays are the targets of discrimination and physical attack. Given the opposition of several major established religions and many governments, official UN protection for gays and lesbians in international law is unlikely in the near future. The UN High Commissioner Louise Arbour is pressing for extension of human rights to sexual minorities. She has criticized laws criminalizing homosexuality as clear violations of international human rights standards. As she put it in a 2006 speech, "Neither the existence of national laws nor the prevalence of custom can ever justify the abuse, attacks, torture and indeed killings that gay, lesbian, bisexual and transgender persons are subjected to because of who they are or are perceived to be" (quoted in Fleshman, 2007, p. 12).

Human Rights Violations by Nonstate Actors. The emphasis of international work on human rights has been on the public, governmental sphere, although there have been weak attempts to include private militias and rebel groups as targets of human rights advocacy. As social workers are well aware, human rights can be and are violated by multinational and local corporations, by private organizations, and by families and neighbors. Large arenas of human rights violation and potential protection are left ill defined and largely unregulated at the global level.

Human Rights and Social Work

The human rights movement is founded on a fundamental respect for the dignity and worth of every human being. This respect for human dignity and the worth of individuals is at the very heart of social work. Thus, there is a profound harmony between social work and human rights, leading the International Federation of Social Workers (1988) to introduce their policy papers with the statement: "social work has, from its conception, been a human rights profession, having as its basic tenet the intrinsic value of every human being and as one of its main aims the promotion of equitable social structures, which can offer people security and development while upholding their dignity." The involvement of social work in human rights is addressed in several chapters of this book, especially Chapter 7 and the concluding chapter. It is particularly significant that human rights are included in the three major international social work policies of the early twenty-first century: the Global Definition of Social Work, the statement of ethical principles, and the *Global Standards for Social Work Education and Training* (IASSW, 2004).

CONCLUSION: LINKING DEVELOPMENT AND HUMAN RIGHTS

In many ways, the principle of indivisibility can be extended to link development and human rights—especially for social work practice in the international arena. The definition of social development cited earlier in this chapter includes enjoyment of human rights as a component of development (UN, 2002). Among the many UN declarations and conventions on human rights is the Declaration on the Right to Development (United Nations, 1986). This statement

> proclaims that development is an inalienable human right, entitling all persons to participate in, contribute to and enjoy economic, social, cultural and political development in which all human rights and fundamental freedoms can be fully realized. The Declaration also states that *the human person is the central subject of development* and should be an active participant and beneficiary of the right to development. (UN Centre for Human Rights, 1994, p. 23, [emphasis added])

According to Peter Uvin (2004), at the "highest level, development and human rights become inseparable aspects of the same process, like two strands of the same fabric. The boundaries between human rights and development disappear, and both become conceptually and operationally inseparable parts of the same processes of social change" (p. 175). Thus, human rights include the right to development, and development must include protection and respect for human rights, as entitlements and in development processes. Integrating human rights into development processes and projects means "an absolute requirement of participation and transparency" (p. 182); both are important principles for international social work and in harmony with professional ethics.

If development is people-centered and poverty is accepted as a particularly outrageous violation of human rights, then an appropriate mandate for international social work can indeed be the simultaneous promotion of development and human rights.

REFERENCES

Agere, S. (1986). Participation in social development and integration in Sub-Saharan Africa. *Journal of Social Development in Africa, 1*(1), 93–110.

Amnesty International. (1996). Declaration on the role of health professionals in the exposure of torture and ill treatment. Issued 1996. Accessed December 31, 2007, at www.amnestyusa.org

Amnesty International. (2006). *About Amnesty International*. Accessed September 15, 2006, at www.amesty.org

Annan, K. (2006). *Meeting the challenges of a changing world: The annual report on the work of the organization*. New York: United Nations.

Boulding, E., with Dye, J. (2002). Women and development. In M. T. Snarr & D. N. Snarr (Eds.), *Introducing global issues* (2nd ed., pp. 179–194). Boulder, CO: Lynne Rienner Publishers.

Bryant, C., & Kappaz, C. (2005). *Reducing poverty building peace*. Bloomfield, CT: Kumarian Press.

Carr, R. (2003). On "judgments": Poverty, sexuality-based violence and human rights in 21st century Jamaica. *Caribbean Journal of Social Work, 2*, 71–87.

Council of Europe. (1961). European Social Charter. *European Treaties* ETS No. 35, Turin, 18.x.1961. Accessed January 25, 2000, at www.coe.fr/eng/legaltxt/35e.htm

Council of Europe. (1996). Revised Social Charter. *European Treaties*, ETS No. 163, Strasbourg, 3.v.1996. Accessed January 25, 2000, at www.coe.fr/eng/legaltxt/35e.htm

Donnelly, J. (1993). *International human rights*. Boulder, CO: Westview Press.

Donnelly, J. (2002). Human rights, globalizing flows, and state power. In A. Brysk (Ed.), *Globalization and human rights* (pp. 226–241). Berkeley and Los Angeles: University of California Press,.

Drinan, R. F. (2001). *The mobilization of shame: A world view of human rights*. New Haven, CT: Yale University Press.

Earth Charter. (2000). Accessed June 12, 2007, at www.earthcharter.org

Eckstein, S. E., & Wickham-Crowley, T. P. (Eds.). (2003). *Struggles for social rights in Latin America*. New York: Routledge.

Estes, R. (2005). Global change and indicators of social development. In M. Weil (Ed.), *The handbook of community practice* (pp. 508–528). Thousand Oaks, CA: Sage.

Food and Agriculture Organization (UN), International Fund for Agricultural Development, United Nations Centre for Human Settlements, World Food Programme (UN). (2006, November 15–16). *Reducing hunger and extreme poverty: Towards a coherent strategy*. Paper presented at the International Forum on the Eradication of Poverty, New York.

Fleshman, M. (2007). African gays and lesbians combat bias. *Africa Renewal, 21*(1), 12–13, 21.

Fox, D. J. (1998). Women's human rights in Africa: Beyond the debate over the universality or relativity of human rights. *Africa Studies Quarterly: The Online Journal of African Studies, 2*(3). Accessed May 23, 2007, at http://web.africa.ufl.edu

Gay rights: Until death do us part. (2006, December 2). *The Economist*, p. 64.

Human Rights Watch. (2006a) *About Human Rights Watch*. Accessed September 15, 2006, at www.humanrightswatch.org

Human Rights Watch. (2006b). *U.S. immigration law inhumane to same-sex couples*. Accessed December 3, 2006, at http://hrw.org/english/docs/2006/05/02/usdom13290.htm

Ife, J. (2001). *Human rights and social work: Toward rights-based practice*. Cambridge, UK: Cambridge University Press.

International Association of Schools of Social Work. (2004). *Global Standards for Social Work Education and Training*. Accessed December 30, 2007, at www.iassw-aiets.org

International Criminal Court. (2007). *About the Court*. Accessed May 9, 2007, at www.icc-cpi.int/about.html

International Criminal Court: Let the child live. (2007, January 27). *The Economist*, 59–60.

International Federation of Social Workers. (1988). Human Rights. In *Policy Papers*. Oslo, Norway: Author.

Isbister, J. (2003). *Promises not kept*, Bloomfield, CT: Kumarian Press.

Mattis, A. (Ed.). (1984). *Society for International Development prospectus*. Durham, NC: Duke University Press.

Meadows, D. H., Randers, J., & Meadows D. L. (1972). *Limits to growth*. New York: Universe Books.

Midgley, J. (1995). *Social development: The developmental perspective in social welfare*. Thousand Oaks, CA: Sage.

Midgley, J. (1999). Social development in social work: Learning from global dialogue. In C. Ramanathan & R. Link (Eds.), *All our futures: Principles & resources for social work practice in a global era* (pp. 193–205). Belmont, CA: Brooks/Cole.

Mutua, M. (2000). *The African human rights system: A critical evaluation* (UNDP Background Papers for the 2000 Human Development Report). Accessed May 24, 2006, at http://hdr.undp.org/docs/publications/background_papers/MUTUA.pdf

Omer, S. (1979). Social development. *International Social Work, 22*(3), 11–26.

Paiva, J. F. X. (1977). A conception of social development. *Social Service Review, 51*, 327–336.

Reichert, E. (2003). *Social work and human rights: A foundation for policy and practice*. New York: Columbia University Press.

Sanders, D. (1982). *The developmental perspective in social work*. Manoa: University of Hawaii Press.

Sandholtz, W. (2002). Humanitarian intervention: Global enforcement of human rights? In A. Brysk (Ed.), *Globalization and human rights* (pp. 201–225). Berkeley and Los Angeles: University of California Press.

Sen, A. (1999). *Development as freedom*. New York: Anchor Books.

Snarr, D. N. (2002). The changing face of global human rights. In M. T. Snarr. & D. N. Snarr (Eds.), *Introducing global issues* (pp. 53–70). Boulder, CO: Lynne Rienner Publishers.

Sterling, T. (2004). The global view of gay marriage. Accessed August 4, 2006, at www.cbsnews.com/stories/2004/03/04/world/main604084.shtml

Stoesz, D., Guzzetta, C., & Lusk, M. (1999). *International development*. Boston: Allyn & Bacon.

Streeten, P., & Burki, S. J. (1978). Basic needs: Some issues. *World Development, 6*(3).

ul Haq, M. (1990). United Nations Development Programme. In *Human Development Report 1990*. New York: United Nations Development Programme.

UNICEF. (1990). *The state of the world's children 1990*. New York: Oxford University Press.

United Nations. (1948). *Universal declaration of human rights*. New York: Author.

United Nations. (1986). Declaration on the Right to Development. Accessed June 3, 2007, at www.un.org

United Nations. (2002, February 7–8). *Financing global social development: Report*. Paper presented at International Forum for Social Development, New York.

United Nations Centre for Human Rights. (1994). *Human rights and social work: A manual for schools of social work and the social work profession* (Professional Training Series No. 1. Developed with the International Federation of Social Workers and the International Association of Schools of Social Work). Geneva, Switzerland: Author.

United Nations Department of Public Information. (2005). *The millennium development goals report 2005.* New York: Author.

United Nations Development Programme. (2000). *Human development report 2000.* New York: Oxford University Press.

United Nations Development Programme. (2003). *Human development report 2003: MDGS: A compact among nations to end human poverty.* New York: Oxford University Press for UNDP.

United Nations Development Programme. (2006). *Human development report 2005.* New York: Palgrave Macmillan for UNDP.

United Nations Economic and Social Council (ECOSOC). (2003). Committee on Economic Social and Cultural Rights, 30th session, State Party Report of Brazil, New York, E/C.12/2003.SR.8

United Nations Educational, Scientific and Cultural Organization. (2005). *United Nations decade of education for sustainable development 2005–2014: Draft international implementation scheme.* New York: Author.

United Nations News Centre. (2006). "Lauding disability convention as 'dawn of a new era,' UN urges speedy ratification." Press release issued 13 December 2006. Accessed December 31, 2007, at www.un.org

United Nations Office of the High Commissioner for Human Rights. (2004). Annex 3: A brief introduction to international human rights law terminology. In *ABC: Teaching human rights—Practical activities for primary and secondary schools.* New York and Geneva, Switzerland: United Nations. Accessed May 8, 2007, at www.ohchr.org

United Nations Office of the High Commissioner for Human Rights. (2005a). *Civil and political rights: The Human Rights Committee* (Fact Sheet No. 15, Rev. 1). Geneva, Switzerland: Author.

United Nations Office of the High Commissioner for Human Rights. (2005b). *The United Nations human rights treaty system: An introduction to the core human rights treaties and the treaty bodies* (Fact Sheet No. 30). Accessed May 18, 2006, at www.ohchr.org

United Nations Office of the High Commissioner for Human Rights. (2006). Accessed May 2006, at www.ohchr.org

United Nations Office of the High Commissioner for Human Rights. (2007). *Convention on the rights of persons with disabilities.* Accessed December 31, 2007, at www .ohchr.org

Uvin, P. (2004). *Human rights and development.* Bloomfield, CT: Kumarian Press.

World Commission on Environment and Development. (1987). *Our common future.* New York: Oxford University Press.

Wronka, J. (1995). Human rights. In R. Edwards (Ed.), *Encyclopedia of social work* (19th ed). Washington, DC: NASW Press.

Wronka, J. (2003, April 28). *Social action strategies toward creation if a human rights culture.* Workshop presentation at Human Rights Conference, University of Connecticut School of Social Work, West Hartford, CT.

CHAPTER 4

GLOBAL SOCIAL ISSUES

This chapter will briefly explore global social issues of concern to social workers. The treatment is necessarily brief and selective but serves to orient the reader to the substance of international social work. In many respects, these problems and issues make up the agenda for international professional action. Social workers have much to contribute to address and alleviate these problems through professional practice and as advocates and policy makers at the national, regional, and global levels. The issues presented here extend the discussion of migration and HIV/AIDS in Chapter 2; further information on work with refugees and immigrants and on international adoption will be addressed later in the book.

What makes a problem a global problem or issue? As defined in this book, problems are identified as global problems either because of causal factors or forces for solutions or, often, both. For some issues, status as a global issue is more evident than for others. Migration, discussed in Chapter 2, is an example of an obvious international issue, as it involves the movement of people from one country to others. The international nature of international human trafficking and international adoption is also readily evident. For other issues, there are complex global forces and structures that contribute to the development and severity of the problem: child labor, for example, exists in part because of the pressures of the global economy and the existence of world markets for low-cost child-produced goods. Similarly, poverty, although experienced locally, is linked to global trade, legacies of international colonialism, and the debt crisis. AIDS is experienced individually and nationally in terms of impact on economies and infrastructure; it is global because of the ways the epidemic spread rapidly through international contact and because solutions involve international agreements on patents for pharmaceuticals and intellectual property (for example, search for vaccines and treatments) as well as relationships of aid giving and receiving. Thus, the conceptualization of a problem as global involves aspects of its causation, shared experience, and the institutions and structures available, involved, or required for redress.

As explained by George and Page (2004), global social problems are defined by meeting the following criteria: "1. The cause of the problem should be found in global rather than national processes. 2. Such problems can spread across national borders despite the efforts of sovereign states. 3. The problem is increasingly difficult to resolve at a national level. 4. Supranational bodies have emerged in order to assist nation-states in dealing with the social problems concerned" (p. 2). They, too, recognize that some problems "are more 'global' than others" (p. 2).

The following issues are addressed in the chapter: poverty; status of women, including poverty, reproduction and health, gender violence, and human trafficking; children in difficult circumstances and in need of protection, including child labor, street children, child soldiers, and AIDS orphans; aging; and natural and man-made disasters.

POVERTY

In addition to the problems whose very nature and substance are shaped by interdependence, there are many problems that can be classified as global in nature in that they are shared by many or all nations and require mutual assistance in their solution. One of the most pervasive is poverty. Widespread poverty is now a global phenomenon and certainly one of the greatest challenges to international social work and to the world community. As Bryant and Kappaz (2005) explained, "poverty must be seen as global in nature given the cross-border causes and implications of poverty" (p. 160). Of all the global problems, poverty is the most fundamental and intractable. It is the root of many if not most other social problems: poverty plays a strong role in migration, it is a growing factor in the spread of AIDS, it is linked to drug production and use, and it is the direct cause of street children, homelessness, child labor, and malnutrition. Mary Robinson, former United Nations (UN) High Commissioner for Human Rights, declared that poverty is the greatest single violation of human rights worldwide. According to UN Development Programme (UNDP; 1996), "poverty is no longer contained within national boundaries. It has become globalized. It travels across borders, without a passport, in the form of drugs, diseases, pollution, migration, terrorism and political instability" (p. 2). In 1990, the World Bank estimated that the number of people living in poverty was 1.2 billion people; half of these were estimated to be living in absolute poverty, defined as having insufficient resources to obtain basic daily requirements of water, food, fuel, and shelter (Estes, 1997). The numbers have only grown; an International Labour Organization (ILO) survey reported that half of the world's workers—1.5 billion people—were living on less than $2 per day in 2006 (Seager, 2006), while the total number of people living on less than $2 per day is at least 2 billion (UNDP, 2005).

The gap between rich and poor has also been growing. The share of the world's income controlled by the richest one-fifth of the world's population has increased to 75%; at the same time, the share for the poorest one-fifth decreased from 2.3% in the early 1960s to a meager 1.5% today (UNDP, 2005).

Figure 4.1 Eking out a living selling produce on the street in Karachi.

Poverty has been reduced in East Asia, especially in China, and poverty rates, but not numbers, have declined in South Asia. However, "for most of the world's poorest countries the past decade has continued a disheartening trend: not only have they failed to reduce poverty, but they are falling further behind rich countries" (UNDP, 2005, p. 36).

Poverty must be understood as more than lack of income. Children suffer disproportionately when they are born into poverty. UNICEF (UN Children's Fund) (2005) defines *child poverty* as the experience of one or more forms of severe deprivation of nutrition, sanitation, health, shelter, education, and information. Thus, 16% of children under age 5 (U-5) are severely malnourished and in some countries, as many as one third of all children are moderately or severely underweight. In the most populous countries of South Asia—India,

Pakistan, and Bangladesh—one-third of U-5 children are underweight. In the developing world, 25% of preschoolers are Vitamin A deficient and face risks of blindness; severe anemia in pregnant women is strongly linked to maternal death, whereas chronic anemia saps human energy and is a barrier to development (Perez-Escamilla, 2006). Four hundred million children, especially rural children, have no access to clean water, and one in three in developing countries live with no sanitation facilities. Education is critical to a child's future, yet 140 million children of school age have never been to school; girls are especially vulnerable to lack of schooling. Finally, UNICEF (2005) identifies information deprivation as a dimension of poverty that is growing in importance in the twenty-first century. Large numbers of children are growing up with no access to TV, radio, computers, or even newspapers. They are poorly equipped to participate in life in the twenty-first century (UNICEF, 2005).

If there is any good news about poverty it is that it is possible for very poor countries to avoid famine and to achieve acceptable levels of human well-being (Sen, 1993). Conversely, as explained in Chapter 3, achieving higher national income is not sufficient to guarantee improvements in life expectancy, infant mortality rates, or education and nutritional statuses. UNDP differentiates income poverty from human poverty, a broader measure of well-being. Concurring with Sen (1993), the agency states that human poverty can be addressed, even in countries with very low income. Sen (1993) cited the example of Kerala State in India, with a population of 32 million. Life expectancy is more than 73 years compared to 63.3 for India as a whole and women have comparable life chances with men (State Planning Board, Government of Kerala, 2005). Literacy rates are high for men (90.9%) and women (87.7%) (Office of the Registrar General, India, 2001). These achievements have come about through state-level policies of expanded public education, an emphasis on universally provided basic health services, and subsidized nutrition, even though the gross national product (GNP) per capita is lower in Kerala than the average for India. Similar policies and results are true in Sri Lanka, Costa Rica, Jamaica, and China, although structural adjustment has hindered and even reversed progress.

UNDP's Human Poverty Index (HPI-2) for industrialized countries comprises four statistics: the percentage of people not expected to survive to age 60; the percentage of people age 16 to 65 who are functionally illiterate; the percentage below 50% of median personal income; and social exclusion as measured by the number of long-term unemployed as a percentage of the total labor force. Using this measure, the United States has the second greatest incidence of human poverty among the 18 Organization for Economic Cooperation and Development (OECD) countries—15.4%—followed by Ireland (15.2%) and the United Kingdom (14.8%). Sweden has the lowest at 6.5%, and Italy has the worst rate at 29.9%, fueled by its high rates of functional illiteracy (UNDP, 2005).

Poverty-Reduction Interventions

There are several recent innovations in poverty reduction strategies. Success has been reported from programs that give grants directly to poor households to reinforce behaviors that ultimately may reduce consequences of severe poverty. In Mexico, Oportunidades is a government program that was targeted to reach 5 million households in 2004. It provides cash transfers directly to poor mothers for school fees and supplies, food, and health care. Proof of school attendance and regular health clinic visits are required to continue to receive the grants. Grants are higher for students in upper grades and students of working age to prevent dropouts for child labor. According to UNICEF (2004), the program has had considerable success in increasing school attendance and retention and lowering maternal mortality and under-five morbidity.

In Brazil, the Bolsa Familia provides a "conditional cash transfer" to poor parents who ensure that their children attend school and get regular health clinic check-ups. The program is a large one, reaching one-fourth of the population. Bolsa Familia, along with reduced inflation, has resulted in reduction of the number of Brazilians living in poverty and a narrowing of the significant income inequality in the country. "The share of national income going to the poorer half of society increased from 9.8% to 11.9%" in just the years between 2002 and 2006 ("Rich Man, Poor Man," 2007, p. 11); obviously, the gap is still significant between rich and poor.

Microcredit and microenterprise projects have been successful in ameliorating household poverty and occasionally community poverty. Through extending small loans to individuals (often women), or through creating savings clubs on which members can draw, microfinance enables poor people to start small income-generating projects (Raheim, Noponen, & Alter, 2005). These range from traditional activities, such as crafts, sewing, and egg production to more "modern projects" such as setting up a telephone "booth" in a rural village through purchasing a cell phone and renting it out for calls. Microlending projects have often targeted women and have enhanced family well-being; microlending should not, however, be used in place of equal access to traditional forms of credit. Estimates are that 92 million people are served by microfinance services, 80% of them women (UN Population Fund, 2006). Evaluative data support the claim that microcredit is an important strategy for poverty reduction and is capable of reaching the very poor. Impressively, "a study of Grameen Bank clients in Bangladesh found that after eight to ten years in the program, 57.5 percent of participant households were no longer poor" (UN Population Fund, 2006, p. 9). Another study in 2005 also found impressive poverty reduction results for villages as well as individuals served by the program.

Poverty does not respect equal opportunity. The poorest of the poor are mostly women and their children, especially those living in rural areas of developing countries. Poverty is a cause and result of the disadvantaged position of women around the world.

THE STATUS OF WOMEN

Women and Poverty

Throughout the world, the status of women is another issue of common concern to social work. Although some have observed that for women there may not be any truly developed countries, women fare much worse in some countries than in others. The increasing feminization of poverty is recognized worldwide. Women-headed households are poorer in all countries; women's poverty affects the lives of their children and is a major contributor to special problems of disadvantaged children.

Illiteracy accompanies poverty as a major barrier to women's advancement. Women are two thirds of the world's illiterates; the male–female literacy gap is largest in South Asia, Sub-Saharan Africa, and the Middle East. In South Asia, for example, only 45% of women are literate compared to 70% of men; in the Middle East and North Africa, the percentages are 57% and 77%, respectively (UNICEF, 2005); 45% of women in India are illiterate (Kapoor, 2006). Even lower percentages of girls have access to secondary or higher education.

Although the Convention on the Elimination of All Forms of Discrimination Against Women was adopted by the UN in 1979 and has been fairly widely ratified, women continue to suffer many forms of discrimination. A few will be highlighted here.

Health and Reproductive Issues

Maternal mortality—deaths due to complications of childbirth and pregnancy—claims more than 500,000 lives a year; almost all of the deaths are in poor countries. In Sub-Saharan Africa, 1 in every 13 women dies from pregnancy/childbirth related causes, while the rate in Canada is only 1 in 7,700. In Ethiopia, where only 6% of births are attended, the maternal mortality rate is over 800 per 100,000 births ("Ten Years Hard Labour," 2004). In countries where all or almost all births are assisted by medical personnel, maternal death is rare.

Illegal abortion contributes to women's death toll, too. According to World Health Organization (WHO) estimates, 46 million of the 80 million unplanned pregnancies in the world are voluntarily terminated each year— 27 million legally and 19 million illegally. Many of these pregnancies result from lack of access to family planning information and services. Where abortion is illegal or severely restricted, it is likely to be unsafe and associated with maternal injury and death (WHO, 2004, p. 1). Abortions are unsafe when they are performed by untrained or poorly trained personnel and in unsanitary conditions; both are associated with illegal abortion. In the year 2000, WHO (2004) estimates that almost 68,000 women died from unsafe abortion. And "in some countries, it is not uncommon to find that half of all obstetric admissions are for complications of unsafe abortion, which undoubtedly compromises other maternity and emergency services" (p. 5). Conversely, when induced abortion is performed by qualified persons using correct techniques and in sanitary conditions, it is a very safe surgical procedure. In the USA, for example, the death rate from abortion is 0.6 per 100,000 procedures, making it as safe as an injection of penicillin. In developing countries, however, the risk of death following unsafe abortion procedures may be several hundred times higher than that of an abortion performed professionally under safe conditions. (p. 5)

Romania is cited as a particularly telling case. Under the Ceausescu regime, abortion policy was manipulated to force Romanians to have larger families:

the number of abortion-related deaths increased sharply after November 1966, when the government tightened a previously liberal abortion law. The figure rose from 20 to 100,000 live births in 1965 to almost 100 in 1974 and 150 in 1983. Abortions were legalized again in December 1989 and, by the end of 1990, maternal deaths caused by abortion dropped to around 60 to 100,000 live births. (WHO, 2004, p. 3)

This dramatic example indicates that women desperate to end their pregnancies will seek unsafe means if necessary, and that unsafe abortion is often a lethal choice.

Legal abortion can also disadvantage women in societies with strong male preference. Amartya Sen (1993) shocked the world when he announced that 100 million women were missing from global population figures, the victims of overt and violent discrimination against female children through sex-selection abortion and infanticide combined with the "staunch antifemale bias in health care and nutrition" (p. 46). In India, Sen (1999) notes that there is considerable evidence that "female children are neglected in terms of health care, hospitalization and even feeding" (p. 106). He also cites "new, ominous signs in China, such as the radical increase in the reported ratio of male births to female births—quite out of line with the rest of the world" (p. 107). Here, sex-selection abortion is a major contributor—a sad joining of modern technology with age-old antifemale attitudes and government restrictions on family size, such as the one-child policy introduced as a development initiative. Sex-selection abortion and infanticide plus extreme neglect of girl children have led to a sex ratio of only 933 females to 1000 males in India as of 2001; as one activist explained, "some are not allowed to be born and others not allowed to survive" (Kapoor, 2006).

The lower value accorded to girls is also reflected in their poorer nutritional status. In families in some parts of the world, girls eat last. A study in the Punjab region of India showed that 20% of girls were malnourished as compared to only 0.1% of boys (MacCormack, 1988). Poor nutrition and less access to health care result in higher death rates for girl children than for their brothers; the World Bank estimates that every sixth infant death in India is due to gender discrimination.

Gender Violence

Girls who survive early childhood may be subjected to other forms of gender violence. In all countries of the world, domestic violence and rape continue to be major threats to women's health, security, and survival. Women are at most risk in their intimate relationships and in their own homes. Home is far from a place of safety and security for many women. In the WHO 10-country study on women's health and violence completed in 2005, respondents in the countries reported incidence of intimate partner physical violence of from 13% to 61%; in most of the countries, between one-fourth and one-half of women reported physical abuse (World Health Organization, 2005). Studies report high rates in rich countries (Finland, 30%) and poor ones (Ethiopia, 49%). Abuse includes physical violence—beatings, chokings, stabbings, burning, and killing—sexual violence, and emotional abuse. Abuse can be lethal. A study conducted in Australia, Canada, Israel, South Africa, and the United States showed that "40%–70% of all female murder victims were killed by their husbands or boyfriends" (UN Report of the Secretary-General, 2006, p. 38). Another study showed that in Columbia, a woman is killed every six days by her partner (UN Report of the Secretary-General, 2006). Other studies have estimated the staggering costs of domestic violence in medical treatment, lost work, counseling, police intervention, shelters, and other services. A 1993 study in Jamaica, based on a survey of victims who sought treatment at Kingston Public Hospital, estimated yearly costs of medical treatment for interpersonal violence at $1.1 billion; a 1999 study in Switzerland estimated that €60 million are spent yearly on medical care, shelters, police, and victim support for battered women (UN, 2006).

Intimate partner violence begins early. In Canada, 54% of girls between the ages of 15–19 reported "sexual coercion" in dating relationships in response to a survey (UN, 2006, p. 42). In the United States, estimates are that 22% of high school age students and 32% of college students have experienced violence while dating.

Traditional Practices. The UN study also outlined the impact of violence caused by traditional practices. Chief among these is female genital mutilation (FGM) or cutting. According to the UN Report of the Secretary-General (2006), 130 million females alive today have been subjected to genital mutilation/cutting and two million girls a year suffer female genital cutting/mutilation (UN Fund for Population Activities [UNFPA], 2005), labeled by UNICEF (1996) "one of the worst violations of the Convention on the Rights of the Child." Although 75% of cases of FGM are in only six countries (Egypt, Ethiopia, Kenya, Nigeria, Somalia, and the Sudan), the practice has migrated with its practitioners and has become "prevalent among immigrant communities in Europe, North America and Australia" (UN, 2006, p. 39), prompting laws against FGM in a number of countries. In 2006, an Ethiopian immigrant was convicted of aggravated battery and cruelty to children for circumcising his two-year-old daughter. This conviction by a court in the state of Georgia is believed to be the first conviction for FGM in the United States ("Father Jailed for US Mutilation," 2006). The first conviction in Scandinavia was also in 2006 in Sweden, where a Swedish citizen was convicted of forcing his daughter to undergo circumcision during a trip to Somalia. Sweden passed a law outlawing FGM on its own territory in 1982 and expanded the law to prohibit taking children abroad for the procedure in 1999 ("Sweden Jails Circumcision Father," 2006). As of 2006, 15 of the 28 African countries where FGM is prevalent had passed laws making the practice a crime; full implementation and compliance lag far behind.

Early and forced marriage, honor killings, dowry deaths, and abuse of widows also take a toll on women. In Ethiopia, 19% of girls are married by the age of 15; in Nepal, 40% are married by age 15, and 7% of these before the age of 10 (UN, 2006). One-half of the marriages in Kyrgyzstan "were the result of kidnappings." The out-of-balance gender ratios in India and China raise fears that bride kidnapping will increase in these areas. The UN Secretary-General's report (2006) estimated that each year there are about 5,000 so-called honor killings—killings of women and girls by their own relatives because of some behavior (including being a rape victim) that shames the family. In India, over 6800 deaths in 2002 were attributed to killings over dowry disputes (UN, 2006).

Violence in Armed Conflict. Although women suffer widespread violence in times of peace, their condition worsens in conflict situations. Rape is now seen as a weapon of war. Sexual violence against women and girls has been rampant in recent wars. In Bosnia, rape was used as a tool of ethnic cleansing, and rape has been widely documented in conflicts in Liberia, Sierra Leone, Darfur, and many other modern conflicts. In a documentary on the "lost boys" of Sudan, one young man comments that the attackers carried away the girls, including his sister: "they took her away and used her up" (Mylan & Shenk, 2003). A special UN Security Council resolution, Resolution #1325, addresses sexual and gender violence in conflict and postconflict situations. The International Criminal Court can try crimes of sexual violence "when committed as part of a widespread or systematic attack directed at a civilian population" (UN, 2007, p. 3).

Human Trafficking

Human trafficking has been greatly exacerbated by globalization. According to the World Commission on the Social Dimension of Globalization's 2004 *Fair Globalization* report,

> Another side-effect of globalization has been a sharp increase in the level of illicit cross-border activities. This has included increased tax evasion and the rise of multinational crime syndicates engaged in money laundering, trafficking in people, and the sex and drug trades . . . the sharp fall in transportation costs and the growth of mass tourism has made the smuggling of people and drugs less costly and more difficult to detect. (p. 49)

Human trafficking has also been fed by increased disparities between rich and poor (supply) and by communications technology that has facilitated Internet pornography. According to the U.S. Department of Health and Human Services (USDHHS; 2005), "after drug dealing, human trafficking is tied with the illegal arms industry as the second largest criminal industry in the world today and it is the fastest growing." Criminals have discovered that, unlike drugs, humans are a "reusuable commodity" and there are high profits to be made in trafficking of people. An estimated 600,000 to 800,000 people are trafficked across borders each year; the U.S. Department of State estimates that between 14,500 and 17,500 of these are brought into the U.S. yearly (USDHHS, 2005). The UN estimates that human trafficking yields about $10 billion a year—a "profit" of about $10,000 per victim (Kapstein, 2006) while the ILO estimates global profits at more than 4 times that amount (Salett, 2006). The total number of people in slavery globally may be any-where from 12 to 27 million (Salett, 2006). This modern horror of trafficking and slavery is "undermining the legal and ethical foundations of the global economy" (Kapstein, 2006, pp. 114–116).

The most common forms of trafficking are sex trafficking and labor trafficking. Women, children, and men are forced against their will into prostitution, pornography, domestic service, sweatshop labor, or agricultural work. Victims may be abducted or, more often, tricked into slavery through advertisements for work overseas as maids, waitresses, or other jobs. Women and girls, especially, are forced into the sex trade (Roby, 2005). They are kept in conditions of modern-day slavery through violence and other forms of coercion, isolation, and threats. As Kapstein (2006) described modern slavery: "Slavers typically recruit poor people in poor countries by promising them good jobs in distant places" (p. 106). Traffickers usually give victims a "loan" to cover transport. On arrival, they confiscate identity documents and force the victims into the sex industry or forced labor; victims may be threatened with being reported to police as illegal immigrants or as prostitutes and are often threatened with violence. Often, those who labor under these conditions receive little or no pay for their work. Thus, victims' level of vulnerability is extreme, preventing help seeking.

According to the USDHHS (n.d.-a), "women and children are over-whelmingly trafficked in labor arenas because of their relative lack of power, social marginalization, and their overall status as compared to men." In-creases in trafficking in India are linked to the out-of-balance sex ratio re-ported above. Women are increasingly trafficked to be sold as wives in areas with too few females (Kapoor, 2006).

Governments are taking steps to reduce trafficking through law en-forcement and services to victims. The United States enacted the Trafficking Victims Protection Act of 2000 (TVPA) to strengthen prosecution of traffickers and protection for victims. Severe sentencing guidelines were adopted for trafficking that involves kidnapping, aggravated sexual abuse, or exploitation of children under age 14. Of particular note is that the law defines "subtle means of coercion," such as trickery and seizure of documents as aspects of the crime (USDHHS, n.d.-b). Passage of the TVPA has resulted in more arrests and convictions for trafficking; police still report that the law is difficult to implement and victims are still often too fearful to cooperate (Kapstein, 2006).

In a recent case in the state of Connecticut, laborers from Guatemala won a settlement from a tree nursery and were given back wages. The men were promised jobs in North Carolina planting trees but were taken to Connecticut against their will, housed in squalid conditions, and forced to work long hours for a fraction of the legally required minimum wage. Their passports were taken from them, and they had few options for escape until a law clinic found out about their plight. Trafficking charges are pending against the company that issued the original labor contracts (Spencer, 2007).

The U.S. Department of Health and Human Services issues an annual *Trafficking in Persons Report* and targets countries that are making weak efforts to intervene with traffickers. Countries currently on the U.S. "Tier 3" list as particularly weak on trafficking are Belize, Burma, Cuba, Iran, Laos, North Korea, Saudi Arabia, Sudan, Syria, Uzbekistan, Venezuela, and Zimbabwe (Kapstein, 2006). In 2000, the UN General Assembly adopted the Protocol to Prevent, Suppress, and Punish Trafficking in Persons, Especially Women and Children; it is the main international agreement on trafficking.

Roles for social workers include identification of victims, treatment and rehabilitation, advocacy, and education of vulnerable groups. One former trafficking victim advised social workers to look for the child who is always alone, wears ill-fitting clothes, is often late or absent from school and behind in school work. Once trafficking is suspected, the social worker or other adult must work to develop a relationship of trust before taking any more drastic actions (Slattery, 2006). Typical intake interviews must be done slowly, often in several stages; in addition to usual questions, suspected victims should be asked if they have their own passports or identification papers, and whether their families know how to contact them (Salett, 2006). Considerable caution must be used in engaging interpreters to ensure that they are not connected to traffickers and will maintain confidentiality. In some countries, such as the United States, once someone is certified as a trafficking victim, that person is eligible for benefits and protected from deportation. Therefore, it can be beneficial to cooperate with law enforcement personnel.

Ultimately, preventing trafficking will include poverty alleviation strategies as well as more vigorous prosecution. Some countries with significant numbers of labor emigrants are establishing protective policies and services to assist their nationals abroad when promised jobs turn out to involve slave-like conditions. The Philippines is one leader in setting up such services.

Global Action on Violence Against Women. In 1993, the UN adopted the Declaration on the Elimination of Violence Against Women. This document clearly stated that violence against women is a violation of human rights and includes violence within the family as well as community violence. The WHO has also recognized violence against women as a major cause of health problems. Yet the 2006 UN Secretary-General's report concluded: "while the number of United Nations bodies that now list violence against women as one of their concerns is impressive, the amount of resources and attention given to this issue is still small and the work lacks effective coordination" (p. 20).

Social workers are playing active roles in victim services throughout the world. Only in the last 30 years have shelters for women become commonplace; these emergency services developed in the United Kingdom and United States in the 1970s and have spread to many other countries. Social workers have been instrumental in developing shelters, in providing training to police and court officials on the needs of victims of violence, in counseling and offering concrete services to victims, and in self-esteem building projects to encourage women to believe that they have a right not to be abused. Counseling techniques have moved assertively toward support and planning for alternatives. In some places, social workers have also initiated counseling and groupwork with abusers to promote violence prevention and reduction. The area of least success and greatest need is in promotion of violence-free intimate relationships. As research continues to show the devastating effects on children from growing up in a violent home, progress in reducing domestic violence must be made.

PROBLEMS OF CHILDREN IN DIFFICULT CIRCUMSTANCES

Child Mortality

Closely connected to poverty and its associated ills is child mortality. In the United States and northern Europe, child deaths are 2%–3% of total deaths. Worldwide, child deaths represent about one-third of the total number of deaths per year. According to Kent (2002), the median age at death in 1990 was 5 or younger in 13 countries (Angola, Burkina Faso, Ethiopia, Guinea, Malawi, Mali, Mozambique, Niger, Rwanda, Sierra Leone, Somalia, Tanzania, and Uganda); that same year, the median age at death in the United States was 76 and in Japan was 78 (p. 203). UNICEF (2005) reports that approximately 10 million U-5 children die each year from preventable causes. The largest numbers are in South Asia and Sub-Saharan Africa. Rates of U-5 child mortality reveal gross differences between levels of child well-being. They range from a worst of 283 per 1000 live births in Sierra Leone to a world best rate of 3 achieved by Iceland and Sweden (UNICEF, 2005). Among the causes are pneumonia (19%), diarrhea (17%), malaria (8%), measles (4%), and AIDS (3%); neonatal deaths are 37% of the total. Malnutrition, inadequate sanitation, and unclean water contribute to many of these child deaths. Thus, the main causes of child mortality are preventable through simple health interventions, sanitation initiatives, nutrition, and education. Although not listed by UNICEF as a major cause of child mortality, it appears that conflict plays a role in worsening child mortality. Among the 12 countries with U-5 rates of 200 or over are Sierra Leone, Angola, Afghanistan, Liberia, Somalia, the Democratic Republic of the Congo, and Rwanda. All have been severely affected by armed conflict in the near past. Iraq has a current rate of 125; in 1990, Iraq's U-5 mortality rate was 50 (UNICEF, 2005). The cumulative impact of economic sanctions and war on children has been devastating.

Millennium Development Goal (MDG) 4 is to reduce child mortality by two-thirds by 2015. Sixty countries that together account for 94% of all U-5 mortality have been targeted. Of these, only seven (Bangladesh, Brazil, Egypt, Indonesia, Mexico, Nepal, and the Philippines) are on pace to meet their MDG goals (UNICEF, 2007). At current rates of progress, many children will continue to die needlessly long after 2015. This is not to deny that progress is being made. In Ethiopia, for example, U-5 mortality was 204 in 1990 and had been reduced to 166 by 2004. It is still a long way to the target of 68 for 2015, and at current rates of reduction, the goal will be missed by a large margin.

Although the contributions of medical and engineering professions are key, social workers also can play a significant role in reducing child mortality through outreach and education about the importance of individual health and sanitation practices. They can also be instrumental in engaging community participation and support for community-level health and sanitation projects to dig wells and pit latrines.

Child Labor

As a global problem, the term *child labor* is used to refer to "children working in conditions that are excessively abusive and exploitive" (Kent, 2002, p. 196), although other experts would surely delete the word *excessively*. Children work in mines, carpet factories, agriculture, brick-making plants, on remote fishing platforms, as domestics, and as forced beggars, among other forms and settings. Even worse forms of child labor include prostitution and armed conflict (discussed separately below). Among the abuses suffered by working children are dangerous conditions, where injuries, exposure to harmful chemicals and particulate matter, and even death are common; long hours of work that deprive the child of opportunity for education; and physical and sexual abuse by supervisors. For their suffering, most child laborers are paid very little. They are often separated from their families and live in wretched conditions in dormitories or sleep on the floors of homes in which they are servants.

One form of child labor is bonded labor, in which a family with a debt is bonded to the creditor in order to "pay off" the loan through labor. Most often, the child must labor for years with no pay or discovers that the cost to meet interest charges on the loan is more than the pay earned. Thus, the debt can never be paid off, and the child becomes permanently enslaved by the debt. In Pakistan alone, it is estimated that there are 7.5 million child-bonded laborers (Kent, 2002, p. 197).

The ILO (2007) states that more than 200 million children are doing work that is "damaging to his or her mental, physical and emotional development."

Figure 4.2 A young seller in the San Blas Islands, Panama, displays a mola, a brightly colored reverse appliqué.

Child labor is difficult to eradicate because children work because their families depend on their wages for survival, even if the wages are minimal. Two ILO conventions are aimed at the elimination of child labor. Convention Number 182 binds ratifying countries to take immediate steps to eliminate the worst forms of child labor; Convention Number 138 sets a longer time frame for widespread elimination of child labor. In addition, conditional income transfer programs such as those in Mexico and Brazil described earlier assist by compensating families for potential child labor wages lost. The ILO reports that the number of child laborers has fallen since 2000, with a 26% reduction in hazardous work by children. In Latin America, for example, projects are under way targeting children working in sugar cane in Bolivia, fireworks industries in El Salvador and Guatemala, mining in Colombia, domestic labor in Haiti, child scavengers in Nicaragua, and commercial sexual exploitation of children in numerous countries (ILO, n.d.).

Street Children

Globally, poverty and worsening economic conditions have caused an increase in the number of street children. Some of these children are part of homeless families; others may live only part of the time on the streets, working to add marginal amounts to a family's subsistence income. In fact, most street children are not orphans but are still in contact with their families. The most disadvantaged, however, have no home other than the streets and little or no contact with families. They may be the gaminos of Columbia, boys who sleep on the streets, stealing or carrying out small jobs for money, and sniffing glue to dull the pain of their existence; they may be the street children of Brazil, facing extreme oppression and for a time even death at the hands of police executioners bent on ridding the streets of these small nuisances; they may be the barrel children of Jamaica, left by mothers who emigrated and who are supporting themselves by selling the barrels of goods their mothers send to them (Crawford-Brown & Rattray, 2001); or they may be adolescent runaways in the cities of America, living in shelters or turning to prostitution to survive or runaways in any country who have left home to escape abuse. In articles by Lusk (1992) and Raffaelli (1997), children in these different situations are labeled as children in the street—those who work selling things or washing windshields but still live at least part of the time with their families—and children of the street, those who have left home and survive by begging or stealing. This latter group is in the most dangerous circumstances; Lusk found that in Rio de Janeiro only about 7% of them attended school, 60% engaged in illegal activities, and 80% admitted to using drugs.

Figure 4.3 Street boys in Colombia eat leftovers taken from a restaurant.

UNICEF (2005) is concerned that even the "term 'street children' is problematic as it can be employed as a stigmatizing label" (p. 40). There is no exact count of the number of street children; however, the numbers are large—estimated by UNICEF at tens of millions. It is clear that "every city in the world has some street children, including the biggest and richest cities of the industrialized world" (UNICEF, p. 41). Most street children are male, perhaps, UNICEF says, because "girls seem to endure abusive or exploitive situations at home longer" (p. 41). As children live in the street or spend increasing amounts of their time away from parental supervision and engaged in petty labor, they are at risk for falling prey to many dangers, including exploitation and trafficking, drug use, violence, crime, and even targeting by police. Usually out of school, they grow up without skills to assume a place in mainstream society.

In a review of interventions with street children, Dybicz (2005) identified levels of prevention efforts, depending on the needs of the children. Primary prevention targets the family living in extreme poverty whose children are not yet on the street. Interventions include income-generation projects and efforts to improve housing and other living conditions. For the large group of street children who work on the streets but are still in contact with families, effective interventions include microenterprise projects that allow children to earn money without criminal activity, and educational programs to "raise awareness in street children of the numerous risks accompanying street life" such as HIV, gangs, and violence (p. 775). Other interventions include drop-in shelters that provide food, shelter, and a safe haven. A program for child prostitutes in Addis Ababa, for example, provides a day center where girls can rest, wash their clothes, receive some basic education and health care, and eat (personal communication/field visit, January 2005). Dybicz's review found that the least effective programs seem to be the residential/rehabilitative programs aimed at hard-core street children—they yield "a low success rate in reintegrating the individual back into the community" (p. 766). The program director at the Addis Ababa project noted that there is a residential component for those girls who are committed to leaving street life; only small numbers take advantage of this. Yet others question whether outreach interventions can help children in the streets transition to safe adulthood. Raffaelli (1997) quotes an expert who said, "there is no rehabilitation on the streets" (p. 98).

Social work interventions can help in several ways. Although poverty is an important factor leading to street children, family violence and child abuse are also significant. The studies cited by Raffaelli (1997) revealed that much higher percentages of children in the streets reported abuse at home than children who returned to their families. Social work services to address child abuse are needed to encourage children to remain in the family.

Youth Unemployment. Although the younger children who are permanently on the street are extreme cases of poverty and abandonment by families and societies, the problems of many street children differ only by degree from the much larger problem of undereducated, unemployed youth. Youth unemployment and social exclusion are growing problems from Europe to the Caribbean islands. According to the ILO, 50% of the world's unemployed are between the ages of 15 and 24 (Seager, 2006). The numbers are staggering and total about 89 million worldwide, ranging from one-third of youth in eastern Europe to one in seven in the United States and Europe. Hopelessness— youth without a vision of a future—leads to drug use and violence in many cases. These problems of homeless and futureless children are among the most pressing for social work attention around the world and are another piece of the shared agenda in social welfare.

Child Soldiers

The image of the child with an AK 47 machine gun has come to symbolize the child soldier. The majority of the world's armed conflicts involve children under the age of 18 and some as young as 8 years old. Children have been involved in combat from South America to Asia; indeed, Burma/Myanmar has the single largest number (Becker, 2006). Attention to the situation of child soldiers, however, has focused on conflicts in Africa, from Angola to Eritrea and more recently Sierra Leone, Liberia, and Northern Uganda. The current estimate according to Human Rights Watch is that 250,000–300,000 children are in armed conflict in 20 countries, serving in government armies, government-backed militias, and rebel armies (Becker, 2006).

Children are recruited primarily because they are easy to control and indoctrinate. They may in fact be sent on particularly dangerous missions because they are considered expendable, as they are not skilled fighters and receive little training. Some are abducted or conscripted by force; some join because they have lost their families and homes to the conflict and have few options for survival; and others probably join "willingly" because of the lure of guns and uniforms (Becker, 2006). Girls are also abducted into armies, some to serve as soldiers, others for sex, and often both.

Clearly a "worst form of child labor," child soldiers suffer maiming and physical injuries and emotional and psychological trauma from the horrors they have witnessed and perpetrated and from sexual abuse. In addition to trauma, their lack of education and civilian job and living skills create huge challenges for adapting to a more normal postconflict life. "They ruined me" said one girl in Uganda, cited by Human Rights Watch (Becker, 2006).

Former child soldiers need services and rehabilitation. In northern Uganda, for example, a reception and rehabilitation center has been serving demobilized child soldiers. At first, the focus was on basic needs and recreation. Family contact was initiated with a goal of reunification and psychosocial support provided in culturally acceptable ways. This process is often difficult, and the staff have found that using rituals is helpful, especially in contexts not accepting of Western ideas about mental health. Children may gather in a group and burn their uniforms and military gear as a way of rejecting that part of their lives, for example, or cleansing rituals may be used. Building tangible skills is also an essential part of reintegration social work

(Ojera, 2006). A Christian Children's Fund project in Sierra Leone focused on girls who were victims of sexual violence either as child combatants or civilians. The project formed community groups to protect the girls from harassment. The groups were originally called Sexual Violence Committees; however, the girls themselves objected to the name; they renamed the groups Girls' Welfare Committees to recognize that they are human beings with multiple needs, not just victims of sexual violence (Wessels, 2006). Through use of local healers and cleansing rituals coupled with health care, protection, and income generation, the project has been rated a success by participants who report being able to get on with life activities (Wessels, 2006).

Wessells (2006) cautions that it is essential to see the whole person in his or her environment and not focus only on the soldiering experience. Child soldiers suffer from joblessness, stigma, lack of education, and health and disability issues, as well as the poverty and HIV/AIDS pandemic that may affect their communities. China Keitetsi (2006), former child soldier, emphasizes the need for healing for families as well as the former child soldiers. She also noted that the process of reintegration is challenging, as former child soldiers usually have no education, no skills, poor health, and many have lost their families. Families may have suffered directly from the often-brutal acts committed by child soldiers and need assistance if reintegration is to take place. Programs should also take care in offering special benefits to child soldiers that are not available to other children, as resentment can inhibit community willingness to participate in reintegration (A. Turay, personal communication, April 12, 2007).

Orphans

Becoming orphaned has always created a situation of severe risk to children, as parents are the primary line of defense against poverty and exploitation. Although some causes of early parental death have been overcome, AIDS has led to increases so large that an orphan crisis has been declared, especially in Sub-Saharan Africa. According to UNICEF (2005), which defines an orphan as a child under the age of 18 who has lost one or both parents, there were 143 million orphans as of the end of 2003; the number increased by 16 million in just a single year (p. 39). The 15 million of these who have been orphaned by AIDS may seem like a small percentage; however, the number of AIDS orphans grew from 11.5 million to 15 million in just a 2-year period; the projected number by 2010 is 25 million AIDS orphans (Joint UN Programme on HIV/AIDS [UNAIDS], 2007). In addition to Africa, home to 12.3 million of the 15 million current orphans, there is growing concern about orphans in South and East Asia where incidence of AIDS is increasing rapidly.

Becoming an AIDS orphan is often a long and difficult journey for a child. Prior to losing the parent to death, the child is likely to have experienced the parent's long illness and growing debilitation. As parents become too ill to work, family poverty increases. Siblings, especially infants, may have died, and the child himself or herself may be infected. In areas with high infection rates, other relatives may have died or be ill with AIDS, leaving few adult caretakers. In many instances, the child becomes the caretaker and is burdened physically and emotionally with caring for a seriously ill parent and facing the prospect of the parent's death. A project was initiated to assist child carers in Zimbabwe, a country that is estimated to have 1.3 million orphans, close to one million of them due to AIDS (Dhlembeu & Mayanga, 2006). Among the comments Martin (2006) reported from child caregivers: "It is difficult for me to lift my parent who is big and I am small" (p. 121) or "my mother's expectations of me are too much" (p. 119) or, from a 9-year-old boy, "I clean the house. I found cleaning difficult because I had never done it before" (p. 118). The emotional toll may be more severe. One project in Zimbabwe found a boy, aged 12, who was caring for his older brother all by himself after both parents and a baby brother had died of AIDS. "Also infected with HIV, his greatest fear and sadness was who would care for him when his time came" (Martin, 2006, p. 109).

In addition to burdens of care and grief, AIDS orphans and children living with seriously ill parents are vulnerable to other practical problems, especially poverty and reduced access to school. Thus, even if not HIV positive, AIDS orphans face reduced life chances as they frequently miss school or drop out, leaving with no skills and a limited future. They are at risk of becoming street children or being exploited by others.

When both parents die, some children remain in child-headed households, as high death rates from AIDS lead to breakdown in traditional patterns of substitute parental care. During the filming of *Pandemic: Facing AIDS* (Kennedy, 2003), the film crew interviewed 7-year-old James in Uganda who was living in his rural home alone with his younger sister. Neighbors helped at times providing food, and James sometimes managed to get to school. Yet the situation of the two small children was desperate; their only bedding was a pile of rags, and James was interviewed wearing a tattered T-shirt. He said he did have one better shirt for school. James told the film crew that his biggest fear is that someone would come and take them away.

Martin (2006) reports that it is astounding how strong and resilient many of the children are. Many not only care for their ill family members or for siblings but also maintain the household and even negotiate with authorities for any entitlements that may be due. Clearly, leaving children alone to cope is not an optimal solution to the orphan issue. Governments may not want to admit that child-headed households exist, so officials have not done as much as they could to address the problem. Martin (2006) notes that neither the 1999 Zimbabwe National Orphan Care Policy nor the 2004 National Plan of Action for Orphans and Other Vulnerable Children addressed the issue of child caregivers. There is a need for services to help these children with their physical and emotional burdens; however, the idea of training child carers is controversial. It is important not to let controversy interfere with reality, while other, better solutions are sought. The three overarching principles of the Convention on the Rights of the Child (CRC) are survival, development, and protection. How can these be best guaranteed to AIDS orphans?

Some orphans are cared for in institutions; however, institutional care is often impersonal, and building and staffing good-quality institutions is beyond the capacity of impoverished countries, especially those with large numbers of children to place. Yet, in Zimbabwe and other countries, nongovernmental organizations (NGOs) and foreign evangelical churches have constructed orphanages, often in the outmoded dormitory style (Powell, 2006). Large institutions are often detrimental to children's development and remove them from any remaining connections to community. Thus, institutions cannot be seen as the solution to the orphan crisis. The increased availability of antiretroviral treatments is an important orphan-prevention strategy, as even delaying parental deterioration and death until children mature would help significantly (Zimbabwe's current life expectancy of 35 indicates the need to address this).

Social workers have played important roles in orphan care and orphan service planning and more remains to be done.

AGING

From 1950 to 2002, the average life expectancy at birth increased by 20 years to 66 (UN, 2003). This stunning accomplishment has resulted in growth in the numbers of aged persons throughout the world. In 2000, there were about 600 million people older than the age of 60; projections for 2050 are for more than 3 times this number—2 billion. While Europe, North America, and Japan lead the demographic shift toward older populations, developing countries are also seeing significant increases in the proportion of their populations classified as aged. According to the UN (2003), the percentage of older persons in Asia and Latin America will rise to 15% by 2025. Although Africa will see some increase, it is projected to lag significantly behind, largely because of the impact of AIDS.

The impacts of an increased aged population will be considerable. Already, the countries of Europe (where the UN projects that 28% of the population will be over age 60 by 2025) worry about sustaining welfare state provisions with dependency ratios that are changing rapidly (dependency ratio is the number of working-age adults to the numbers of children and aged). The fastest growing segment of the aging population is the "old old"—those over age 80. This suggests the need for increased supportive services to sustain persons with disabilities and need for assistance with tasks of daily living.

Aging is projected to become a major social issue in developing countries within the next few decades. The challenge will be to find ways to sustain progress in development and provide for the aged in new ways. The report of the Second World Assembly on Ageing in Madrid (United Nations, 2003) pointed out that more aged in developing countries live in rural areas, rather than urban. This presents additional challenges for provision of needed services, especially as younger family members migrate to cities or emigrate to find better employment opportunities. Remittances will help but will not

Figure 4.4 Resident of a home for the aged in China.

provide the assistance with daily living that may be a growing need. Women make up the larger number of aged and are more likely to be poor, in industrialized and developing countries. Among white aged in the United States, for example, only 5.8% of men are below the poverty line compared to 10.2% of women (U.S. Bureau of the Census, 2006). Minority populations are also disproportionately poor. In the United States, 23.9% of black aged live below the poverty line (U.S. Bureau of the Census).

Policy and practice challenges for the future (and present, in many places) include,

• Addressing poverty in old age, especially special needs of women
• Ensuring participation and integration into society (special challenges of rural aged, as above)
• Provision and financing of health care
• Social protection
• Ending age discrimination
• Addressing needs for supportive environments—services to assist with activities of daily living and environments that facilitate this.

The Political Declaration and Madrid International Plan of Action on Ageing identified three priorities for global attention: aging and development, health in old age, and "ensuring enabling and supportive environments" (UN, 2003, foreword). Social workers play particularly important roles in connecting the elderly with needed services and helping families to plan for supportive environments.

NATURAL AND MAN-MADE DISASTERS

This final global social problem differs from the others considered here because it is the only one that is often not preventable through human intervention. This point should, however, be qualified, as lack of care of the environment is contributing to global warming, and scientists believe this in turn is increasing the severity of hurricanes and other storms. Human-caused erosion also worsens damage caused by floods. Other natural disasters—earthquakes and volcanic eruptions—cannot be prevented, so interventions must focus on preparedness and recovery.

A disaster has been defined by Brathwaite as "an event which seriously disrupts the normal functioning of the affected society causing widespread human, material or environmental losses which exceed the ability of the affected society to cope, using its own resources" (cited by Rock & Corbin, 2007, p. 386). A more comprehensive definition is that a disaster has seven elements that when all are present distinguish it from other tragedies. These are that a disaster *(1)* "involves the destruction of property, injury or loss of life"; *(2)* "has an identifiable beginning and end"; *(3)* "is sudden and time-limited"; *(4)* "affects a relatively large group of people"; *(5)* is "public" and affects more than one family; *(6)* "is out of the realm of ordinary experience"; and *(7)* "is psychologically traumatic enough to induce stress in almost anyone" (Rosenfeld, Caye, Ayalon, & Lahad, 2005, p. 11).

A rash of severe natural disasters in the early twenty-first century met all these criteria and focused new attention on the social impacts of natural disaster. The Caribbean basin, for example, was hard hit by hurricanes in 2004, culminating in Hurricane Ivan that devastated Grenada, destroying or damaging 90% of the buildings on the island and leaving one-third of the population homeless (Rock & Corbin, 2007). A cataclysmic tsunami hit Southeast Asia in December of 2004, killing almost 250,000 people and causing death and destruction from Indonesia to India to the coast of East Africa. Then, in the fall of 2005, Hurricane Katrina hit the southern coast of the United States, leading to death and unprecedented dislocation and shaking faith in the capacity of the most powerful country in the world to respond to human need on its own territory. Killing close to 2000, Katrina was the costliest storm in U.S. history with damage estimated at $125 billion (*World Almanac*, 2007). A huge earthquake in Pakistan and Kashmir killed far more people (80,000) in October 2005 but competed for the attention of a disaster-weary world community.

Dislocation caused by natural disaster can be so severe that in the case of the earthquake that hit Armenia in 1988, it contributed to Armenia's break with the Soviet Union and forced new ways of thinking and coping. The

ongoing eruptions of a long-dormant volcano in Montserrat covered two-thirds of the island in lava and ash, obliterated the capital, and forced the emigration of about 70% of the population (Ring & Carmichael, 2006). For the people of Montserrat, their country no longer exists as they once knew it. The psychological as well as economic impacts have been severe. Social workers play many roles in disaster response and recovery and are increasingly interested in disaster prevention and mitigation (taking steps to reduce the impact of natural disasters that may occur). A mixed focus on meeting immediate basic needs and attention to psychosocial trauma is indicated. Indeed, recent lessons learned strongly suggest that the majority of children who experience even a major disaster will "regain normal functioning once basic survival needs are met, safety and security have returned and developmental opportunities are restored within the social, family and community context" (*Psychosocial Care and Protection of Tsunami Affected Children, 2005*).

There are also human-caused disasters that meet some or all of the criteria outlined above. These have included nuclear accidents such as the explosion in Chernobyl, Ukraine; chemical leaks such as the Union Carbide leak in Bhopal, India, that killed more than 3000 people in 1984; and large-scale terrorist bombings, such as the attack on the World Trade Center in New York in 2001. Harding (2007) describes the "current war in Iraq, following years of economic sanctions, U.S. military intervention in 1990–1, the Iran-Iraq war and decades of government repression" as a case of human caused disaster (p. 295). Many years of violence have killed thousands, destroyed much of Iraq's infrastructure, and caused a flood of refugees to neighboring countries. Large-scale famines, such as the 1984 famine in Ethiopia that killed as many as one million people, are the result of environmental and human factors. It and other famines are large-scale international disasters that involve response from dozens if not hundreds of NGOs and governmental agencies from numerous countries. The impact on property and people and the response required in responding to human-caused disasters are often similar to natural disasters.

Disaster response and social work roles will be discussed further in Chapter 10.

CONCLUSION

Of necessity, the range of global social problems treated in this chapter has been modest. Other issues, including conflict and postconflict recovery, substance abuse, child abuse, challenges of people with disabilities, and more are equally compelling. Hopefully the reader has gained an understanding of the increasingly global nature of the social problems that face social workers wherever they practice. Understanding the global forces involved in etiology and redress is required for international social work to make a significant impact in practice and policy development.

REFERENCES

Becker, J. (2006, June 9). *Child soldiers*. Paper presented at Smith College School of Social Work Conference on Child Soldiers, Northampton, MA.

Bryant, C., & Kappaz, C. (2005). *Reducing poverty building peace*. Bloomfield, CT: Kumarian Press.

Crawford-Brown, C. P. J., & Rattray, J. M. (2001). Parent child relationships in Caribbean families. In N. Boyd Webb (Ed.), *Culturally diverse parent-child and family relationships* (pp. 107–32). New York: Columbia University Press.

Dhlembeu, N., & Mayanga, N. (2006). Responding to orphans and other vulnerable children's crisis: Zimbabwe's national plan of action. *Journal of Social Development in Africa, 21*(1), 35–49.

Dybicz, P. (2005). Interventions for street children: An analysis of current best practices. *International Social Work, 48*(6), 763–771.

Estes, R. (1997). World social situation. In R. L. Edwards (Ed.), *Encyclopedia of social work* (19th ed., 1997 Suppl., pp. 343–359) Washington, DC: NASW Press.

Father jailed for US mutilation. (2006, November 2). *BBC News*. Accessed June 4, 2007, at http://newsvote.bc.co.uk/

George, V., & Page, R. M. (Eds.). (2004). *Global social problems*. Cambridge, UK: Polity Press.

Harding, S. (2007). Man-made disaster and development: The case of Iraq. *International Social Work, 50*(3), 295–306.

International Labour Organization. (2007). International Programme on the Elimination of Child Labor. Accessed May 15, 2007, at www.ilo.org

International Labour Organization. (n.d.). *Child labour in Latin America and the Caribbean*. Accessed January 5, 2008, at http://ilo.org/dyn/declaris/DECLARATION WEB.DOWNLOAD_BLOB?Var_DocumentID-6198

Joint United Nations Programme on HIV/AIDS. (2007). *Report on the global AIDS epidemic*. New York: Author.

Kapoor, A. (2006, October 24). *Violence against women in India*. Panel presentation at the 7th Annual UNESCO Chair and Institute of Comparative Human Rights Conference, University of Connecticut, Storrs.

Kapstein, E. B. (2006). The new global slave trade. *Foreign Affairs, 85*(6), 103–115.

Keitetsi, C. (2006, October). *Child soldiers*. Presentation to the UNESCO Chair Conference on Human Rights, University of Connecticut, Storrs.

Kennedy, R. (Producer and Director). (2003). *Pandemic: Facing AIDS* [TV mini-series]. United States: Moxie Firecracker Films.

Kent, G. (2002). Children. In M. T. Snarr & D. N. Snarr (Eds.), *Introducing global issues* (pp. 195–213). Boulder, CO: Lynne Rienner Films.

Lusk, M. (1992). Street children in Rio de Janeiro. *International Social Work, 35*, 293–305.

MacCormack, C. P. (1988). Health and social power of women. *Social Science and Medicine, 26*(7), 677–683.

Martin, R. (2006). Children's perspectives: Roles, responsibilities and burdens in home-based care. *Journal of Social Development in Africa, 21*(1), 106–129.

Mylan, M. (Producer/Director) & Shenk, J. (Producer/Director/Cinematographer). (2003). *Lost boys of Sudan* [Motion picture]. United States: Actual Films/Principe Productions.

Office of the Registrar General, India. (2001). *Census 2001*. Accessed October 14, 2006, at www.censusindia.net

Ojera, S. (2006, June 9). *Workshop on reintegration of child soldiers in Northern Uganda.* Paper presented at the Smith College School of Social Work Conference on Child Soldiers, Northampton, MA.

Perez-Escamilla, R. (2006, October 24). *Nutrition & food security: The indivisibility of human rights.* Keynote presentation to the 7th Annual UNESCO Chair and Institute of Comparative Human Rights Conference, University of Connecticut, Storrs.

Powell, G. (2006). Children in institutional care: Lessons from Zimbabwe's experience. *Journal of Social Development in Africa, 21*(1), 130–148.

Psychosocial care and protection of tsunami affected children: Guiding principles. (2005) Principles adopted by the International Rescue Committee, Save the Children UK, UNICEF, and UNHCR.

Raffaelli, M. (1997). The family situation of street children in Latin America: A cross-national review. *International Social Work, 40*(1), 89–100.

Raheim, S., Noponen, H., & Alter, C. F. (2005). Women's participation in community economic development: The microcredit strategy. In M. Weil (Ed.), *The handbook of community practice* (pp. 548–566). Thousand Oaks, CA: Sage.

Rich man, poor man. (2007, April 14). *The Economist* [In Special Report on Brazil]. pp. 11–13.

Ring, K., & Carmichael, S. (2006). Montserrat: A study of Caribbean resilience. *Caribbean Journal of Social Work, 5,* 9–28.

Roby, J. L. (2005). Women and children in the global sex trade. *International Social Work, 48*(2), 136–147.

Rock, L., & Corbin, C. (2007). Social work students' and practitioners' views on the need for training Caribbean social workers in disaster management. *International Social Work, 50*(3), 383–394.

Rosenfeld, L. B., Caye, J. S., Ayalon, O., & Lahad, M. (2005). *When their world falls apart: Helping families and children manage the effects of disasters.* Washington, DC: NASW Press.

Salett, E. P. (2006, November). *Human trafficking and modern-day slavery. Human rights and international affairs practice update.* Washington, DC: NASW.

Seager, A. (2006, January 25). Global jobless rise hampers efforts to cut poverty. *The Guardian,* p. 23.

Sen, A. (1993, May). The economics of life and death. *Scientific American,* 40–47.

Sen, A. (1999). *Development as freedom.* New York: Anchor Books.

Slattery, M. (2006, November 3). *Human trafficking: A victim's story.* Paper presented at the Conference on Human Trafficking and Modern Day Slavery. University of Connecticut School of Social Work, West Hartford.

Spencer, M. (2007, June 26). Settlement ends workers' suit. *The Hartford Courant,* pp. B1, B9.

State Planning Board, Government of Kerala. (2005). *Human development report 2005 Kerala.* Accessed October 14, 2006, at www.undp.org.in/hdrc/shdr/kerala/Keral%20HDR%20Book.pdf

Sweden jails circumcision father. (2006, June 26). *BBC News.* Accessed June 5, 2007, at http://newsvote.bbc.co.uk

Ten years' hard labour. (2004, September 4). *The Economist,* pp. 74–76.

UNICEF. (1996). *The progress of nations 1996.* Wallingford, UK: P&LA for UNICEF.

UNICEF. (2004). *The state of the world's children 2005.* New York: Author.

UNICEF. (2005). *The state of the world's children 2006: Excluded and invisible.* New York: Author.

UNICEF. (2007). Millennium Development Goals. Accessed May 18, 2007, at www.unicef.org

United Nations. (2003). *Political declaration and Madrid international plan of action on ageing* (Second World Assembly on Ageing, Madrid, Spain). New York: Author.

United Nations. (2007). *Ending impunity for violence against women and girls* (International Women's Day United Nations Backgrounder). New York: UN Department of Public Information.

United Nations Development Programme. (1996). *Human development report 1996.* New York: Oxford University Press for UNDP.

United Nations Development Programme. (2005). *Human development report 2005.* New York: Oxford University Press for UNDP.

United Nations Fund for Population Activities. (2005). *Violence against women: Fact sheet 2005.* Accessed June 4, 2007, www.unfpa.org/swp/2005/presskit/factsheets/facts_vaw.htm

United Nations Population Fund. (2006). *From microfinance to macro change: Integrating health education and microfinance to empower women and reduce poverty.* New York: Author.

United Nations Report of the Secretary-General. (2006, July 6). *In-depth study on all forms of violence against women, 2006* (61st session of the General Assembly). New York: Author.

U.S. Bureau of the Census. (2006, August). *Current population report: Income, poverty and health insurance coverage in the United States: 2005.* Accessed May 29, 2007, at www.census.gov

U.S. Department of Health & Human Services. (2005). *Human trafficking fact sheet.* Washington, DC: Author.

U.S. Department of Health and Human Services. (n.d.-a). *Labor trafficking fact sheet.* Washington, DC: Author.

U.S. Department of Health and Human Services. (n.d.-b). *Trafficking Victims Protection Act of 2000 fact sheet.* Washington, DC: Author.

Wessels, M. (2006, June 9). *Child soldiers reintegration and community resilience following armed conflict.* Paper presented at the Smith College School of Social Work Conference on Child Soldiers, Northampton, MA.

World almanac and book of facts. (2007). New York: World Almanac Books.

World Commission on the Social Dimension of Globalization. (2004). *A fair globalization: Creating opportunities for all.* Geneva, Switzerland: International Labour Organization.

World Health Organization. (2004). *Global and regional estimates of the incidence of unsafe abortion and associated mortality in 2000.* Geneva, Switzerland: Author. Accessed November 10, 2006, at www.who.int/reproductivehealth/publications/unsafe_abortion_estimates_04/estimates.pdf

World Health Organization. (2005). Summary report: WHO multi-country study on women's health and domestic violence against women. Geneva, Switzerland: Author.

CHAPTER 5

INTERNATIONAL SOCIAL WELFARE ORGANIZATIONS AND THEIR FUNCTIONS

The challenges of globalization outlined in Chapter 2 and the global problems discussed in the previous chapter are addressed by a wide range of international organizations that work in the social welfare field. These organizations are at work on projects such as planning and implementing income-generation projects to address poverty; providing emergency food, clothing, and medical care in crisis situations; conducting education and prevention campaigns to slow the spread of HIV; promoting low-cost primary education models; developing standards to encourage equal rights for women; and tackling child labor through standards setting and negotiation. Although comprehensive descriptions are not feasible here, this chapter provides an overview of a selected number of international organizations to increase understanding of the context of international social work. Selection is challenging because international social welfare activities are conducted by myriad organizations. Some specialized organizations deal only with international issues related to social welfare. Other international social welfare activities are carried out by domestic organizations with international linkages and by international organizations in other fields of specialty, such as economics, health, or agriculture. Three major groups of organizations are the intergovernmental agencies of the United Nations (UN) system, governmental agencies of individual countries, and private or nongovernmental organizations (NGOs).

Most international agencies do not have a specific set of roles or functions labeled "social work." However, they are engaged in development or social development work, the enhancement of social welfare, the promotion of standards for social and economic well-being throughout the world, and the sponsorship of professional exchanges. Thus their work fits within the definition of international social work used in this book, and understanding the functions of these organizations is essential for professional action in an interdependent world.

INTRODUCTION TO DEVELOPMENT AND
DEVELOPMENT ASSISTANCE

Most international social welfare organizations are involved in development and/or promotion of human rights. These two movements have been priorities in post–World War II international relations. As discussed in Chapter 3, the emergence of numerous newly independent countries in the 1960s— countries that had poorly developed economies, mass poverty, and little physical or institutional infrastructure—led to identification of development as a priority.

The provision of development assistance has spawned a large network of international organizations. Development assistance can be provided through bilateral agreements—the provision of aid or technical assistance by one country to another—or through multilateral efforts. Although bilateral aid can address humanitarian objectives and is based partly on notions of obligation of the rich nations to assist the poor, the foreign policy goals of the donor country are often intertwined with the more explicit program goals. At least partly for this reason, recipient countries often prefer multilateral aid— assistance provided through intergovernmental organizations with varied members, often including the recipient country. Although they exist, there are fewer foreign policy "strings" and obligations attached to multilateral aid, and at the broadest level, the concept of *global cooperation* is present. Bilateral and multilateral governmental organizations also channel development assistance through NGOs similar to the way national and state government agencies deliver programs domestically through private agencies by means of grants and contracts.

Individual descriptions will be provided for key intergovernmental agencies and selected governmental agencies. Because of the large number of NGOs, relatively few examples can be included; the section on NGOs will be organized to describe the major functions carried out by such bodies: relief and development, advocacy, development education, exchange, and cross-national- and international-related casework.

UNITED NATIONS AGENCIES AND ACTIVITIES

The UN and its agencies are major players in international social welfare and the provision of multilateral assistance. Indeed, some scholars identify accomplishments in the social field as the most significant successes of the UN, rather than its intended major goals of peace keeping and conflict resolution. As noted by Altschiller (1993), "the founders of the United Nations gave it . . . a wide mandate in economic and social affairs" (p. 196).

Activities within the social mission were among the first UN activities. Prior to the official establishment of the UN, a number of countries worked through the UN Relief and Rehabilitation Administration (UNRRA) to provide relief and reconstruction in war-torn Europe and Asia. These efforts will be described in Chapters 6 and 7. As noted, social work experts were substantially involved in the UNRRA programs and leadership, and for many social workers, experience gained through UNRRA launched their careers in international social welfare. The activities and success of UNRRA provided an important backdrop for the evolution of the social development mission of the UN.

Current UN Structures and Agencies

The UN was created with the signing of the charter on June 26, 1945 (effective October 24, 1945). The charter defines the following as the purposes of the UN:

> 1) to maintain international peace and security; 2) to develop friendly relations among nations; 3) to achieve international cooperation in solving international problems of an economic, social, cultural, or humanitarian character and in promoting respect for human rights; and 4) to be a center for harmonizing the actions of nations in the attainment of these common ends. (U.S. Government Manual, 1998, p. 754)

The third purpose—wide in scope—legitimizes the many social welfare/ social development efforts of the UN.

There are presently 192 member nations, up dramatically from the 51 founding members. The work of the UN is done thorough the General Assembly, comprising all member states; the Security Council, whose 15 members are charged with the responsibility of maintaining international peace and security; and the Economic and Social Council (ECOSOC), which is described below. A substantial amount of the UN development effort is carried out by the specialized agencies and special bodies of the UN, including UNICEF (the UN Children's Fund), the World Health Organization (WHO), and the UN Development Programme (UNDP). After the description of the ECOSOC, the major UN agencies related to social welfare are described, followed by a discussion of how the UN uses special events and commemorations to extend its impact on the problems of special groups, such as women, children, and families.

The Economic and Social Council. ECOSOC reports to the General Assembly and has been given coordinating functions over a range of economic and social matters (Altschiller, 1993). According to its charter, its purposes are to promote higher standards of living, full employment, and conditions of economic and social progress and development; solutions to international economic, social, health, and related problems and international cultural and educational cooperation; universal respect for and observance of human rights and fundamental freedoms for all without distinction as to race, sex, language, or religion (United Nations, 1945). ECOSOC has representatives from 54 member states and operates through four standing committees:

Program and Coordination, Human Settlements, Non-Governmental Organizations, and Negotiation with Intergovernmental Agencies (United Nations, 1998). It also utilizes Regional Commissions, Functional Commissions, and additional expert bodies. Among the nine Functional Commissions are the Commission for Social Development, the Commission on Population and Development, the Commission on Sustainable Development, the Commission on the Status of Women, the Population Commission, and the Commission on Narcotic Drugs (United Nations, 2007). ECOSOC's functions include coordination of the activities of the specialized UN agencies in the social field.

A major social welfare report, *The Report on the World's Social Situation,* is issued every 4 years by the Department of Economic and Social Development of the UN, and endorsed by ECOSOC. The 2005 report in the series that began in 1952 focuses on the theme "the inequality predicament" (United Nations, 2005). It states concern over the "worldwide asymmetries resulting from globalization" and calls for expanded efforts to reduce poverty, improve working conditions for those in the informal economy, and to promote "social integration and cohesion as key to development, peace and security" (p. iii).

The Centre for Social Development and Humanitarian Affairs, previously located in Vienna, had been a focal point of social welfare activity in the UN, serving, among other capacities, as the organizing force behind the 1987 Interregional Consultation (described later in this chapter). In 1991, ECOSOC adopted a resolution calling for strengthening and restructuring the Centre for Social Development, noting the growth in interest and activities in the social development arena. The Centre has now been reorganized, with most of its functions incorporated into the new Division for Social Policy and Development.

UNICEF (the UN Children's Fund). UNICEF is an important agency of the UN. Founded in 1946 for post-war relief in Europe and China, it became a permanent agency with a focus on development. UNICEF operates programs in most of the world's countries, 157 in 2004, with total expenditures in 2004 of over $1.6 billion, of which 93.9% was for program support (United Nations, 2006). The agency's goal is "to improve the lives of children and youth in the developing world by providing community-based services in primary health care, social services, water supply, formal and nonformal education, nutrition and emergency operations" (Hoy, 1998, p. 88). Since the passage of the Convention on the Rights of the Child by the General Assembly and its subsequent ratification by almost all nations of the world, UNICEF's major emphasis has been "to ensure the survival, protection and development of children within the framework of the Convention" (United Nations, 1997b, p. 1034).

UNICEF's efforts in the area of child protection are of particular interest to social work. The agency has addressed issues of abuse and exploitation through its initiative on Children in Especially Difficult Circumstances; it is now working to integrate these efforts "into mainstream programs, leading to a holistic response" (United Nations, 1997b, p. 1203). UNICEF assists children affected by armed conflict, hazardous or exploitative child labor, sexual exploitation, childhood disability, and those children and families affected by HIV/AIDS. UNICEF has supported NGO programs on prevention, protection, and rehabilitation regarding sexual exploitation of children in Brazil, Costa Rica, and Thailand; a national trauma recovery program for war-affected children in Rwanda; and a coordinated project providing alternative care, education, and life skills training for AIDS orphans in Uganda.

A major compiler of statistics on the status of children, UNICEF publishes useful data for comparative research and planning in its annual report, *State of the World's Children*.

UNICEF has achieved some notable successes. In 1991, UNICEF and the WHO announced that they had surpassed their goal of immunizing 80% of the world's children against six major killer diseases (United Nations, 1992). The campaign for simple interventions in cases of diarrheal disease—oral rehydration therapy (ORT)—has gained ground in many countries. UNICEF's success in drawing attention to children's issues was underscored by the UN's adoption of the Convention on the Rights of the Child in 1989, by the World Summit for Children, held in 1990, and the 2002 General Assembly Special Session on Children. All have been major tools for advocating for children and will be briefly discussed below. Successful advocacy by UNICEF through its campaign for "Adjustment with a Human Face" forced lending institutions and governments to recognize the human and social costs of structural adjustment (Cornia, Jolly, & Stewart, 1987).

Unfortunately, UNICEF has had to devote a large share of its funds and efforts to emergency relief. In 2004–2005, UNICEF spent 20%–30% of its budget in armed conflict situations and during natural disasters. This is up from only 8% in 1990 (United Nations, 1997b, 2006).

United Nations Development Programme. UNDP was created in 1965 and by the mid-1990s was the largest source of multilateral grant assistance, "providing a greater variety of services to more people in more countries than any other development institution" (Hoy, 1998, p. 84). UNDP is the largest operational development agency in the UN system and plays a coordinating role among all the UN entities involved in development. UNDP works in 166 countries (UN, 2006). The agency focuses on five areas: "reducing human poverty; fostering democratic governance; energy and environment for sustainable development; crisis prevention and recovery; and responding to HIV/AIDS" (UN, 2006, p. 876). UNDP is currently a strong advocate for the Millennium Development Goals (MDGs) and works to integrate the MDGs and strategies to meet them in national plans.

In 1986, UNDP set up the Division for Women in Development, responding to criticisms that development programs not only overlooked the role of women but sometimes worsened their condition. It administers the UN Development Fund for Women (UNIFEM), a special fund to support projects for low-income women in poor countries. UNIFEM has identified four "strategic areas" for its activities: (1) reducing poverty among women; (2) ending violence against women; (3) reducing HIV/AIDS in women and girls; and (4) "achieving gender equity in democratic governance" in peace and war (UNIFEM, 2007).

The annual UNDP publication, *Human Development Report*, a volume referenced liberally in this book, provides useful information for international social work. A feature of the reports is a rating of countries' progress on the Human Development Index (HDI), a rating that combines life expectancy, adult literacy, mean years of schooling of the population, and Gross Domestic Product (GDP) per capita. Development of this index has been significant in increasing the recognition that development must include social and human resource elements, not just economics.

World Health Organization. WHO is another specialized agency of the UN. The goal of WHO is to encourage the greatest possible level of health for all. As such, this agency monitors international health issues, works to control communicable diseases, sets international health standards in such areas as drugs and vaccines, conducts research, and engages in more direct efforts to solve health problems and strengthen national health systems (Morrison & Purcell, 1988). A special focus is primary health care, a campaign launched in recognition of the fact that the most gains in overall health status come from simple interventions in sanitation, water, immunization, and maternal–child health.

WHO has now been called on to lead in the campaign to control the spread of HIV. With the estimated number of persons living with HIV in 2005 at 38.6 million, including almost 4.1 million new cases in that year, AIDS education, prevention, and research have become major WHO priorities (Joint UN Programme on HIV/AIDS, 2006). Africa, with the highest rates of HIV infection and grossly inadequate health resources, is a special target. Increasing attention is also being paid to the enormous social welfare impact of AIDS, especially the growing population of orphaned children and other disruptions in normal family roles and responsibilities.

Malaria remains a stubborn and serious problem and a major cause of death and disability. WHO is credited with a major role in the successful eradication of smallpox. It has been working to eradicate polio, as part of the long-term Health for All by the Year 2000 campaign—a campaign to provide basic health services to all people in the world and to make progress on eradicating major preventable diseases. New diseases such as severe acute respiratory syndrome (SARS) have added new challenges for WHO.

United Nations Fund for Population Activities. UNFPA is the largest source of funds for family-planning-related programs in developing countries (Hoy, 1998). More than two-thirds of program funds go into reproductive health services. Smaller amounts are spent on education and on collection of population data, with emphasis on developing countries (Morrison & Purcell, 1988). Recently, the agency has emphasized the importance of linking family planning and reproductive health with development goals, following the recommendations from the 1994 UN International Conference on Population and Development. The concept of demographic targets has been deemphasized in favor of meeting the family planning needs of individuals (Hoy, 1998). Another accomplishment has been to provide family planning and reproductive health services in refugee crisis situations.

Funding support from the United States was greatly curtailed beginning in 1984 when the United States government cut off all funds to organizations that supported or permitted abortion services. This ban was reversed in 1993 and reinstated by President George W. Bush at the beginning of his term.

The United Nations High Commission for Refugees. UNHCR celebrated its 50th anniversary in 2001. Originally created as a temporary agency, the UNHCR shows no sign of completing its tasks of protection and service to refugees. In 2004, for example, the agency had responsibility for the fate of about 19.2 million people. In addition to refugees, other populations under UNHCR programs are the internally displaced, returnees following disasters or conflict, and others with special humanitarian needs (United Nations, 2006). The functions of the UNHCR include refugee protection, assistance and aid to refugees in transit, voluntary repatriation where possible, resettlement, and integration into countries of first asylum. In 1995, for example, the agency assisted about 800,000 people to repatriate, primarily to Afghanistan, Rwanda, and Myanmar. In 2004, 30,000 people were resettled. During the same year, 1.5 million refugees returned to their home countries while others fled new conflicts (UN, 2006). UNHCR works on standards regarding the treatment of refugees worldwide in addition to its direct work to solve specific refugee problems of relief and settlement. In fact, for the first few decades of its existence, the agency emphasis was on setting standards for the identification and treatment of refugees, rather than provision of assistance. UNHCR became more involved in direct work during the 1975 crisis when Cambodian refugees flooded into Thailand.

UNHCR beneficiary needs are expected to reach $3 billion in 2007 (UNHCR, 2006).

Food and Agriculture Organization (FAO) and World Food Program. The first of the UN specialized agencies created, the FAO's goal is to work toward global food security. The organization provides technical assistance and advice on agricultural planning, production and food distribution, and, through a Global Information and Early Warning System, it identifies areas at risk of food shortage. With the UN, the FAO sponsors the World Food Program, which supplies 25% of the world's food aid. The goal of the program is to not only provide food for crisis situations but also to support development. In the mid-1980s, about two-thirds of the food aid was used to support development. By 1994, 70% was being used for emergency situations. The primary role of the agency now is "the coordination of large scale relief operations"

(Hoy, 1998, p. 90). The agency continues to have to devote the majority of its aid to emergencies.

There are other UN organizations that conduct activities related to social welfare. However, a complete and comprehensive description of these is beyond the scope of the present volume. Through the *Yearbook of the United Nations*, other UN publications, and the many Web sites maintained by the organization, readers can expand their knowledge about UN agencies and activities.

Special Years, Conferences, Declarations, and Conventions

The UN utilizes designations of special years and decades and global conferences both to draw attention to important issues and to bring world leaders together to work on acceptable strategies and commitments (see, e.g., Bennett, 1988; Taylor & Groom, 1989). Many of these have emphasized social welfare. Some have resulted in significant forward-looking plans of action. Historically, two special meetings stand out in their importance to international social work: the UN Conference of Ministers Responsible for Social Welfare, held in 1968, and the Interregional Consultation on Developmental Social Welfare Policies and Programmes, held in 1987.

The UN International Conference of Ministers Responsible for Social Welfare, held at the UN headquarters in New York in 1968, is viewed as a watershed event. The conference brought together 89 high-level national delegations, including many government ministers. Additional representatives attended as observers from eight other nations, from UN agencies, and from other international bodies and NGOs in consultative status with ECOSOC (United Nations, 1969). The conference focused global attention, at the very highest levels of government, on social welfare needs and strategies. In addition to specific recommendations, the conference unanimously adopted a resolution underscoring that "effective social welfare policy and programmes have a vital role to play in national development" and that "social progress, higher levels of living and social justice are the ultimate aims of development" (United Nations, 1969, p. 23).

The next global intergovernmental meeting on social welfare took place nearly two decades later in Vienna in 1987—the Interregional Consultation on Developmental Social Welfare Policies and Programmes. Official representatives from 91 countries, including 30 government ministers, participated along with representatives of UN organizations and of more than 50 NGOs (United Nations, 1987). The meeting resulted in adoption of "Guiding Principles for Developmental Social Welfare Policies and Programmes in the Near Future" (United Nations, 1987). As described by the director general of the UN Vienna office, the adoption and subsequent endorsement by the General Assembly of the "Guiding Principles" "denotes growing international consensus on the vital importance of social issues in any genuine and sustainable development process" (United Nations, 1987, preface). It also clearly identified social development as the thrust of the UN in the area of social welfare, a focus that continues to the present.

Recent Special Years and Conferences of Significance. In 1995, two major social welfare events occurred, the World Summit for Social Development (Copenhagen) and the Fourth World Conference on Women (Beijing). The Social Development summit, a landmark event in the future of social development and social welfare, convened heads of state to develop means to put the needs of people, especially the poor, at the center of development efforts. According to Kofi Annan, Secretary-General of the UN, this Summit "represented a turning point in our collective consciousness regarding social issues" (United Nations, 1997a, p. v.). Issues addressed included achieving sustainable development with social justice, enhancing social integration, reducing poverty, and expanding opportunities for productive employment (United Nations, 1993b). NGOs participated actively in preparations for the summit (the ICSW's involvement is discussed in Chapter 7) and in the NGO Forum held in conjunction with the actual meeting. An important outcome of the summit was agreement on "Ten Commitments" by the participating governments, including commitments to work for eradication of poverty, full employment, promotion of social integration, respect for human dignity and achievement of equality and equity for women, and universal access to education and primary health care (United Nations, 1995a). The work done at the Summit on Social Development was partially eclipsed by the Millennium Summit held in September 2000. The Millennium Declaration included adoption of the MDGs, discussed in Chapter 3.

The other 1995 meeting was the Fourth World Conference on Women, held in Beijing, China, in September. The focus of this meeting, with a theme of "Action for Equality, Development and Peace," was a second 5-year review of the plan adopted in Nairobi at the World Conference to Review and Appraise the Achievements of the UN Decade for Women in 1985, the "Nairobi Forward-Looking Strategies for the Advancement of Women to the Year 2000" (United Nations, 1991). The conference called for universal ratification of the Convention on the Elimination of All Forms of Discrimination Against Women (CEDAW), by 2000 (United Nations, 1995b). Its work was updated in 2005 in the "Beijing Plus 10" reports.

The World Summit for Children, which in 1990 was the first world gathering of heads of state to focus on children, adopted goals to improve the lives of children, including reduction in child deaths, improved nutrition, basic education for all children, and extension of family planning services. The children's agenda was expanded at the General Assembly Special Session on Children held in 2002. Among other major conferences that have recently focused the world's attention on issues important to social work are the 1992 UN Conference on Environment and Development, held in Rio de Janeiro, which explored the interrelationships between environmental preservation and sustainable development; the 1993 World Conference on Human Rights; the 1994 Conference on Population and Development; the World Conference

Against Racism, Racial Discrimination and Xenophobia and Unrelated Intolerance, held in Durban, South Africa, in 2001; and the Second World Assembly on Aging, Madrid 2002, that yielded far-reaching goals for an aging globe. Fewer of these large conferences are expected in the future, as some member nations, led by the United States, have protested the expenses involved in staging such events.

The UN also designates international years and international decades to call attention to issues and to mobilize planning and action. The goals of the International Year of the Family in 1994, for example, were to increase awareness of family issues and "to improve the institutional capability of nations to tackle serious family-related problems with comprehensive policies" (United Nations, 1993a, p. 18). The recommendation for the year was developed at the 1987 Interregional Consultation on Developmental Social Welfare Policies and Programmes, described above. The International Year of Older Persons, 1999, was designated to "recognize humanity's demographic coming of age and the promise it holds" (United Nations, 1993a, p. 17).

Declarations and Conventions as International Social Policy

Policy documents issued by the special meetings, developed in preparatory work, and those developed at the UN take a variety of forms. The most significant are the conventions, which are statements of international law ratified by member nations as explained in Chapter 3. In 1989, the UN adopted the Convention on the Rights of the Child, a major piece of international "legislation" in the area of child welfare that identifies standards for survival, protection, and development of children. As of 2007, all but two countries (Somalia and the United States) have ratified the convention, making it the most widely ratified piece of international law. This follows other significant conventions on human rights, including CEDAW (1979) and the Convention on the Elimination of All Forms of Racial Discrimination (1969). Declarations such as the Copenhagen Declaration of the World Summit for Social Development and the Millennium Declaration state the goals to which country leaders commit themselves. Declarations do not include the monitoring and enforcement provisions of conventions, but they state goals and principles.

World Bank and International Monetary Fund

The World Bank and IMF are not social welfare organizations. Because of the significance of their loans and policies, however, they deserve brief mention here. In 1944, representatives from the United States and Europe met in Bretton Woods, New Hampshire, to establish new economic policies to address the needs of the post–World War II world. The World Bank, IMF, and a series of trade agreements resulted from these meetings; the financial institutions are sometimes called the Bretton Woods organizations, in reference to the historic meetings.

The IMF and World Bank have similar philosophies, members, and activities. Their major goals differ however. The IMF provides technical assistance to countries on banking, balance of payments, taxation, and related matters. The major goal of the World Bank is "to provide loans to encourage economic development, whereas the IMF oversees monetary and exchange rate policies" (Hoy, 1998, p. 77). Therefore, the World Bank can be viewed as a development organization, whereas the IMF aims to ensure an orderly world economic system. Both organizations make loans, but there are differences in their loan policies. Any member country can borrow from the IMF—usually to address balance-of-payments problems—but only developing countries can borrow from the World Bank.

Several organizations comprise the World Bank group, including the International Bank for Reconstruction and Development (IBRD), and the International Development Association (IDA). The IBRD loans money for economic development. The terms of these loans are only "slightly better than average market rates and only slightly concessional; thus, they are not considered official development assistance" (Hoy, 1998, p. 46). Because of this, the poorest nations can seldom afford IBRD loans. They borrow instead from the IDA, often interest-free and with lenient terms. These loans are considered to be development assistance and go to countries that cannot borrow elsewhere; funds for the loans come from donor nations (Hoy, 1998).

The majority of loans have been devoted to infrastructure projects, but the World Bank also funds projects in rural and urban development, housing, education, health and nutrition, and population planning. UN member countries are members of the World Bank, but the United States, Japan, and the EU control 55% of the votes. World Bank influence was substantial in the 1970s and is still considerable in some countries. Overall, its influence has lessened due to the strong role of private capital. In 2004, the World Bank lent $20.1 billion to developing countries for 245 projects (World Bank, 2007). In 1995, $170 billion was invested in these countries by private companies (Hoy, 1998). Private investment seldom flows to countries considered poor risk; in these countries, the World Bank remains the primary source of credit.

The loan policies of the World Bank group and the IMF greatly affect the development prospects of poor nations and the climate within which international social welfare efforts are made. As explained in Chapter 2, since the 1980s, the IMF has insisted that nations with poor balances of payments and large debt adopt programs of "structural adjustment" to qualify for additional credit. Requiring broad-scale changes in economic structure, structural adjustment often leads to cutbacks in publicly supported, universal services, such as health and education, and worsens the plight of the poor within the poorest countries. As such, monetary policies have negatively affected social welfare conditions in much of Africa and Latin America, as least in the short run (Cornia et al., 1987; Jacobson, 1989). The impact of the IMF's policies falls largely on poor countries. As summarized by Hoy (1998): "Its power over developing countries is immense, but it has little more than the power of advice over the economies of industrialized nations" (p. 69).

GOVERNMENTAL AGENCIES

Governments carry out international programs through their national agencies and through participation in multilateral organizations, including those just described. International social welfare functions of governments include foreign assistance, professional and educational exchange in social welfare and social work, research on comparative social welfare, direct services to international populations, such as refugee assistance, and participation in various international programs and conferences.

In the United States, social welfare was included in the government's very first technical assistance program. Established by the Technical Assistance for Foreign Countries Act passed by Congress in 1939, the Department of State, the Children's Bureau, and the American Association of Schools of Social Work collaborated in a program that brought 15 directors of Latin American schools of social work to the United States for training (Hilliard, 1965). Thus at the very earliest stages of giving aid, the importance of social work was recognized.

Key U.S. government agencies in international aspects of social welfare today are the International Development Cooperation Agency and the Department of Health and Human Services (DHHS). They, as well as agencies from other countries, will be explained briefly below.

Governmental Bilateral Aid Programs and Agencies

The Nature of Bilateral Foreign Assistance. Foreign aid, or international development assistance, in part fulfills a social welfare function. Aid is viewed as one mechanism, along with investment and favorable trade prospects, that can assist poor countries in their development efforts. In 1968, the Pearson Commission, an international panel appointed by the president of the World Bank to recommend improved policies for international development, set a target for the level of aid effort for industrialized nations of 0.7% of each nation's gross national product (GNP)—a figure adopted by the UN as part of its strategy for the Second Development Decade (Isbister, 1998). Aid effort is the amount of aid given as a proportion of the donor country's GNP. Few nations, however, have ever contributed at the recommended level—to date only Denmark, Luxembourg, the Netherlands, Norway, and Sweden have met this goal (Organization for Economic Co-operation and Development [OECD], 2007).

It is important for social workers to understand that international assistance serves many purposes for the donor nations and that humanitarianism is often not the major consideration. Bilateral aid in particular is an instrument of foreign policy, used to gain allies and shape policy decisions in other countries. During the cold war era, aid was used by Western countries to build allies against communism and by the Soviet Union and China as a tool to secure allies for the communist bloc. Aid also may be used to open up new markets for donor country products. Hoy (1998) charges that in the United States, "replacing the cold war rationale for aid as a means to contain communism is today's rallying call for international aid to help the United States compete successfully in the global marketplace" (p. 40). In justifying giving aid to an increasingly skeptical Congress and public, the U.S. Agency for International Development (described below) boasted that 70% of bilateral aid money is spent in the United States and fully one-half of the money the United States allocates for multilateral aid is spent on U.S. goods (Hoy, 1998). Historically, U.S. generosity in distributing surplus food has been important to maintenance of farm prices at home. Thus aid is used partly to benefit the domestic economy; these considerations may lessen the effectiveness of the international mission of assistance by increasing the cost of commodities and services donated, adding excessive regulations about utilization of U.S. carriers and businesses, and by depriving countries in the recipient country's region of much-needed business. In addition, the end of the cold war did not end the use of assistance for security and military reasons. Recipients are often selected for strategic reasons rather than on a basis of need for help. For many years, therefore, Israel and Egypt topped the list of recipients of U.S. aid dollars, receiving almost one-half of the aid budget while the world's poorest countries receive only about one-fourth (Isbister, 1998). More recently, large amounts of U.S. aid have gone to Afghanistan, Iraq, and Pakistan. Top recipients of U.S. overseas development assistance (ODA) in 2005 were Iraq, Afghanistan, Egypt, Sudan, and Ethiopia, in that order (OECD, 2007).

Bilateral Aid Agencies: The U.S. Agency for International Development (US-AID). In the United States, the foreign aid program is administered by the USAID, which is part of the International Development Cooperation Agency. The Overseas Private Investment Corporation is a separate part of the umbrella agency; it facilitates U.S. private investment to promote economic development in 150 countries. USAID currently administers economic and humanitarian aid programs in Africa, Asia, Latin America, and the Caribbean, the Near East, Europe, and Eurasia. Although an emphasis on strengthening private sector development shifted USAID away from traditional social welfare projects during the 1980s, the agency remains involved in many social initiatives.

    USAID is frequently reorganized and redirected to meet the foreign policy goals of the administration in office. In a reorganization of USAID in the early 1990s, five goals for the agency were defined: *(1)* Provision of humanitarian relief; *(2)* stabilization of population growth; *(3)* promotion of democracy; *(4)* environmental protection; and *(5)* broad-based economic growth (Hoy, 1998). USAID also encouraged "building indigenous capacity, enhancing participation and encouraging accountability, transparency, decentralization, and the empowerment of communities and individuals" (cited in Hoy, 1998, p. 35). Clearly, these are very compatible with social work methods and purposes.

When President Clinton took office in 1992, he expressed a commitment to restoring U.S. leadership in aid for true development. This promise was not realized. Instead, the aid budget was repeatedly cut, and the poorest countries are receiving an even smaller share. The USAID focus in the mid to late 1990s was on strengthening democracy and capitalism, especially in the countries of the former Soviet bloc. In 1996, the former Soviet republics received 17% of the U.S. bilateral aid budget, while all of Africa, undeniably the area where need is greatest, received less than 12% (Hoy, 1998).

USAID provides a number of types of assistance: technical assistance and capacity building; training; food aid and disaster relief; infrastructure construction; small-enterprise loans; credit guarantees and other types of support (USAID, 2007a). In 2005, nine principles were enunciated to promote the objectives of economic growth, democracy, and social transition. The nine principles are: ownership through participation; capacity building; sustainability; selectivity in allocating resources (based in "need, local commitment and foreign policy interests"); assessment to ensure best practices; results; partnership, including governments, NGOs, the private sector, and international organizations; flexibility; and accountability and transparency to prevent corruption (USAID, 2007b).

In 2006, Secretary of State Condoleezza Rice announced a change to an emphasis on "transformational diplomacy" to "build and sustain democratic well-governed states." The new goals for foreign assistance are to ensure that foreign aid is used to "meet our broad foreign policy objectives"; and to "demonstrate that we are responsible stewards of taxpayer dollars." While falling far short on humanitarian ideals, Rice has made the often-hidden purposes of foreign aid explicit.

The United States is the largest donor of ODA in terms of total dollars but is among the least generous in aid effort. At times in recent years, the United States has been last among industrialized nations in amount given as a percent of the national income. In 2005, the ratio of ODA to gross national income (GNI) was 0.22% (OECD, 2007), far below the target of 0.7%. New twenty-first-century aid initiatives include the Millennium Challenge and the Global AIDS Office.

USAID carries out some of its international relief and development work by providing funding to NGOs. Recognizing the need to build a constituency of support for aid, development education has also been part of the agency's agenda.

Peace Corps. The U.S. Peace Corps is an unusual program that fits both in the category of development assistance and in the category of exchange. Established to involve Americans directly in providing assistance in poor nations, many have asserted that the Corps is really an international cultural exchange effort, with benefits largely flowing to the volunteers themselves in terms of cultural enrichment and career preparation.

When the Peace Corps was founded in 1961, social work organizations attempted to play a major formative role and to convince Peace Corps founders that the building of social services in developing countries should be a major component of Peace Corps services. Their efforts were largely unsuccessful (Katz, 1962). Nonetheless, through the Peace Corps, the United States conducts volunteer projects, some of which are related to social welfare, such as primary health care promotion, urban development, and community development. The Peace Corps was made an independent agency by the International Security and Development Cooperation Act of 1981.

Bilateral Aid in Japan, Nordic Countries, and Canada

Bilateral aid is provided by many nations, including all of the industrialized countries. There are some differences in approach in various nations. In 1989, Japan became the largest donor of bilateral aid in terms of absolute funds, but its share has since declined. In 2006, Japan's net official development assistance was only about one-half that given by the United States. Japanese aid tends to emphasize large infrastructure projects rather than capacity-building ones. And there is a heavy regional emphasis to its aid. Seven of the top 10 recipient countries of Japan's aid are in Asia; in 2005, Japan was particularly generous in providing tsunami relief aid (OECD, 2007). As is true for U.S. aid, Japanese aid is often tied to the purchase of Japanese goods.

"Sweden, Finland, Norway, and Denmark are commonly perceived as having the most pro-development, altruistic and progressive aid programs" (Hoy, 1998, p. 32). Sweden, Norway, and Denmark are leaders in level of effort, consistently surpassing the target of 0.7% of GNP. In addition, their aid agencies have focused on development goals and have conceptualized recipient countries as partners. They also strongly support multilateral agencies such as UNICEF. Denmark, for example, gave a large share of its ODA to least-developed countries and other low-income countries—more than 50%. Top recipients were Tanzania, Vietnam, Mozambique, Uganda, and Ghana. Although many countries are directing more of their aid to bilateral programs than multilateral organizations, Denmark's 64% share bilateral compares to 92% for the United States, again suggesting more cooperation with international organizations (OECD, 2007). In 2005, Denmark gave .81% of its GNI in development assistance.

The Canadian International Development Agency (CIDA) was established in 1968. The agency's ideals stress cooperation with recipient countries in order to contribute to economic growth and improve social systems. Following an important review of Canadian foreign assistance efforts in 1987, the resulting Charter on Overseas Development Assistance defined four key principles: (a) putting poverty first—helping the poorest; (b) helping people to help themselves; (c) priority for development goals in setting aid objectives rather than other foreign policy considerations; and (d) partnership between Canada and people and institutions in the third world (Gilcrest & Splane, 1995). Furthermore, this document defined poverty as "a lack of choice," a "lack of access," and "inequity in opportunity in the distribution of the benefits of growth and in social justice" and "underdevelopment of human potential" (as cited in Gilcrest & Splane, 1995, p. 583). Social workers in Canada hailed this progressive definition of poverty as well as the CIDA emphasis on putting poverty first.

At the same time, Canada reaffirmed its earlier commitment to meet the 0.7% target for assistance. However, that figure has not been achieved to date; instead, Canada, like other countries, has reduced its level of spending in the face of economic difficulties at home. In an assessment of the aid program, social work authors Gilcrest and Splane (1995) said that the important goals expressed in the 1987 charter are not likely to be reached "in this century" (p. 584). Rather, Canada's program has the characteristics criticized in a UNDP report, *The Reality of Aid:* a decline in aid budgets, of "increased diversion of aid from long-term development projects to short-term emergency relief; diversion of aid from Africa to eastern and central Europe; and the continuing use of aid to promote domestic imports from industrialized countries" (as cited in Gilcrest & Splane, 1995, p. 583). In 2005, Canada gave 0.34% of its GNI in official development aid (OECD, 2007). CIDA's program priorities include an emphasis on democratic governance, anticorruption, and women's rights. Expanded support to women's groups in Africa and increased roles in Latin America and the Caribbean are planned.

A unique feature of governmental aid in Canada is that provincial governments also give aid. The national government permits provinces to sponsor aid projects as long as they are consistent with overall Canadian social and foreign policies. Thus the government of Alberta, for example, spent about $2 million on projects in 56 countries in 1992/93 (Gilcrest & Splane, 1995).

Government Agency Exchange Efforts

National governmental agencies play important welfare-oriented functions in international exchange, policy setting, and implementation. In addition, national agencies relate to the United Nations and other intergovernmental bodies related to their spheres of interest and expertise. Within the U.S. government, for example, the State Department and the Department of Health and Human Services are significantly involved in international social welfare activities.

Department of Health and Human Services. Within DHHS, the international affairs staff in the Office of Public Affairs of the Administration for Children and Families (ACF) has been the contact point for the international activities of the U.S. government most closely related to social work. The office organizes U.S. participation in intergovernmental international meetings and organizations, administers several bilateral programs in social welfare, is involved in comparative research, and arranges the programs of international visitors in social welfare.

The ACF has participated with social welfare ministries in several countries in cooperative social welfare projects. In the 1990s, several special initiatives focused on Eastern Europe and the countries of the former Soviet Union. ACF regularly participates in meetings of international organizations, such as UNICEF, ECOSOC, and the European Centre for Social Welfare Policy and Research. Additionally, ACF provides experts for special UN efforts; one example is the provision of support and expertise to the UN group that developed the Declaration on Social and Legal Principles Relating to Adoption and Foster Placement of Children Nationally and Internationally (U.S. DHHS, 1993).

The Social Security Administration, also part of DHHS, conducts research on social security programs worldwide. The research is published in a biennial volume, *Social Security Programs Throughout the World.* The agency also serves as the U.S. link to the International Social Security Association.

The State Department oversees international child abduction policies, human trafficking, and international adoption. It has been the lead agency in work to bring the United States into compliance with the Hague Convention on international adoption and now issues an annual report on global human trafficking. Within the State Department, the Bureau of Education and Cultural Affairs sponsors numerous exchange programs, including exchanges in social work and social welfare. The Fulbright program that has sent U.S. scholars to study and teach abroad and brought foreign scholars to U.S. institutions is one of the sponsored programs. Some of these programs were previously organized under the United States Information Agency; that agency was abolished and its functions transferred to the U.S. State Department in 1999.

Agencies Dealing With Migration and Refugees

The Office of Refugee Resettlement (ORR) is part of the ACF, within DHHS, and has responsibility for planning and directing the implementation of national programs to resettle refugees in all the states and advising the secretary of DHHS on resettlement policies (U.S. DHHS, 2007). Among the programs for which ORR is responsible are Refugee and Entrant Resettlement, Refugee Cash Assistance, Unaccompanied Refugee Minors Program, Services for Survivors of Torture, and Assistance to Trafficking Victims. Within the State Department, the Bureau of Population, Refugees and Migration is charged with developing policies on refugees and migration and for overseeing programs for refugee admissions. In addition, this bureau administers U.S. contributions to agencies that serve refugees around the world, including UN organizations and NGOs. Further, the bureau "coordinates U.S. international migration policy within the U.S. government and through bilateral and multilateral diplomacy" (*U.S. Government Manual*, 1998, p. 397). Resettlement will be discussed in more depth in Chapter 11.

Other agencies are involved in international social welfare. These include the Department of Labor, the lead agency on International Labour Organization (ILO) matters, and extensive programs in international health administered by the National Institutes for Health, Fogarty International Center, and the Office of International Health at the Public Health Service. The Department of Agriculture shares responsibility for international food assistance efforts with USAID. Key programs in agriculture include the Food for Peace Program, established in 1966, and the more recently founded Food for Progress Program to provide food to developing democracies.

NONGOVERNMENTAL ORGANIZATIONS

NGOs play a significant role in international social welfare. Also called *Private Voluntary Organizations* (PVOs), they are organized to serve a range of functions, including:

• relief and development
• advocacy for causes such as human rights and peace
• development education
• exchange
• international networks of social and youth agencies
• the cross-national work of domestic agencies targeted at international problems such as adoption, child custody, and refugee resettlement
• professional associations (as described in Chapter 7).

In addition to their major functions, many of these NGOs have consultative status in the UN (defined in Chapter 7) and its specialized bodies and may collaborate with and receive funds from intergovernmental and national government agencies to conduct their work. Too numerous to describe all, this section will give examples of NGOs that fulfill the functions just identified. (The international professional organizations are described in Chapter 7 and will not be covered here.)

Relief and Development

NGOs plan and implement relief and development work in developing countries, and, increasingly, in poverty-stricken areas of industrialized nations. One of the earliest private relief organizations was the International Committee of the Red Cross, which was founded in 1863 to provide relief services and ensure humane wartime treatment of prisoners and civilians.

The Red Cross has been joined by numerous international private organizations emphasizing relief to refugees, famine victims, and victims of war and natural disasters. Usually provided under emergency conditions, relief involves provision of basic necessities of food, water, shelter, clothing, and medical care to sustain life. Increasingly, the large-scale relief organizations have worked to refocus their efforts toward development—the initiation of self-sustaining efforts that will contribute on a long-term basis to improvements in quality of life. Some examples of development activities are forming local co-operatives and introducing improved farming techniques, preventive health care projects, and local sanitation improvements, such as digging wells and building latrines. Some NGOs have moved further into what has been called *sustainable systems development* (Morrison & Purcell, 1988). In this approach, more interventions target policy and institutional changes at the regional or national level to create an environment in which sustainable people-centered development is feasible. The line between relief and development is seldom absolute. Most development NGOs still engage in some relief work, especially in times of crisis and, as much as possible, relief agencies add a development focus to their work. This stems from the recognition that development is impossible without the guarantee of human survival. As expressed by Mabub ul Haq (1982), former head of UNDP, if an individual dies from hunger, there is no chance that he can be developed.

Among the larger U.S.-based NGOs in development work are CARE (the Cooperative for American Relief Everywhere, now known by its acronym), Catholic Relief Services, Save the Children, and the Christian Children's Fund. All have annual budgets of hundreds of millions of dollars. Most receive considerable amounts of government funding to carry out relief and development work on-site in developing countries. Innovative work, often in politically difficult climates, is also done by smaller NGOS, such as the American Friends Service Committee (AFSC), Oxfam, and the Unitarian Universalist Service Committee. Many of these agencies do not accept government money in order to remain free to advocate for policy changes and to assist in areas not approved by government agencies. The AFSC, for example, began projects in Cambodia shortly after the fall of the Khmer Rouge, during a time when the U.S. government prohibited official aid to Cambodia.

There is increasing realization that development efforts must be self-sustaining in order to have impact. This favors participatory, community-level efforts that are "bottom-up"—strategies planned and implemented with and by people experiencing the problems being addressed. There is a perception that NGOs are more innovative, flexible, and cost-effective and that they are better able to reach the poor through grassroots work than is true for governmental or intergovernmental organizations. In general, NGOs are less bureaucratic and are less tied to the changing priorities of legislatures than the bilateral agencies. For those with significant dependence on government funding, these advantages are partially erased; these NGOs also become limited by the priorities and "strings" of government regulations.

The work of international NGOs is complemented by Southern NGOs—those based in developing countries. Some Southern NGOs are very small, village-based organizations, whereas others are national cooperatives, environmental groups, or women's organizations. Among the more well-known NGOs are the Grameen Bank of Bangladesh, an organization that has spurred microenterprise development, especially for women, and the Green Belt Movement in Kenya, a women's environmental movement in which over 50,000 women have participated in planting more than 10 million trees to stem soil erosion (Hoy, 1998). There are also some international organizations based in the South. Development Alternatives With Women for a New Era (DAWN), based at the University of the West Indies in Barbados, is a network of third world women activists. These developing country NGOs are important players in development successes and their activities—both independent projects and partnerships with Northern NGOs—need to be encouraged.

SAVE THE CHILDREN USA: A DEVELOPMENT AND RELIEF NGO

Save the Children USA, is one of many relief and development NGOs based in the United States. It stands out as one of the older and larger agencies, founded more than 75 years ago. The agency mission is "to create lasting positive change in the lives of children in need in the United States and around the world" (Save the Children, 2007a). Save the Children works in more than 50 countries, with its largest programs in Africa and Asia. Its programs also operate in the United States, including a current post-Katrina response program. Program divisions are: Emergencies and Crises, Primary Health, Education, Economic Opportunities, HIV/AIDS, and Food Security and Resource Management. All are based on the principles of "child centered, woman-focused, participatory and empowering" approaches.

Save the Children was founded in the United States in 1932 and originally targeted children in need at home. During World War II, the child sponsorship program began to address children affected by the war in Europe. The organization continued to expand its scope, opening field offices in Africa and Latin America during the 1960s. Today, it is truly a global organization. Save the Children USA, is part of a global network, the International Save the Children Alliance, all inspired by the work of Eglantyne Jebb (featured in Chapter 7). Its 28 member organizations work in more than 110 countries.

The total annual budget of Save the Children USA was about $332 million in 2006. The agency reports that 90% of funds are spent on programs, with 6% on fund raising and 4% on management expenses. More than one-third of annual revenues come from grants and contracts from the U.S. government. Government aid programs deliver some of their development and relief assistance through NGOs, especially the larger NGOs. The remainder of Save the Children's income comes from private donations, including child sponsorships.

Several new initiatives are under way. The Rewrite the Future project was launched by the International Alliance to bring education to children caught up in conflict situations. Save the Children USA is part of this

(continued)

initiative, with education projects in Afghanistan, Ethiopia, Nepal, and Sudan. With funding from a private foundation, the Bill and Melinda Gates Foundation, Save the Children USA has begun a program to provide better health care to newborns in areas with high infant mortality. Child survival remains a critical foundation for development. And long-term recovery projects with children at the center are under way in Aceh, Indonesia, and the Hurricane Katrina affected areas of the United States.

More on the specific program work of Save the Children USA can be found in case examples in Chapter 1 and Chapter 10.

Sources: InterAction. (2007). *Save the Children agency profile.* Accessed July 23, 2007, at www.interaction.org; Save the Children. (2007a). *Annual report 2006.* Westport, CT: Author; Save the Children. (2007b). *75 years of Save the Children.* Westport, CT: Author. Accessed July 23, 2007, at www.savethechildren.org

To further their goals, Northern NGOs have formed several coordinating bodies. InterAction is a coalition of more than 160 U.S. NGOs that have joined together to coordinate their work in disaster situations, to work toward improved U.S. development assistance and general development policy, and to collaborate in development education efforts (InterAction, 2007a). The U.S. National Association of Social Workers (NASW) has joined InterAction. InterAction has developed and published PVO standards covering governance, finance, and management practices (InterAction, 1993). The International Council of Voluntary Agencies (ICVA) is an international membership organization for national and international PVOs engaged in development work. The organization provides information exchange and management assistance, as well as serving as a liaison to UN bodies.

These coordinating bodies have been particularly active in assisting NGOs to carry out their supplementary purposes of policy advocacy and development education, which are presented in the following sections.

Advocacy

Most NGOs include advocacy as one of their functions. Increasingly, U.S.-based NGOs have identified the need to serve as voices for more effective international assistance programs and for responsible international policies in general. InterAction has campaigned to encourage U.S. ratification of the UN Convention on the Rights of the Child, unfortunately without success. NGOs led a successful campaign against the sale of baby formula in developing countries in the 1980s through massive public education on the value of breast feeding and the dangers of using baby formula in areas with poor sanitation. The campaign included pressure on multinational corporations involved in the manufacture and promotion of baby formula. A more recent campaign is the One Campaign aimed at poverty eradication. More typical of the NGO lobbying agenda is advocacy for development priorities and adequate funding for foreign assistance.

Another form of advocacy is carried out at the intergovernmental level through consultative status with the UN. More than 2,300 NGOs were accredited by the UN for participation in the Copenhagen World Summit for Social Development, and the Beijing Conference on Women included participation of more than 4,000 NGOs.

Some NGOs are devoted primarily to advocacy, especially in human rights. An example is Amnesty International, an organization that documents abuses of human rights and sponsors campaigns to improve human rights treatment and obtain prisoner release. Another human rights NGO, Defense for Children International, was active in the 1980s and early 1990s in over 60 countries to monitor and advocate for children's rights. The organization was a major actor in the campaign to draft and adopt the UN Convention on the Rights of the Child.

Development Education

Many NGOs conduct development education programs—efforts to educate the public on conditions in the developing world and to motivate action on behalf of the needs of the world's poor. Partly motivated by the need to appeal to donors and the realization that there is large-scale public ignorance of development realities, agencies also recognize the contribution they can make in sharing their knowledge and experience in development with the general public. Between 1982 and 1993, the Biden-Pell Amendment to U.S. foreign aid legislation provided special grants for development education. The Young Women's Christian Association (YWCA) and NASW were among the organizations that received these grants from USAID; funds were used for materials and educational campaigns on global issues aimed at their memberships. Development agencies were also involved. Save the Children (SC), for example, produced educational materials to sensitize children to the needs of other children around the world and implemented action projects in schools. Bread for the World is an organization dedicated solely to development education and advocacy, with a focus on world hunger. This Christian-based citizens' group produces action alerts, background papers on hunger issues, and videos for education; it also lobbies the government on domestic and world hunger policies.

The American Forum for Global Education is an NGO that sponsors and promotes development education. It sponsors an annual forum on development education and publishes books, manuals, teaching aids, and a newsletter to assist educational efforts.

Exchange Programs

Exchange is used in social welfare, as in other fields, as a mechanism for transfer of knowledge and service models as well as a means of bridging cultural barriers and increasing understanding. The Council of International Programs (CIP) is one example of an exchange organization. Founded in 1956, CIP sponsors educational exchanges for human service professionals and youth leaders. Participants are engaged in both educational seminars and fieldwork in social agencies and youth programs. The placements and seminars are operated by local affiliates that are linked to universities. Professionals from more than 147 countries have participated in CIP exchanges (CIP, 2007).

Agencies such as World Learning, founded in 1932 as Experiment in International Living, have sponsored youth exchanges to enhance cross-cultural understanding. Academic exchanges, some in the social welfare field, are supported under the Fulbright Scholar program. The Fulbright program has been one of the major sources of support for U.S. scholars to teach, consult, and do research in other countries. In Europe, the European Union has sponsored numerous professional and educational exchanges. In addition, many exchanges have developed between universities or from personal contacts between professionals.

Social and Youth Agencies With International Counterparts

Although they will not be discussed in depth here, there are a number of social and youth development agencies that have branches in many nations. These include the Boy Scouts, the Girl Scouts, the YMCA, the YWCA, the Salvation Army, the Red Cross, and others. Each has functions that relate to status as an international organization. The U.S. YWCA, for example, maintains World Mutual Service committees in many of its branches and has a headquarters division to address collaborative efforts with the World YWCA. Red Cross branches in many nations send volunteers to assist in disasters in other parts of the world.

Agencies Engaged in Cross-National Social Work

A growing number of private nonprofit social welfare agencies are engaged in cross-national social work, including international adoption, child custody problems, divorce and other family problems involving citizens and laws of more than one country, and sponsorship and resettlement of refugees. Although some agencies specialize in such work, others are introduced to international dimensions of social welfare through their involvement with individual cases.

International Social Service (ISS), located in Geneva with branches in 16 countries, specializes in cross-national casework. With an emphasis on migration, the agency intervenes in individual and family problems that can be solved only through coordinated efforts in several countries. The agency maintains a documentation center on migration, refugees, family law, and children's rights (*Encyclopedia of Associations*, 1999).

Many international adoptions are arranged through social agencies and all such adoptions in the United States involve a home study, as required by government regulations. Agencies such as Holt International Children's Services, founded in 1956, specialize in international adoption. Such services, however, are also available from many general adoption agencies. The adoption of children from other countries is also common in Europe. Wherever it occurs, the practice of international adoption involves agencies in cross-national work.

Refugee resettlement programs have also engaged many private social agencies in international work. Although not always conceptualized as international social work, competent refugee work is impossible without knowledge of the refugee's culture of origin, international transit experiences, and the receiving country's policy regarding refugees, including reunification and family sponsorship issues. Among the agencies significantly involved in refugee resettlement in the United States are Migration and Refugee Services of the U.S. Catholic Conference, Lutheran Immigration and Refugee Service, and many specialized agencies serving particular national, religious, or ethnic groups. Practice issues concerning refugee resettlement, immigration, international adoption, and intercountry casework will be discussed in Chapter 11.

CONCLUSION: MOVING FORWARD

The social work-related functions of international organizations cover an enormous scope, and there are many such organizations. Assessments of need and the growing importance of social factors in development suggest that the level of activity is likely to increase significantly in the future.

All recent surveys of current social welfare needs in the international context indicate that a full agenda remains and grows. Basic-needs issues persist: Food, shelter, primary health care, and primary education are still inadequately provided in much of the developing world. Ensuring respect for the rights of children, women, persons with disabilities, and minority ethnic and racial groups remains a challenge. At the same time, demographic changes and modernization influences are causing new concerns with issues of aging, mental health, and substance abuse. Wars and natural disasters create new areas of need. There is a continuing recognition that the social dimensions of development decisions and policies are key to meeting the ultimate objectives of development strategies—improved living standards for all. Thus social welfare and social development should grow in importance.

If there is a counterindication, it is that trends in reducing domestic social safety nets and curtailing the Western welfare state are having and will have an impact on development assistance. As explained by Roger Riddell (1996) in a study of the role of aid:

[A] factor adversely influencing aid lies in the ripple effects of changing perceptions within donor countries about the nature of the state, the welfare state, and
society; the nature of responsibility for assisting those which do not have the
means to help themselves; and how best to prioritize the use of state funds.... As
state aid, including hand-outs, are viewed less and less sympathetically as solutions to domestic problems, it is asked why these solutions should continue to be
used to help solve development problems of poorer countries. (p. 2)

These "ripple effects" are further evidence of the social policy emulation
discussed in Chapter 2. Clearly, emphases on privatization, increased role of
the market, and reduced social welfare roles for governments are already
having an impact on attitudes and practices in international development.

To move forward, the organizations involved in international social development and social work must appropriately assess accomplishments and
failures. The problems facing the field of international social welfare appear
overwhelming—seemingly intractable poverty, especially in Africa; the
devastation of AIDS in suffering, costs, and family disruptions; ethnic conflicts; and a continuing flow of refugees. However, there have been major
successes, such as lengthening the life span, eliminating diseases such as
smallpox, reducing hunger in Asia, increasing the number of literate adults,
recognizing standards for human rights, and introducing new strategies to
improve child survival. The social mission of the UN has been one of its major
successes. Governments have demonstrated a willingness to come together
and work on strategies for human betterment, even if with imperfect results.
Early in the new century, governments have pledged to work toward the
important targets set forth in the MDGs. International agreements have been
reached on the broad outlines of human rights policy covering women,
children, persons with disabilities, and racial and ethnic minorities. While
implementation lags, it is no small achievement to have secured wide international agreement on principles of human rights and human development.
There have also been millions of small social development successes in terms
of individual lives saved, refugees resettled, villages mobilized to help
themselves, artisans helped to start small businesses, and persons educated
about HIV risks.

Thus in considering the future of international social welfare efforts, it is
important that both the successes and the failures, the challenges and the
victories, be reported and analyzed.

Chapter 10 will look more specifically at practice in international social
development and implications for social work. Although there are many
challenges ahead for international social welfare, one that may shape social
work participation in international work is success in reducing the dichotomy
between international and domestic social welfare issues. There are currently
two separate fields with different personnel, terminology, and policy concerns. Particularly in the United States, social work, the dominant profession
in domestic social welfare, has remained minimally involved in international
social development agencies, and mostly untouched by the development

education movement. Chapter 10 will detail the roles and functions involved in development work that are relevant for social work. It will also identify the lessons learned from international development that can be applied to social work wherever it is practiced.

REFERENCES

Altschiller, D. (1993). The United Nations' role in world affairs. *The Reference Shelf* (Vol. 65, No. 2). New York: H. W. Wilson Company.

Bennett, A. L. (1988). *International organizations: Principles and issues* (4th ed.). Englewood Cliffs, NJ: Prentice Hall.

Canadian International Development Agency. (2007). *Estimates 2007–2008: Part III, Report on Plans and Priorities*. Accessed June 12, 2007, at www.acdi-cida.gc.ca/cidaweb/acdicida.nsf/En/JUD-829101441-JOC

Cornia, G., Jolly, R., & Stewart, F. (Eds.). (1987). *Adjustment with a human face*. New York: UNICEF.

Council of International Programs USA (2007). About us. Accessed December 29, 2007, at www.cipusa.org/about_us.asp

Encyclopedia of associations: International organizations. (1999). Detroit, MI: Gale Research.

Gilcrest, G., & Splane, R. (1995). Canada's role in international social welfare. In J. Turner & F. Turner (Eds.), *Canadian social welfare* (3rd ed., pp. 574–596). Scarborough, Canada: Allyn and Bacon.

Hilliard, J. F. (1965). AID and international social welfare manpower. In *Proceedings of the Conference on International Social Welfare Manpower, 1964*. Washington, DC: U.S. Government Printing Office.

Hoy, P. (1998). *Players and issues in international aid*. West Hartford, CT: Kumarian Press.

InterAction. (1993). *InterAction PVO standards*. Washington, DC: Author.

InterAction. (2007a). *About InterAction*. Accessed June 15, 2007, at www.interaction.org

InterAction. (2007b). *InterAction member profiles* Washington, DC: Author.

Isbister, J. (1998). *Promises not kept: The betrayal of social change in the third world*. West Hartford, CT: Kumarian Press.

Jacobson, J. (1989, July–August). Paying interest in human life. *WorldWatch*, pp. 6–8.

Joint UN Programme on HIV/AIDS. (2006). *2006 Report on the Global AIDS Epidemic*. Accessed June 15, 2007, at www.unaids.org

Katz, A. (1962). Social work's contribution to the Peace Corps. In *Proceedings of the 1962 Annual Program Meeting CSWE* (pp. 75–85). New York: Council on Social Work Education.

Morrison, E., & Purcell, R. B. (Eds.). (1988). *Players and issues in U.S. foreign aid*. West Hartford, CT: Kumarian Press.

Organization for Economic Co-operation and Development (2007). *Data on gross bilateral ODA 2004–2005*. Accessed June 26, 2007, at www.oecd.org

Riddell, R. (1996). *Aid in the 21st century* (Discussion Paper Series No. 6). New York: UNDP.

Taylor, P., & Groom, A. J. R. (Eds.). (1989). *Global issues in the United Nations' framework*. New York: St. Martins Press.

ul Haq, M. (1982, July). *Beyond the Cancun Summit.* Unpublished presentation at the Society for International Development Conference, Baltimore, Maryland.

UNIFEM. (2007). *About UNIFEM.* Accessed June 19, 2007, at www.unifem.org/about

UNHCR. (2006). *UNHCR's Annual Program Budget 2007.* Accessed June 19, 2007, at www.unhcr.org

United Nations. (1945). United Nations Charter. Available at www.un.org

United Nations. (1969 September 3–12). *Proceedings of the International Conference of Ministers Responsible for Social Welfare.* New York: Author.

United Nations. (1987). *Interregional consultation on developmental social welfare policies and programmes* [Special Issue of the *Social Development Newsletter,* vol. 1987-1-25.] Vienna, Austria: Centre for Social Development and Humanitarian Affairs.

United Nations. (1991). *Women: Challenges to the Year 2000.* New York: Author.

United Nations. (1992). *Yearbook of the United Nations, 1991* (Vol. 45). Dordrecht, Netherlands: Martinus Nijhoff Publishers.

United Nations. (1993a). *United Nations conferences and observances* (Reference Paper No. 32, Communications and Project Management Division and Meetings Coverage Section). New York: Author.

United Nations. (1993b). World Summit for social development to be held in Denmark in 1995. *UN Chronicle, XXX*(1), 82–85.

United Nations. (1995a). *Copenhagen Declaration and Programme of Action. World Summit for Social Development.* New York: Author.

United Nations. (1995b). *Platform for Action and the Beijing Declaration: Fourth World Conference on Women.* New York: UN Department of Public Information.

United Nations. (1997a). *Report on the world social situation 1997.* New York: Author.

United Nations. (1997b). *Yearbook of the United Nations 1995* (Vol. 49). New York: Author.

United Nations. (1998). *Basic facts about the United Nations.* New York: Author.

United Nations. (2005). *The report on the world social situation.* New York: Author.

United Nations. (2006). *Yearbook of the United Nations 2004* (Vol. 58). New York: Author.

United Nations. (2007). *About ECOSOC.* Accessed June 21, 2007, at www.un.org/ecosoc/about/subsidiary.shtml

US Agency for International Development. (2007a). *About USAID.* Accessed June 12, 2007, at www.usaid.gov/about_usaid

US Agency for International Development. (2007b). *Nine principles.* Accessed June 24, 2007, at www.usaid.gov/policy/2005_nineprinciples.html

US Department of Health and Human Services. (2007). Office of Refugee Resettlement. Accessed December 29, 2007, at www.acf.hhs.gov/programs/orr

US Department of Health and Human Services, Administration for Children and Families. (1993, March 30). Staff memo. Washington, DC: Author.

United States government manual 1998. (1998). Washington, DC: Office of the Federal Register, National Archives and Records Service, General Services Administration.

PART II

THE PROFESSION INTERNATIONALLY

CHAPTER 6

THE HISTORY
OF THE DEVELOPMENT
OF SOCIAL WORK

It is difficult to affix a date to the beginning of the profession of social work. The National Association of Social Workers (NASW) in the United States declared 1998 to be the 100th anniversary of the profession; however, that year was actually the anniversary of the first social work training course in the United States, a summer school held in New York in 1898. Earlier training courses existed in England, and perhaps elsewhere, and the first true school of social work was begun in Amsterdam in 1899. In the countries in which social work has developed, helping activities began under a variety of auspices. When can these be labeled social work? Is one hallmark that they became secular rather than exclusively under the control of religious personnel? Or that they were undertaken by individuals who devoted themselves to helping as a regular activity rather than an occasional volunteer one? Van Wormer (1997), for example, reports that the first recorded employment of a social worker was the hiring of Mary Stewart, a trained Charity Organization Society (COS) worker, in 1895 by the Royal Free Hospital in London. Her task was to determine whether patients were eligible for free treatment. Another explanation is that social work became a profession when those providing such helping services began to systematize their efforts and to train others to provide services in a similar way.

Clearly, the easiest date to identify is the beginning of formalized training for social work. It can indeed be argued that this is the point at which social work becomes a profession. Earlier markers include the establishment of agencies such as settlement houses and the Young Women's Christian Association (YWCA), founded in 1855 in England and in 1858 in the United States. Founding of these agencies represented organized efforts to provide social services, often through paid staff who devoted themselves to this work as their main enterprise.

INTERNATIONAL DEVELOPMENT

In describing the origins of social work around the world, an effort will be made to discuss services and education. It should be recognized, however, that the founding of a school of social work or even a formalized training program is much more likely to be well documented and can therefore be reported with more accuracy.

Two distinct patterns in the evolution of social work are evident. Social work schools emerged almost simultaneously in London, Amsterdam, New York City, and Berlin around 1900 (de Jongh, 1972). For a long time it has been thought that this was a spontaneous development; new research into correspondence and papers from her day shows that Mary Richmond, a pioneer in social casework in the United States, not only read British works on the COS movement but also attended committee meetings in London at which the training course was being planned (Kendall, 2000). Formal training in the United States and Europe was organized to meet the needs of staff providing social services that had been developed to address the human needs that were by-products of the industrial revolution. Family services, settlement houses, and assistance to orphans, widows, immigrants, and young working women sprang up in response to harsh employment conditions. In contrast, de Jongh (1972) says: "I do not know of any developing country in which social work education was an original product of national develop-ment; the origins can always be traced back to strong foreign influences" (p. 23). Thus we have two patterns: Social work evolving in the United States and much of Europe as an indigenous response to the conditions of late nineteenth-century life, and social work being introduced into countries in Asia and Africa by American and European experts to address the problems of "underdevelopment." A third pattern, which emerged after de Jongh's work, is the introduction, or reintroduction, of modern social work in the countries of the former Soviet Union and Eastern bloc, including Russia, the nations of Eastern Europe, China, and Vietnam; this process has also involved substantial foreign influence.

Social Work Services Emerge in Europe and the United States

As summarized by Van Wormer (1997), "two social movements in social welfare that began at the end of the nineteenth century shaped the devel-opment of the profession of social work: the Charity Organization Societies (COSs) and the settlement house establishments" (p. 162). Each developed as a response to the social ills of the times, but they differed in philosophy and approach. Both institutions began in London, the Charity Organization So-ciety in 1869 and the first settlement house, Toynbee Hall, in 1884. Within less than a decade, each was transplanted to the United States—remarkable ex-amples of early technology transfer in the human services. The first COS in the United States began in 1877 in Buffalo and was followed by rapid de-velopment of societies in other cities. Hull House was founded in Chicago in

1889, following Jane Addams's visit to Toynbee H
of social work was strongly influenced by the sett
the United States and Europe. The COS workers
needy individual and the combination of "sc
friendly visiting, were the forerunners of socia'
for more formal training led to the establish'
mentioned above, in 1898.

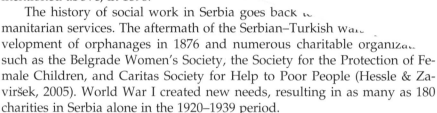

The history of social work in Serbia goes back ᴜ
manitarian services. The aftermath of the Serbian–Turkish waɪ̯
velopment of orphanages in 1876 and numerous charitable organizaᴜ
such as the Belgrade Women's Society, the Society for the Protection of Female Children, and Caritas Society for Help to Poor People (Hessle & Zaviršek, 2005). World War I created new needs, resulting in as many as 180 charities in Serbia alone in the 1920–1939 period.

Services developed in other parts of the world, as well, often as a result of colonial activities. Jamaica provides an interesting example:

> The extent to which services established in the then British West Indies colonies were conceived as export models from the mother country is reflected in the names of the programmes established in the Region. None demonstrates this more completely than the Kingston Charity Organization Society founded in 1900 which was promoted with a view to rationalizing the delivery of private charity in the community. It did not however assume the central prominence in the development of social services and the systematizing and ultimate professionalizing of social work service delivery that was achieved by the original London Charity Organization Society of the 1850's or the transplanted varieties in Buffalo, New York, Montreal and other prominent northern American and Canadian cities. The K.C.O.S. settled into being essentially a private relief-giving agency. (Maxwell, 1993, p. 9)

Social Work Education Develops

Professional education may well be the cornerstone of the establishment of a profession. In 1899, the first school of social work was begun in Amsterdam, the Institute for Social Work Training. According to its prospectus, this was a 2-year course that aimed "at the methodical, theoretical and practical training of those who wish to dedicate themselves to certain important tasks in the field of social work" (United Nations, 1958, p. 109). Five fields of study were offered: welfare of the poor, housing management, "Toynbee work" (settlement house work), child care for orphans and deserted children, and social work in factories and workshops.

This comprehensive program followed efforts elsewhere to offer series of lectures for training of social workers. Octavia Hill was conducting training in England as early as 1873. Series of lectures followed in London throughout the 1890s. In 1895, a summer institute was sponsored in Chicago by Hull House. Then, in 1898, the New York COS began a summer school in philanthropic work after Mary Richmond had urged more organized training in

the 1897 National Conference on Social Work. Seen as the begin-
ofessional social work education in the United States, the sum-
titute had become a 1-year full-time course by 1904 and eventually
e the Columbia University School of Social Work (United Nations,
). In the previous year, 1903, the School of Sociology in London began a
year course of theory and practice that grew from the efforts of the COS
and its "professionalizing effect." On the European continent, Alice Salomon
began a training course for young women interested in doing social work in
1899 and founded the first school of social work in Germany (in Berlin) in
1908 (Wieler, 1988). Thus, as noted by de Jongh, social work education
emerged almost simultaneously in Britain, the United States, and the European continent at the turn of the century, quickly progressing in each location
from lectures to full-time training.

Further east in Europe, the Training School for Social Work was founded
at the Free University of Poland in Warsaw in 1925 by Madame Helene
Radlinska. Its 2-year program, too, was preceded by several short courses in
social work (Radlinska, 1929). Madame Radlinska commented to the educators assembled in 1928 for the First International Conference of Social Work
that she found it difficult to balance theory and practice. "In fact, there are
very few professors who combine practical experiences with academic
qualifications; therefore it is difficult to correlate the practice and theory of
social work" (Radlinska, 1929, p. 92). This, indeed, has been and continues
to be a challenge everywhere in the early years of developing professional
education in social work.

The Spread Beyond Europe: Early Social Work and Social Work Education in Latin America, Asia, and Africa

By the 1920s, international influences had begun to play a major role in the
spread of professional social work. The School of Social Work at Santiago,
Chile, the first school in Latin America, was founded in 1925 by Alejandro del
Rio, a physician, with assistance from another physician, René Sand of Belgium. It was founded after a visit to Europe by Dr. del Rio to examine the
roles social workers played there in assisting physicians. His chance meeting
with Dr. Sand on the ship led him to include a stop at the Central School of
Social Studies in Brussels (Kendall, 2000). The first principal of the school in
Chile was Madame Bernier from Belgium, recruited by Sand at del Rio's
request. Dr. del Rio remained affiliated with the school until 1932 and continued to seek assistance from Dr. Sand, as documented in letters exchanged
between the two (Kendall, 2000).

A similar pattern followed in neighboring Argentina where doctors investigated the idea of using "hygiene visitors," which they had observed in
Europe. In the early 1930s, a school was founded in connection with the
School of Medicine at the University of Buenos Aires to train auxiliaries for
doctors. Early influences on the development of Argentine social work came

from Belgium, France, and Germany and emphasized charity work and social work as auxiliary to other professions (R. Teubal, personal communication, March 13, 1997). A tradition of charity work in Argentina long preceded the establishment of the school. In 1823, for example, a women's organization called the Charity Society was established and given authority to administer institutions for children, women, and the aged. In existence until 1948, this organization has been described as "by far the most powerful charity organization in the 19th century" (Queiro-Tajalli, 1995, p. 92). Until the 1940s, Argentine social work and social work education were influenced by European ideas and by their own religious and charity traditions. From the 1940s to the 1960s, U.S. influence grew, introducing psychology and concepts of psychotherapy to Argentine social work.

The first schools in Africa began at opposite ends of the continent, in South Africa in 1924 and in Egypt in 1936. In South Africa, social work training began to address the problems of "poor whites"; theory for the training was borrowed from North America and Europe with little attention to adaptation (Mazibuko, McKendrick, & Patel, 1992). The 1924 course was founded at the University of Cape Town. Within a decade, it had been joined by social work programs in Pretoria and Stellenbosch; in 1938, the Joint Universities Committee on Social Studies was established to promote the study of social work in South Africa (Ntusi, 1995). While there was an opposing tradition of liberalism that advocated diversity and openness, early social work education was also linked to Broederbond, an Afrikaner advancement movement that opposed any cultural assimilation. As explained by Ntusi (1995):

> The provision of social work services to the poor whites served two purposes. It unified and strengthened the ethnic boundaries and gave rise to a certified professional elite, loyal to the government and all out to achieve the government's goal of stamping out white poverty. (p. 263)

In this tradition, Dr. Verwoerd established a department of sociology and social work at the University of Stellenbosch in 1932. The two traditions of liberalism—focusing on poverty in general—and the Afrikaner focus on services to whites—continued unchanged in South African social work education for decades.

The first school to focus on educating nonwhites for social work was the Jan H. Hofmeyr School of Social Work, founded in 1941 with assistance from the Young Men's Christian Association (YMCA) (Kendall, 2000). It was the result of the work of Hofmeyr, a South African philanthropist who believed in equal opportunity, and Ray Phillips, a Congregationalist missionary with a PhD from Yale; Phillips was committed to the "absolute equality of men and women of every race and condition," and his work in founding the school was one way to put his beliefs into action (Kendall, 2000, p. 85).

Social work education in the Middle East/North Africa was begun in Cairo in 1936, the year that Egypt gained recognition as an independent nation. According to Ragab (1995), in the early stage of development, "the American model was successfully transplanted into Egypt" (p. 281). The founders, including several foreign-born and -trained social workers, were confident that the many social problems facing the new nation could be handled with an approach to social reform based on sound theory and research. "The school was an instant success . . . as the country was teeming with idealistic, enthusiastic youth searching for a role in national reconstruction and development" (Ragab, 1995, p. 284). Social services also became more formalized and job opportunities grew as the government established the Ministry of Social Affairs and Labour in 1939 to provide public social services. Prior to 1939, social services in Egypt were entirely voluntary, organized by mosques and NGOs (Walton & El Nasr, 1988). While several other schools developed in Egypt, only in 1975 did social work education move into the university when the Higher Institute of Social Work in Cairo became a part of the new Helwan University.

A settlement house–like agency, the Nagpada Neighborhood House, was founded in 1926 in the slums of Bombay, India, by Dr. Clifford Manshardt, an American missionary. An ordained Congregational minister, Manshardt was rejected when he first applied for missionary work because church officials found him to be "commendably idealistic but religiously inadequate" (Manshardt, 1967, p. 9). Especially troubling to the church were his views on the brotherhood of man, which he saw extending to all, no matter what their faith. He was finally appointed to a social work post and told that with his unorthodox views, he could not be used in regular church work with Indian Christian families because his ideas "might disturb their faith"; in a social work role, however, the church deemed that he "could do little harm—and very likely considerable good" (Manshardt, 1967, p. 11).

From his work in the settlement, Manshardt (1941) was convinced "that the standard of social work in India could not be raised appreciably until a permanent School of Social Work was set up to engage in a continuous study of Indian Social Problems and to offer training for social work on a graduate basis" (p. 15). With financing from the trust of an Indian industrialist, Manshardt opened India's first professional school, the Sir Dorabji Tata Graduate School of Social Work, in Bombay in 1936. The faculty consisted of a German Jewish refugee, an American visiting professor, and two Indians, one with a background in education and theology and the other a sociologist (Desai, 1987). The school focused on urban problems and pioneered in training labor welfare officers to cope with the new factory labor force as families moved into Bombay from rural villages. Labor welfare has continued to be important in Indian social work. A second school, the Delhi School (originally located in Lucknow), came into existence in 1946 "under the auspices of the National Y.W.C.A. of India, Burma and Ceylon with substantial assistance from the Foreign Division of the Y.W.C.A. of the United States" (Yelaja, 1969, p. 365). In keeping with the pattern identified by de Jongh (1972), discussed earlier in the chapter, India is another case in which the "birth and early growth of social work and its professionalization . . . was not the product of indigenous inspiration" (Kudchodkar, 1963, p. 96). Indian social work education was heavily influenced by U.S. models for many years.

The first recognized social work service in China (as recorded in the literature) were medical social work services in a hospital social work department in Beijing, established in 1921 by American social worker Ida Pruitt. The department provided social casework services, adoption work, and rehabilitation services; in addition, in-service training was provided for social workers—probably the first social work training in China. American professors from Princeton set up a sociology department at Yanjing University (now Beijing) in 1922, a department that became the Department of Sociology and Social Services just a few years later (Leung, 1995). Social work and social work education were heavily influenced by American missionaries and related organizations such as the YMCA and YWCA; although there was some work in rural areas, the emphasis was on urban clinical practice, a model poorly matched to the pressing needs of China (Leung, 1995).

Further Developments in the 1930s. In those countries in Europe where social work education was developed after the "first wave," foreign influences also played a role. In Denmark, for example, the first school was founded in 1937 in Copenhagen by Manon Luttichau. Working with a private organization called Care for Danish Women (Danske Kvinders Velfaerd) during the 1920s and early 1930s, Luttichau had traveled to the United States on a study tour and while there realized that social workers needed a professional education. Returning to Denmark, she wrote that while common sense is important, it is not enough to make one a social worker. She also traveled to Germany and encouraged others interested in social work to travel and learn. She was convinced that no social worker can sit in his or her own country to develop social work but must visit other places to exchange ideas (Hjerrild, personal communication, April 17, 1997).

Efforts to Gain Recognition as a Profession

It was not easy for social work to achieve recognition as a profession. In 1915, Abraham Flexner dismayed his audience at the U.S. National Conference of Charities and Correction by stating that social work was not a profession because it did not have a body of educationally transmissible techniques and because the boundaries of social work were too broad (Popple, 1995). In about the same period of history, Alice Salomon, seeing the increased demand for social workers in Germany toward the later years of World War I, decided it would be important for schools of social work to have uniform standards. In Germany, state approval was needed to promulgate uniform standards, as such an action would have required recognition of professional status. Salomon therefore called together representatives of the schools and government representatives from the Ministries of the Interior and of Education.

A PIONEER IN DENMARK: MANON LUTTICHAU

Photo by Anne-Li Engström, 1988.

Manon Luttichau was the most influential individual in the founding of professional social work in Denmark. Born on April 9, 1900, a year after the first school of social work was established in Europe, she became interested in the "preprofessional" social work activities then underway in Denmark. Early work there was being done in settlement houses for young women, some of them pregnant with nowhere to go. Social work was also done as "street work"—assisting women near the train stations, for example. From 1922 to 1932, Luttichau was an assistant with one of these organizations, a private organization called Care for Danish Women (translated). During these years, she also traveled to other countries, including the United States, to gather knowledge and inspiration to establish social work as a profession in Denmark.

On April 1, 1934, she became employed at the Copenhagen Municipal Hospital as a "social worker"—a new title in Denmark that she undoubtedly brought back from her visit to the United States. In 1936, she brought together a group of physicians, lawyers, and others to plan social work education for Denmark. Beginning on January 5, 1937, the classes took place in the hospital auditorium, using donated space and 29 volunteers as teachers. This was originally called the Social School in Denmark. Luttichau was the "dean" for the first two groups of students. She also founded the National Association of Social Workers in Denmark in 1938.

A true internationalist, Luttichau believed that interchange among countries was essential to the process of developing a profession. Learning from the experience of others and exchanging ideas with social workers in other nations were things she highly valued. She herself traveled in Europe and to the United States and participated in at least one of the early international conferences on social work.

The pioneer of professional social work in Denmark, she died on her 95th birthday in 1995.

From information supplied by Inger Hjerrild, Esbjerg School of Social Work, Esbjerg, Denmark, based on her historical research.

They gathered for a morning of discussion about the n€
recognition and standards, but the results were not posi1
   As Salomon (n.d.) wrote in her autobiography: "Tr
public health section of the Ministry, a very stiff and
finally broke out: 'You talk about a number of different
ing for health work—for educational activities—for relie:
labor—and all this you call a profession of social workers. What you talk
about does not exist' " (p. 197). She goes on to say that a similar process
and outcome occurred in France. The first five schools of social work there
and the director of the Public Relief and Hygiene Board in Paris petitioned
the Minister of Health asking for regulation of social work. The reply was
" 'the petition deals with a profession which cannot be defined, which hardly
exists in France, and the character of which makes regulations impossible' "
(p. 197).

   Publication of Mary Richmond's *Social Diagnosis* (1917) was heralded as
an answer to Flexner, giving social work a communicable technique. There is
evidence that this book made an impact in European social work training as
well as an important contribution in the United States.

Gender and the Social Work Profession

Part of the difficulty in securing recognition may have been gender bias
because social work was and still is considered a profession for women. Alice
Salomon (n.d.), referring to the negative reactions of officials to the young
social work profession, said:

> Behind this expression of hostility was the distrust of learned and progressive
> women. They considered out endeavors as part of the struggle ever latent be-
> tween men and women, now transferred to a new sphere of life. They fought
> against a type of school which would prepare for a profession pre-eminently
> suited to women, conceived by women, and formed according to their scale of
> values. So far all professions—that of the nurse and the teacher included—had
> been shaped by men. Most educational institutions were directed by men, in
> conformity with men's notions of women's duties and capacities. The object of
> education for women had been to form men's "helpmates." Our opponents were
> right in guessing that we wanted more. We wanted to make women responsible
> for services in which human needs should be met with a woman's understanding.
> A man brought up in the tradition of German officialdom could not even grasp
> the nature of our aspirations, much less approve. (p. 198)

Early social work was indeed a female profession. As late as 1937, 83 of
the 179 schools of social work in the world were for women only, just 9 were
reserved for men. In some European countries, including Austria, France,
Hungary, Italy, Norway, Portugal, Romania, and Switzerland, the only social
work training institutions were reserved for women. In addition, many of the
pioneers of social work in North America and in Europe were actively involved in the struggle for women's suffrage and broader women's rights.

ts of women within family law, for property ownership, and in the world
work-related issues, such as equal pay, were advocated by the founders
of social work. The extent of the feminine character of early social work is
striking.

Links With Pacifism

Links with the early women's movement also led to international collaborations on behalf of peace. Shortly after the beginning of professional social
work training, professional pioneers from several countries had the opportunity to meet each other at the International Congress of Women in Berlin in
1904 and again in Canada at the 1909 Congress of the International Council of
Women. Here, for example, Jane Addams met Alice Salomon, and the two
began a friendship "strengthened by their mutual commitment to international pacifism" (Lorenz, 1994, p. 60). The link between social work and peace
was clear to Salomon who wrote: "War annihilates everything that social
work tries to accomplish . . . this is the reason why social workers should be
the first ones to facilitate and maintain peace-creating international relations"
(Wieler, 1989, p. 19). During the first 50 years of social work, the commitment
to pacifism was rudely challenged by heightened nationalism and two devastating world wars.

In the United States, social worker Jeannette Rankin turned to politics and
was the first woman elected to Congress. She holds the distinction of being
the only member of Congress to vote against U.S. entry into both world wars.
In the vote to declare war against Japan in 1941, she said, "as a woman I can't
go to war, and I refuse to send anyone else." In 1968, 88-year-old Rankin,
a lifelong pacifist, led a protest march demanding U.S. withdrawal from
Vietnam (Lewis, 1999).

The Depression and Growing Nationalism

The worldwide depression occupied social workers with domestic crises in
many countries during the 1930s. National response in the form of new
policies and services changed the nature and activities of social work. In the
United States, for example, widespread unemployment convinced most that
poverty was not the result of individual inadequacies or traits but was systemic. A social worker, Harry Hopkins, was the architect of many of the New
Deal policy solutions to the crisis. Although the American version of the
welfare state was minimal, the changes altered the environment of social
work practice and influenced future philosophical developments around the
nature of human need.

In other parts of the world, especially Europe and Japan, an increase in
nationalism and militarism was the response to economic hardship or national humiliation, setting in motion the forces that led to World War II.

The unrest of the 1930s was widely felt. Several years of labor unrest
and social protests took place throughout the West Indies, for example. "The

social disturbances of the late 1930s which were explosive expressions of smoldering discontent by a deprived and exploited proletariat in the Caribbean, led to investigations of the root conditions by the famous Moyne Commission of 1938" (Brown, 1991, p. 22). This commission, appointed by the British government, made recommendations for improvement of social and economic conditions in the West Indian colonies, emphasizing social welfare services as "the major means for improving the West Indian quality of life" (Brown, 1991, p. 22). Thus similar to the unrest due to the Great Depression in the United States, social welfare services, and ultimately social work, were bolstered in Jamaica and other West Indian nations.

War, however, interrupted the depression and its resultant focus on social needs.

World War II and the Nazi Period

The late 1930s and early 1940s brought calamity for the world and, at times, brought out the worst in the profession of social work. Active collaboration with the Nazi-controlled government in Germany is almost certainly the darkest episode in social work history. It should be noted that there were also many instances of positive, even heroic, efforts by European social workers during this period. As Alice Salomon (n.d.), born into a Jewish family, reflects in her autobiography:

> The attitudes of my most intimate group of fellow workers, the staff of the School of Social Work and the Academy, most of whom were Protestant in predominantly Protestant Berlin, were typical of educated women. There were instances of human strength and human weakness. Some came out of the battle finer and stronger personalities, others lost whatever moral poise they had ever possessed. There were some women on our staff who would have been considered irreproachable by Nazi standards but for having worked closely with me. They tried to atone for this with redoubled fervor, saying "Heil Hitler" twice where others said it once. (p. 243)

German social work educators also intensely pressured her to resign from the presidency of the International Association of Schools of Social Work, threatening that all German schools would withdraw from the Association if she did not comply (Nitzsche, 1935). Several times Salomon resigned to save the association; however, each time the international membership reinstalled her as president.

The involvement of social workers in collaboration apparently went beyond shunning Jewish colleagues. According to Lorenz (1994):

> It is a fact that the welfare machinery of Nazi Germany, by "doing its duty" willingly or reluctantly, delivered thousands of people into the hands of the henchmen of the regime, caused untold anguish and suffering, deepened divisions at all levels of society and discredited its own humanitarian ideals. The murder of millions of Jewish citizens of Germany and its occupied countries, by

ALICE SALOMON

Joachim Wieler, personal collection

Alice Salomon, called "the Jane Addams of Germany" by Julia Lathrop (Salomon, n.d., p. 180), was a founder of social work education in Europe and a leader in international movements for social work education, women's rights, and peace. Among her accomplishments were the founding of the first school of social work in Germany in 1908, publication of 28 books and about 250 articles and service as the first president of the International Association of Schools of Social Work (Wieler, 1988). Salomon also had many "firsts" for women, including receiving a doctorate from the University of Berlin in 1906. Just a few years after the school she founded in Berlin was named the Alice Salomon School of Social Work to honor her, she was sent into exile in 1937 by the Nazis and died, nearly forgotten and alone, in New York in 1948.

Born in 1872 into a Jewish family, she converted to Christianity in 1914 but continued to be active in Jewish social services. She developed a strong interest in the plight of women, especially in the workplace, and attacked the issue with action and scholarship. She began a training course for young women interested in doing social work in 1899, providing opportunities for training and meaningful work for women, who were denied work in most fields. Simultaneously, she fought to gain admission to the University of Berlin (then closed to women) and was awarded the doctorate for her dissertation *Unequal Payment of Men's and Women's Work*—a very early study of the concept of comparable worth (Wieler, 1988).

A feminist, Salomon's life "was devoted nationally and internationally, in about equal parts to social work and to extensive work with councils of women" (Kendall, 1989, p. 28). She became active in the International Council of Women, rising to a leadership position in the organization. In her autobiography, she emphasizes her commitment to peace and the increasing dissonance she felt living in a militaristic Germany from 1914 until

(continued)

her exile. She became active in the international peace movement, joining with Jane Addams in working through the International League for Peace and Freedom, activities for which Addams eventually won a Nobel prize and for which Salomon was sent into exile. With World War I well under way, she was instrumental in arranging an audience for Jane Addams in Berlin in 1915 with the German chancellor as part of a delegation from a women's peace conference in The Hague, which was dispatched to the capital of each nation at war to try to talk the governments into peace. Needless to say, the mission failed. But how interesting it is to think about the courage and commitment of the women who would meet in Europe during a war and travel to hostile nations to talk about peace.

In her 60th year, Salomon was honored for her work in Germany and internationally. The school she had begun was named after her, she was given an honorary doctorate, and she received the Silver Medal for Merit to the State, bestowed unanimously by the Prussian Cabinet. Within a year, however, Hitler came to power, and the society Salomon had worked to create began to crumble rapidly. She was soon identified as an enemy of the Nazis; she was Jewish under the law, and her work in peace and disarmament, women's rights, and internationalism all conflicted with Nazi doctrine. Social work as a profession had championed reforms on behalf of the disabled, including the retarded and mentally ill—populations now labeled inferior and subject to extermination.

Salomon was stripped of her honors and offices, and her name was removed from the School of Social Work. While under intense pressure and in personal danger, she conducted and published the first international survey of social work education in 1937 under a grant from the Russell Sage Foundation. When she returned to Berlin from a speaking tour in the United States, she was summoned by the Gestapo and, after hours of interrogation, given the choice of leaving Germany permanently or being put into a concentration camp. As reported by *The New York Times* on July 13, 1937, "Alice Salomon, the founder and the distinguished head of the first school of social work in Germany, the Sociale Frauenschule of Berlin, who completed a lecture tour across the American continent last winter and who has visited this country on two other occasions since the war, has now been expelled from the Reich by order of the Nazi secret police" ("Alice Salomon Exiled," 1937, p. 510). After a brief stay in England, she came to the United States where she lived an increasingly lonely existence until her death in 1948. According to Wieler (1988):

> After more than three-quarters of a century of service to and with throngs of people, Alice Salomon died so alone that even the exact time, date and cause of her death were never established . . . the woman who had helped, protected, and taught countless social workers, championed the rights of women and created an international awareness and structure for social work education, went to her final rest with four people in attendance. There was no ceremony. (p. 170)

which the regime is most vividly remembered, was not an isolated case of extremism disconnected from other "achievements": it is the epitome of its politics, including welfare politics.... Once the granting of human rights became conditional..., the logic of discrimination, segregation and exclusion established itself as an unimpeded force in everyday professional discourse and could eventually not stop short of extending the line to extermination. (p. 63)

Lorenz traces the evolution of acquiescence. In the 1920s, possibly due to harsh postwar conditions in Germany, "the distinction between educable and ineducable youngsters—between 'valuable and inferior' persons—was beginning to enter the language and practice of German welfare staff" (Lorenz, 1994, p. 62). This grew to support for sterilization of the mentally ill and handicapped and then to segregation and elimination of other classes of undesirable people. An early Nazi social policy measure allowed sterilization of the mentally ill, alcoholics, and the handicapped and included a mandatory reporting clause that extended to many professions—a chilling early example of the practice of mandatory reporting, now seen as a client protection. "The actual legitimation of the procedure depended essentially on experts such as doctors and social workers making the 'right diagnosis'" (Lorenz, 1994, p. 65). Social work skills and methods of assessment, diagnosis, and report writing were used to identify "unworthy life" whose existence as "parasites is medically and economically unjustified," as stated in directives from the City of Frankfort, published in 1933 (cited in Lorenz, 1994, p. 66).

Such events were not limited to Germany. In Rome, a Higher Fascist School for Social Assistance in Industry was established in 1928. In Spain, the Franco regime set up its own social work schools after closing down the existing school in Barcelona. Social welfare services were supported by the fascists as part of their systems of social control.

Evidence suggests that some collusion was the result of active support for the policies, while others cooperated out of naïveté. There is evidence, too, of resistance from some social workers as they realized how their reports were being used. Involvement of the helping profession in such inhumane actions is difficult to comprehend and assimilate. Yet it is important to examine to prevent recurrence. Lorenz believes that the strong scientific emphasis in social work at the time and promotion of the belief in value neutrality were at least partially to blame. The focus on technical methodologies for dealing with human problems and the absence of a human rights orientation allowed the methodologies of the profession to be used for evil purposes.

Elsewhere in the world, social work also coped with grave restrictions of human rights, such as in the internment of Japanese citizens and resident aliens alike in the United States. Articles in the *Social Service Review* give some indication of social work action—or inaction—over the internment:

It is easy for us to forget about the Japanese—aliens and citizens—who were evacuated so many months ago. And the rejoicing over the Attorney General's announcement that Italian Americans who are still aliens would not be considered enemy aliens reminds us that the large numbers of Japanese-Americans, citizens and aliens alike, are still waiting for justice in our American republic. ("Child Welfare Problems and Japanese Evacuation," 1942, p. 673)

So complete was the suppression of Japanese rights in the West that even Japanese children were evacuated from orphanages and moved to the internment camps.

The Postwar Period

The postwar period brought several profound changes to social work around the world. First, communist takeover of Eastern Europe led to the end of social work in several countries and the retarded development of social work throughout the communist bloc. Second, devastation brought opportunities for social workers to become involved in the enormous relief and rehabilitation efforts in Europe and China. And third, nationalist and independence movements throughout the developing countries of Asia, Africa, and the Caribbean led to the birth of many new social work programs to accompany the birth of new nations.

Professional social work, as indicated by the presence of social work training institutions, had developed in Czechoslovakia, Hungary, Yugoslavia, China, and other countries later to fall under communism. Soon after the Soviet takeover of Eastern Europe, social work was officially abolished as an unnecessary and bourgeois profession. The Chinese followed this pattern after the 1949 revolution. The Secretary's Report of the International Committee of Schools of Social Work in July 1950 reveals the beginning impact of the cold war on social work education while showing unrealistic optimism about the situation in China:

> From the Tsechoslovakian Schools, who were members before the last war, we hear no more. Of the East of Europe only the School of Mrs. Radlinska at Lodz in Poland has remained loyal to us. It may interest you to hear that Miss Schlatter received a letter from Dr. Chen of Nanking, mentioning that his School did not in the least suffer from the new order. (Moltzer, 1950, p. 3)

Note that Miss Schlatter is Dr. Marguerite Schlatter of the School of Social Work in Zurich, Switzerland, and member of the International Committee of Schools of Social Work.

The secretary was correct about Poland. Although it did not flourish, social work continued in Poland throughout the era of Soviet domination. In Yugoslavia, in contrast, social work expanded, as the country broke with the Soviet Union and developed its own form of socialism. From earlier roots (there were at least five delegates from the Kingdom of the Serbs, Croats, and Slovenes at the First International Conference of Social Work in 1928), schools of social work were established in 1952 in Zagreb, 1955 in Ljubljana, and 1958

IRENA SENDLER

Irena Sendler, a social worker from Poland, has been nominated for the Nobel Peace Prize. Her story is one of heroism in the face of extreme oppression. Sendler, born in 1920 in a suburb of Warsaw, Poland, is credited with saving more than 2,500 Jewish children from the Warsaw ghetto during the Holocaust. A Catholic, she worked for the Warsaw City Council Welfare Department and, as a social worker, had access to the Ghetto. The Warsaw Ghetto was a 16-square-block area that was enclosed in 1940 to contain the 450,000 Jews who had been forced into the area and were kept there before being deported to death camps. Sendler convinced Jewish parents to give her their children so that she could save them from the Nazi death camps. Using various means, she and her colleagues in the underground movement smuggled children out of the Ghetto and into homes of Christian Polish families or convents. She invented new non-Jewish identities for the children but buried the original birth certificates and other documents in jars and bottles in her garden so that she could reunite children with their parents after the war. Although she dug up the bottles and tried to find the children's parents, most of them had died at Treblinka (Wieler, 2006).

Sendler was arrested on October 20, 1943, and imprisoned at the Pawiak prison. She was tortured there and received a death sentence but never divulged the locations of the children. The Polish underground, however, bribed her captors and she escaped. She lived hidden during the rest of the war. The petition to the Nobel Prize committee, supported by the International Federation of Social Workers (IFSW) includes the following: "She is one of the last heroes from the generation of our parents and our grandparents, who when confronted by the unparalleled evil of twentieth century totalitarianism, revealed great bravery, simple conviction, and the power of human will and intention" (Urbaniak, 2007).

Persecution of Sendler continued after the war. Sendler was apparently also not impressed with communist dictatorship and oppression and maintained contact with the Polish government in exile and the underground movement. She was again sentenced to death, but again, saved from the sentence. She kept a low profile, and her wartime activities on behalf of children only came to light after Poland emerged from the era of Soviet domination (Wieler, 2006). When interviewed, she said she didn't think people should make such a fuss about her efforts.

in Belgrade, Sarajevo, and Skopje (Hessle & Zavirsek, 2005). Social work was seen as a way to "bring to life and enforce advanced socialist legislation and, in a rational manner, be able to manage the substantial funds that our country has reserved for the social protection and better life of our labour class"

(Minister, Council of People's Health & Social Policy, Croatia, quoted in Hessle & Zavirsek, 2005, p. 37).

Commenting on the period of the 1950s in Croatia, Eugen Pusic said:

> The introduction of the social worker profession has contributed to the humanization of governance in general. Before, people just looked at documents and thought that the task of administration is to deal with paperwork and decisions. . . . To step out into real life, to reach out and see what was really going on in the field was a completely strange concept. The social worker profession humanized the administration. (cited in Hessle & Zavirsek, p. 38)

Pusic also noted the important contribution of social work to promotion of the idea of the worth of each individual human being.

In China, however, social work was soon abolished as an unnecessary and bourgeois profession. In still other cases, such as Armenia, Soviet domination isolated its republics and satellites from professional contact, thereby preventing the introduction of social work.

Devastation and Relief

The war brought devastation to the countries of Europe and to China and much of Southeast Asia. As Friedlander (1975) describes the situation in Poland:

> Poland was the most ravaged European country at the conclusion of the Second World War. Its railroads, power stations, highways and bridges had been destroyed, its ports made unusable, its factories stripped of machinery or burned, its livestock killed. Over six million Poles had died in the war and at least as many had been deported as slave laborers to Germany and to concentration camps. Almost the entire Jewish population had been murdered by the Nazis. (p. 14)

Social work, of course, did not escape, as the following plea for help for the Polish School of Social Work demonstrates:

> I appeal most warmly in the name of the Board, especially the French, English and German speaking countries to make their members send all they possibly can collect, books, papers reports, etc. regarding social work to Mrs. Helena Radlinska, one of the founders of our Committee, professor of the State University of Lodz (Poland). Mrs. Radlinska had the great misfortune to see destroyed besides her private house, the School of Social Work, founded by her at the University of Warsaw as well as the University itself, and to lose by death two-thirds of the teaching staff. In spite of this great misfortune starting anew at the age of 75 years Mrs. Radlinska does what she can to rebuild a School of Social Work at the University of Lodz. We cannot remain indifferent seeing this rare energy. (Moltzer, 1948, p. 2)

Devastation brought the need for relief and rebuilding. More interesting for social work history is that the need for extensive relief efforts were predicted and planned for long before hostilities ceased. Although it will be discussed more fully in the next chapter, social work involvement in the United Nations Relief and Rehabilitation Administration (UNRRA) programs in Europe was a high point of international social work activity. In November 1943, UNRRA was established by 44 nations, promising to organize relief and rehabilitation for the nations invaded by the Axis powers as soon as liberation occurred (Kollwitz, 1943). As soon as countries were liberated, relief efforts began. Efforts focused on the restoration of public services—water, sanitation, electricity, transportation—and reconstitution of health and social services. In many places, food relief was needed. It was an enormous undertaking. During its several years of operation, UNRRA was the largest exporter in the world and at its peak had a staff of 25,000 (Friedlander, 1975). The welfare division was set up in 1946. The emphasis was on aid to displaced persons, especially in Germany, Austria, Italy, Greece, North Africa, and, later, China. In Europe alone, 21 million persons had had to flee their countries or had been taken to Germany as prisoners or slave laborers. Special services were also developed to serve orphans and other needy children.

"For social work and social welfare, the restoration period following World War II can be described as a rich cornucopia filled with international programs, projects and opportunities" (Kendall, 1978, p. 178). A number of American social workers became involved in the relief and rehabilitation efforts of UNRRA in Europe and China. This was the first systematic program to send social welfare experts abroad to assist other countries in developing social legislation and social service programs. Training of indigenous social work personnel was a component of these efforts. The active consultation and training programs begun under UNRRA would continue for several decades under the auspices of the newly formed UN. Social workers also continued international work through the programs for children, refugees, and health care that were transferred to UN agencies such as the World Health Organization (WHO) and UNICEF (the UN Children's Fund).

Expanding Social Work in Developing Countries

Building on the UNRRA programs in social work education that sent educational consultants to devastated countries and provided funding for scholars to study in the United States and elsewhere, the UN soon became the largest contributor to the spread of professional social work throughout the world, taking responsibility for starting schools of social work in a number of developing countries (Younghusband, 1963). While the UN was only in its infancy, the then-temporary Social Commission of the Economic and Social Council (ECOSOC) encouraged attention to the training of social workers and to provision of technical assistance in social welfare. A series of studies and publications were initiated under the title "Technical Assistance for Social Progress" (vander Straeten, 1992). One of these, *Training for Social Work: An International Survey* by Katherine Kendall, was issued in 1950, the first of five comprehensive studies in the field. Then, in 1959, the ECOSOC of the UN

asked the secretary-general to do "everything possible to obtain the participation of social workers in the preparation and application of programs for
underdeveloped countries" (Garigue, 1961, p. 21).

The 1950s and 1960s were periods of independence movements throughout Africa, the Caribbean, and those parts of Asia still under colonial rule.
Social welfare was identified as an important component of preparation for
self-governance, as it was clear that populations held out hope for better
standards of living under self-rule. In Jamaica, for example, Norman Manley,
one of the "fathers of Jamaican independence," was responsible for the creation of Jamaica Welfare Limited in 1937, an organization devoted to community development. Through the political movement that grew out of the
unrest of the 1930s, Manley secured an agreement for a tax on the export of
bananas to fund community development programs (Maxwell, 1993). Community development was astutely selected for its contributions to community
betterment while building an empowered populace crucial in moving independence forward. It became and remained a component of social work and
social work education in Jamaica at the University of the West Indies and at
the Social Welfare Training Centre.

In her discussion of Africa, Asamoah (1995) observed:

> Perhaps the most significant event in the 1960s for both social work practice and
> social work education in Africa was the first International Conference of Ministers
> Responsible for Social Welfare, held in 1968. . . . The 1968 Conference of Ministers
> recommended that priority in developing countries be given to social welfare and
> that social welfare training prepare workers for carrying out developmental roles.
> (p. 225)

This conference, organized and held under the auspices of the UN, brought
together top government officials in social welfare from 89 countries and
observers from other nations and NGOs (United Nations, 1969). It is viewed
as a landmark event in global social welfare.

Many countries in the developing world received consultative assistance for establishing social work training. Others secured fellowships to
send faculty abroad for advanced training. In addition, grants through the
UN and other sources directly assisted in establishing social welfare programs and social work training. Uganda, for example, established its social
work program at Makerere University in Kampala with a UNICEF grant that
financed the school through its first 4 years (Rao, 1984).

Era of Indigenization: The 1970s

The intense period of consultation, transplantation, and borrowing that occurred during the 1950s and 1960s was followed by a reaction characterized
by rejection of Western models and a search for an indigenous form of social
work. As proclaimed at the 1972 world meeting of social workers: "We have
entered the era of 'indigenization'—of indigenous development based on the

SYBIL FRANCIS: A MODERN PIONEER OF JAMAICA

Photo from personal collection of Sybil Francis

Sybil Francis is widely regarded as a central figure in the establishment of social work services and training in Jamaica and the Caribbean region. Born in 1914, her special talents were noticed early; she placed second in Jamaica in her High School Senior Cambridge examination. After several years of work experience in Jamaica, her talents were recognized and she was given a scholarship by the Colonial Development and Welfare Organization to study at the London School of Economics in 1943. Her schooling there actually took place in Cambridge, as the London school was evacuated to Cambridge due to the bombings during the war (Johansen, 1999).

Francis began her work at the YWCA of Jamaica. Next, she worked as a secretary in the Land Department with a land settlement program for small farmers. When a social welfare section was formed, she was appointed to the position and began organizing women's groups, community organizations, and a settlers' association. All this was before Jamaican independence, but signs of change were apparent. She remembers sitting up in the mountains talking with farmers, speculating with them about what it would mean to live in an independent country. She also served as assistant secretary in the Social Welfare Ministry, working as liaison with the nongovernmental organization (NGO) sector and as administrator of the Child Care Division.

It is for her long career with the Social Welfare Training Centre at the University of the West Indies, which she headed from 1962 to 1989, that Sybil Francis is particularly well known. The core activity of the Training Centre was, and still is, to provide short-term training to social welfare personnel from the many countries in the Caribbean area. So thoroughly has the Centre done this that Francis once told a government minister that she could close down all the social services in the Caribbean by calling a strike of the graduates of her 4-month certificate course.

(continued)

A particularly remarkable feature of Francis's work at the Social Welfare Training Centre, however, is the number of other social service programs that were developed through her efforts and that continue today. These include the Child Development Centre, which grew out of UNICEF-sponsored efforts and now includes a day care center with research and education on the young child; WAND, the Women and Development program (now centered in Barbados), an organization doing research, publication, community development, and training on women and development; and a family planning project, initially taken on by Sybil under IASSW auspices and eventually transferred to Social and Preventive Medicine.

Now retired, Sybil Francis is tackling the topic of aging and is chair of the Jamaica National Council on Aging. She was a member of the Jamaican delegation to the World Assembly on Aging, representing her country on the main committee.

A side journey took her to the UN as part of newly independent Jamaica's delegation in 1963. Here, she became a member of the Third Committee at the time work was being done on the Declaration on the Elimination of All Forms of Racial Discrimination. A particularly proud aspect of her service was that Jamaica proposed that 1968 be designated as International Human Rights Year.

She remains optimistic about social work and the potential for its contributions. Although dedicated to Jamaica and the Caribbean, she has also been a true internationalist. Francis served as vice president of the International Association of Schools of Social Work and was a member of the board of directors of the International Council on Social Welfare. A special feature of the 4-month training course at the Social Welfare Training Centre was the required cross-cultural field experience. A short-term project was completed in Jamaica by students from the other islands while Jamaican students were sent to Puerto Rico to do their projects. In this way, she shared her beliefs in international exchange with her students; she believes that each gained enormous insight about their own country through working in another.

Based partly on personal communication with Sybil Francis, April 24, 1997.

needs and resources and the cultural, political and economic landscape of each society—and the schools of social work are taking the lead, as they must, in carving out such new directions" (Stein, 1972, p. 161).

Latin America began the indigenization trend. As described by an Argentine educator, the 1960s were perhaps the "most creative phase" as social work attempted to "grow from our own social reality" (R. Teubal, personal communication, March 13, 1997). According to Sela Sierra, "during the reconceptualization period, Latin America stopped searching for answers from Europe and the United States of America and engaged itself in the discovery of its own authentic potential to become a free continent" (cited in Queiro-Tajalli, 1995, p. 97). Strong anti-American feelings developed along with a rejection of the process of borrowing and using models from the industrialized countries. Social work became more political, more radical, and more focused on political consciousness. All social action was seen as having a political dimension. Whether the practitioner is conscious of it or not, the social worker is always siding with someone. The new message was that either you are on the side of the poor or you are not. Called the *reconceptualization movement*, it developed in two streams: the radical, which rejected capitalism, and the moderate, which moved away from the three accepted U.S. social work methods of casework, groupwork, and community organization toward a holistic perspective. In both streams, social work took on a more macro and more historical perspective (R. Teubal, personal communication, March 13, 1997). The ideas of Paulo Freire, a Brazilian educator exiled to Chile, helped Latin American social work develop a new emphasis on participation, organization, and consciousness-raising as methodologies (Jimenez & Aylwin, 1992). Liberation theology—the reinterpretation of Christianity through the eyes and experiences of the poor—as developed by Latin American Catholics also influenced social work.

As social work developed, radicalization was often more a topic of discussion than an action agenda. It may have been the reestablishment of the dictatorship in Argentina or the coup in Chile in 1973 that overthrew elected President Allende and ushered in the repressive Pinochet era that curtailed the move to active radicalism. All freedom of speech was suppressed and numerous social workers and social work students were persecuted, imprisoned, tortured, and "disappeared" by these regimes.

The Vietnam War intensified anti-Americanism around the world and brought new discussion of the dangers of imperialism. An intellectual campaign, waged in professional journals and at conference presentations, condemned the impact of the borrowing of American and British models of social work in Africa, Asia, and Latin America as irrelevant at best, damaging at worst. In some countries, the result was little more than protest, while in others, indigenization efforts yielded production of useful local case studies and teaching materials and the first development of culturally specific theories. In still other countries, there was more violent reaction against Western influences. As described in the brief biography of Sattareh Farman Farmaian, the Islamic Revolution in Iran resulted in the violent takeover of the school of social work. While attention to indigenization continues, it has been joined by more mutual efforts to cope with interdependence and by a new wave of borrowing set off by the dissolution of the communist bloc.

The Fall of the Eastern Bloc and the End of the Cold War

The gradual thaw and then the dramatic end of Soviet domination in Eastern Europe set in motion an avalanche of new opportunities to establish social work services and educational programs in Eastern Europe and the former republics of the Soviet Union. As noted above, except in Poland and Yugoslavia, social work had officially been nonexistent in all countries of the Eastern bloc since World War II.

Social work in some form did exist in the USSR in the 1920s; indeed, representatives of the Soviet Union participated in the First International Conference of Social Work in Paris in 1928 where they were outspoken against the individual charity approach and against religious influences on the profession. In the 1930s, however, social work was "condemned as a bourgeois artifact and eliminated" (Guzzetta, 1995, p. 197).

The end of the cold war brought a flood of consultants to Eastern Europe. As Guzzetta (1995) observed:

> For vacationers and "consultants" from the West, the Central and Eastern European countries were a dream come true. Prices were unbelievably low and outsiders were treated as honored guests, every utterance receiving attention and belief totally beyond the experience of academics in their home institutions. Once the borders were opened and the word was out, the stampede was on. (p. 200)

While much of the consultation has been useful, other advice has been given uncritically and without understanding of the context. It is likely that another era of indigenization will emerge for the countries of the East.

A more gradual but still substantial opening up in China has occurred. Following the communist takeover in 1949, all social sciences were banned from Chinese universities by 1952, labeled bourgeois/capitalist subjects. For almost 30 years, there was no contact between China and world, relating to social work. Following the reestablishment of social sciences in Chinese universities in the early 1980s, explorations of social work began. By 1988, four universities had been given approval by the state to develop social work courses, and books and journals began using the term *social work* (Leung, 1995). The University of Hong Kong engaged in a 3-year cooperative project with Zhongshan University in China, involving teaching and fieldwork development. Chinese scholars were permitted to attend international social work meetings, and in 1988, China hosted the Conference on Social Work Education in the Asia and Pacific Region (Leung, 1995). Although the situation in China remains more controlled than in Eastern Europe, developments have been rapid since the mid-1980s and there are now many social work programs.

The other major event of the 1990s was European unification. Its impact on social work has been considerable, especially on issues of personnel mobility and comparability of standards. As political and economic forces have brought about successively stronger agreements for a united Europe, a degree of professional integration is becoming necessary. Provisions now exist for the right to work in any member country, requiring mutual recognition of professional qualifications. "The European issue is now less the celebration of

SATTAREH FARMAN FARMAIAN:
FOUNDER OF SOCIAL WORK IN IRAN

Photo by L Healy

When Sattareh Farman Farmaian returned to her native Iran to begin the first school of social work there, there wasn't even a word for social worker in the Persian language. Therefore, she invented one: *madadkar*, one who helps. She describes the tasks facing this new profession: "Social work in Iran would not be a desk job. It was going to be hard and dirty, practiced in discouraging circumstances amid conditions of the utmost wretchedness in a slum, a village or a public institution for the poor" (Farman Farmaian, 1993).

The personal story of this modern social work pioneer parallels the modern history of her country. She was born into the family of a prince of the Qajar family, the 15th of her father's 36 children. During her childhood, the family lived well in their compound in Tehran, but with uncertainty, as the new ruler, Reza Shah Pahlavi, was confiscating property of the Qajars and had briefly imprisoned Farman Farmaian's father after the fall of the Qajar dynasty. In her autobiography, she describes life in the harem and her close relationships with her mother, several of her father's other wives, and with many siblings and half-siblings (Farman Farmaian, 1992).

Her father, contrary to Muslim tradition, insisted that his daughters be educated as well as his sons. Sattareh was an enthusiastic student; during World War II, she left her sheltered home and traveled to the United States, where she became a student at the University of Southern California (USC) in 1944. She earned a BA and MSW from USC and began her career in social work.

For 4 years she worked with the UN in the Middle East, primarily as a social welfare consultant to the government of Iraq for the UN Educational, Scientific and Cultural Organization (UNESCO). She describes her experiences, first among the Bedouin and later in Iraq: "I had performed welfare work, training and research among the reed-hut slums of Baghdad, the mud dwellings of the Nile farmers, and in the dreadful Palestinian refugee camps in Lebanon" (Farman Farmaian, with Munker, 1992, p. 206).

(continued)

Then, in 1958, she returned to Iran, determined to put her knowledge and experience to work for her own country. With the backing of the Shah's government, she opened a 2-year professional school of social work in Tehran and accepted her first class of 20 young Iranians for social work training later in 1958. The selection process was challenging. As she puts it, "a madadkar had to be a person whom I could teach to believe in something more than just himself and the future of his family and I could not afford to squander our meager resources on anyone uncommitted or opportunistic" (Farman Farmaian, 1993, p. 3). Her first task was to help the students—recruited from diverse social class, ethnic, and religious backgrounds, and sitting in a classroom with the opposite sex for the first time—accept each other.

The school became actively involved in social reform, tackling first the terrible conditions they discovered in an orphanage and a mental institution. Several years later, the School of Social Work established the Family Planning Association of Iran, introducing modern family planning into Iranian society. It took great skill in strategic accommodation and negotiation for this pioneer to further her agenda of family's and women's rights in a religious and very traditional society. The work, accomplished with help from an International Association of Schools of Social Work (IASSW) pilot project in family planning, was lauded in an IASSW report: "As a pioneer in the family planning movement in the country, it [the Tehran School of Social Work] has demonstrated to an unusual degree the effectiveness of social workers in promoting progressive policies, establishing effective programs, and providing needed service to a wide range of recipients" (Kendall, 1977, p. 20).

For 20 years, she devoted her efforts to furthering social work in Iran and to contributing to social work internationally. The Islamic Revolution in 1979 brought an end to her career in Iran and very nearly cost Farman Farmaian her life.

She arrived at work one morning to be told by one of the gardeners that students were waiting inside to kill her. Instead, they arrested her and delivered her to the headquarters of Ayatollah Khomeini. Among the charges leveled against her was that she had raised the living standard in Iran. By lifting many Iranians out of poverty, it was claimed that she had made them complacent and thereby delayed the overthrow of the Shah. Had the consequences not been so grave, it was a charge that would delight a social worker. After hours of waiting and of interrogation, she was released because another Ayatollah had interceded on her behalf. Warned to leave the country, she left Iran and went into exile in the United States.

common values, knowledge and skills than how to best implement the right of social workers to practice in other member states" (Harris, 1997, p. 429). Numerous programs have offered grants to bring European social workers and social work educators together in joint programs. Interest in "European social work" has grown in the member states.

CONCLUSION

For social work in the early years of its second century, challenges abound and new opportunities are evident. The promise of the end of the cold war has been diminished by continued conflict and regional wars, including a costly war in Iraq, creating new casualties, destruction, and displacement, and a renewed peace movement. Worldwide fascination with the market economy and the resulting consequences of increased unemployment and greater personal insecurity for many hamper progress toward elimination of poverty. Cutbacks in welfare state commitments and lingering effects of financial crises in developing countries have led to continued scarcity of resources for meeting human needs and, therefore, to the widening gap between rich and poor. Yet during this period, social work has expanded to almost every nation and has increased its involvement in human rights and other significant international movements. New challenges and renewed attention to older ones are involving social workers in the HIV/AIDS pandemic, human trafficking, and disaster response. Regional cooperation has increased, especially in Europe, creating new opportunities for cross-fertilization in the profession. Organized efforts at international action throughout the history of the profession will be discussed in more depth in the next chapter. Understanding the global history of the development of the profession and of its international involvement will assist in charting the course of social work for the future.

REFERENCES

"Alice Salomon exiled" (1937) *Social Service Review, XI* (3), 510–511.

Asamoah, Y. (1995). Africa. In T. D. Watts, D. Elliott, & N. S. Mayadas (Eds.), *International handbook on social work education* (pp. 223–239). Westport, CT: Greenwood Press.

Brown, G. (1991). The programme in the School of Continuing Studies. In J. Maxwell & E. Wint (Eds.), *Contemporary social work education: A Caribbean orientation. Summary Proceedings of Social Work Symposium held May 27–29, 1991* (pp. 21–26). Mona, Jamaica: University of the West Indies, Department of Sociology & Social Work.

Child welfare problems and Japanese evacuation. (1942). *Social Service Review, 16*(4), 673–676.

de Jongh, J. F. (1972). A retrospective view of social work education. In International Association of Schools of Social Work (IASSW), *New themes in social work education* [Proceedings] (pp. 22–36). XVIth International Congress of Schools of Social Work, The Hague, Netherlands, August 8–11, 1972. New York: IASSW.

Desai, A. (1987). Development of social work education. In *Encyclopedia of social work in India* (pp. 208–219). New Delhi: Government of India, Ministry of Welfare.

Farman Farmaian, S. (1993, February). *Social work in Iran.* Paper presented at the meeting of the Council on Social Work Education Annual Program, New York, NY.

Farman Farmaian, S., with Munker, D. (1992). *Daughter of Persia: A woman's journey from her father's harem through the Islamic revolution.* New York: Crown Publishers.

Friedlander, W. (1975). *International social welfare.* Englewood Cliffs, NJ: Prentice Hall.

Garigue, P. (1961). Challenge of cultural variations to social work. *Proceedings of the Ninth Annual Program Meeting* (pp. 9–22). New York: Council on Social Work Education.

Guzzetta, C. (1995). Central and Eastern Europe. In T. D. Watts, D. Elliott, & N. S. Mayadas (Eds.), *International handbook on social work education* (pp. 191–209). Westport, CT: Greenwood Press.

Harris, R. (1997). Internationalizing social work: Some themes and issues. In N. S. Mayadas, T. D. Watts, & D. Elliott (Eds.), *International handbook on social work theory and practice* (pp. 429–440). Westport, CT: Greenwood Press.

Hessle, S., & Zaviršek, D. (Eds.), (2005). *Sustainable development in social work—The case of a regional network in the Balkans.* Stockholm, Sweden: Stockholm University Department of Social Work.

Jimenez, M., & Aylwin, H. (1992). Social work in Chile: Support for the struggle for justice in Latin America. In M. C. Hokenstad, S. K. Khinduka, & J. Midgley (Eds.), *Profiles in international social work* (pp. 29–41). Washington, DC: NASW Press.

Johansen, M. (1999, June 26). Sybil Francis reminisces on life and career. *The Daily Observer*, pp. 15, 17.

Kendall, K. (1977). *Final report: International development of qualified social work manpower for population and family planning activities.* New York: IASSW.

Kendall, K. A. (1978). The IASSW from 1928–1978: A journey of remembrance. In K. Kendall (Ed.), *Reflections on social work education 1950–1978* (pp. 170–191). New York: IASSW.

Kendall, K. (1989). Women at the helm: Three extraordinary leaders. *Affilia, 4*(1), 23–32.

Kendall, K. A. (2000). *Social work education: Its origins in Europe.* Alexandria, VA: Council on Social Work Education.

Kollwitz, K. (1943). The United Nations relief and rehabilitation administration begins its work. *Social Service Review, 17*(4), 486–488.

Kudchodkar, L. S. (1963). Observations. *Indian Journal of Social Work, 24*(2), 96.

Leung, J. (1995). China. In T. D. Watts, D. Elliott, & N. S. Mayadas (Eds.), *International handbook on social work education* (pp. 403–419). Westport, CT: Greenwood Press.

Lewis, J. J. (1999). *Jeannette Rankin.* Accessed May 18, 2007, at http://womenshistory .about.com/library/bio/blbio-jeannette_rankin.htm?p-1

Lorenz, W. (1994). *Social work in a changing Europe.* London: Routledge.

Manshardt, C. (1941). Education for social work. *Indian Journal of Social Work, II*(1), 12–22.

Manshardt, C. (1967). *Pioneering on social frontiers in India.* Bombay, India: Lalvani Publishing House for the Tata Institute of Social Sciences.

Maxwell, J. A. (1993, June). *Caribbean social work: Its historical development and current challenges.* Paper presented at the Caribbean Regional Social Work Conference, St. Michaels, Barbados.

Mazibuko, F., McKendrick, B., & Patel, L. (1992). Social work in South Africa: Coping with apartheid and change. In M. C. Hokenstad, S. K. Khinduka, & J. Midgley (Eds.), *Profiles in international social work.* Washington, DC: NASW Press.

Moltzer, M. J. A. (1948, March 12). *Correspondence to members of the International Committee, Bloemendael, Holland.* IASSW Archive, Social Welfare History Archives, University of Minnesota, Minneapolis, MN.

Moltzer, M. J. A. (1950, July). *Secretary's report.* International Committee of Schools of Social Work. IASSW Archive, Social Welfare History Archives, University of Minnesota, Minneapolis, MN.

Nitzsche, E. (1935). *Letter to Alice Salomon.* IASSW Archives, Social Welfare History Archives, University of Minnesota, Minneapolis, MN.

Ntusi, T. (1995). South Africa. In T. D. Watts, D. Elliott, & N. S. Mayadas (Eds.), *International handbook on social work education* (pp. 261–279). Westport, CT: Greenwood Press.

Popple, P. R. (1995). Social work profession: History. In R. Edwards (Ed.), *Encyclopedia of social work* (19th ed., pp. 2282–2292). Washington, DC: NASW Press.

Queiro-Tajalli, I. (1995). Argentina. In T. D. Watts, D. Elliott, & N. S. Mayadas (Eds.), *International handbook on social work education* (pp. 87–102). Westport, CT: Greenwood Press.

Radlinska, H. O. (1929). Training for social work in Poland. In *International Conference of Social Work* [Proceedings] (Vol. II, pp. 85–93). First Conference, Paris, July 8–13, 1928.

Ragab, I. A. (1995). Middle East and Egypt. In T. D. Watts, D. Elliott, & N. S. Mayadas (Eds.), *International handbook on social work education* (pp. 281–304). Westport, CT: Greenwood Press.

Rao, V. (Comp.) (1984). *World guide to social work education* (2nd ed.) New York: Council on Social Work Education for the International Association of Schools of Social Work.

Richmond, M. (1917). *Social diagnosis.* New York: Russell Sage Foundation.

Salomon, A. (n.d.), *Character is destiny.* Unpublished manuscript. (Available at the Leo Baeck-Institute, New York).

Stein, H. D. (1972). Cross-national themes in social work education: A commentary on the sixteenth IASSW Congress. In IASSW, *New Themes in Social Work Education* (pp. 155–164). New York: IASSW.

United Nations. (1958). *Training for social work: Third international survey.* New York: Author.

United Nations. (1969). *Proceedings of the International Conference of Ministers Responsible for Social Welfare.* New York: Author.

Urbaniak, M. (2007, January 14). Polish righteous gentile nominated for Nobel Peace Prize. *European Jewish Press.* Accessed May 18, 2007, at www.ejpress.org/article/news/western_europe/12906

vander Straeten, S. (1992). *Oral history interview of Katherine Kendall.* Unpublished transcription of the interviews.

Van Wormer, K. (1997). *Social welfare: A world view.* Chicago: Nelson-Hall.

Walton, R. G., & El Nasr, M. (1988). The indigenization and authentization of social work in Egypt. *Community Development Journal, 23*(3), 148–155.

Wieler, J. (1988). Alice Salomon. *Journal of Teaching in Social Work, 2*(2), 165–171.

Wieler, J. (1989). The impact of Alice Salomon on social work education. In *60 Jahre IASSW* (pp. 15–26). Berlin, Germany: Fachhochschule fur Sozialarbeit und Sozialpadagogik.

Wieler, J. (2006). The long path to Irena Sendler—Mother of the Holocaust children. *Social Work & Society, 4*(1) .

Yelaja, S. A. (1969). Schools of social work in India: Historical development 1936–1966. *Indian Journal of Social Work, 29*(4), 361–378.

Younghusband, E. (1963). Tasks and trends in education for social work: An international appraisal. *Social Work* (London), *20*(3), 4–11.

CHAPTER 7

INTERNATIONAL PROFESSIONAL ACTION
A Selective History

In this chapter, the discussion of history continues with a focus on episodes of international professional action by social workers and with in-depth discussions of the brief notes that follow:

- more than 2,000 members of a new profession gather in Paris in 1928 to participate in the First International Conference of Social Work
- a social worker with the UN Relief and Rehabilitation Administration (UNRRA) meets with Mao Tse-tung and Chou En-lai to negotiate for delivery of postwar relief supplies in civil war–torn China in 1946
- the UN sponsors five major world surveys of social work education between 1950 and 1971
- a social worker advises the U.S. embassy in Brazil on important social conditions in 1963
- social work educators in Iran, Jamaica, the Philippines, and 17 other countries participate in an International Association of Schools of Social Work (IASSW) international project to develop curriculum on family planning in the 1970s
- in 1993, members of the International Council on Social Welfare (ICSW) Executive Committee approve an ambitious plan for involvement in the UN Summit for Social Development
- members of the International Federation of Social Workers meet in New York for an evening of letter-writing to Saddam Hussein, asking for the release of a Kuwaiti social worker
- in 2004, social work delegates at the general meetings of the IASSW and the International Federation of Social Workers in Adelaide, Australia, approve global standards for social work education.

As the chapter title indicates, this will be a selective history, and one that will not follow a neat chronological order. The intent is to communicate some of the more interesting examples of social workers in action on the international scene and to discuss areas in which impact was considerable. After introductory remarks about social work involvement in social movements at the turn of the last century, the chapter begins with a discussion of the first effort to hold a worldwide social work conference, the 1928 First International Conference of Social Work. This meeting spawned the three major international social work organizations, now known as: the International Association of Schools of Social Work (IASSW), the International Federation of Social Workers (IFSW), and the International Council on Social Welfare (ICSW). Each organization will be discussed and a brief synopsis of their purposes and major activities will be given. One aspect of each organization's past or present work will be highlighted to illustrate how social work organizations have been differentially involved in international action, often having significant impact on social conditions. Selected for examination are (a) the family-planning project conducted by IASSW in the 1970s, (b) the human rights work of the IFSW, and (c) ICSW's use of its consultative status with the UN to influence the Social Development Summit in the 1990s.

Three additional examples of particular importance to the history of international social work will also be presented. In UNRRA, social workers held a range of direct service, administrative, and planning positions in direct relief work in postwar Europe and China. The lessons of this experience suggest that social work skills can be successfully applied to relief and development work. In the early decades of the UN, social workers were involved as employees, trainers, consultants, and sponsored trainees in activities that spread social work education throughout much of the developing world. As "insiders," they had important opportunities to influence program directions at the UN. Finally, as an interesting example of policy influence, the experiences of the social welfare attachés in the U.S. State Department will be described. It demonstrates the potential value of social work in foreign policy.

Although the reader is reminded that this is far from a comprehensive history of social work's international involvement, the examples selected communicate a rich history of professional effort and impact. These will be further illustrated through several brief biographies of pioneers in international action.

ANTECEDENTS: ACTIVISM IN THE SOCIAL MOVEMENTS OF THE EARLY TWENTIETH CENTURY

The seeds of international professional action were sown by social work participation in the important international issues of the early twentieth century. Women's issues, world peace, and labor conditions were dominant

TIMELINE: HISTORY OF INTERNATIONAL PROFESSIONAL ACTION	
1915	Social workers involved in Women's Peace Conference, The Hague
1919	Save the Children founded
1923	Jebb drafts Children's Charter
1924	Charter adopted by the League of Nations as Declaration on the Rights of the Child
1928	Social Welfare Fortnight held in Paris, including First International Conference of Social Work
1928–29	Founding of predecessors of ICSW, IASSW, IFSW
1932	Second International Conference of Social Work—Frankfurt
1936	Third International Conference of Social Work—London
1944–47	UNRRA conducts relief programs in Europe and China
1945	UN established
1946	Consultative status system for nongovernmental organizations (NGOs) at UN established
1948	Fourth International Conference of Social Work—Atlantic City
1950	First UN survey of social work education
1955	Second UN survey of social work education
1958	Third UN survey of social work education
1963	Social welfare attachés appointed to U.S. embassies in Brazil and India
1965	Fourth UN survey of social work education
1971	IASSW family planning project begins
1971	Fifth UN survey of social work education
1976	IFSW Code of Ethics adopted
1970s	Inter-University Consortium for International Social Development (IUCISD) founded
1988	IFSW forms Human Rights Commission
1988	IFSW publishes policy papers
1994	IFSW/IASSW UN Manual on Human Rights published
1994	IFSW adopts *Revised Declaration of Ethical Principles*
1995	UN World Summit for Social Development held in Copenhagen
2000	IFSW and IASSW adopt new Global Definition of Social Work
2004	IFSW and IASSW adopt new ethics document and *Global Standards for Social Work Education and Training*

social concerns at the international level, and members of the new profession of social work were active in each of the related social movements. Through these movements, leaders in the social fields from different countries had opportunities to meet and exchange ideas while working for improved conditions for women and for workers. As noted in Chapter 6, among the

Figure 7.1 Women's Peace Congress at The Hague, 1915.
Sophia Smith Collection, Smith College, photographer unknown. Used with permission.

social work pioneers who were also leaders in international women's organizations and international pacifism were Jane Addams and Alice Salomon. The two met at the 1909 International Congress of the International Council of Women in Canada (Lorenz, 1994) and were, with others, founders of the Women's International League for Peace and Freedom. Addams was a leader of the Women's Peace Conference at The Hague in 1915 and continued her involvement in pacifism in spite of heavy criticism. Social workers were also concerned about conditions for children. Eglantyne Jebb led efforts for improving children's lives, through the Save the Children Fund, and initiated the first international policy on children's rights, a declaration adopted by the League of Nations in 1924.

It may have been from a natural outgrowth of these involvements that social work formed its own world organizations. There are indications that these social workers were in communication and visited with each other to examine developments in other countries. Seeking additional mechanisms for professional exchange and communication led to the call for a world conference and then for formal organizations. Within 30 years of the founding of professional social work, an international conference was held and the major international social work organizations were founded. Although earlier conferences provided opportunities for international exchange (e.g., the European International Conference on Charity and Welfare, founded in 1856, and the meeting on charities held in 1893 in conjunction with the Chicago World's Fair), the 1928 conference is seen as a watershed in the organization of international social work.

SOCIAL WORK TAKES THE WORLD STAGE: INTERNATIONAL ORGANIZATIONS

The idea for organizing an international conference of social work was suggested by European and Japanese social workers who were invited to attend the National Conference of Social Work held in the United States in 1919 and in 1923. An official proposal was made by Dr. René Sand of Belgium in a January 15, 1923, letter to Julia Lathrop; Dr. Sand was invited to attend the 1923 conference in Washington to explain his idea further. The conference approved the idea in principle and the endorsement by the American Association of Social Workers soon followed. Support was secured from the League of Red Cross Societies in 1925. In September 1926, an organizing committee met in Paris with representatives from 17 countries from Europe, the Far East, and North America and from the League of Nations, the International Labour Organization (ILO), the League of Red Cross Societies, the International Congress on Statutory and Voluntary Assistance, the International Migration Service, the Save the Children Fund International Union, and others. Funding was secured from various foundations, including Rockefeller and Russell Sage. Dr. Alice Masarykova of Prague led the conference and Dr. René Sand was secretary general.

PIONEERS IN INTERNATIONAL ACTION: EGLANTYNE JEBB

Save the Children

Although she died at the relatively young age of 52, Eglantyne Jebb contributed extensively to international social action; she founded a major international NGO and drafted a document on children's rights that became the foundation for the 1989 Convention on the Rights of the Child. Jebb was born in 1876 in Shropshire, England, into a prosperous family. She was educated at Oxford and then took training as a teacher. However, she taught only briefly, soon becoming involved in social work with the Charity Organization Society (COS). In 1906, she conducted a study of poverty in Cambridge, "Cambridge: A Study in Social Questions," that is still recognized as sound and insightful research. Her career directions changed in 1913, when she went to Macedonia to do relief work after the Balkan Wars. It was during this visit that she found her life's work—emergency and development help to children in need—after seeing the appalling conditions of refugees displaced by the war.

Two accomplishments stand out among the many that can be attributed to Jebb. The first is the founding of the Save the Children Fund. News of the suffering caused by the Allied blockade in Europe at the end of World War I began to reach England. With her sister Dorothy, Eglantyne began to raise money to provide direct help to children in war-devastated Europe and called the effort the Save the Children Fund. Many thought it treasonous to assist enemy children. One of Jebb's supporters was well-known playwright George Bernard Shaw, who responded to criticism of his support of the enemy by saying, "I have no enemies under seven" (Graham, 1978). Jebb was a masterful fundraiser. One story tells of her arrest and conviction for publishing photographs of suffering children in Austria without proper permission from the censor still in place after the war. She was fined after vigorous prosecution but managed to talk the prosecutor into giving a donation to the Save the Children Fund (Graham, 1978). She foresaw the phenomenon of "compassion fatigue" when she said "we have to devise means of making known the facts in such a way as

(continued)

to touch the imagination of the world. The world is not ungenerous, but unimaginative and very busy."

The Save the Children Fund became an international alliance that continues to this day. Jebb's ideas about aid, relief, and development were truly visionary; she advocated policies that are seen as the hallmarks of forward-looking development assistance for the twenty-first century. Two of the principles of the Fund was that aid should be based on need and that children should not suffer due to wars they had no part in. Jebb also believed that aid should be self-sustaining, be given in such a way as to stimulate self-help, and based on planning and research. She was concerned about mutuality, saying that: "The system of world organization . . . was not based on the principle of dividing up the countries into those which gave and those which received but on the policy of requiring the recognition of dual duty from all countries."

Jebb's other major accomplishment was the drafting of the "Declaration on the Rights of the Child" in 1923. It was adopted by the League of Nations and became the first in a series of global documents on children's rights, leading to the 1989 Convention on the Rights of the Child.

Jebb participated in international social work events and wrote about the nature of social work and globalism. The following quote exemplified her thinking: "Every social worker ought to be a scientist, and social workers all over the globe should feel that they are all members of one body engaged in laying the foundation of the civilisation of the future, working shoulder to shoulder and drawing upon a fund of common knowledge."

She suffered from chronic poor health and apparently from periodic depression. At times, her life seemed somewhat aimless, and she spent periods traveling with her mother. But during the last 9 years of her life, when her health was quite fragile, she pursued her mission to help children of the world vigorously. As noted above, it was during this 9-year period that she made her mark on social work, international development, and children's rights.

Her concerns for children were truly global. Prior to her death, she had intended to organize a conference on the needs of children in Africa and was studying Chinese to help with another project in the planning stages to develop alternatives to child labor in China. The conference she planned on Africa was held in 1931. Jebb intended to participate in the 1928 International Conference on Social Work in Paris but poor health prevented her from attending. However, the paper she prepared was read; in it she defined the essentials of international social work (Jebb, 1929). She died shortly after the conference in 1928.

In addition to the references noted, the biographical sketch of Jebb was prepared using documents from the archives of the International Save the Children Federation, including Save the Children, 1994, Information Sheet 15; Quotes from Eglantyne Jebb; 34 Facts About Eglantyne Jebb, and Save the Children Facts.

Following several subsequent planning meetings in Paris and Prague, more and more social organizations asked to hold their conferences at the same time. Thus the planned event grew to become the International Social Welfare Fortnight and included not only the first international social work conference but also meetings of the International Child Welfare Congress, the International Congress on Voluntary and Statutory Assistance, and the International Housing and Town Planning Congress. Funds for the Fortnight came from foundations in the United States, from the Czech and Japanese Red Cross Societies, and from national committees in Germany, Poland, and Spain.

The event itself was well attended. The International Conference of Social Work was held from July 8 to 13, 1928, in Paris, and drew 2,481 delegates from 42 countries, including 279 from the United States (Organization of the International Conference of Social Work, 1929, p. 14). One section of the conference was devoted to social work education.

The 1928 Fortnight initiated what would become regular world meetings on social work and social welfare. The second conference was held in Frankfurt in 1932 in the midst of a worldwide depression. Discussions focused, not surprisingly, on the impact of unemployment on the family. The third conference in 1936 in London was also shaped by economic depression and unemployment, although the official theme was "Social Work and the Community" and featured discussion of the "new concept of community organization" (Katzki, 1988, p. 13). Ominous forewarnings were felt as representatives of the Nazi regime in Germany attended the conference and presented on the virtues of Nazi philosophy. Indeed, the war that followed interrupted all international activities and meetings until 1946, when remnants of social work and social welfare leadership came together in Paris to plan for the future. Conferences resumed in 1948, with the fourth conference in Atlantic City, New Jersey. The social work and social welfare professional organizations have held biennial conferences since 1948, continuing the important activities of knowledge sharing and professional networking across nations. In the two decades following the Atlantic City conference, milestones were the holding of world conferences in India (1952), Brazil (1962), and Kenya (1974); these events signified the expansion of social work organizations beyond Europe and North America to worldwide bodies.

The three major international social work organizations—IASSW, IFSW, and ICSW—developed out of the 1928 conference and remain active today. They share some purposes in common and collaborate on a number of activities. All have an interest in promoting human rights and social development and further these goals through representation on United Nations NGO committees and commissions. IFSW and IASSW jointly sponsor an annual Social Work Day at the United Nations in New York. Each organization holds a biennial conference; throughout the past few decades these have sometimes been joint or co-located conferences and at other times held separately. The organizations have agreed to hold a single large conference beginning in 2010. The three organizations co-sponsor *International Social Work*, a journal

INTERNATIONAL SOCIAL WORK ORGANIZATIONS

International Association of Schools of Social Work
Acronym: IASSW
Founded in: 1928
Previous name: International Committee of Schools of Social Work
Members: Social work educational programs at the tertiary level throughout the world. Individual memberships also available
Purpose: To promote and develop quality education, training, and knowledge for social work practice worldwide, to encourage exchange among educators and to represent social work education globally

International Federation of Social Workers
Acronym: IFSW
Founded in: 1928 (predecessor organization); reassembled in 1956
Previous name: International Permanent Secretariat of Social Workers
Members: National professional associations make up the membership; individuals may join as Friends of IFSW
Purpose: To promote social work as a profession; to support national associations; to encourage and facilitate contacts between social workers of all countries; to represent the profession on the international level

International Council on Social Welfare
Acronym: ICSW
Founded in: 1928
Previous name: International Conference on Social Work
Members: National committees, other national associations, and specialized international organizations; individual memberships in national committees
Purpose: An interdisciplinary organization to promote social development and social welfare; to serve as a forum for exchange of knowledge in these areas; to maintain active liaison with the UN on social development matters

International Consortium for Social Development
Acronym: ICSD
Founded: In the late 1970s; inaugural symposium held in 1980
Previous name: Inter-University Consortium for International Social Development
Members: Institutional members (mostly educational institutions) and individual members
Purpose: An interdisciplinary organization founded by social work educators to promote social development, ICSD brings scholars, practitioners, and students from the human services together to advance social development through teaching, practicing, researching, and networking

initiated by IASSW and ICSW in 1958 and joined by IFSW in 1959. Each will be discussed in the next section.

International Association of Schools of Social Work

Although Dr. René Sand was the prime mover behind the first conference, he asked Alice Salomon of Germany to lead a section on social work education. It was during this meeting that Dr. Moltzer of the Netherlands recommended that a committee be formed "to write to all the training schools of social work asking them whether they would be prepared to become members of an International Association of Schools," thus giving birth to the IASSW ("Fifth Question," 1929, pp. 233–234). Joining Salomon as founders of the International Committee of Schools of Social Work were Dr. M. J. A. Moltzer, the Netherlands; Mme Mulle, Belgium; and Mme Wagner-Beck and Mlle M. de Meyenburg, Switzerland. Miss Sophonisba Breckinridge and Mr. Porter Lee of the United States, Miss Elisabeth Macadam and Miss Elinor Black of England, Mme Edouard Fuster of France, and Professor Helena Radlinska of Poland were soon brought into the leadership group (Kendall, 1978). The letter of invitation to join a new organization of schools of social work that Dr. Salomon sent to the 111 identified schools of social work resulted in 46 founding member schools from 10 countries. By 1939, the number had grown to 75 member schools from 18 countries, including 29 schools from the American Association of Schools of Social Work (Kendall, 1978). By then, however, all German schools had dropped their membership in protest against the leadership of Dr. Salomon, a German of Jewish background.

The association (then named the International Committee of Schools of Social Work) immediately began to reach out to intergovernmental organizations. A working relationship was developed with the Commission on Social Questions of the League of Nations. The International Labour Office (Geneva) set up a Centre of Documentation for schools of social work to pull together statistics, research reports, and reports of seminars from schools of social work. Thus the setting up of working relationships with international intergovernmental bodies was identified very early as a strategy for international social work action.

Another early and continuing strategy for action, as noted above, is the holding of international conferences and seminars to facilitate interchange of information and ideas and the building of relationships across borders. This type of exchange is particularly important to an association of educators, which are seen as responsible for building knowledge and for research in the field. Exchange of information also contributes indirectly, if not directly, to the development of implicit general standards for social work education. In addition to the periodic world conferences, in the early years, international summer schools were held by the committee in Europe, focusing on various areas of social service (e.g., protection of minors, housing, and care and education of persons with disabilities) (Kendall, 1978).

World War II had a devastating, but temporary, impact on IASSW. Kendall (1987) notes that "the European network was shattered by World War II," (p. 992), leading to leadership changes in the organization. The founding president, Dr. Salomon, had been driven into exile and was not able to revive the board from her exile in the United States. She died in 1948, the year the IASSW met in Atlantic City in its first real postwar meeting. René Sand, still active after more than 30 years, became president until his death in 1953. The association began to mature into a world organization as it expanded its leadership group beyond Europe and added to the board members from Australia, Guatemala, Japan, and India in 1956. IASSW set up an independent secretariat in 1971, led by the first paid secretary general, Katherine Kendall.

The formation of a secretariat made it possible for the organization to take on expanded functions. A program initiative launched in the 1970s—a population and family planning curriculum project—demonstrates how social work education can contribute to international social change and development.

Family Planning in the IASSW: Program Development to Reshape Services. The IASSW population and family planning project provides an example of social work action through direct program development and implementation. Beginning in 1971, IASSW initiated a 5-year contract (extended to a 6th year) with the U.S. Agency for International Development (USAID) to develop qualified personnel for population and family planning work in developing countries. (The following section is summarized from the final project report; see Kendall, 1977.) The need for the program was defined at the International Conference on Social Work Education, Population and Family Planning held in 1970 and was twofold. First, population control and family planning were growing in importance as part of development programs; however, the approach of population experts was on meeting quantitative targets, with little attention to the human and cultural dimensions. Second, although social workers were strategically positioned to play important roles in family planning, there was little in social work education at the time to prepare them for these roles. The project goals were to define family planning in the context of social development and to prepare social workers for effective professional practice in family planning as part of their professional roles.

During the project, activities were carried out in 31 schools of social work in 13 developing countries, with less involvement in 7 other countries. In each of the project schools, population and family planning were formally added to the curriculum. Seminars and workshops (more than 100 over the life of the grant) were held to train faculty members to teach family planning, IASSW resource teams provided short-term consultation on curriculum development, and reference and teaching materials were provided to each school. The main activity was teaching social work students to use family planning information in their social work practice. Continuing education programs were developed for graduates and for related personnel. The project also resulted in interorganizational work at the IASSW level and for the participating schools of social work, bringing social work into closer contact with governmental agencies and NGOs in population and development work. An important outcome was that social work defined its own approach to family planning: "Social workers hold the promotion of human welfare as a major goal of the profession; thus, they are concerned with family planning as a human right, as an essential element in family health and welfare, and as a significant aspect of social development. This means that the project has been just as much concerned with placing family planning into the full range of social welfare services as in placing social workers into family planning clinics" (Kendall, 1977, p. 3).

An impressive feature of the project was its geographic reach. Pilot schools were located in Turkey, Iran, Korea, the Philippines, Thailand, Indonesia, Jamaica, Sri Lanka, Bangladesh, Vietnam, Pakistan, Ecuador, Hong Kong, Sudan, Zambia, Ghana, Egypt, and Kenya. Project leadership was also diverse. Secretary general Kendall served as project director and was aided by a team that included Angelina Almanzor from the Philippines, E. Maxine Ankrah from Uganda, Barry Rigby, George Walmsley, Jacqueline Atkins, and Katherine Oettinger. The one area of disappointment was Latin America where the project failed to take hold. The one program established in the area was discontinued as performance was not satisfactory. In Asia, Africa, and the English-speaking Caribbean countries considerable success was achieved. Asian schools reported that 7,000 students had been reached by the project. There were also increases in family planning–related field placements, in faculty community service activities, and in graduates securing related employment.

Another important outcome of the project was the strengthening of the national relevance of the social work curriculum as a whole. To prepare for integration of family planning content, many schools did a total curriculum review and used the challenge of integrating family planning and social development to link social work more closely with national social and economic development plans. Thus the family planning project strengthened the move toward indigenous curriculum, especially in the Asian schools. Regional differences in emphasis emerged; social development was accepted as the goal among Asian schools, whereas the African schools preferred an emphasis on family life education with a strong emphasis on community rather than the individual. The evaluators note that a later start limited African schools from realizing the full benefits of the project, although considerable progress was made.

The project generated a series of publications, some of which had lasting impact. An early publication was *Population and Family Planning: Analytical Abstracts for Social Work Educators and Related Disciplines* (1972, IASSW, New York). This volume brought acclaim from other professions and was deemed so useful that it was translated into Spanish by the Pan-American Health Organization. In 1973, a casebook was published of 22 Asian vignettes on social work in family planning: *Social Work in Action: An International Perspective on Population and Family Planning* (IASSW, New York). Proceedings of various international conferences and the regional seminars further enhanced the literature, especially the publication of volumes from regional perspectives in Asia and Africa. These include *A Developmental Outlook for Social Work Education* (1974) and *Asian Social Problems: New Strategies for Social Work Education* (1976) from the Asian region and *Education for Family Welfare: A Component of Development* (1977) and *Family Welfare in Africa: Educational Strategies* (1977) from seminars held in Africa (all published by IASSW, New York). Jamaica made a special contribution to the project in sharing its success with training paraprofessionals in social welfare and family planning. Through hosting an international workshop on paraprofessional training and publication of a manual on the subject, the work of the Social Welfare Training Centre at the University of the West Indies influenced similar developments in Asia.

The project was not without problems. Indeed, as mentioned earlier, efforts to establish pilot schools in Latin America failed; the project faced opposition to family planning from the established church and from leftists who denounced family planning as an effort to limit populations of developing countries. Even in some of the schools with successful programs, small groups of students opposed family planning content on ideological grounds. Overall, however, the project provides an excellent example of international action to improve human well-being through the use of a curriculum and education project. The summary paragraph from the final report states:

> The project has laid the basic foundation for the development of qualified social work manpower for population and family planning responsibilities in Asia. An excellent beginning has been made in Africa. The IASSW view of family planning as positive family welfare and an integral aspect of social development has led to significant educational change in both regions. As a grassroots operation, the project has led to indigenous curriculum development related to national needs and priorities. This response to national development concerns through the new emphasis on family planning has broadened the purposes and scope of social work education to embrace a variety of community-based activities. (Kendall, 1977, p. 42)

In the 1980s and 1990s program efforts have included further work on indigenous curriculum, assistance to the development and expansion of social work education in Eastern Europe and the former Soviet Union, attention to gender and women's issues in social work education, and an ambitious census project to catalog extensive information on social work education throughout the world.

In 2000, the Board of Directors adopted a new mission statement specifying four goals: *(1)* to develop and promote excellence in social work education, research, and scholarship globally to enhance human well-being; *(2)* to create and maintain a dynamic community of social work educators and their programs; *(3)* to support and facilitate participation in mutual exchanges of information and expertise; and *(4)* to represent social work education at the international level (IASSW, 2000). The statement also reiterated IASSW's commitment to human rights, social justice, and social development. An example of implementation of the mission is through a new program of project grants. Small international projects among member schools are funded as a way to further exchange and promote innovation and quality in social work education.

Development of standards for social work education worldwide was perhaps the most important association activity in the early twenty-first century. Extensive work, with many national and regional consultations and member input, resulted in a final draft of *Global Standards for Social Work Education and Training* in 2004. The drafting and consultation effort was led by IASSW under the leadership of Vishanthie Sewpaul of South Africa, but with ongoing participation of IFSW in a joint task force. Both organizations adopted the *Standards* at their 2004 meetings held in Adelaide, Australia. As adopted, the *Standards* are regarded more as guidelines to assist countries and schools in achieving quality educational program. At the time of writing, there is no global social work educational accrediting process and considerable division of opinion within the profession as to the desirability of such a system. The *Standards*, however, represent a major step forward in defining quality social work education.

Co-sponsorship of the journal *International Social Work*, representation with the UN and UNICEF (the UN Children's Fund), and regular biennial conferences continue. Additional activities are carried out by regional associations.

International Federation of Social Workers

The IFSW, an international organization of professional social workers, was founded in 1956. Its predecessor, the International Permanent Secretariat of Social Workers, was initiated in Paris in 1928 by social workers from England, France, Scandinavia, Switzerland, and Czechoslovakia; provisional statutes for the organization were approved at the Second International Social Work Conference in Frankfurt in 1932 by eight founding member countries (Belgium, Czechoslovakia, France, Germany, Great Britain, Sweden, Switzerland, and the United States) (Secretary General Tom Johannesen of the IFSW, personal communication, July 16, 1999). The Secretariat was active until the beginning of World War II; a conference planned for Prague in 1940 never took place. By 1950, plans began for a new organization, building on the legacy of the Secretariat—the International Federation of Social Workers.

The primary aim of the IFSW is to promote social work as a profession with professional standards and ethics. Thus, one of the major achievements of the organization has been development of ethical standards for the global profession. The International Code of Ethics was initially adopted in 1976 and represented the first code of ethics adopted to apply to social workers around the world. A number of national organizations have used the code as their own. In 1994, new ethical documents were adopted, the International Ethical Standards for Social Workers and the International Declaration of Ethical Principles of Social Work (IFSW, 1994). These were superseded by the *Ethics in Social Work: Statement of Principles* in 2004 (see Appendix A).

Another major goal of the IFSW is to "encourage contacts between social workers of all countries" and "to provide the means for discussion and exchange of ideas" (Johannesen, 1997, p. 154). Therefore, like the other professional organizations, the IFSW sponsors regular conferences at the regional and international levels to promote communication and exchange among social workers.

An important part of IFSW's work has been to represent social work's views on major world issues through development of policy position papers and through its consultative status with the UN. As defined in its constitution, the IFSW aims to ensure social work involvement in international social policy, by supporting national organizations in participating in social planning and policy formulation, nationally and internationally, and by presenting the point of view of the profession on an international level through liaisons with various international organizations in the social welfare field (Johannesen, 1997). Through development and promulgation of policy positions on a number of significant global issues, IFSW has increased social work visibility on global policy. Among the problem areas addressed are: HIV/AIDS, migration, peace and disarmament, advancement of women, refugees, human rights, and indigenous people (IFSW, 1988).

Beginning in the late 1980s, IFSW adopted a strong program focus on human rights. Through case advocacy, policy advocacy, and member education, the Federation is making an impact in this important arena.

Human Rights: A Case of International Advocacy by the Profession. As explained by Secretary General Tom Johannesen (1997):

> Human rights are inseparable from social work theory, values, ethics, and practice. It is therefore difficult to perform social work in a society in which basic human rights are not met. The recognition of the interdependence between human rights and social work practice has led IFSW to focus its work in this area. (p. 155)

Although some activities began earlier, IFSW established its Human Rights Commission in 1988, with a human rights commissioner for each of the association's regions. The commission has an official liaison to Amnesty International. In 1996, the federation's policy statement on human rights was promulgated and publicized among members and related organizations (IFSW, 1996).

An important part of the IFSW's human rights program is direct advocacy on behalf of professional social workers and other social service workers who are victims of violations of human rights. An intensive campaign focused on Chile in the 1980s and South Africa in the latter part of that decade. IFSW sent a representative to Chile twice to investigate disappearances of social workers and social work students during the Pinochet regime. More recent efforts have focused on social workers who are being held as political prisoners in Iraq, Myanmar, and other countries. Using the methods popularized by Amnesty International, IFSW uses publicity and letter writing to

---

CASE 7.1

In 2000, IFSW took on the case of Phyliss Coard. Coard, a social worker practitioner and lecturer for 18 years and Deputy Minister for Women's Affairs in Grenada, was convicted of murder along with 17 others in 1983. The highly political trial was denounced by observers as "a travesty of justice." In addition, Grenada passed a special law denying the group the right to appeal—a law that applied only to this case. IFSW advocacy for Coard was not based on her trial, but rather on the inhumane aspects of her long imprisonment. When in 2000 she was diagnosed with colon cancer and needed chemotherapy, there was none available in Grenada. IFSW and other advocacy groups pressed the government of Grenada to release Coard for treatment. She was temporarily released and allowed to receive chemotherapy. IFSW advocacy continued until 2003 (IFSW, 2007).

---

governments and other human rights bodies to call attention to the situation of those being illegitimately held for speaking out on injustices and other similar actions.

The IFSW, along with the IASSW, collaborated with the UN Centre for Human Rights on a curriculum project on human rights, resulting in the publication of a manual, *Human Rights and Social Work: A Manual for Schools of Social Work and the Social Work Profession* (United Nations, 1994). The manual was the first in a UN series planned to target human rights information to various professions and groups and served to expand the Centre's program of information and training beyond legal and criminal justice professionals. In the foreword to the manual, the assistant secretary general for human rights explains that it has been published "with the specific purpose of adding to the knowledge and understanding of this important professional group in respect of all aspects of human rights and the international mechanisms that have been developed to protect those rights" (p. iii).

The manual stresses the relevance of human rights to all levels of social work concern—the microlevel of the individual, the mesolevel of community, and the macro- or societal level. Social workers are encouraged to "examine the world and their role through a social justice lens" (p. 3). The recommended curriculum presents human rights as "inseparable from social work theory, values and ethics, and practice" (p. 5). Therefore, social workers are mandated to advocate for human rights even in authoritarian and oppressive contexts where it is dangerous to do so. The IFSW developed a follow-up publication on the rights of the child.

In addition to the intrinsic importance of the work itself, IFSW's human rights efforts increase the visibility and credibility of social work in the community of international organizations. For the future, IFSW plans to regularly update its policy papers, expand its human rights work, and engage with new issues such as professional mobility (Healy & Hall, 2007).

International Council on Social Welfare

The third of the three organizations founded in 1928, the ICSW (first named the International Conference on Social Work) is now a "world organization for the promotion of social development" (Lally, 1987, p. 982). It does this by serving as a forum for exchange on knowledge on social welfare and social development; through liaison with relevant intergovernmental organizations, such as those of the UN, on social development matters; and by encouraging positive developments in social welfare around the world. Its mission statement defines its action strategies as follows:

> ICSW's main ways of pursuing its aims include gathering and disseminating information, undertaking research and analysis, convening seminars and conferences, drawing on grass-root experiences, strengthening non-governmental organizations, developing policy proposals, engaging in public advocacy and working with policy-makers and administrators in government and elsewhere. (ICSW, 1994)

Membership in the ICSW is largely through national committees. Other national associations and international organizations can also belong to the Council; current NGO members include the International Social Service, the International Organization for Migration, and the Salvation Army. ICSW reaches beyond any particular profession to involve practitioners from various disciplines and laypeople interested in social welfare. This differentiates it from the work of its "sister" organizations, IFSW and IASSW.

ICSW has held conferences regularly, except for the years during World War II. The organization has worked to ensure that work continues between conferences and has made efforts to increase the action components of its agenda (see Box on René Sand). From 1964 to 1966, the organization considered ways to expand beyond a forum for biennial debate and exchange of ideas and to venture into action programs. In 1966, the name of the organization was officially changed to the International Council on Social Welfare to underscore that its scope is not limited to any one profession. The addition of a descriptive phrase to its name in 1982—International Council on Social Welfare: A World Organization Promoting Social Development—underscores the efforts of the organization to identify with the development movement and more closely identify with UN priorities (Katzki, 1988).

ICSW has always maintained relationships with major world organizations. It has successfully used its consultative status with the UN to increase the voice of social welfare in important recent deliberations, as will be explained next.

United Nations Consultative Status: Action to Influence Global Policy. ICSW maintains consultative status in Category I (explained below) with the UN, allowing the organization to participate with UN bodies in New York,

RENÉ SAND: ORGANIZATION FOUNDER

Social Welfare Archives, University of Minnesota

Dr. René Sand was a founder of the ICSW and the IASSW, an inspiration for the beginning of social work education in Chile, and a contributor to social work in his native Belgium; in addition, he made outstanding contributions in the field of social medicine. Truly a renaissance man, he was a leading figure in social work and social welfare for more than 3 decades and a leading figure in medicine for almost 5 decades.

Sand was born in Ixelles, Belgium, in 1877; he studied medicine at the University of Brussels and undertook postgraduate studies in hospitals in Berlin and Vienna. One of his early posts was as a medical consultant to an insurance company dealing with accidents in the workplace. There he became aware of the everyday hazards in the life of ordinary workers, and his interest in social medicine was born. During World War I, he worked with the Red Cross of Belgium and aided refugees in London, deepening his social commitments. He was elected secretary general of the League of Red Cross Societies in 1921, an association he continued long into his career.

Sand made many trips abroad. He visited the United States twice in the years after World War I and was a presenter at the U.S. National Conference on Social Welfare. In 1924, he visited South America where he gave lectures in social medicine at the University of Santiago. As mentioned in Chapter 6, it was on his return to Europe that he met Dr. Alejandro del Rio and became involved in setting up the first school of social work in Chile. Working with the League of Red Cross Societies, he was involved in the creation of a number of international organizations, including the International Committee of Mental Health and the International Hospitals Association. In describing his special qualities as a leader, his obituary in *Lancet* read: "He had the knack of suppressing trouble-makers with a piece of well-timed and discriminating flattery; and he could shift readily from one language to another and produce a bon mot in each" ("René Sand," 1953, p. 576).

(continued)

Social workers, however, remember Sand for applying these gifts to his founding activities in the field of social work. Sand was a prime mover in organizing the 1928 First International Conference of Social Work. In a paper he wrote proposing the conference, he expressed his belief in the importance of having those in the same field from different countries come together to share information about their daily practice and to meet each other. He worked with others for more than 4 years to make the conference a reality. Later, he said that the conference has "conferred on the social work profession a dignity and an authority that it had not enjoyed previously" (Anciaux, 1988, as translated from the French). He served as president of the ICSW from 1932 to 1948 and was president of the IASSW from 1946 until his death in 1953. He was credited with having been the "central source of power and inspiration behind the establishment" of both organizations (Kendall, 1978).

In 1937, Sand became secretary general of the Ministry of Public Health in Belgium. During World War II, he was taken prisoner by the Nazis in 1940 when they invaded Belgium and held in Tyrol, Austria, until May 1945 when he was liberated by the U.S. Seventh Army ("Obituary of René Sand," 1953). He returned to his activities in social medicine and social work. He stepped down from the presidency of the ICSW in 1948, insisting that a younger member be named. But he continued on as honorary president and had, by then, been pressed into service as president of the IASSW to reorganize it after the war. Presiding at the 1952 Conference of Social Work in Madras, India, he oversaw the transformation of social work organizations into truly worldwide bodies.

Sand was also significantly involved in the founding of the World Health Organization (WHO). He presided over the committee of experts put together by the new UN to develop an international health organization; in 1950, he was appointed chair of the WHO expert committee for professional and technical education.

He died suddenly in 1953, and members of many organizations mourned his loss. In addition to his legacy of organizational leadership, he left extensive writings on the many topics of his expertise, including *The Advance to Social Medicine, La Medecine Sociale,* and *Health and Human Progress.* As noted in his obituary in the *British Medical Journal,* Sand "will be long remembered not only for his conceptions of the potentialities of international collaboration in medicine but also for his ideas of the part that medicine, as an art, should play in the social structure of every country" ("Obituary René Sand," 1953, p. 572). He believed that medicine would be fully developed only "if social and psychological aspects received a proper place in the training of medical students" ("Obituary René Sand," 1953, p. 572). His ideas on both international collaboration and on the importance of social factors in health are still current today. An award was established in his name by the ICSW and is awarded every other year to an

(*continued*)

individual or organization that has given outstanding service in social welfare.

Upon hearing of his death, Katherine Kendall, of the CSWE and later the secretary general of the IASSW, wrote:

> Dr. Sand was a hero to me and almost a myth long before I ever met him. From social work friends in Latin America, I had heard about him as the "father" of social work education there. They told me how he had traveled from one country to another awakening a deep and lasting interest in establishing schools for the preparation of social workers. When I did meet him at last, immediately after the war, the easily perceptible greatness of the man explained the myth and I knew why my South American friends had spoken of him with love and a respect amounting to reverence. ("In Memoriam," 1953).

Geneva, and Vienna. Indeed, ICSW was one of the first NGOs to receive consultative status with the UN shortly after its founding. The system for NGOs to interact with the UN was established in 1946 and remains largely unchanged today. Organizations are permitted to apply for consultative status with the Economic and Social Council (ECOSOC) if they meet several conditions: They must focus on issues related to ECOSOC, have aims consistent with the UN Charter, and broadly represent those in their field (with a preference for worldwide organizations rather than national bodies). NGOs can be accepted into one of three classifications, with varying privileges. ICSW is a Category I organization, designated as an organization "with a basic interest in most of the activities of the Council" (Willetts, 1996, p. 32). Category II organizations are those with competence in selected areas of ECOSOC's scope and are granted fewer privileges of interaction. Still other organizations are placed on the roster, a list of specialization organizations that ECOSOC may consult on an ad hoc basis.

Over the years, efforts have been made to limit the number of NGOs with consultative status and to put some restrictions on their activities. In the specialized work of the UN, however, the importance of NGO contributions and expertise is recognized. As a Category I organization, ICSW can attend ECOSOC meetings, circulate written statements to members, and address a council committee and, if recommended, the full council. In addition, Category I organizations can submit agenda items for ECOSOC consideration. Access to information is an important benefit of consultative status; NGOs have access to UN documents and have passes to enter UN facilities, although recent concerns with security may limit the number of persons with access.

Social Development Summit (1995): Effective Use of Consultative Status. The specialized conferences held by the UN have created additional opportunities for NGO participation. One of these was the World Summit for Social Development, held in Copenhagen in 1995. Falling squarely within the expertise of ICSW, the organization mobilized and implemented a series of special efforts to make an impact on world deliberations and, beginning in 1993, made the summit its major priority. Since the summit, the ICSW program has emphasized follow-up efforts to implement its plan of action.

Activities began several years prior to the actual summit, as the optimal time to influence UN deliberations is during the preparatory work that precedes major world meetings. Working with other key NGOs, ICSW developed plans at its February 1993 executive committee meeting to organize an NGO consultation meeting during the first UN Summit Preparatory Committee meeting and to organize a global NGO preparatory meeting to coincide with the 1994 International Conference on Social Welfare in Finland (ICSW, 1993). A special summit newsletter was initiated; over the next several years, six issues were produced and thousands distributed to members, NGOs, governments, and intergovernmental agencies. The NGO preparatory meeting drew over 60 NGO leaders for a 3-day meeting in Helsinki in July 1994. Later that summer, ICSW participated in the second preparatory committee meeting for the official UN Summit. At the meeting, it organized an NGO issues forum and disseminated several thousand copies of ICSW speeches and policy papers related to poverty and other Summit topics (ICSW, 1995). Through this lengthy process of monitoring official deliberations, disseminating speeches and policy suggestions, and organizing NGOs for participation, ICSW was able to influence the official plan of action of the UN meeting. According to Julian Disney, chair of the ICSW Summit Working Group, "ICSW widely circulated about a dozen policy papers and proposals for inclusion in the Summit agreements and we are pleased that many of our recommendations are reflected in the final documents" (ICSW, 1996).

Activities continued after the summit, focusing on implementation of the summit recommendations and plan of action. ICSW initiated the *Social Development Review*, a quarterly publication dedicated to summit follow-up and other social development issues. Following the summit, ICSW developed a policy paper on social development to guide its actions in the field (ICSW, 1998). Another important activity was the organization of regional follow-up meetings for NGOs to work on implementation issues and seminars on summit implementation for each ICSW regional meeting.

In 1997, a "Memorandum of Understanding Between the U.N. Development Programme and the International Council on Social Welfare" was adopted to realize greater collaboration between the UN body and the Council. As stated in the document: "The principal areas for collaboration and interaction will concern reduction and eradication of poverty throughout the world, with special emphasis on pursuing and monitoring implementation of the relevant agreements made at the World Summit for Social Development and other global conferences" (ICSW, 1997, p. 1). The memorandum committed the two organizations to work together to implement the summit recommendations on the eradication of poverty by promoting the use and discussion of UNDP's annual *Human Development Report* and ICSW's *Social Development Review*, producing and distributing expert papers on strategies for poverty reduction, increasing NGO involvement in intergovernmental meetings relating to poverty eradication, and preparing for the year 2000 UN General Assembly review of progress on the implementation of the Summit plan (ICSW, 1997).

Since 2000, the UN has focused on the Millennium Development Goals (MDGs). In its regular submissions to the UN Commission for Social Development ICSW has been critical of the narrow definition of poverty expressed in the MDGs. The Council has called for inclusion of the full range of principles from the Summit Commitments, including the role of decent work for all (ICSW, 2007).

Thus, through this work, ICSW has successfully launched and maintained an action agenda focused on influencing global policy and mobilizing other NGOs to do likewise. The ICSW experience is a useful example of effective use of UN consultative status, which is discussed again in Chapter 12.

DIRECT WORK IN INTERNATIONAL ORGANIZATIONS: THREE EXAMPLES

UNRRA: A Case Example of Direct Social Work in Relief and Development

Social workers continue to make an international contribution through direct work in relief and development, and the UNRRA (discussed briefly in Chapter 6) was a particularly important international direct service experience for the profession. It was not the first such experience, however; social workers had been active in voluntary organizations such as the Red Cross and the international YWCA for decades prior to World War II. Social workers also participated in the founding of the Save the Children Fund in 1919, and in 1924, founded the International Migration Services, later renamed International Social Service, to aid those displaced by World War I and the Great Depression that followed. The work of this organization demonstrated the value of social casework techniques in addressing problems of migration and family separation.

UNRRA, however, was active during a unique period in the history of international social work. Social workers joined in the postwar relief efforts, especially under UNRRA, giving many professionals their first experience in international social work.

> UNRRA organized the first systematic program to delegate experts in social welfare on the request of governments of liberated nations where UNRRA missions started the training of key workers, in order to enable them to organize their own welfare and health services. (Friedlander, 1949, p. 207)

Although much of the work of the UNRRA was to manage large-scale import of relief supplies and to rehabilitate public utilities and the infrastructure for transport, the necessity for relief services was also recognized. Most UNRRA social workers were involved in work in relief services, defined in the council resolution as:

> health and welfare; assistance in caring for, and maintaining records of, persons found in any areas under control of any of the United Nations who by reason of war have been displaced from their homes and, in agreement with the appropriate governments, military authorities or other agencies, in securing their repatriation or return; and such technical services as may be necessary for these purposes. (Howard, 1944, p. 5)

The need for qualified personnel was recognized. "First consideration must be given to technical competence. Whether the task is to care for orphaned or other disadvantaged children; to provide for aged or disabled persons; to feed masses of men, women, and children; or to render any of the wide variety of services likely to be needed, the primary requisite should be knowledge of the work to be done and skill in its performance" (cited in Howard, 1944, p. 6). The requisites for international social work are further identified and remain true today:

> Second in importance only to technical competence is a sympathetic understanding of the economic and social situation of the people among whom welfare work is to be done . . . and a knowledge and an appreciation of the normal customs and ways of life of the people among whom they work. . . . Furthermore, since UNRRA is a truly international organization, its welfare staff should be comprised only of persons possessing an international viewpoint and willing to dissociate themselves from any national interests or objectives which might conflict with their responsibility to the family of nations by which they are employed. (cited in Howard, 1944, p. 7)

Voluntary social service agencies joined the international relief efforts. At least 40 private agencies formed the American Council of Voluntary Agencies for Foreign Service to coordinate planning for relief among themselves and with government agencies. By mid-1944, the council had recruited 67 experienced social workers from the staffs of member agencies to work in the UNRRA, with their salaries continuing to be paid by their employing voluntary agencies (Larned, 1945). The council formed working committees on geographic areas, on displaced persons, and on material aid. An important aspect of its work was to set personnel standards and, in liaison with UNRRA, to encourage careful selection of welfare workers.

Social workers participated in UNRRA work throughout Europe and held some leadership roles; Irving Fasteau, an American social worker, directed the UNRRA program in Finland (Friedlander, 1978).

UNRRA was also active in China. According to Howard (1946a, p. 310), there were probably 100 "highly competent American social workers" in-

DONALD HOWARD: SOCIAL WORKER IN UNRRA

Social Welfare Archives, University of Minnesota

Many social workers left their regular posts to join the UNRRA in the years between 1944 and 1946. One of them was Donald Howard, who took a leave from the Charity Organization Department of the Russell Sage Foundation to join UNRRA in 1944. Over the next 2 years, he made significant contributions to postwar relief efforts.

Howard helped to draft materials for the UNRRA council that defined the relief and welfare functions of the organization. His first official UNRRA assignment was in the Washington office, where he headed up research and planning for the Welfare Division. Next, he was deployed to London and Paris. There he helped to develop the postwar welfare programs for Eastern Europe. The Welfare Division focused on assisting displaced persons and addressing the breakdown of social services infrastructure in countries that had been occupied. However, sound planning for resettlement and for infrastructure development were often overshadowed by pressing needs for relief supplies. Arranging for delivery and distributions of food and medicines occupied much of UNRRA staff's attention.

After 6 months in England and France, Donald Howard was transferred to China as the chief welfare officer for the China office. Soon, he was named deputy director of the UNRRA China Mission in charge of health, welfare, and displaced persons services.

His UNRRA assignments led to some unusual social work experiences. In Europe, Howard worked with SHAEF—the Supreme Headquarters, Allied Expeditionary Forces. All planning for welfare services to displaced persons in Germany had to be done in coordination with the U.S. Army (Howard, 1946b). Logistical problems increased with the increasing East/ West divide in Europe; political problems also intensified as citizens in the West grew less supportive of sending supplies to Soviet-controlled areas. Work in China was greatly complicated by the ongoing civil war between the Nationalist forces and the Communists. UNRRA's mission was to distribute aid equitably, without regard to political allegiances. In his 1946

(continued)

article about relief work in China, Howard discusses an important meeting he held with Mao Tse-tung, Chou En-lai, and Nationalist representatives to arrange for relief to be allowed into communist-held territory (Howard, 1946a). Through his writings on UNRRA for social work journals, Howard conveyed the difficulties of the work. A worldwide food shortage and tremendous need for relief resulted in famine conditions in China. Relief workers were called on to decide who could be saved by a ration of scarce food: "The decision to abandon the principle of aiding those persons who are in greatest need is perhaps the most difficult choice a relief worker can ever be called upon to make. And, once he has determined that these shall be saved but that those shall be allowed to die, a worker feels a sickening sensation, as if something vital inside him had given way, as if something sacred had been debased" (Howard, 1946a, p. 308).

After the UNRRA mission, Howard returned to the Russell Sage Foundation as director of the Department of Social Work Administration, overseeing studies in domestic, international, and foreign social welfare. He was elected president of the AASW in 1947. During his presidency, he remained extensively involved in international affairs. Under his leadership, the AASW developed policy statements on major international issues of the day. His correspondence files include drafts for AASW policy statements on foreign relief and on long-term aid to displaced persons. To these he applied the principles learned through the UNRRA experience, advocating aid without regard to politics and the importance of addressing human needs. He highlighted the similarities between administration of foreign aid and sound social work principles that had evolved from the depression-era programs.

Howard helped to draft the postwar constitution for the International Conference of Social Work and was a leader in efforts to organize and implement the long-delayed Fourth International Conference of Social Work. Originally planned for Brussels in 1940, the conference was cancelled due to the war. It was finally held in Atlantic City, New Jersey, in 1948. The Social Welfare Archives house an extensive file of letters written by Howard to solicit speakers for the conference. Those about the emergence of the rift with the Eastern Bloc and the deteriorating situation in China are particularly illuminating.

Howard's international interest may have derived from his parents. He was born in Tokyo, Japan, in 1902, where his parents were serving as missionaries. He returned to the United States at the age of 10 and was educated in Ohio. Howard received degrees from Otterbein College in Ohio and the University of Denver; and a PhD in 1941 from the University of Chicago School of Social Service Administration. Prior to beginning at Russell Sage Foundation in 1936, he worked at community organizing in Colorado and worked as director of adult activities at a settlement house in Chicago. In the mid-1930s, Howard worked for the Emergency Relief

(continued)

Administration in Colorado. Howard left the Russell Sage Foundation in 1948 to become the founding director of the University of California at Los Angeles (UCLA) Department of Social Welfare (UCLA, 1948); within a year, the program became the School of Social Welfare, and Howard's title changed to dean (UCLA, 1988).

volved in relief efforts in postwar China. These included general relief workers plus specialists in such areas as child welfare, work with the aged, work relief projects, and work with refugees.

> These ambassadors of American social work are achieving signal success, not only in helping to work out technical methods of meeting China's staggering needs, but also in providing the spark and impetus so essential to get relief work under way in areas where wide-scale and fast-moving operations are a novelty. To see these workers in action gives one a new appreciation of the validity of American social work principles, of the soundness of our technical skills. (Howard, 1946a, p. 310)

In the article, Howard also discusses the difficulties of ensuring distribution of relief in China due to the ongoing conflict between the communists and nationalists for control of territory. He describes his own involvement in negotiations with the communists:

> The most heartening experiences which the writer enjoyed in China included visits with Mao Tze-tung and Chou En-lai to discuss possibilities of getting relief to Communist areas; more detailed discussion with lesser Communist officers; and finally, conferences between local Communist representatives and Nationalist army officers to plan means of getting relief supplies into a specific Communist area. (Howard, 1946a, p. 300)

As noted by Wickwar (1947), the achievements of the UNRRA Welfare Division "are highly instructive to all who have at heart the further development of international welfare action" (p. 363). It is also clear from the accounts of participants that the UNRRA experience launched many social workers into international careers; others continued a part-time interest in internationalism through teaching, consultation, and research. Social workers who began their careers in the 1940s cite UNRRA as the most significant force in expanding internationalism within social work. Some of the work, especially consultations and aid to social work education, were continued under the UN and its constituent agencies.

Inside Influence at the United Nations

Precedent for liaison with the UN was established earlier under the League of Nations and the ILO. Grace Abbott chaired the League Committee on the Traffic in Women and Children and served as the first U.S. delegate to the ILO

(Abbott, 1947). Social workers from various countries participated in discussions of international social questions with the League. Within the various sections and committees of the League, social workers were "frequently invited to sit with government officials as observers or to participate as experts, thus affording opportunity for fusion of official and voluntary agency points of view" (Larned, 1945, p. 194). Involvement of the international professional organizations in the UN through consultative status has already been described, but in the early years, social workers were directly involved in the work of the UN as employees and consultants. Kendall talks of her work at the temporary headquarters of the new body at Lake Success, New York:

> It was a fabulous experience working at the U.N. in those early days of 1947 as all the programs were shining new and idealistic. We were located at Lake Success in a barn of a building that had produced material for the war effort and now it was a peace factory. In that period, people there were so imbued with the promise of the U.N. that there they had no question that the world would eventually, if not soon, be safe from the scourges of war and other evils." (Billups, 1997, p. 68)

In another speech, she added: "We were there as international civil servants and we were international. If we did not think and act as internationalists we could not have survived in the heady international atmosphere of those first years. It was really quite wonderful" (Kendall, 1994, p. 7).

For at least 2 decades following the World War II, the UN "was unquestionably the most significant of the internationalizing influences on the social work profession, not only in this country [U.S.] but throughout the world" (Kendall, 1994, p. 6). At its first meeting in 1947, the Social Commission of ECOSOC followed up on the work of UNRRA by encouraging development of social work and social services.

In 1950, the UN Social Commission adopted an important resolution on the necessity of training for social work. The resolution read:

> that social work should in principle be a professional function performed by men and women who have received professional training by taking a formal course of social work theory and practice in an appropriate educational institution . . . and that these courses, whether provided in universities or special schools, should be of the highest possible quality and should be sufficiently comprehensive to do justice to both the variety and the unity of social work. (cited in Billups, 2002, p. 154)

The resolution was sent to ECOSOC and to the General Assembly; it was adopted in 1950. This put the UN on record as recognizing social work as a profession requiring specialized training—an important development (Billups, 2002).

In 1959, the ECOSOC expanded its interest in social work and asked the UN secretary-general to do "everything possible to obtain the participation of social workers in the preparation and application of programs for underdeveloped countries" (Garigue, 1961, p. 21). These strong statements demonstrate that in the early days of the UN, social workers had important roles inside the organization as employees and consultants working on expansion of social work education and development of social programs. Eileen Younghusband (1963), too, acclaimed the UN's role as the biggest contributor to the spread of social work education around the world and, therefore, because of the close link between training and profession, to the spread of the social work profession. Major world surveys of social work training were conducted and published by the UN in 1950, 1955, 1958, 1965, and 1971; training seminars were held on social work; and social welfare officials from developing countries were given UN support to study social work in the United States and Great Britain. The UN lent support to several conferences exploring aspects of international social work education, sending representatives to the 1964 Conference on International Social Welfare Manpower (Washington, D.C.) and to the 1970 Conference on Social Work Education, Population and Family Planning (Hawaii).

Social work involvement in the early UN inspired the careers of some important actors in international social work, as the following quotation indicates. A social worker from Egypt, who became chief of social welfare at the UN and then chief of UNICEF for Europe, explained her introduction to international work in this way:

> My interest was stimulated when I was a student at Bryn Mawr from 1946–50. The U.N. was developing during this time period and this was a frequent topic of discussion at the School of Social Work. Some of the social work pioneers at the U.N. came to speak to us; others had developed materials for teaching from their U.N. experiences. Professors were involved in training relief workers for the Quakers to work in war torn areas and this affected their teaching of us. There were quite a few foreign students enrolled in the social work program. We both caught the excitement of these international developments and then contributed to it through sharing our ideas. (A. Gindy, personal communication, September 22, 1982)

Decline of Inside Influence. Positions as staff and consultants enabled social workers to have a direct impact on design and implementation of UN programs. More recently, social work influence and activity inside the UN has declined greatly. Several reasons can be advanced. One is that the UN shifted its emphasis away from human resources to economic development, a field to which social work has less to offer. Even as the focus moved toward social development, social work was slow to adapt to the development movement and was unable to compete in the interdisciplinary environment. As one expert expressed it: "We spent too much time promoting social work instead of promoting strategies to meet human need" (S. Pettis, personal communication, November 11, 1982). Was this due to lack of experience with the mass poverty characteristic of developing nations? To the individual focus of dominant models of social work? To overconcern with protecting social

PIONEERS IN INTERNATIONAL ACTION:
DAME EILEEN YOUNGHUSBAND

Katherine Kendall; personal collection

Dame Eileen Younghusband of Great Britain "changed the character of social work education in her own country and, as a consultant and author of the third U.N. international survey of social work education she contributed enormously to the development of schools of social work around the world" (Kendall, 1989, p. 24). Born in 1902 in London, her father was a mountaineer and explorer. Younghusband studied sociology and social studies at the London School of Economics and joined the faculty there (Quam, 1995).

Younghusband's international contributions were many. Her primary arenas for international action were the UN and the IASSW. She also had a significant but controversial career in Britain, where she played a major role in establishing the social work course at the London School of Economics. The conclusions she drew in her major survey of social work in Britain (sponsored by the Carnegie U.K. Trust) were that training was deficient in lack of emphasis on fieldwork and practical aspects of the profession, that there was a serious lack of literature and research, and most significantly, that social work was splintered into many separate specializations and lacked a core identity. She advocated a general approach rather than specialization, saying: "It would be dangerous to overstress divisions within the course; it may be that they are a concession to our ignorance rather than to our knowledge" (Jones, 1984, p. 54). The recommendations were unpopular, especially with psychiatric social workers and almoners who had considerable clout within social work. Thus at the time, much of Eileen's leadership was rejected by her colleagues in Britain, and she was chided by the psychiatric social workers in particular for her lack of a social work credential. As her biographer noted, "To say, as the professional social workers did, that she 'wasn't qualified' was rather like complaining that Florence Nightingale was not a State

(continued)

Registered nurse. She was creating the profession they belonged to" (Jones, 1984, p. 60).

On the international scene, she was almost venerated as a leader and friend to social work educators. Soon after World War II, Younghusband began to get involved in international social work activities. She worked with the UNRRA and attended the first postwar International Conference on Social Work in the Netherlands in 1947. She spent part of 1948 in Geneva as a consultant to the Social Welfare Fellowship program of the UN Bureau of Social Affairs. During this year, she also traveled to UN headquarters, which was then at Lake Success, New York. There she met Katherine Kendall, another pioneer in international action, and the two began a long friendship and productive professional association. It particularly flourished through their involvement in the IASSW. Younghusband participated in the 1950 congress in Paris and was soon identified as a leader in the IASSW; she served as vice president from 1954 to 1961, as president from 1961 to 1968, and then as honorary president until her death (Quam, 1995).

From 1956 to 1959, the UN engaged Younghusband to conduct and write the *Training for Social Work: Third International Survey*, produced in 1959. The report remains "one of the most thoughtful, exhaustive and thorough attempts to analyzes the nature of social work education, the teaching methods, the content and the objectives" (Jones, 1984, p. 96). As Kendall explained, "As the author of a landmark U.N. study that dealt in depth with the organization and content of social work education, she helped to give the social work curriculum a distinguishing identity, thus making it possible for social work to claim legitimacy as an international discipline" (Kendall, 1989, p. 30).

It is not surprising that Younghusband was sought after as an international consultant on social work. She assisted many countries—including Hong Kong, Jamaica, and Greece—in their efforts to improve the profession and professional education. As she reflected: "It was a time for world experts. Colonialism was being phased out and the newly independent nations still looked to the West for help and support" (as quoted in Jones, 1984, p. 92).

In her work in Britain and throughout the world, she viewed social work as a "gestalt" in which knowledge from many fields was brought together and the result was a synthesis that was more than its individual parts: "This knowledge may be comparatively elementary in any one of the social or behavioral sciences, but the total synthesis results in an understanding of man and his social functioning, refined by constant practice, which is certainly not elementary" (as quoted in Jones, 1984, p. 97).

Younghusband died in a traffic accident in 1981 at the age of 79 while on a visit with friends in the United States. She left a wealth of important publications on British and international social work. At her memorial

(*continued*)

service held in the beautiful church of St. Martin-in-the-Fields in London, hundreds of colleagues and friends from the United Kingdom and other countries paid tribute to her unique place in the history of social work in Britain and in the world (Kendall, 1982). Tributes to her outstanding contributions to international action continue, especially through the bi-ennial Eileen Younghusband memorial lecture at the world congresses of the IASSW.

work's sphere of influence? Whatever the mix of reasons, the profession was not successful in specifying how it could contribute to the goal of develop-ment and therefore was left behind in the mainstream movement toward development programs within the UN. The failure to define social work responsibility in the international arena, beyond spreading social work edu-cation around the world, was a shortcoming that ultimately brought a de-cline in influence. As another expert sadly noted, "The fading influence of U.N. activities in the field of social welfare is an example of what can happen when the vision is gone and only the bureaucracy remains" (Kendall, 1978, p. 191).

The Social Welfare Attaché Program

An even more short-lived but interesting opportunity for work and influence was realized in the social welfare attaché program in the United States. Al-though the impact of the attaché program was limited due to the brevity of the experiment, the lessons of the relevance of social work expertise to foreign policy are important. Embassy positions, called attachés, exist for experts in fields such as labor and military affairs to advise the embassy staff on key matters. In the 1960s, the U.S. State Department experimented with a pro-gram that placed social welfare attachés in two U.S. embassies. There was an earlier version of this program just after World War II when there were welfare attaché positions in France and India. Mary Catherine Jennings was appointed attaché to the Brazilian embassy in 1963; shortly thereafter, Ruby Pernell was appointed to be social welfare attaché to the embassy in India under Ambassador Chester Bowles. Bowles was ambassador to India after World War II when that embassy had a social welfare attaché. He valued the contribution so highly that he specifically requested reinstitution of this po-sition when he accepted a return assignment in India in the 1960s (Bowles, 1965). The profession was enthusiastic about the appointments. An article in the *NASW News* reporting the appointment of Jennings indicates that the professional association had lobbied for this: "This appointment is the first tangible result of the years of work done by NASW in co-operation with the U.S. Department of Health, Education and Welfare (DHEW) since the two positions for social welfare attachés established in 1947 were discontinued" ("Mary Catherine Jennings," 1963, p. 1).

The overall function of the attaché was to provide the ambassador and other staff members with reports based on observation and evaluation of social conditions and social services. The attachés were to maintain contacts with local social agencies, interpret and represent U.S. social welfare policies and services, provide consultation to the embassy on intercountry services, increase U.S. participation in international social welfare activities, and promote exchanges in the field of social welfare. The job description also indicates that they may be called on to provide consultation to the U.S. Agency for International Development to evaluate requests for social development aid and to provide consultation to the staff of the embassy on intercountry social service issues, such as repatriation of stranded Americans, intercountry adoptions, or arranging for social services for separated families. This last task was limited; the attachés had to be on guard not to become social workers to the embassy staff (M. C. Jennings Holden, personal communication, March 4, 1997).

One benefit of the program to the U.S. government was that social welfare attachés were in contact with groups that did not normally interact with the embassy. In Brazil, for example, Jennings was an important link to movements for social progress and to the Catholic Church. This, she believed, helped to balance public perception that U.S. interests in Brazil were about militarism and materialism. One of the key functions of the attaché was to observe and report what was going on in social development. The topic was of interest to the State Department and other government agencies at the time, as President Kennedy's Alliance for Progress initiatives had a social development component. Therefore, a study of social work education in Brazil that illuminated attitudes toward social development was shared with the Department of Health, Education and Welfare (DHEW) as well as the State Department.

The posts were evaluated very positively by the ambassadors. Recommendations were made to add social welfare attachés at other key embassies in the developing world, including the Philippines and Indonesia. Instead, by the late 1960s, the program fell to budget-cutting pressures. Jennings left her post in Brazil in 1968 to become chief of the International Training Section at DHEW; she was not replaced. The position in India ended at about the same time. Quite possibly these budgetary pressures were complicated by the political environment of the times, with substantial unrest at home and domestic and worldwide antiwar agitation over the Vietnam War, then at its height. These events diminished support for international interventions.

The social welfare attaché program is an important model for international action. In an evaluation of the importance of the post, the ambassador in India noted that the social welfare attaché broadened the embassy's contacts with government and the wider society, building relationships that no other unit in the embassy had. Perhaps surprisingly, the attaché was seen as important in building a positive image of the United States. "Due to the earlier work of the first Social Welfare Attaché, a tremendous amount of goodwill towards the United States had been created which, without a social welfare specialist, we were unable to continue to cultivate" (Bowles, 1965). Social work brought expertise to a wide range of important issues, including status of women, children, and youth; poverty; and social planning. The example and lessons of the social welfare attaché program should not be forgotten, whether or not they can ever be revived in the same format. The value of provision of social welfare expertise to governmental bodies in international relations and the centrality of issues of social development to social, economic, and political relations should be promoted in all nations.

CONCLUSION

The profession of social work has had a long history of international action, beginning almost at the inception of the profession. There have been impressive accomplishments, by organizations and by individuals. If there is a negative side, it is that it is a history of ups and downs, not a seamless story of progress. The diminution of inside involvement in the UN represents a loss of professional influence and a reduction in the centrality of social welfare in UN work. Presently, social work influence in the UN is primarily external, through the consultative status of the professional organizations and participation in many other international NGOs. The UN has relatively few social work employees and no special social work programs.

Responsibility for this reduction rests within the UN and within the profession. When the UN turned away from the promotion of social work education and social welfare programs toward development and then toward an emphasis on special populations through its special years and conferences (see Chapter 5), social work lost its arena of uncontested leadership. The profession was not successful in defining a new role in development or in taking the lead in its areas of expertise on women, children, and poverty. Recently, UNICEF has increased its emphasis on child protection. This may well open new avenues for more direct social work involvement.

Initially, social workers made their international impact in broad global social movements, such as the peace and women's movements at the beginning of the twentieth century. It appears that social work leadership in major global movements has lessened, although it may be too soon to fully evaluate this. And there are examples of significant individual involvement, such as the work of social workers from Africa and the United States in world AIDS work, and organizational involvement, such as the work of ICSW on social development described above.

On the positive side, the international social work organizations have shown remarkable resiliency, and certainly their survival and continued work are important. They have been particularly successful in actions to ensure exchange of professional knowledge by regularly holding world conferences and by sustaining publication of *International Social Work* for more than 50 years. Recently, the organizations have shown renewed initiative by using their consultative status with the UN and by joining with other NGOs in preparatory work and NGO forums at some of the special UN world conferences.

Continued development of vehicles for professional action is another positive action. A fourth vibrant international social work organization was founded less than 30 years ago, the Inter-University Consortium for International Social Development, now the International Consortium for Social Development (ICSD). It was originated by a group of U.S. social work educators in response to what they saw as neglect of the critical issues of social development by the established social work organizations. It has grown into an international, interdisciplinary organization with a focus on development theory, research, teaching, and practice. The addition of ICSD has created additional opportunities for international involvement and may well have spurred increased attention to development by the older social work organizations.

Important successes of the past may inform action for the future. The IASSW family-planning project demonstrated how a concerted response to a social need through the seemingly modest strategy of curriculum development can make an impact on the shape of social and health services. If significant funding had been available more recently, could similar levels of success have been achieved in other areas, such as HIV/AIDS?

The positive evaluation of the brief social welfare attaché program points to the value of advisory roles for social workers in international relations. While it may never be revived in the exact form of the attaché experiment, the profession and individual professionals may use lessons learned to identify new advisory roles through which contributions can be made.

As international organizational action for the future is considered, the policy role may well grow in importance. Policy advocacy in human rights and other areas should continue. Social work professional organizations also need to develop national action agendas on their own nations' foreign policy. In 1947, in discussing postwar relief proposals for aid to Europe and China before Congress, Howard (1947) told the social work profession in the United States:

> Because of deep interest in and special knowledge of social welfare needs and services, social workers must take a leading part in helping the American people fully to understand the issues at stake and to do all in their power to see that the course taken by our government is the best that can be pursued under prevailing circumstances. (p. 7)

His message led to a resolution of support for foreign assistance by the AASW. Today, it can be applied to the social work profession in all countries where governments take action that has international impact. Now more than ever, the global arena needs international social work professional action.

REFERENCES

Abbott, E. (1947). Three American pioneers in international social welfare. *The Compass, XXVIII*(4), 3–7, 36.

Anciaux, A. (1988). Rene Sand—Fondateur de L'ICSW. In ICSW *1928–1988: ICSW, Celebration of the 60th anniversary* (pp. 25–28) Vienna, Austria: International Council on Social Welfare.

Billups, J. (1997). Reflections on a professional's life as an internationalist: An interview with Katherine A. Kendall. *Reflections,* 3(2) 65–85.

Billups, J. (2002). *Faithful angels: International social work notables of the late 20th century.* Washington, DC: NASW Press.

Bowles, C. (1965, Sept. 15). Correspondence to D. Wilken, Director, Inter-departmental Relations Staff and GAO Liaison, Department of State.

Fifth Question: Co-education or separate schools for men and women. The plan for an International School of Social Work. (1929). In *International Conference of Social Work* [Proceedings] (Vol. II, pp. 223–238). First Conference, Paris, July 8–13, 1928.

Friedlander, W. A. (1949). Some international aspects of social work education. *Social Service Review, XXIII*(2), 204–210.

Friedlander, W. A. (1978). *International social welfare.* Englewood Cliffs, NJ: Prentice Hall.

Garigue, P. (1961). Challenge of cultural variations to social work. In *Education for Social Work* [Proceedings] Council on Social Work Education (Ninth Annual Program Meeting), 9–22.

Graham, J. (1978, December). Saviour to the world's children. *Readers Digest,* 121–128.

Healy, L. M., & Hall, N. (2007). International professional organizations in social work. In L. Wagner & R. Lutz (Eds.), *Internationale Perspektiven Sozialer Arbeit: Ein einfuhrendes Handbuch* (pp. 223–242). Frankfurt am Main, Germany: IKC.

Howard, D. S. (1944). U.N.R.R.A.: A new venture in international relief and welfare services, *Social Service Review, XVIII*(1), 1–11.

Howard, D. S. (1946a). Emergency relief needs and measures in China. *Social Service Review, XX,* 300–311.

Howard, D. (1946b, June). *Personal vitae.* Social Welfare Archives, NCSW Collection Box 7-folder 5.

Howard, D. S. (1947, May). Urgent international welfare measures—Our responsibility. *The Compass,* reprinted in "From the archives" (1998). *Journal of Progressive Human Services* 9(1), 65–72.

In memoriam: Dr. René Sand, 1877–1953. (1953). *Social Service Review,* 27(4), 427– 428.

International Association of Schools of Social Work. (2000). *Mission statement.* Accessed June 19, 2007, at www.iassw-aiets.org

International Association of Schools of Social Work. (2004). *Global standards for social work education and training.* Accessed June 19, 2007, at www.iassw-aiets.org

International Council on Social Welfare. (1993). Executive Committee Meeting, Draft Minutes. Vienna, February 10–14, 1993. (Available from ICSW, 5 Tavistock Place, London, UK.)

International Council on Social Welfare. (1994). *ICSW Mission Statement.* Accessed July 31, 1998, at www.icsw.org/mission.htm

International Council on Social Welfare. (1995). *Report of the Activities of the General Secretariat, January 1994–March, 1995.* Prepared for the Executive Committee

Meeting, Copenhagen, March 13–15, 1995. (Available from ICSW, 5 Tavistock Place, London, UK.)

International Council on Social Welfare. (1996). *Biennial report, 1994–1996.* Montreal, Canada: Author.

International Council on Social Welfare. (1997). *Memorandum of understanding between the United Nations Development Programme and the International Council on Social Welfare.* Accessed July 31, 1998, at www.icsw.org/policy_memorandum.htm

International Council on Social Welfare. (1998). *Policy paper on social development.* Accessed July 31, 1998, at www.icsw.org/policies_social.htm

International Council on Social Welfare. (2007 February 7–16). *Unabridged version of the Statement to United Nations Commission for Social Development.* Utrecht, Netherlands: Author.

International Federation of Social Workers. (1988). *International policy papers.* Geneva, Switzerland: Author.

International Federation of Social Workers. (1994). *The ethics of social work.* Oslo, Norway: Author. (Full text available at www.ifsw.org)

International Federation of Social Workers. (1996). *International statement on human rights.* Accessed November 8, 1998, at www.ifsw.org/4.5.6.pub.html

International Federation of Social Welfare. (2007). *Human rights cases.* Accessed June 14, 2007, at www.ifsw.org

Jebb, E. (1929). International social service. In *First International Conference of Social Work* [Proceedings] (Vol. I, pp. 637–655). First Conference, Paris, July 8–13, 1928.

Johannesen, T. (1997). Social work as an international profession: Opportunities and challenges. In M.C. Hokenstad & J. Midgley (Eds.), *Issues in international social work* (pp. 146–158). Washington, DC: NASW Press.

Jones, K. (1984). *Eileen Younghusband: A biography.* Occasional Papers on Social Administration Number 76, London: Bedford Square Press. (Note: Jones quotes Younghusband throughout the biography but does not identify the works from which the quotes are taken.)

Katzki, K. (1988). 60 Years of ICSW. In ICSW, *1928–1988: Celebration of the 60th Anniversary* (pp. 11–20). Papers from the conference, Frankfurt and Berlin, July 29–August 2, 1988. Vienna, Austria: ICSW.

Kendall, K. (1977). *Final report: International development of qualified social work manpower for population and family planning activities.* New York: IASSW.

Kendall, K. (1978). The IASSW 1928–1978: A journey of remembrance. In K. Kendall (Ed.), *Reflections on social work education* (pp. 170–191). New York: IASSW.

Kendall, K. (Guest Editor). (1982). *International Social Work, XXV*(1).

Kendall, K. A. (1987). International social work education. In A. Minahan (Ed.), *Encyclopedia of social work* (18th ed., pp. 987–996). Silver Spring, MD: NASW Press.

Kendall, K. (1989). Women at the helm: Three extraordinary leaders. *Affilia, 4*(1), 23–32.

Kendall, K. A. (1994). The challenges of internationalism in social work: Past, present, and future. In L. Healy (Ed.), *The global-local link: International challenges to social work practice.* West Hartford, CT: University of Connecticut School of Social Work, Center for International Social Work Studies.

Lally, D. (1987). International social welfare organizations and services. In A. Minahan (Ed.), *Encyclopedia of social work* (18th ed., pp. 969–986). Silver Spring, MD: NASW Press.

Larned, R. (1945). International social work. In *Social Work Yearbook 1945* (pp. 188–194). New York: Russell Sage Foundation.

Lorenz, W. (1994). *Social work in a changing Europe.* London: Routledge.

Mary Catherine Jennings is appointed new social welfare attaché in Brazil. (1963). *NASW News,* 8(3), 1.

Obituary of René Sand. (1953). *Journal of the American Medical Association, 153,* 1028, 1111.

Obituary of René Sand, M.D. L.L.D. (1953). *British Medical Journal, 4835,* 571–572.

Organization of the International Conference of Social Work. (1929). In *International Conference of Social Work* [Proceedings] (Vol. I, pp. 5–17). First Conference, Paris, July 8–13, 1928.

Quam, J. K. (1995). Younghusband, Dame Eileen (1902–1981). In R. Edwards (Ed.), *Encyclopedia of social work* (19th ed., p. 2619). Washington, DC: NASW Press.

René Sand. (1953). *Lancet* (London) *265,* 576.

United Nations. (1994). *Human rights and social work: A manual for schools of social work and the social work profession* [Professional training series No. 1]. Geneva, Switzerland: UN Centre for Human Rights.

University of California, Office of Public Information, Biography—Donald Howard, 9/1/48. Social Welfare Archives, AASW Collection, Box 21.

University of California at Los Angeles. (1998). Issue on the 40th Anniversary of the UCLA School of Social Welfare [Special issue]. *UCLA Social Welfare,* 3(1).

Wickwar, W. H. (1947). Relief supplies and welfare distribution: UNRRA in retrospect. *Social Service Review, XXI*(3), 363–374.

Willetts, P. (Ed.). (1996). *The conscience of the world: The influence of non-governmental organisations in the U.N. system.* Washington, DC: Brookings Institution.

Younghusband, E. (1963). Tasks and trends in education for social work: An international appraisal. *Social Work* (London) *20(3),* 4–11.

CHAPTER 8

SOCIAL WORK AROUND THE WORLD TODAY

> The term social work includes every effort to relieve distress due to poverty, to restore individuals and families to normal conditions of living, to prevent social scourges and to improve the social and living conditions of the community, through social casework, through group activities, through community action in legislation and administration, and through social research.
>
> First International Conference of Social Work, 1929, p. 5

> The social work profession promotes social change, problem solving in human relationships and the empowerment and liberation of people to enhance well-being. Utilising theories of human behaviour and social systems, social work intervenes at the points where people interact with their environments. Principles of human rights and social justice are fundamental to social work.
>
> Definition adopted by IFSW and IASSW, 2000

The social work profession has sought international commonalities since its early years. The quotations above are two international definitions of social work, one developed for the international conference held in 1928 and the current definition adopted 72 years later in 2000. In examining social work in various countries around the world, one is struck by similarities and differences. Although indigenization has increased local variations in method and increased attention to local problems, globalization has heightened professionals' awareness of common issues and increased opportunities for communication and exchange.

There are many commonalities in social work throughout the world. Recognition of these commonalities took a major step forward in 2004, when voluntary global standards for social work education were adopted by the International Association of Schools of Social Work (IASSW) and International Federation of Social Workers (IFSW) (2004): *Global Standards for Social Work Education and Training,* as mentioned in the previous chapter. One important common thread in the profession is that social work everywhere recognizes a dual emphasis of responsibility to individuals in need and responsibility for social reform or social change. Another is that throughout the world, values play an important part in defining social work, with human dignity as the core value. And social work practice in all countries is strongly influenced by the social environment and the larger political-economic context. This last commonality, the strong environmental or contextual component of social work, leads to unique local patterns. Thus, one of social work's most important and distinguishing common features—that it is *the* profession that recognizes the interaction of individuals with their environments—leads to differences in social work practice among countries and regions. In addition, resource availability is a facilitating or constraining factor that varies greatly by country.

In this chapter, examples of current social work practice and issues will be discussed, drawing on countries facing many different social problems with varying levels of economic and professional resources. These range from Denmark, a high-income country where social work is practiced in the context of a universal welfare state, to Jamaica, a relatively resource-poor country that has achieved respectable standards of health and education yet where social workers have struggled with the impact of structural adjustment. Mauritius can best be described as a society in transition, creating new challenges for a 35+-year-old profession. Ethiopia, another African country, suffers overwhelming social and economic problems yet is experiencing an exciting rebirth and expansion of social work education. Social workers in Argentina have worked, along with the rest of civil society, to overcome the effects of their long period of military oppression, while facing new challenges of privatization. In Armenia, the profession of social work has emerged since 1990 to cope with war, extreme political change, and resource shortages. And in Japan social workers address the problems of a postindustrial, consumer-oriented society that has undergone a demographic transition. Through these examples, similarities, and differences in social work will be illustrated. A brief analysis of common and divergent themes will conclude the chapter.

DENMARK

Social workers in Denmark practice within the context of a comprehensive, universalist welfare state. The proportion of the population living in poverty is relatively small, estimated to be almost 10% if *poverty* is defined as a family with less than 50% of the median income, or about 8% of families who have difficulty paying their bills (Strauss, 2006). Usually, poverty is only temporary, especially for children, and poverty is particularly severe for ethnic minority groups. Families are protected by a set of universal welfare programs that provide for health care, education, and protection from poverty due to unemployment, illness, or old age. In addition, the social welfare system takes a preventive approach to problems that arise from normal living, providing, for example, a system of health visitors to provide support to new parents and advise on child rearing and child health matters.

The majority of social workers are employed by local social service agencies run by municipalities or by counties. A new structure that took effect in 2007 will shut down the county level and allow some of the smaller municipalities to join together in larger units. The health services, general and mental hospitals, employ social workers, as do the prisons. Social work with the elderly is relatively new but is growing with the aging of the Danish population. Smaller numbers of social workers are employed by private organizations, such as battered women's crisis centers, foster home agencies, users' interest organizations, and settlement houses. In Denmark, however, a relatively small number of agencies are private, and even these get some public funds. Although it is important to underscore that most social work services are delivered by public agencies, policy changes are under way. Corporations are now being encouraged by the Ministry of Social Affairs to take social responsibility for their employees; and, as a result, some are employing social workers to assist with this function. Revisions to the Social Services Act adopted in 1997 included provision for active cooperation of the public sector with various private organizations in the municipalities. However, there are many unresolved problems in efforts to establish a mixed public and private sector welfare system, and it has not become usual practice to allow private organizations to take over more social work functions as a way of addressing the growing costs of the welfare state (H. Strauss, personal communication, January 2006). Issues for the future include the division of labor between the sectors, and "myths and prejudices within these two sectors" (Halskov & Egelund, 1998, p. 19).

The major functions of social workers are social counseling and case management, especially those employed by Municipal Social Services. Referral is another important social work function, assisting the client to access the available benefits and services. Referrals are made to services offered by the public sector and by private organizations. Therapy is not considered part of the social work task and function. Perhaps 10%–15% of social workers do become therapists, but only after receiving advanced training; they then typically find work in hospitals, family care centers, crisis centers for women or men, and other treatment institutions. In such settings, a part of being a social worker is being able to offer professional therapy (I. Hjerrild, personal communication, April 17, 1997).

In Denmark, only trained persons with diplomas in social work can call themselves social workers or be hired by the authorities to do social work. Social pedagogy here is a narrower field, emphasizing training to care for children and disabled adults in day care and other institutions.

Social Work Education

Social workers are educated at four National Danish Schools of Social Work at Esbjerg, Odense, Aarhus, and Copenhagen and in a program at Aalborg

University. The programs at the National Danish Schools accept students who have completed secondary school exams. Reflecting changes as of 2003, social work education is now a 3½-year, postsecondary course, leading to a bachelor of profession. As have many other European countries, Denmark has joined the Barcelona Convention, which validates educational comparison and allows student mobility. This system is facilitated by a joint European Credit Transfer System (ECTS points). Social work study consists of 210 ECTS points of which 36 are for two practice placements. Education combines academic courses in social work methods and theories, social welfare legislation, psychology and sociology, economics, and law with field placement. Use of problem-oriented projects in groups is regarded as a valuable pedagogic method that encourages students to do their own studies, with guidance. Students write reports about their work that usually include interviews with service users and social workers related to their chosen topic. Typical field placements are in the social welfare and health services of local authorities, including social and health service departments, hospitals, correctional services, trade unions, housing associations, and residential institutions. The goal is to prepare students with critical and analytic competence related to social problems who can select appropriate methods and work for social change in cooperation with service users. Students are expected to have the skills to carry out their tasks and make decisions taking into account the demands of the law, the situation of the user, and the practice of the agency or department. They are also expected to be able to work for change within organizations, take part in social research, and work with quality assurance measures (H. Strauss, personal communication, January 2006). Social workers and related professionals (teachers, nurses, pedagogues) can obtain a diploma in special areas of social work, such as family and children, multicultural social work, and psychiatric social work. In 1996, a government act introduced modifications in the academic program and governance structure of social work education ("Social Work Education in Denmark," 1998). A stronger emphasis on interdisciplinary education has been required. Teams of faculty from various disciplines were required to develop curriculum in the four main areas of social work: counseling theory and practice; human development; law; and political science, economics, labor, and other supporting social sciences. The law also demanded higher order integration of theory and practice and required evaluation of students' practice and personal competencies, as well as their academic progress. Local boards made up of local political representatives and social service agency representatives, faculty, and a student were to be established to govern schools of social work (I. Hjerrild, personal communication, April 17, 1997).

The Danish Association of Social Workers, with approximately 10,000 members (95% of all professional social workers), negotiates with the government at local and national levels on pay and working conditions (*Information Sheet on Danish Association of Social Workers*, 2000). In addition, the

Association runs conferences and becomes involved in legislative issues affecting social work.

Future Issues

In the future, social workers in Denmark will continue to work on identity issues and intend to work to strengthen research. Changes in Danish society are posing new professional challenges, especially a new conservatism in the political-economic culture and an increase in the number of the unemployed and of minorities in society. Unemployment is 4.3%, the lowest rate in Europe. However, unemployment strikes unevenly and is particularly severe among young immigrants; unemployment among young immigrants is 25%, and many of these youth have poor prospects for future employment because of low levels of education (H. Strauss, personal communication, January 2006). New strategies aimed at "activating" the unemployed and other marginalized populations are being developed, along with a strong emphasis on employment. The general caseload tends to include more low-income clients. Will this signal a turn away from the universalism that has brought social harmony to Denmark? (I. Hjerrild, personal communications, April 1997; June 1998). A concern about the emphasis on employment is that it "ignores the need for broader and more personally-targeted initiatives in relation to more vulnerable young people—for instance young, single mothers" (Halskov & Egelund, 1998, p. 15).

There is also concern that many people in Denmark see refugees as a big problem, although most are well integrated. Policies on immigration have been tightened in recent years as the public has become less welcoming. The welfare state has depended on wide acceptance of community social norms, and therefore, the Danish approach to refugee resettlement has emphasized integration. This includes integration not only into schools and the labor market but also in integrated interpersonal relations and "Danish behavior" to maintain a coherent society (Strauss, 2006). Some recent refugees are less willing or less able to become fully integrated. As unemployment grows among sectors of the population, there is concern about multigeneration social exclusion, as youth may receive a negative "social inheritance" when they are raised in homes of unemployed, single-parent, non-Danish speaking families (Strauss, 2006). The current content of social work education may not prepare professionals adequately for work with ethnic minority youth, although programs are beginning to focus more attention on immigrant populations.

Finally, a change of paradigm over recent decades is affecting the profession. Although financial help from the state was previously regarded as a gift, the client today is expected to give something in return to the state. This can be described as a change from welfare to workfare. Social work is increasingly linked to contracts, standardized methods spelled out by the state, decentralization, and privatization—not unlike trends in less universalist welfare states (Buss & Strauss, 2004).

JAMAICA

In Jamaica, the majority of professionally trained social workers are employed in government programs, especially probation and correctional services and children's services. Some of the major hospitals, including the Children's Hospital and psychiatric hospital, have social workers; and at the University Hospital in Kingston social workers are deployed in such areas as sickle cell disease, AIDS, and detoxification, and in a new violence prevention program. The number of social workers employed in schools is increasing. A few pilot employee assistance programs existed in selected industries such as a bauxite company that employs a professionally trained social worker as a "welfare officer." Approximately three-fourths of trained social workers are in the public sector, primarily with the services named above, with slightly less than 25% in nongovernmental organizations (NGOs), often as managers, consultants, and researchers. There are only a few who work in the private, for-profit sector, usually in human resource development (J. Maxwell, personal communication, May 31, 2007).

Although many of the problems social workers deal with are common to any society, others reflect the particular circumstances of Jamaica. Migration to the United States and Canada is a common phenomenon and often separates families, sometimes for years. Social workers encounter children whose parents are overseas or who are preparing to migrate themselves. Care arrangements may be inadequate or unstable and children may feel abandoned. Children are an important focus for social work, and government and Jamaica's NGO community have mobilized to implement the Convention on the Rights of the Child (CRC). New legislation, the Child Care and Protection Act, is an important government response to the CRC. Attention is now being paid to trafficking and child labor, and to child abuse as interest in child protection and parenting have increased in recent years. Restructuring of the Children's Services was an important development in the social services, and the service is a major employer of social workers in Jamaica. An Office of the Child Advocate has been newly established and a professional social worker appointed to the post. This, too, reflects Jamaica's increased commitment to improvement of children's well-being.

Drug abuse and AIDS have created demands for new social work services over the past few decades. As Maxwell (2002) indicates, use of hard drugs such as cocaine and heroin increased and led to treatment and prevention initiatives, spearheaded by the National Council on Drug Abuse. HIV/AIDS is a significant concern in the Caribbean, and Jamaica has the third largest population living with HIV in the Caribbean. An AIDS program has been developed at the University Hospital and includes social work services. Other initiatives have addressed community violence and, especially, its impact on children. Community violence is a significant problem and affects social workers and their clients. The murder rate in Jamaica soared from 33 per 100,000 in 1997 to 56 per 100,000 in 2004 (Levy, 2005). Many were committed by gangs, some by criminal gangs, but others by what Levy (2005) called "corner crews" or community gangs—groups of young people in inner-city ghettos who see little future. Some social service providers have launched initiatives to promote peace building among these gangs that rule low-income settlements and engage in periodic gun battles. For the social worker attempting to serve those in the inner city, the challenges are "how to do mediation and counseling, how to build institution and community, how to reach through a vortex of violence, crime and garrison politics towards peace and development" (Levy, 2005, p. 15).

Identity and Contributions

Social work leaders in Jamaica see many universals in social work practice. However, they also note that social workers in Jamaica, especially those who are untrained, tend to be more directive and prescriptive than social workers in the United States. This is explained partly by the pressures of large caseloads but is also due to cultural expectations on the part of clients who expect the expert to have knowledge and to solve their problems. In addition, the ability to truly use a democratic empowerment approach is societally determined. The ideal is present in Jamaica; however, its practice may be hampered by traditions of social stratification and traditional authority patterns (J. Maxwell, personal interview, April 1997). Others believe that social work principles, though generally applicable across nations, have been interpreted

Figure 8.1 Bringing early childhood services to inner-city Kingston, Jamaica.

One experienced social worker described her career as follows. For years, she was employed by an NGO named VOUCH—Voluntary Organization for the Upliftment of Children. Here, she worked with families experiencing problems with child rearing. The clients were inner-city families living in poverty; often, they were long-term clients of the agency. She did casework, assisting parents (usually mothers) in working out solutions to their children's distresses, and did referrals for other services. At that time, the agency temporarily assigned its social workers to work two days a week in the maternity hospital and the children's hospital. As a result, these hospitals have since added social work services. Now employed by the United Way, she sees her function as educating corporate people and United Way volunteers about the social problems of Jamaica and consulting with private voluntary agencies to help them to improve their programs (S. Nicholson, personal communication, April 22, 1997).

through the "filters of the culture and with a particular Jamaican scene" (S. Francis, personal communication, April 24, 1997).

Another area of contribution has been through involvement in community development (although it is not the area of major social work employment in Jamaica). Beginning in the years of unrest and political awakening in the 1930s, community development has been important in involving social workers in attacking severe rural poverty and, later, urban problems. An early organization was Jamaica Welfare, founded in 1937 by Norman Manley (founder of one of Jamaica's two major political parties and second premier from 1955–1962) with funds negotiated from the Banana Producers' Association. The organization established that the funds were "not for charitable purposes . . . but for real help in the development of the island and its peasants" (Girvan, 1993, p. 7). As early as 1940, Jessie Irwin, "an outstanding social worker," advocated for the focus to be on community organizing at the village level to strengthen local capacity, rather than on the building of community centers (Girvan, 1993, p. 10). This was accomplished through many organizations: farmers organizations, women's groups, cooperatives, study clubs, and youth groups. Community development continues to be a social work function today in a number of small NGOs throughout the island. In the late 1980s, the Association of Development Agencies in Jamaica utilized a community development approach to rebuilding after Hurricane Gilbert, mobilizing residents to engage in self-help reconstruction and institution building, rather than passive relief work. Case 8.1 illustrates the development approach.

In a more recent community development effort, social workers affiliated with the University of the West Indies worked in a squatter community on leadership development and community capacity building to enable the community to plan for its relocation (Shillingford, 2005). In Jamaica, large

CASE 8.1: COMMUNITY DEVELOPMENT AFTER A DISASTER

A social worker heading the Association of Development Agencies (ADA) in Jamaica was faced with a practice dilemma in the wake of Hurricane Gilbert in 1988. Gilbert was a devastating hurricane, causing the worst destruction in Jamaica in 30 years. Needs for assistance were enormous. Yet ADA was a development agency, committed to enhancing community capacity for self-help. Its challenge after Gilbert was to sustain this focus in the face of such great need and donor pressure to engage in relief—the distribution of commodities.

Devastation was particularly bad in poverty areas, where poorly constructed dwellings were no match for high winds. ADA therefore decided to organize a series of shelter clinics to teach local agencies and residents how to build or rehabilitate homes to make them less prone to hurricane damage. A team was put together, including architects and a builder from the Women's Construction Collective—selected purposefully to increase female participation. Funding was quickly secured from several external and regional funders.

The clinics included preparatory meetings in the community to define roles and responsibilities, a community-wide workshop to mobilize participation, workdays to construct a building, and an evaluative workshop that included evaluation of the extent of learning about disaster preparedness and about community building. Community participants learned by doing—by constructing a simple structure with a hurricane-resistant roof to be given to a particularly needy individual or used as community space. Before construction could begin, the community had to decide the disposition of the finished product. During the project, ADA held 13 clinics in "rural to deep rural" locations, with an average of more than 50 participants in each. Outcomes included more than 600 residents having learned safe building skills, increased personal efficacy, and the development of new and/or strengthened community organizations in most locations.

Social work roles for the director and her associates were many. The most important may have been to guide the agency to stay true to mission in difficult times and to find a way to use crisis to strengthen, rather than divert, the agency. Social work beliefs in resiliency and empowerment were definitely put into practice. Much time was spent in coalition building and in guiding and facilitating local involvements, being vigilant not to take control of community decisions. Finally, the project was designed and implemented to pay attention to the needs of those often left out: women, rural residents, and the disabled. The model's success led to a request to take it to Montserrat the next year after Hurricane Hugo hit the Eastern Caribbean.

Case adapted from Baker, 1998.

numbers of people are living on land that they do not own or formally rent; these settlements are commonly referred to as squatter communities.

Current leaders in the profession assess the contributions of social work to national development positively. One commented that through the work of social work NGOs "we have jolly well kept the lid on the kettle" in many instances, by tackling issues the government won't or can't deal with. If these efforts had not been made, catastrophic problems could have resulted (S. Nicholson, personal communication, April 22, 1997). Another stated that social work has made a particularly important contribution to Jamaica's development by making people more aware that things can be done to improve conditions. Social work's stance is that people can change, that they can be helped, and that they can learn to help themselves; through this message, social work has done a lot for Jamaica, and it is recognized, even by government (E. Sayle, personal communication, April 24, 1997).

Social Work Education

Social work education was initiated at the University of the West Indies in 1961 as a 2-year certificate course. A baccalaureate degree has been offered since 1969–1970 (or 1973–1974 in current form), and a master's degree was begun in 1993 (Maxwell, Williams, Ring, & Cambridge, 2003). The master's program is small yet offers three areas of specialization—clinical practice, administration and management, and community organization/policy—in alternating years. Recently, a social work program has begun at Northern Caribbean University.

The majority of trained social workers receive their education through the baccalaureate program in the Department of Sociology, Psychology and Social Work. Approximately 150 are enrolled at any one time, and by 1991, it was estimated that about 600 social workers had been educated by the department. That number has likely grown to well more than 1,000. Content includes core courses in sociology and other social sciences, psychology of the individual and society, and social work methods and practice, taught in academic classes and in field practica. Caribbean realities are addressed throughout the curriculum and in several focused courses. However, indigenous social work literature is less available. As Maxwell (1991) indicated,

> there remains, still largely unanswered, a challenge to develop local theoretical formulations as a basis for advancing the understanding of . . . the Caribbean personality, individual and interpersonal behavior patterns, the effectiveness of techniques directed at assisting individuals, groups and community to improve social functioning or to effect changes on oppressive environmental forces. (p. 20)

Short-term, more paraprofessional training has been available in social services through the Social Welfare Training Centre, established in the Department of Extra Mural Studies at the University of the West Indies in Mona in 1962. This "four month course in the principles and practice of social work" was first offered in 1963, to 12 students from 5 Caribbean countries (Brown, 1991). The Training Centre (now part of the School of Continuing Studies) continues to offer the 4-month course and other short-term, practical training to persons working in social services throughout the English speaking Caribbean. A one-year certificate is now offered at community colleges and at the Social Welfare Training Centre. Social work training is beginning to be offered at other colleges; in addition, there has been considerable expansion of degree-level social work education at the other campuses of the University of the West Indies and elsewhere in the Caribbean including Guyana, Belize, and the Bahamas (J. Maxwell, personal communication, May 30, 2007).

The Jamaica Association of Social Workers (JASW) is the professional association. Educators from the Mona campus have taken lead roles in creation of a regional educational association, the Association of Caribbean Social Work Educators (ACSWE) in 1997, and in the launch of a professional journal, *The Caribbean Journal of Social Work* in 2002. The latter development should be of particular help in generating local literature.

Challenges

There are a number of challenges facing social work in Jamaica. Regional educators identify locally relevant theory development as "the most critical and urgent challenge confronting current development efforts" (Maxwell et al., 2003, p. 26). There is also a need for more social work involvement in advocacy on public policy issues, such as poverty, homophobia, domestic and community violence, and funding for social services and education. To strengthen professional voice and leadership, JASW needs to become a more active and vigorous body. Finally, Jamaica must also contend with the continued out-migration of professional social workers. Along with others with tertiary and professional education, significant numbers of social workers leave Jamaica for better employment opportunities in North America. This exodus diminishes the capacity of the profession in Jamaica to address the challenges it faces.

MAURITIUS

Mauritius, an island nation in the Indian Ocean, has undergone tremendous change over recent decades. After years of colonization by France and Britain, independence was achieved in 1968. More recently, the biggest change has been a shift from a predominantly agricultural economy overwhelmingly dependent on a single crop (sugar) to an economy with a sizable manufacturing sector and considerable tourism. The growth of manufacturing, initially textiles, brought job opportunities for women, ushering in changes in gender and family roles. Mauritius is therefore described as a society in transition, from an agricultural to manufacturing economy, from an unskilled to skilled labor force, from extended families to nuclear families, and toward status as a "NIC"—newly industrialized country (UNICEF & Republic of Mauritius, 1994). More change is underway as tourism and the service sector are becoming more important domains for income generation and employment (S. Ragobur, personal communication, August 19, 2006). It is not surprising that the president of the Mauritian Association of Social Work said that "at the threshold of the third millennium, the social work profession in Mauritius is preparing to face the challenges of change affecting every sphere of life of the Mauritian citizen" (Ramgoolam, 1996, p. 1).

UNICEF describes Mauritius as in transition from a society concerned with child survival to a society concerned with child development and protection (UNICEF & Republic of Mauritius, 1994, p. 2). This description is useful in examining changes in social work functions and priorities, in Mauritius and in other countries at similar levels of development. Originally focused on community development, then on probation services, social work is increasingly concerned with behavioral and emotional aspects of individual and family well-being. Mental health counseling, work with families experiencing domestic violence, child protection, and suicide prevention are services now beginning to attract social work attention. This transition can be observed not only in Mauritius but also in many developing countries as they successfully reduce infant mortality, improve literacy and sanitation, and wipe out widespread malnutrition. Once the survival issues are satisfactorily addressed, quality of family life and developmental issues can be tackled.

Figure 8.2 Women's group in Mauritius. Women study patterns for an income generation project.

Service needs and roles for social workers continue to evolve. Elder abuse and neglect are beginning to surface as the population ages, and mental health concerns are growing as life in a changing environment grows more stressful. Social workers are also providing services in poverty alleviation and efforts to fight social exclusion. The major government poverty alleviation program, the Trust Fund for Poverty Alleviation, includes efforts to develop community assets and empower poor and unemployed persons through enterprise development (S. Ragobur, personal communication, August 19, 2006).

Social work is a relatively recent profession in Mauritius; however, social welfare entitlements and social services have a long history. An old Poor Law provided indoor and outdoor relief as early as 1830, and the modern Mauritian welfare system was influenced by British Fabian socialism. Several decades before independence, Labour Party leader and future prime minister Seewoosagur Ramgoolam began to advocate for food subsidies, health insurance, publically financed education, and old-age pensions ("Mauritius: The Welfare System Environment," 1986). Labour Party support was bolstered by the two influential social welfare studies conducted in Mauritius around 1960. The first, conducted by J. E. Meade, examined the economic and social structure of Mauritius; the second, by Richard Titmuss and Brian Abel-Smith, focused on social and demographic issues (Meade et al., 1961; Titmuss & Abel-Smith, 1961). The reports led to development of strong programs in family planning and related social services, and to social welfare legislation. Although constrained by the International Monetary Fund's (IMF's) structural adjustment requirements in the 1980s, the commitment to social welfare remains strong. Examination of the welfare indicators for Mauritius in Table 1.1 (Chapter 1) will show the island's success in child survival, with an infant mortality rate of 14 and life expectancy of 72. As noted above, current "typical social work cases" show increased concern with child development, family life, and mental health.

Most social workers in Mauritius are civil servants, and the largest numbers are employed in Social Security and in the Probation Service. A network of social welfare centers and community centers throughout the country employ social workers, who engage in a variety of roles to encourage community action to solve problems. There are a few medical social workers in the major hospitals, and a small number at the mental hospital. A smaller number of social workers are employed by the larger nongovernmental agencies, including the Mauritius Family Planning Association and the Mauritius Alliance of Women.

Certainly no single case is typical of social work in a country. The following case is included because it illustrates Mauritian social work in transition, recognizing child development needs, yet hampered by incomplete service development and lack of resources.

The case such as Jean's could occur in many societies. It illustrates the functions of the social worker in investigation, efforts at family intervention, referral, and finally case advocacy to secure needed services for the client. It points out the need for further advocacy for service development to ensure

---

CASE EXAMPLE: A CASE OF CHILD NEGLECT
IN A FAMILY IN POVERTY IN MAURITIUS

Jean is a 4-year-old boy who lives with his father, 7-year-old sister, and grandmother in a three-room corrugated iron-sheet house. The parents are separated, and mother lives elsewhere. The case was reported to the Child Development Unit of the Ministry of Women, Family Welfare and Child Development by a medical worker in the hospital. A caseworker visited and found that Jean, mentally retarded, was being "grossly neglected." The house was filthy; according to the grandmother, the father is an alcoholic, and she said she is too old to care for such a child who needs constant care. The caseworker discovered that Jean could not speak. He made noises and followed the caseworker everywhere, touching him frequently. The child seemed to the worker to be deprived of affection. Making a second visit, the caseworker interviewed the father. The father said he had no objection to the child being placed in a home. Mother was summoned to the office, but she refused to take Jean.

The caseworker tried to admit Jean to an institution but could not find a vacancy in a place equipped to care for handicapped children.

Soon thereafter, Jean was left tied to a bed, unfed and unattended. He became ill and was admitted to a hospital. During his 2-month stay, no relative visited him. Discharge planning was challenging, as no placement could be found. The caseworker attempted to admit Jean to the Shelter for Women and Children in distress, a temporary shelter. However, the agency refused him admission, as they claimed they were not equipped to cope with Jean's multiple needs. The caseworker took the case to the Ministry's Permanent Secretary and to the magistrate to get an order to admit Jean to the shelter. Now, he is waiting while SOS Children's Village determines whether it will admit him for longer term care (Boodajee, 1997).

---

that the needs of children with disabilities can be addressed. The case also illustrates the transition being experienced in Mauritian social work. Rather than focusing on child survival, the caseworker is focusing on child protection. As more appropriate services can be developed, child development will increase in importance.

The successes and future challenges Mauritius faces are indicated by UNICEF's decision to conclude its work there in 2003, because of the country's success in improving child welfare. Cited were the 2005 under-5 (U-5) mortality rate of 15, down from 23 in 1990, and the universal access to public health care, safe water, and primary education. As noted in the UNICEF (2007) country brief:

> The end of UNICEF's programme of cooperation, however, doesn't mean there are no challenges still facing children. Pockets of poverty remain, and child abuse

and violence against women, sexual exploitation, increasing drug and alcohol dependency among young people and the exclusion of children with disabilities all are cause of concern. Services to support children in need of protection are not yet sufficient: there are scarcities of trained social workers, counsellors, rehabilitation specialists and child psychologists and there is a need for better coordination between non-governmental organizations, civil society and the private sector.

Unlike most other countries, social work in Mauritius has been a male profession. However, the number of females has increased significantly, and female social work students now outnumber their male counterparts in the classroom. The most likely factor influencing this change is the changing role of women in society.

The Mauritius Association of Professional Social Workers was formed in 1984 and is affiliated with the International Federation of Social Workers. Its structure calls for an Executive Committee of representatives from the six major areas of social work: social security, probation, youth, medical social work, municipality welfare, and social welfare. Given the expansion of new settings for social work discussed above, some modifications may be expected in the future.

Social Work Education

Social work education is offered at the University of Mauritius. Until 1995, the highest credential offered was a diploma in social work studies, earned through a 2-year course of academic classes and field placement. In the diploma program, only students with at least 2 years of social work experience were admitted, and slots were allocated to various ministries and agencies, including the Ministry of Social Security, the Ministry of Reform Institutions, the Ministry for Women's Rights and Family Affairs, Mauritius Family Planning Association, the Sugar Industry Labour Welfare Fund, and the Mauritius Council on Social Service. The professional association and personnel from social agencies lobbied for several years for upgrade to a degree program, citing the need for upgrading of skills and improved status, and "the need in our society for intervention by professional social workers in various problems thrown up by the complexity of life in present day Mauritius" (Manrakhan, 1990). In 1995, the University responded and began a degree program, leading to a BSc in social work. The first students graduated in 1998.

ETHIOPIA

Also an African country, socioeconomic conditions in Ethiopia contrast sharply with those in Mauritius. Ethiopia is the second most populous country in Sub-Saharan Africa and one of the poorest countries in the world,

with a Human Development Index ranking of 170th out of the 177 countries ranked in 2005 (UN Development Programme [UNDP], 2005). U-5 mortality is 166, 20th worst among nations listed in the 2006 *State of the World's Children* (UNICEF, 2006), and up to 70% of the population is considered "food insecure" meaning that any misfortune can tip a family or individual into hunger. Ethiopia suffered from a particularly severe and well-publicized famine in 1984 in which hundreds of thousands of people died. Lack of rains in 2007 again caused widespread hunger and need for food aid.

Civil war and regional conflicts have been a regular part of Ethiopian reality since the 1960s, including a 30-year war leading to the independence of Eritrea in 1993; simultaneously, Ethiopia has often hosted refugees from other regional conflicts, adding to the burden on resources. A brief but difficult experiment with Marxism further complicated the Ethiopian condition. Yet Ethiopia also boasts a rich tradition of art, culture, and religion and is the home of "Lucy" a human ancestor dated 3.2 million or more years old. Important and advanced civilizations flourished in earlier times, including the ancient kingdom of Aksum from approximately 1–700 A.D.

Present-day Ethiopia presents numerous challenges for social work. Asked to identify the social problems existing in Ethiopia, the dean of the School of Social Work in Addis Ababa quipped that it would be easier to list what are "not problems" (Tasse, 2005). Some of the issues are evident from UN statistics: poor health conditions leading to high infant mortality, low levels of literacy, and large numbers of the population living in severe poverty. Impeding easy solutions are the environmental challenges of arid land and poor soil conditions, as well as large sections of the country that cannot be farmed. The president of Addis Ababa University, Andreas Eschete, identified numerous areas of critical need for social work, including problems of "women, persons from disadvantaged regions, and the urgent need for counseling for students from rural regions in their transition to urban, college life" (Johnson-Butterfield & Linsk, 2005, p. 15). He also identified serious unmet need for mental health and counseling services, as there were generally little or no such services available at the beginning of the twenty-first century, except for one mental hospital. Other areas identified as important priorities for social work include maternal and child health, women's and children's rights, rural development, health, and microenterprise (Johnson-Butterfield & Linsk, 2005, p. 15).

UNICEF has called for attention to early marriage, abduction of women and girls, and female circumcision, all of which reduce life chances of girls. A growing AIDS epidemic further threatens human well-being; there is little treatment available for those who become infected.

Social Work Education

A School of Social Work was begun as a unit of Haile Selassie I University (now Addis Ababa University) in 1959 by the Ministry of Public Health. Assistance was provided by the UN Technical Assistance Board and a 2-year diploma course began. In 1961, the School became a member of the IASSW as an independent unit at the University (Sedler, 1968). The program became a faculty with a mix of foreign and Ethiopian lecturers. At the beginning of the offering of a BA degree in 1966, there were three Ethiopians among the seven faculty members. The Ethiopian faculty became leaders in the region and in IASSW, with Seyoum Gebreselassie elected as an IASSW vice-president; the 1974 Congress of the IASSW was scheduled to be held in Addis Ababa. Sadly, unrest and then a coup disrupted the plans and disrupted social work education for some time.

The BA program was closed by the military region in 1975. However, social work faculty changed the names of their courses and continued to teach social work "underground" within the sociology department. Oppression ended the ability of Ethiopian educators to continue their regional and international leadership in the field until conditions improved.

Through an international partnership, a master's in social work (MSW) program was begun in September 2004 at Addis Ababa University. Thirty-nine students enrolled in the first class and graduated in the summer of 2006. Of the first 39, 7 were women. According to the project, the MSW curriculum is intended to prepare social workers "to manage community-based services and develop new programs in the areas of health, poverty reduction, child welfare, HIV/AIDS, and community development" (Johnson-Butterfield & Linsk, 2005, p. 3). The program has been taught by a remarkable array of international lecturers along with Ethiopian colleagues. A planned doctoral program was initiated in 2006, enrolling a small number of the MSW graduates. This will allow Ethiopia to train its own faculty to expand social work education and should permit reopening the BA program.

Social Work Roles

Social workers are working in areas of critical need in Ethiopia, including HIV/AIDS, women's programs, refugee work, and work with street children and other vulnerable children. Some hold management positions in large NGOs and in intergovernmental organizations, such as UNICEF. Challenges for the future include sustaining the remarkable progress that has been made, and taking advantage of the rebirth of Addis Ababa as the center of African regional organizations and leadership.

ARGENTINA

The roots of social work in Argentina are in the early work of charity groups, religious organizations, and mutual aid societies. Formal education for social work, as mentioned in Chapter 6, was adapted from European models and emphasized the role of social worker as assistant to other professions, especially medicine. Religious traditions remain influential, as does a focus on the family. The theme of freedom from oppression is also significant— initially freedom from repressive governments, more recently replaced by the oppression of international debt (Queiro-Tajalli, 1995). In January 2006, Argentina paid its entire debt to the IMF ahead of schedule, using reserves from the Argentine Central Bank. It is hoped that the country will be relieved of the unbearable demands from the IMF and will be able to focus on reconstruction of the economy (I. Queiro-Tajalli, personal communication, July 2, 2006).

Social workers work in a variety of fields of practice, including schools, family and children's services, mental health, health, gerontology, and in the judicial system, working with juveniles, or in jails and courts. Other employment opportunities are in general and mental hospitals and with the aged. Excellent work with the aged was done for many years as part of government programs. However, with cutbacks in funding, some of the benefits for the aged have disappeared, and poverty among the aged is a growing problem. There are macro-roles for social workers in community work, planning, and administration. Little clinical work is done by social workers in Argentina, as the profession does not emphasize therapy. For many years, Argentine social workers have practiced within a welfare state, and 95% were employed by the government. Now, however, the numbers of government employees are reduced as part of world trend toward privatization and the restructuring required by the IMF. A sizable number of social workers are still employed by the national, state, and municipal governments. In response to the funding and service cutbacks, marginalized peoples "created grassroots projects to survive the devastating effects of neoliberal policies" (Queiro-Tajalli, 2005, p. 9). Social work programs became involved in these grassroots projects, offering technical assistance and student interns.

Social work is about 90% female, although about 40% of social work professors are male. Identification as a women's profession has kept salaries low. In addition, "the profession's roots in charity work, its primary mission of helping the poor and the oppressed, and its dependence on other disciplines do not help to improve the public image of social work" (Queiro-Tajalli, 1995, p. 93). Legislation adopted in 1989 does recognize broad functions as part of social work including supervision, research, planning, and programming as well as direct services; agency and nonagency-based practice are recognized (Queiro-Tajalli, 1995).

Social workers are organized in numerous associations, grouped by the Federación Argentina de Asociaciones Profesionales de Servicio Social (I. Queiro-Tajalli, personal communication, July 2, 2006). The profession was described by one professor as "politically minded but not politically active" (R. Teubal, personal communication, March 13, 1997). There is a strong philosophical belief that social workers in practice are either on the side of the poor or they are on the side of the rich. This is reflected in the definition of social work advanced by Sela Sierra, an Argentine educator: "Social work is a change process seeking the humanization of social conditions and a progressive social liberation" (quoted in Queiro-Tajalli, 1995, p. 97). Thus, a macrovision exists, yet there is little overt social reform or social action. This is probably explained by several realities: the very high percentage of government employees among professionals; fear of losing jobs in this era of cut-backs; and the residue of the oppression of the 1970s. To understand current macro-practice, one needs to remember the sociopolitical events of the 1970s. Argentina lived through one of the darkest chapters of its history when the military took power and entered a "long, horrifying journey of terrorism, counter-terrorism, riots, abductions and tortures" (Queiro-Tajalli, 1995, p. 98). The military dictatorship that ruled from 1976 to 1983 waged a "dirty war" in which somewhere between 13,000 and 30,000 were killed or "disappeared" and others kept in concentration camps ("Argentina," 2006). Liberal and radical ideas, such as those of Paulo Freire that had changed social work in Latin America, were banned. Social workers tell of burning their books to avoid suspicion, spies in the classroom, and colleagues who were "dis-appeared." Social work educators and practitioners were among those who were fired, jailed, killed, or had to flee into exile. Not only was advocacy suppressed, even the teaching of group work was dangerous. Social work educators had to be sure not to promote radical action by students that could result in the students being killed. Thus, for survival reasons, social work would "think radically, but act conservatively" to paraphrase the more usual saying (R. Teubal, personal communication, March 13, 1997).

Nonetheless, today frontline social workers are very much involved in working with impoverished communities to help them emerge from the devastating effects of structural adjustment and economic crisis. Social work scholars are once again reviewing social work theories 40 years after the well-known reconceptualization movement (see Alayon, 2005).

Social Work Education

From its beginnings in 1930, social work education has expanded consider-ably and is now offered at 62 schools of social work (Queiro-Tajalli, 1995). These include schools at two levels, university degree programs and those programs offered by religious and governmental organizations. As noted above and in Chapter 6, the content of social work education has been influenced by philosophical and political developments within the country. The emphasis is on "integrating theory and practice, the need to work at the micro- and macro-levels, and the necessity of interventions that respond to the socioeconomic and political realities of those being served" (Queiro-Tajalli, 1995, p. 101). Students in university programs receive broad education in the social sciences, including sociology, psychology, and scientific thought, con-tent on Argentinian social problems, research, social work practice, and field practica. Placements are in such settings as community centers, health clinics, and schools. In the 1990s, the University of Buenos Aires had its students begin with macro-practice and move to more micropractice settings, with a first placement in community work, a second in groupwork, and the final placement in work with individuals and families (R. Teubal, personal com-munication, March 13, 1997). With student participation in governance re-stored, a renewed focus on relevance and indigenous concerns can be expected, tempered, however, by economic realities of reduced educational funding and scarcity of professional jobs.

ARMENIA

On September 21, 1991, Armenia ended 70 years of Soviet rule and voted to declare itself a sovereign state. Reforms and changes that had begun earlier intensified, particularly the move from a centrally controlled economy to free enterprise. Today, as described by Humphreys and Haroutunian (2004), Armenia is "a newly independent small landlocked Christian country in the southern Caucasus region" (p. 33). Although transition to independence and free enterprise has been difficult in many parts of the former Soviet empire, Armenia has faced particularly enormous challenges. Conflict with neighboring Azerbaijan led to an influx of refugees and to a blockade of Armenia by Turkey as well as Azerbaijan. This caused extreme shortages of fuel and raw materials, further devastating the economy. In addition, Armenia was still reeling from the effects of a 1988 earthquake that killed 25,000, left 500,000 homeless, and destroyed most of the country's second largest industrial city (Manjikian, 1996, p. 29). Ironically, the earthquake planted some of the seeds for the development of social work, as will be explained.

Figure 8.3 Refugee mother and child in refugee housing await permanent settlement in Armenia. (Photo by Thomas Felke)

As part of the Soviet system, the state controlled social welfare and provided a set of subsidies and cash payments to protect against social and medical crises. Government was the only source of solutions to problems outside the family. No private charitable organizations existed or were permitted; indeed, even the Armenian church did not have a well-developed tradition of charitable works. Armenia, therefore, like the other former Soviet republics, suffered from significant gaps in human service infrastructure to support the introduction of social work.

The crisis created by the 1988 earthquake shocked Armenians into realizing how unprepared they were to deal with needs for social services. This great tragedy has also been described as an opportunity. "It might sound callous to characterize such a tragedy as an opportunity, it was in the sense that it shook and collapsed social and political structures as effectively as it did material structures" (Moushigian, 1991, p. 1). Although Armenia was still under Soviet control, international aid organizations moved in to help, as "the disaster crumbled the barriers of this garrison state" (Moushigian, 1991, p. 2). Among these were the International Committee of the Red Cross, UNICEF, UN High Commissioner for Refugees, Oxfam, the Peace Corps, and aid agencies of the European Union. The external assistance—with modern medical technologies and mental health and trauma counseling—revealed just how unprepared and ill equipped the Soviet system was to cope with the emergency. Thus, in Armenia, the earthquake opened the way to outside influences, including the introduction of mental health and social services, in advance of the coming dissolution of the Soviet Union. The earthquake also brought aid from Armenians in the diaspora. Some contributed money, while "hundreds, perhaps thousands, of Armenians from the diaspora came to Armenia to help with the aftermath of the effects of the earthquake" (Humphreys & Haroutunian, 2004, p. 37). Humanitarian aid and remittances from Armenians living abroad have become important sources of revenue to independent Armenia.

Rapid change has shaped the context for the introduction of social work to Armenia. In the larger political and economic arenas, Armenia has moved rapidly toward a market economy and democracy. The first few years of independence brought the birth of a dozen political parties, initiation of a free press, privatization of farms, housing, and small business, introduction of a national currency, opening of a stock exchange, and a new tax system (Manjikian, 1996). The rapidity of change, coupled with the blockade and the earthquake, resulted in a 55% decline in national income from 1988–1992. The living standards of most Armenians fell significantly, just as expectations were rising.

With no prior history of social work nor even a religious charitable tradition, the majority of the Armenian population had no understanding of what social work is or how this newly introduced profession could contribute to the society. Yet, in just a few short years from 1991–1998, a profession has been established. Social work education has not only begun but has moved into full university status.

Social Work Education

Efforts to establish the profession began in 1990 when Dr. Ludmila Haroutunian, head of the Department of Applied Sociology at Yerevan State University and active in women's affairs in the USSR, began to organize training for social workers. Dr. Haroutunian had some prior knowledge about social work from an earlier stay in France in the 1970s. Faculty members received training at the London School of Economics where they studied social work for 6–12 months and gained practical experience in social welfare settings. Important contacts were also initiated with the University of Connecticut in the United States, which led to design and implementation of 6-month training courses for employees of the Ministry of Labor and Social Welfare. With the graduation of the first 15 trainees in June of 1994, Armenia had its first group of trained social workers. An undergraduate social work major has now been introduced at Yerevan State University, and the first group of baccalaureate social workers graduated in Spring 2000.

As in other eastern European countries and former Soviet republics, establishing field placements was initially a challenge. Yet, by the spring of 1998, there were 41 students in field placements. Settings included children's residential programs, an old age home, children's hospitals, a juvenile detention facility, the civil and criminal courts, the Ministry of Social Welfare, a mental health facility, and a community-based agency serving battered women. This last agency was founded by a faculty member and is staffed by social work graduates and current field students (N. A. Humphreys, personal communication, February 1999). Accompanying the development of social work has been the formation of numerous NGOs providing social services. Some were founded with the assistance of international agencies, while others were self-help or mutual aid organizations. Several have been founded, as the example above, by faculty members at Yerevan State University, helping the largely sociology-trained social work faculty to gain firsthand experience with social work (Humphreys & Haroutunian, 2004). With the help of the University of Connecticut, and an Armenian American social worker, staff at Yerevan State University have written a field work manual and provided training and orientation to the new field instructors. Most of the field instructors are psychologists; orientation and training provided has emphasized the differences and similarities between their profession and the "new" profession of social work (N. A. Humphreys, personal communication, February 1999).

The current social work education programs in Armenia include a 4-year undergraduate social work degree, a newer one-year MSW program that provides graduate education, and a number of distance learning sites that deliver some social work training.

Roles for graduates continue to expand. Social workers work in hospitals, schools, and in the newly established NGOs. Children's services are a growing area. The government has made a commitment to close the orphanages and is working to create a foster care system. Foster care will be essential as Armenia transitions from institutional to noninstitutional as the dominant model of care. In this as in other areas of service development, European Union standards are influential. Although Armenia has a considerable number of refugees and displaced persons, this is not a major area of social work practice.

An Armenian Association of Social Workers has been established as a division of the Armenian Society of Social Scientists. Particularly noteworthy is the initiation of a scholarly professional journal, *Social Transitions*.

An Armenian Model

Significant challenges remain; however, Armenian social workers and social work educators are confident that progress has been steady, if not remarkable. Early in the initiation of social work, one observer defined Armenia as a "case example of a country subscribing to a world culture," viewing the establishment of social work as part of the effort of Armenia "to establish itself in the world community by modeling other programs which are regarded as successful" (Manjikian, 1996, p. 42). An alternative explanation is the functional argument that views the initiation of social work as a response to the enormous social and economic dislocation brought about by the dissolution of communism, the earthquake, and the conflict with Azerbaijan. New problems arose or were being documented for the first time, and established programs and patterns of help were disrupted by change. Social work, with its theories of helping and practical skills, emerged through a combination of local and borrowed initiations to fulfill the helping function.

Developing an Armenian model of social work is and has been one of the most important foci of work on the profession. This has remained at the forefront throughout the consultations provided by the American partners; "an important aspect of the collaboration has been to insure that the profession develops in a way that is compatible with the Armenian culture" (Humphreys & Haroutunian, 2004, p. 45). Professional social work in Armenia has been developing rapidly through contact with many countries, especially the United Kingdom, Germany, and the United States. After exposure to so many different models and approaches to social work, the Armenians have realized that they must shape social work to fit their own culture and local issues. Ludmila Haroutunian (personal communication, August 2006) explains that in some ways,

> developing, testing and codifying an Armenian Model comes from the fact that Armenia itself is struggling to create a country that recaptures, celebrates, and, in some instances, invents what it means to be Armenian. During Soviet times, there was an emphasis on everyone doing things the same way. Creating social work in a way that fits Armenian culture is part of a society-wide effort to make things Armenian.

The recognition of social work as an occupation in the new Armenian Constitution should assist future efforts.

JAPAN

Social work in Japan is caught between tradition and demographic change, and both are influencing the roles and functions of professionals. Social welfare services have been established and organized through a set of major national laws, and most social work is practiced in agencies established by these laws. Three of the laws were passed in the immediate postwar period: Child Welfare Law (1948), Law for the Welfare of Physically Handicapped Persons (1949), and Daily Life Security Law (1950). During the 1960s, three more were added: Law for the Welfare of Mentally Retarded Persons, Law for the Welfare of the Aged, and Law for Maternal and Child Welfare (Okamoto & Kuroki, 1997). Although Japan does not have a comprehensive welfare state, Article 25 of the constitution guarantees the right to an acceptable standard of living: "The state has the responsibility to ensure that the people maintain a minimum standard of wholesome and cultural living" (Maeda, 1995, p. 395). Trained social workers, chiefly graduates of baccalaureate programs, work mainly in child welfare, services for the disabled and the elderly, and government services; other settings include hospitals and health centers, youth organizations, and community agencies (Maeda, 1995). Many social workers practice in residential institutions, either child care institutions or nursing homes for the elderly. Staff at child guidance clinics investigate child abuse cases. However, the clinics are public institutions, and staff members are civil servants of local governments, not necessarily social workers. Urban areas are more likely to have trained staff; in rural areas, social workers may have their first contact with abused children only after the children were placed in institutions.

The major social work functions are social casework and case management; community work exists but plays a secondary role (Matsubara, 1992). Social casework is the common method in welfare offices, hospitals and health care centers, and child guidance centers. The approach to public assistance combines financial assistance with counseling of clients. Case management is growing in importance, especially in the field of welfare of the elderly. The increased popularity of case management is attributed to lack of coordination and cooperation among social welfare institutions, inefficient services, lack of knowledge of services among the populace, and cultural rejection of counseling as negative and stigmatizing (Matsubara, 1992). Thus, referral, service advocacy, coordination, and reassurance are more common and acceptable social work roles than in-depth counseling to individuals.

As noted above, community work is less common. However, there are important roles for community work within the profession: to identify needs for social services, to promote the establishment of more nonprofit agencies to provide needed services, and capacity building in local communities to expand "mutual support and assistance" (Matsubara, 1992, p. 90).

The profession is organized and recognized in law. Social workers are nationally certified through the Center for Social Welfare Promotion and National Examination under the Ministry of Health, Labour and Welfare. The following certifications exist: certified social worker, certified psychiatric social worker, and certified care worker (Japanese Association of Schools of Social Work [JASSW], 2006). Only students who have had fieldwork in relevant settings—aging, children, disabilities, hospitals, and government welfare offices—are eligible to take the certification exams (T. Akimoto, personal communication, February 2006). Confidentiality is protected by the Center for Social Welfare (CSW) law, and the certification laws and exams have increased the recognition of social workers as qualified professionals.

There are four professional associations affiliated with the International Federation of Social Workers (IFSW): the Japanese Association of Certified Social Workers (with approximately 21,100 members), the Japanese Association of Certified Psychiatric Social Workers (4,600 members), the smaller Japanese Association of Social Workers in Health Services, and the Japanese Association of Social Workers (IFSW, 2006; JASSW, 2006).

Social Work Education

Education for social work is provided in colleges and universities and junior colleges, with some lower-level social work education included at the high school level. The JASSW was founded in 1955 to upgrade educational standards and to join the IASSW. JASSW (2006) purposes as stated in the Constitution are "to promote the quality of social work education, to enhance academic research development, and to represent and promote better social work education in Japan." Annual seminars are held to address curriculum and educational methods. JASSW curriculum standards require education in four areas: foundation (history, principles, policies and services of social welfare, social security, and helping methods and skills), advanced/application (advanced courses in foundation areas and fields of practice such as family and children, aging, disabilities, medical, and international), fieldwork, and related disciplines (economics, law, sociology, psychology, philosophy, medicine, rehabilitation) (T. Akimoto, personal communication, February 2006). The government exerts considerable control over the social work curriculum.

The number of schools of social work has grown rapidly. At the founding of the JASSW, there were 17 member schools. Current membership in JASSW (accounting for the majority, but not all training institutions) include 144 four-year universities, 16 two-year colleges, and 11 vocational schools at the undergraduate level. Graduate education developed more slowly; however, today there are 81 master's courses and 44 doctoral courses (JASSW, 2006). In 1995, Maeda estimated that there were only about 150 students enrolled in graduate education in social work. Thus, until recently, few social workers were trained for leadership roles. Another dilemma is that some students select social work just to get a place in a university, with no intent to practice the profession. A 1983 study showed that more than one-fourth of social work students did not intend to work in social work (Maeda, 1995). There has been considerable expansion of the number of social work programs because the government allowed the development of new educational programs only in nursing and social work. Thus, universities began programs to expand and students select social work to secure a place in the university.

Issues and Challenges

Challenges for Japanese social work grow out of demographic change, the conflicts between tradition and change, and the relatively low status of the profession.

Traditional Japanese culture is family oriented and group oriented. Values that are stressed in the family and in the workplace are loyalty, conformity, and unity (Okamoto & Kuroki, 1997). Yet, Japanese society has been undergoing major changes. Modernization has led to new family patterns; more young Japanese live in nuclear families, rather than remaining with parents. In the mid-1960s, 80% of elders lived with their children (Bass, 1996); however, by 2005, 58.9% of the households in Japan were nuclear households, and 27.6% were one-person households (Ministry of International Affairs and Communications, 2007). "The breakup and perhaps passing of the traditional family in Japan—in other words, the movement in recent decades toward the nuclear family as society's paradigm—is related to Japan's economic success, as more families become transient in the pursuit of employment" (Matsubara, 1997, p. 87). At the same time, the number and proportion of aged in the population has increased dramatically. In 1940, only 4.7% of the population was over age 65. Figures from the United Nations (2006) Population Division report that 27% of Japan's population in 2006 is age 60 or older and 19% are age 80 or beyond, the highest percentages of any country. By 2050, the projections are for a population age 60 and older at 42% of the total; if the predictions hold, Japan will have a support ratio of 1, meaning that there will be only one working person between the ages of 15 and 64 to support the elderly and children. The need for services for the aged has therefore increased and will continue to expand; Matsubara (1992) predicted that 200,000 additional social workers would be needed by early in the twenty-first century just to serve the elderly. As the dependency ratio increases, concern over paying for services will intensify and may result in reductions in social welfare benefits. Yet the government is pursuing policies to insure opportunities for "productive and meaningful aging." According to Bass (1996), the Japanese gerontologic emphasis on "expanding opportunities for enhanced meaning and purpose in life is a far more complex and challenging goal, and one which has received scant attention in Western societies" (p. 11).

It is also possible that demographic realities will cause modifications in traditional attitudes about the roles of families, government, and other service providers as the burden of family care grows more onerous. At the same time, "the system of mutual aid, which has traditionally existed in historically stable communities, is a potential casualty of Japan's new economic prosperity" (Matsubara, 1992, p. 87). Even more than other Japanese, the elderly see using social services as an embarrassment, not a right. Social workers will need to find ways to reach the reluctant elderly and help them to use the services they need. This is an important professional challenge for the present and near future.

Underutilization of social work training is another problem area. Many social work graduates work in residential institutions where they are assigned direct care work. In these roles, there is little or no professional autonomy and professionals are asked to do hands-on care, rather than counseling or case management. Although there are benefits to the clients in that abuse and neglect are rare, "this relative upgrading of the quality of care is achieved at the expense of social workers who are trained to do more" (Matsubara, 1992, p. 91). Lack of job mobility compounds this loss of optimal use of skilled social workers.

Underutilization of social work talent is related to the status of social work and the struggle between professions for authority in the arena of social services (A. Kuroda, personal communication, June 26, 2007). In localities, care planning committees make care plans for the elderly. In terms of knowledge of needs of the elderly and appropriate services, social workers should logically be in charge of these committees, yet social work is overwhelmed by the medical professions in the care planning process. Social work needs to challenge the medicalization of social problems and assert more authority in service planning (A. Kuroda).

Social work services are not provided in schools, and there is little contact between the educational and social service sectors. Yet social work is needed to address growing problems among children caused by intense academic competitiveness.

There is considerable national government control over social services in Japan. A positive effect is that services of equal quality are available to all. The negative impact is that control leads to less variety and less flexibility in designing services to meet special needs (A. Kuroda, personal communication, June 26, 2007). There are current efforts to shift authority to lower levels of government. In addition, a recent law, the Non Profit Organization law, permits the formation of NGOs. It will now be possible for social workers to create organizations to provide innovative services.

Finally, social work in Japan continues to struggle to adapt imported social work theories. The reliance on foreign, mostly U.S. theories has impeded the development of a responsive profession. As a result,

> there is a considerable gap between the theory and the practice of social work. The shared responsibility for this lack of fit lies with the incongruous match between American theories and the Japanese sociocultural environment and culture-bound practice situations. This makes it hard to accommodate theories from cultures foreign to Japanese values in Japanese social work practice. (Okamoto & Kuroki, 1997, p. 279)

Increased attention to theory development is suggested.

SIMILARITIES AND DIFFERENCES IN THE WORLD
OF SOCIAL WORK

Now that social work has been briefly explored as it manifests itself in seven very different countries, we can turn to an analysis of the difficult questions raised by comparative efforts. What, indeed, are the similarities and differences in social work as it is conceptualized, organized, and practiced in our example countries and beyond? Can social work legitimately be called a worldwide profession?

Some of the authors who have commented on the universality–difference question have stated that the similarities in social work worldwide are superficial and exist only at highly abstract levels. It is equally legitimate to argue that it is the differences that are superficial. Social work continues to endure and to expand into a growing number of countries. Identification with a worldwide profession through professional associations has intensified, and many national associations have collaborated with the IFSW to develop a revised Code of Ethics and Statement of Ethical Principles, a manual on human rights, and position statements for the global profession on social issues. Of particular note, in 2000 the new Global Definition of Social Work was adopted and in 2004, global standards for social work education.

Commonalities and Differences Among the Example Countries

A number of specific commonalities and differences in the profession can be identified. To some degree, social work in all countries examined had external roots, yet with differences. The founder of social work in Denmark sought inspiration and knowledge from the United States and Germany; however, social work in Denmark then developed along a particularly Danish path. In Argentina, a sustained and vigorous rejection of foreign theory has led to considerable independent development of professional ideology. Mauritius, Jamaica, and Japan are still heavily influenced by foreign literature and imported models of social services. The Japan case suggests that early introduction of the profession does not automatically lead to its taking root firmly in the culture. The more recent development of social work in Armenia was assisted by educators from Europe and North America, yet an Armenian model is emerging. In Ethiopia, social work education was initiated with assistance from overseas faculty and UN technical assistance; the new MSW program has drawn on a wide range of international lecturers in a highly interactive mode to create an education that is simultaneously international and Ethiopian. The dearth of indigenous literature remains a problem in much of Africa and Asia. In countries such as the United States, Britain, France, and Germany locally produced research and literature have played significant roles in shaping the profession.

Hokenstad, Khinduka, and Midgley (1992) identified four sets of commonalities from their analysis of social work in 10 countries. First, social work takes on a broad range of roles and responsibilities in each country where it is present; second, in all countries examined, social work defines itself as an agent of social change and reform; third, work with the poor is a part of social work in almost all countries (and the authors do not identify any countries where this is not true); and last, there are shared values of "promoting human dignity and social justice, empowering poor and vulnerable peoples, and encouraging intergroup harmony and goodwill" (p. 182). They also concluded that in spite of many differences among nations, social workers face similar issues in most if not all countries. On the other hand, these authors conclude that "the universality of social work does not mean that the pattern of social work's organization, roles and fields of service, modes of educational preparation; or degree of social recognition are uniform throughout the world" (p. 181). The areas of commonality and difference will now be examined in more depth.

Breadth and Variety of Roles and Settings for Practice. Context—including the role of government in social welfare, the pattern of development of complementary professions, and the structure of societal institutions—influences the specific fields of practice and roles of social work. As described above, school social work is prevalent in Argentina but unknown in Mauritius or Japan. In Jamaica, the "school social work function" is assumed by social workers and by counselors trained by teachers' colleges. These realities probably have little to do with social work competence in the various countries but are shaped by societal definitions of the nature of problems of children and structural decisions about where psychosocial problems should be addressed. The involvement of social workers in direct care work in institutions in Japan is a similar type of difference in professional role. In the United States, direct care work is considered nonprofessional or paraprofessional work, and in Denmark it is the work of a separate profession of social pedagogy. Social work roles are therefore influenced by professional status and by the development of other professions in the social welfare arena.

In all countries, social work is broad and has shown flexibility in expanding into new roles and new fields of service. This has been another enduring characteristic of the profession. The definition developed in 1928, quoted at the beginning of this chapter, speaks to social work's wide range of roles in treatment, prevention, and improvement of social conditions. The full range of social work methods—casework, groupwork, community action, legislative work, administration, and research—are included in this definition written almost 80 years ago. Harris (1997) views flexibility as a key to social work's success. He also notes that it is related, perhaps unavoidably, to definitional difficulties: "a precondition for its (social work's) flexibility and utility is a certain lack of precision and an embarrassing degree of definitional elusiveness" (p. 437). Flexibility and growth are amply demonstrated in the case studies cited here, such as the expansion into counseling and mental health work in Mauritius and social work leadership on issues of child welfare and children's rights in Jamaica.

Social Change. The belief in positive change and in people's capacities to change are important hallmarks of social work. As expressed by one of the leaders from Jamaica, social work's stance that people can change, that they can be helped, and that they can learn to help themselves is a valuable contribution to individual, community, and national development (E. Sayle, personal communication, April 24, 1997). In the face of daunting and overwhelming social problems everywhere, social work's optimism and emphasis on possibilities are important commonalities. Empowerment may not yet be a commonality in the way social work is practiced; however, the ideology of empowerment is one of the shared values of the profession. Weiss (2005), in her 10-country study of social work graduates, found "substantial similarity" in respondents' beliefs about the causes of poverty, "the way to deal with poverty, and the goals of the profession" (p. 108). In all 10 countries, there was recognition of the dual responsibilities of social work for promoting social justice and improving individual well-being. However, there were differences in degree of relative emphasis. Respondents from the United States, Canada, and Zimbabwe gave equal weight to the goals of "enhancing individual well-being and promoting social justice." "The Brazilian and Australian students ranked social justice as most important; and the British, German, Hong Kong, Hungarian and Israeli cohorts ranked enhancing individual well being as a significantly more important goal" (p. 108).

Action agendas to bring about change also differ according to the national context. Lobbying and legislative action predominate in the United States, where social reform is seen as part of the profession's dual commitment to client service and societal improvement within a democratic system of government. In Argentina, social workers have a more radical ideology, but a cautious approach to taking action shaped by many years of repressive government. Social workers under apartheid South Africa and military governments elsewhere have struggled to find ways to bring about change when even words and peaceful protest could result in arrest and imprisonment; and in Ethiopia, social work had to be taught as a "disguised subject" during the rule of the military junta and President Mengistu. Thus, social change ideology is universal; social change strategies and the level of the profession's involvement in change efforts are determined by the local context.

Social Problems and Interventions. Social workers are coping with similar social problems in many if not most countries. "The extraordinary similarity of issues that social workers face all over the world is probably the most salient conclusion one can draw from a review of social work in different countries" (Hokenstad et al., 1992, p. 191). Poverty and the related difficulties that poor people experience are important concerns for social workers everywhere.

Other common challenges include child and family problems, cultural diversity and conflict, and social exclusion. Yet differences in scope and severity of these problems cannot be overlooked. Poverty affects only about 8% of Danish residents but is a mass phenomenon in India, Sub-Saharan Africa, and in many countries of the former Soviet Union. Many of the clients of social work services in Jamaica and Argentina are desperately poor, and in Ethiopia, the majority of the population is poor and even food insecure. Differences in the scope of poverty or other problems, in resources available, and in social welfare structures differentially shape the social work response. Mass poverty requires a social or community development approach; individual poverty in a welfare state can be addressed through referrals for entitlements. Thus, common problems provide a global agenda for social work; however, interventions continue to be locally determined.

Malcolm Payne (1998) argues that social work exists and gains societal acceptance because it "allows society to deal successfully with social issues which have been identified and which cannot otherwise be resolved" (p. 447). Globally, social work is therefore a profession that responds to identified social issues, which most scholars believe are becoming more commonly experienced around the world. The specific forms that social work takes in any country, however, are shaped by that society's views of the social issue and by the possibilities for intervention, including resources, institutional supports, and societal approval. "Societies construct the kind of social work that responds to their views of social issues and the way it would be possible to deal with them" (p. 447).

Shared Values. Value commitments and ethical principles are at the core of social work as a profession. At least at the level of general principles, there is commonality of values. Social work in every country stands for respect for the worth and dignity of all people. Social work also shares a concern for vulnerable groups, with particular attention to the poor, and identifies efforts to end discrimination and move toward equal treatment for all as professional goals. As discussed above, a commitment to social reform and change is a universal value of the profession, at least at an abstract level. Participation and self-determination of those being helped are widely accepted principles, although they may be put into practice with different levels of tolerance for paternalism. Values differences are most likely to be expressed in communally oriented societies, where the individualistic values that originated in Western social work have a lack of fit. These similarities and differences will be discussed in depth in Chapter 9.

Theoretical Underpinnings. Determining the common or different theoretical underpinnings of social work is more complex. Social work everywhere draws on a range of social and behavioral sciences to inform its practice. Curricula in social work educational programs across the countries examined include content on human behavior and the social environment from the social and behavioral sciences, content on social service policies and programs, and social research methods. Specific theories emphasized may differ. Lorenz (1994) identifies four philosophical traditions as the key forces that shaped social work in Europe: Christianity, philanthropy, feminism, and socialism. Clearly, as a group, these cannot be claimed as globally relevant dominant theories. The lack of fit is obvious in our example countries of Mauritius with its Hindu majority, Ethiopia with about equal numbers of Muslims and Christians and minimal voice of feminism, Armenia, which lacked a philanthropic tradition, and Japan where feminism has been a late and relatively weak development and where Christianity is embraced by only a minority of the population.

In Latin America, social work has incorporated elements of liberation theology and the conscientization ideas of Paolo Friere. These have given Latin American social work a locally relevant identity that supplements the elements it shares with social work elsewhere. African social workers and social work educators have made efforts to identify social work as social development. Although this has clarified the importance of linking professional goals with development goals, the theory base of social development is vague and draws from many disciplines. Competence in social development requires a theoretical background across many disciplines, with "specific attention to theories of adult education and literacy, social change, social structure, social order, social development and modernization, attitude development and change, motivation, and family systems and kinship networks" (Asamoah, 1997, pp. 310–311).

There is clearly no single theoretical base for social work as a global reality. Instead many theories used have broad relevance and others are locally specific. Although the *Global Standards for the Education and Training of the Social Work Profession* (IASSW/IFSW, 2004) identifies a number of components of core curriculum, no specific theoretical approaches are named. Continued efforts toward practice theory development in Africa, Asia, Latin America, and the countries of the former Soviet Union are needed and will contribute to the evolution of a constellation of applicable theories. As Lorenz (2001) observed: "it is its paradigmatic openness that gives this profession the chance to engage with very specific (and constantly changing) historical and political contexts while at the same time striving for a degree of universality, scientific reliability, professional autonomy and moral accountability" (p. 12).

Examinations of similarities and differences in social work across countries yield a picture of a profession that is at one and the same time global and local. As stated by Weiss (2005), the results of research on the global profession

underscore the impact of centripetal forces that enhance convergence within global social work and lead to similarities in the professional ideologies of graduates of social work training in very diverse cultural settings. At the same time, they also leave little doubt as to the potency of centrifugal forces that encourage divergence. (p. 109)

REFERENCES

Alayon, N. (Ed.). (2005). *Trabajo social Latinoamericano: A 40 Anos de la Reconceptual-izacion.* Buenos Aires, Argentina: Espacio Editorial.

Argentina: The slow battle for justice. (2006, September 16). *The Economist*, 47–48.

Asamoah, Y. (1997). Africa. In N. S. Mayadas, T. D. Watts, & D. Elliott (Eds.), *International handbook on social work theory and practice* (pp. 303–319). Westport, CT: Greenwood Press.

Baker, P. A. (1998). Staying focused on development. In E. Wint & L. Healy (Eds.), *Social work reality* (pp. 46–57). Kingston, Jamaica: Canoe Press, University of the West Indies.

Bass, S. A. (1996). Introduction: Japan's aging society. *Journal of Aging and Social Policy*, 8(2/3), 1–12.

Boodajee, K. Y. (1997). *A critical appraisal of the functioning of the Child Development Unit of the Ministry of Women, Family Welfare and Child Development with reference to case studies showing strengths and weaknesses of the unit.* Social Work Diploma Project, University of Mauritius, Reduit.

Brown, G. (1991). The programme in the School of Continuing Studies. In *Contemporary social work education: A Caribbean orientation* (pp. 21–26). Mona, Jamaica: University of the West Indies, Department of Sociology and Social Work.

Buss, L., & Strauss, H. (2004). The profession of social work. In L. Moos, J. Krejsler, & P. F. Lauersen (Eds.), *Professions of relations.* Copenhagen, Denmark: Danish University of Education.

First International Conference of Social Work. (1929). The organization of the First International Conference of Social Work and of the First International Social Welfare Fortnight. In *The First International Conference of Social Work: Proceedings* (Vol. I, pp. 5–17).

Girvan, N. (Ed.). (1993). *Working together for development: D.T.M. Girvan on cooperatives and community development 1939–1968.* Kingston, Jamaica: Institute of Jamaica Publications Limited.

Halskov, T., & Egelund, T. (1998). Social work in Denmark. In S. Shardlow & M. Payne (Eds.), *Contemporary issues in social work: Western Europe* (pp. 11–24). Hants, UK: Arena Ashgate Publishing Ltd.

Harris, R. (1997). Internationalizing social work: Some themes and issues. In N. S. Mayadas, T. D. Watts, & D. Elliott (Eds.), *International handbook on social work theory and practice* (pp. 429–440). Westport, CT: Greenwood Press.

Hokenstad, M. C., Khinduka, S., & Midgley, J. (1992). *Profiles in international social work.* Washington, DC: NASW Press.

Humphreys, N. A., & Haroutunian, L. (2004). Armenian refugees and displaced persons and the birth of Armenian social work. In D. Drachman & A. Paulino (Eds.), *Immigrants and social work: Thinking beyond the borders of the United States* (pp. 31–48). Binghamton, NY: Haworth Press.

Information sheet on Danish Association of Social Workers. (2000). Accessed February 17, 2000, at http://socialrdg.dk/Startside/engelsk.htm

International Association of Schools of Social Work/International Federation of Social Workers. (2004). *Global standards for the education and training of the social work profession.* Available at www.iassw-aiets.org or www.ifsw.org

International Federation of Social Workers/International Association of Schools of Social Work. (2000). *International definition of the social work profession.* Available at www.ifsw.org or www.iassw-aiets.org

International Federation of Social Workers. (2006). *Member organizations.* Accessed August 20, 2006, at www.ifsw.org

Japanese Association of Schools of Social Work. (2006). *About us.* Tokyo: Author.

Johnson-Butterfield, A., & Linsk, N. (2005, August 21). *Project SWEEP: Social Work Education in Ethiopia Partnership* (Final Report, Institutional Partnerships Program). Chicago, IL: University of Illinois at Chicago, Jane Addams College of Social Work.

Levy, H. (2005). Peace-making on the front line. *Caribbean Journal of Social Work, 4,* 14–27.

Lorenz, W. (1994). *Social work in a changing Europe.* London: Routledge.

Lorenz, W. (2001). Social work in Europe—Portrait of a diverse professional group. In S. Hessle (Ed.), *International standard setting of higher social work education* (pp. 9–24). Stockholm, Sweden: Stockholm University, Stockholm Studies of Social Work.

Maeda, K. K. (1995). Japan. In T. D. Watts, D. Elliott, & N. S. Mayadas (Eds.), *International handbook on social work education* (pp. 389–402). Westport, CT: Greenwood Press.

Manjikian, G. (1996). *The spread of social work education: Case study of Armenia* [Monograph]. Stanford, CA: Stanford University, School of Education, International Educational Administration and Policy Analysis.

Manrakhan, V. (1990, September). Unpublished letter to the University of Mauritius regarding the degree course in social work. The Mauritius Association of Professional Social Workers.

Matsubara, Y. (1992). Social work in Japan: Responding to demographic dilemmas. In M. C. Hokenstad, S. K. Khinduka, & J. Midgley (Eds.), *Profiles in international social work* (pp. 85–97). Washington, DC: NASW Press.

"Mauritius: The Welfare System Environment." (1986, October). Unpublished document. University of Mauritius, School of Administration.

Maxwell, J. (2002). The evolution of social welfare services and social work in the English-speaking Caribbean (with major reference to Jamaica). *Caribbean Journal of Social Work, 1,* 11–31.

Maxwell, J. A. (1991). The Professional Programme in the Department of Sociology and Social Work. In *Contemporary social work education: A Caribbean orientation* (pp. 11–21). Mona, Jamaica: University of the West Indies, Department of Sociology and Social Work.

Maxwell, J., Williams, L., Ring, K., & Cambridge, I. (2003). Caribbean social work education: The University of the West Indies. *Caribbean Journal of Social Work, 2,* 11–35.

Meade, J. E. et al. (1961). *The economic and social structure of Mauritius.* London: Methuen & Co. Ltd.

Ministry of International Affairs and Communications. (2007). *Statistical handbook of Japan* (Chapter 2, Population). Accessed June 29, 2007, at www.stat.go.up/English/data/handbook/c02cont.htm

Moushigian, G. (1991). *Armenia, the earthquake of December, 1988, and the role of American social work.* Unpublished paper.

Okamoto, T., & Kuroki, Y. (1997). Japan. In N. S. Mayadas, T. D. Watts, & D. Elliott (Eds.), *International handbook on social work theory and practice* (pp. 263–281). Westport, CT: Greenwood Press.

Payne, M. (1998). Why social work? Comparative perspectives on social issue and response formation. *International Social Work, 41*(4), 443–453.

Queiro-Tajalli, I. (1995). Argentina. In T. D. Watts, D. Elliott, & N. S. Mayadas (Eds.), *International handbook on social work education* (pp. 87–102). Westport, CT: Greenwood Press.

Queiro-Tajalli, I. (2005, July 25–29). *Local responses to global oppression: The Piquetero movement in Argentina.* Paper presented at the 14th International Symposium, Inter-University Consortium for International Social Development, Recife, Brazil.

Ramgoolam, K. C. (1996, July). *Social work profession meeting the challenges of change in Mauritius—Community workers in action.* Paper presented at the Joint World Congress of IFSW and IASSW, Hong Kong.

Sedler, R. F. (1968). Social welfare in a developing country: The Ethiopian experience, Part III, The role of social work education. *International Social Work, 11*(2), 36–44.

Shillingford, A. (2005). Institutional and cultural challenges in working with the poor and marginalized. *Caribbean Journal of Social Work, 4*, 28–38.

Social work education in Denmark. (1998). Available at www.dshaa.dk/edueng1.htm

Strauss, H. (2006, January). *Denmark.* Paper presented at the IASSW Board Seminar, Hatfield, UK.

Tasse, A. (2005, March). *Social work in Ethiopia.* Presentation as part of the Social Work Around the World Series, University of Connecticut School of Social Work, West Hartford.

Titmuss, R. M., & Abel-Smith, B. (1961). *Social policies and population growth in Mauritius* [Report to the Governor of Mauritius]. London: Methuen & Co., Ltd.

UN Development Programme. (2005). *Human development report 2005.* New York: Oxford University Press for UNDP.

UNICEF. (2006). *The state of the world's children 2006: Excluded and invisible.* New York: Author.

UNICEF. (2007). *At a glance: Mauritius.* Accessed May 9, 2007, at www.unicef.org/infobycountry/mauritius.html

UNICEF & Republic of Mauritius. (1994). *Situation analysis of women and children in Mauritius.* Port Louis, Mauritius: UNICEF.

United Nations. (2006). *Population ageing 2006* (Sales no. E.06.XIII.2). New York: United Nations, Department of Economic and Social Affairs, Population Division.

Weiss, I. (2005). Is there a global common core to social work? A cross-national comparative study of BSW graduate students. *Social Work, 50*(2), 101–110.

PART III

INTERNATIONAL SOCIAL WORK:
VALUES, PRACTICE, AND POLICY

CHAPTER 9

VALUES AND ETHICS FOR INTERNATIONAL PROFESSIONAL ACTION

> It is never the people who complain of human rights as a Western, or Northern imposition. It is too often their leaders who do so.
>
> Kofi Annan, 1997, UN Secretary-General

> Cultural relativity should never be used as a pretext to violate human rights.
>
> Shirin Ebadi, 2004, p. 23, 2003. Nobel Peace Prize Laureate

Values are potentially unifying and divisive factors in international social work. In the search for commonalities in social work around the world, the strong value base of the profession is always cited as one of the key aspects of its universal identity. Social workers in all countries espouse commitment to professional values, and social work professional associations in many countries have adopted or are currently working on codes of ethics. The profession has come together through its international organization, the International Federation of Social Workers (IFSW), to develop and adopt several versions of an international code of ethics, the most recent in 2004, also adopted by the International Association of Schools of Social Work (IASSW). (See Appendix A.) Yet the commonality of values and ethics may be superficial. There is a strong current of criticism that social work values and ethical codes are too grounded in Western-oriented individualistic values to the exclusion of other perspectives. It is undeniable that issues of values and ethics become complex and controversial as one moves among various social and cultural contexts.

In this chapter, values and ethics that relate to the full range of international professional actions—cross-cultural practice, practice in the global arena, professional exchange, and international policy advocacy—are discussed. Questions to be addressed include:

1. To what extent are social work values universally applicable? What are the areas of agreement and the areas of tension and conflict in attempting to define universal social work values?

2. How do these issues within social work relate to the broader philosophical arguments for universalism and the polar position of cultural relativism in the study of values and ethics?

3. If values are not universal, are there alternative values that would inform social work in contexts that differ along the key dimension of emphasis on individuals as contrasted to emphasis on the collectivity?

4. What social work values are needed to support and guide international professional action as defined in this book? To what extent are current national and international codes adequate, and what revisions would be helpful in furthering a global profession?

UNIVERSALISM VERSUS CULTURAL RELATIVISM

An understanding of universalist and cultural relativist perspectives on ethics is a prerequisite to advancing discussion of ethics for the global profession. Can a universal set of social work values be defined that applies to professional work in any country? This question raises philosophical issues with very practical consequences for social workers in practice in multicultural as well as international environments.

Two competing schools of thought within ethics are the deontologist school that "stresses the overriding importance of fixed moral rules," arguing that "an action is inherently right or wrong" and therefore that ethical principles apply to all situations, and the teleologist view that ethical decisions should be made "on the basis of the context in which they are made or on the basis of the consequences which they create" (Dolgoff, Loewenberg, & Harrington, 2005, p. 43). In the language of international human rights, these viewpoints are called the universalist and the cultural relativist, respectively. In the universalist view, "all members of the human family share the same inalienable rights" (Mayer, 1995, p. 176) and "culture is irrelevant to the validity of moral rights and rules" (Donnelly, 1984, p. 400). Cultural relativists, on the other hand, argue that "culture is the sole source of the validity of a moral right or rule" (Donnelly, 1984, p. 400) and that "members of one society may not legitimately condemn the practices of societies with different traditions," especially practices considered culturally based (Mayer, 1995, p. 176). At the extremes, each position is rigid.

Universalism and relativism can more usefully be seen as a continuum. Mixed positions occupy the center of the continuum, combining the notion of a set of universal rights with consideration for the maintenance of cultural traditions. The IFSW 1994 code of ethics identified with this middle ground. In the statement of the purposes of the International Declaration of Ethical

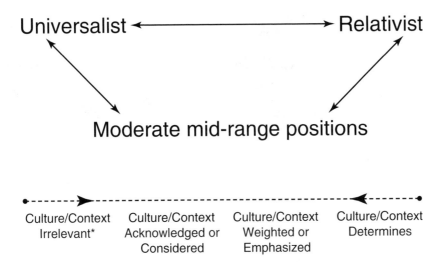

Figure 9.1 The universalist/cultural relativist continuum for ethical decision-making.
From L. M. Healy, "Universalism and cultural relativism in social work ethics," International Social Work, 50(1), p. 12, 2007. Used with permission.

Principles, the first is "to formulate a set of basic principles for social work, which can be adapted to cultural and social settings" (IFSW, 1994, Section 2.1). This idea was expanded in the 2004 document, which is described as a set of general principles. "By staying at the level of general principles, the joint IASSW and IFSW statement aims to encourage social workers across the world to reflect on the challenges and dilemmas that face them and make ethically informed decisions about how to act in each particular case" (IFSW/IASSW, 2004, p. 1).

Adapting principles, however, is not easy. Practitioners in the field often encounter situations that cause moral discomfort and raise ethical dilemmas as they interact with different cultures. They struggle at the practical level with the universalism–relativism debate, asking themselves, "When is different just different and when is different wrong?" (Donaldson, 1996, p. 48). This question suggests a mixed approach, and indeed, Donaldson argues that it is wrong to fully adopt either a universalist or relativist approach.

The universalism–relativism debate is highly relevant to social work values and ethics. Much of this value systems debate has taken place over human rights, concerning issues central to social work interest and practice. These include the rights of children, the disabled, gays and lesbians, ethnic minority groups in many host countries, and, perhaps particularly, the rights of women. The role and status of women and children within the family and within their economies and societies are often at the heart of social work value clashes over the principle of self-determination and the social work commitment to equity. For example:

- A female Cambodian refugee living in a U.S. city asks for help at a shelter for battered women. The local Cambodian Mutual Assistance Association criticizes the shelter, charging that its focus on counseling the woman on her rights and on preparations for independence are destroying the fabric of Cambodian family and social life.
- Iranian social work educators were instrumental in bringing family planning services to Iran in the 1970s. Were the mullahs right that this represented a fundamental threat to the Islamic way of life, or was it essential practice to meet the needs of women and their families?
- West Indian politicians in a U.S. city speak out against the child protection agency's investigations of child abuse in families using corporal punishment, asserting that West Indians don't want their children to grow up undisciplined.
- Local community development workers in Bangladesh encounter a group of enraged local leaders, charging that their microenterprise and literacy programs for women are destroying family roles and violating the Koran.
- Efforts to ensure nondiscriminatory treatment for gays and lesbians encounter hostility in Jamaica, Zimbabwe, the United States, and elsewhere.

These brief examples show that the social work values that drive practice interventions are enmeshed in the dilemmas of universalism versus cultural relativism.

Equality and Culture: Can They Be Reconciled?

As noted above, issues concerning the role and status of women have often been at the heart of the values debate. Social work codes of ethics, including that of IFSW/IASSW, express a commitment to equality and specifically mention gender equality. Feminist human rights scholars warn of the dangers of cultural relativism. Ketayun Gould (1989), a social worker, sees the problem as "advocacy of a 'cultural' viewpoint that assumes a defensive posture by not only tolerating the oppression of women in one's own and other societies, but coming repeatedly to the defense of this oppression in the name of ethnic solidarity" (p. 12). In 1979, the UN adopted the Convention on the Elimination of All Forms of Discrimination Against Women (CEDAW). As of 2005, 180 countries had ratified CEDAW and an additional one had signed it (United Nations Development Programme [UNDP], 2005). But CEDAW has had more reservations entered by countries ratifying than any other human rights treaty, indicating "widespread and deep-rooted resistance to the concept of full equality for women" (UNICEF, 1997). Furthermore, some of these reservations, such as those entered by Bangladesh, Egypt, Libya, and Tunisia contradict the purposes and essential protections of the treaty. Twenty-four

nations filed reservations against Article 16, the guarantee of equality between women and men in marriage and family life. "Such reservations strike
at the heart of CEDAW. They reject the extension of human rights protection
into the private domain and entrench the inferior role of women" (UNICEF,
1997, p. 49). Thus "the UN tolerated a situation where some Middle Eastern
countries would be treated as parties to a convention whose substantive
provisions they had professed their unwillingness to abide by" (Mayer, 1995,
p. 179).

An interesting aspect of CEDAW is that it specifically calls for cultural
change. Article 5 states that ratifying countries should take measures to
"modify the social and cultural patterns of conduct of men and women with a
view to achieving the elimination of prejudices and customary and all other
practices which are based on the idea of the inferiority or the superiority of
either of the sexes or on stereotyped roles for men and women" (United
Nations, 1979, Article 5). Principle 2.2.7 of the IFSW 1994 International Declaration of Ethical Principles of Social Work states that, "Social workers respect the basic human rights of individuals and groups as expressed in the
United Nations Universal Declaration of Human Rights and other international conventions derived from that Declaration," which includes CEDAW.
The 2004 ethics document specifically lists CEDAW as one of the "documents
particularly relevant to social work practice and action" (3.0). It can be argued,
therefore, that the social work ethical codes put social workers on the side of
advocating for changes in cultural practices when those practices are discriminatory or are based on stereotypical ideas of gender roles.

An alternative argument is provided by the Afrocentric scholar Josiah
Cobbah. The Universal Declaration of Human Rights, he charges, is "a
product of Western liberal ideology," adopted during a time when "most of
the population of Africa south of the Sahara was still under colonial domination" (Cobbah, 1987, p. 316). Thus, the declaration is grounded in individualism and its values are a poor fit in the communalist societies of Africa.
Cobbah is concerned that human rights may be a "Trojan horse" sent in to
change African civilizations. "Africans emphasize groupness, sameness and
commonality" rather than individual freedom (Cobbah, 1987, p. 320). The
prosperity of the community is more important than the prosperity of the
individual. The values that emanate from communalism are hierarchy, respect, restraint, responsibility, and reciprocity. Some elements in the mix are
easily embraced by social work, such as generosity and cooperation in daily
life. Others are more problematic, especially the notion of a hierarchical village
and family organization in which social roles are rigidly assigned, almost
invariably assigning women to roles of lesser economic and social influence.
Aspects of the concept of restraint may also be problematic; restraint means
that "a person does not have complete freedom. Individual rights must always be balanced against the requirements of the group" (Cobbah, 1987, p.
321). Would a social worker therefore encourage a client to show restraint in
seeking to resolve a problem, suggesting that the client's individual need
should recede in the interests of group cohesion?

What Is Culture?

One difficulty in assessing the validity of claims for cultural relativism are the vexing questions of what represents culture and who are the legitimate interpreters of a culture. In the following box, Arati Rao suggests considering questions about the nature of culture and participation when faced with a claim for cultural relativism in human rights.

Rao's questions ask practitioners to evaluate the extent to which cultural practices are shaped through participation of all sectors of a population and to examine who benefits from the defense of a particular cultural practice. For example, were women and young girls involved in the definition of female sexuality that gave rise to genital mutilation/female circumcision in East Africa? Although it is true that many women are involved in the continuation of the practice, this does not prove that the practice grew out of female views of sexuality or that women had or have power to shape cultural practices. Women's role in continuation of the practice today may well be more indicative of extreme dependence on male approval and marriage customs for survival than on intrinsic support for the practice. Another aspect of the analysis is to determine whether women benefit from this ritual circumcision. Clearly, many women suffer severe health problems, even death, and others endure lifelong pain and discomfort. The "benefit" to women is continued acceptance into traditional marriage patterns. True beneficiaries of the practice are male society members who continue to control the sexuality of females through circumcision.

The question "What is culture?" can also assist in assessing whether practices should be challenged or defended. Social workers can look, with their clients, at the extent to which the practice in question is core or central to the maintenance of culture. For example, when a West Indian parent says that child beating is important to maintaining the culture, the social worker can encourage exploration of whether it is corporal punishment that is the cultural value or well-disciplined children. Reframed in this way, mutual problem solving may be enhanced and may permit movement beyond culture clash.

Cultural relativists tend to present culture as static. In reality, cultures are dynamic: "Culture is a series of constantly contested and negotiated social

---

EVALUATING CULTURAL CLAIMS

1. What is the status of the speaker?
2. In whose name is the argument from culture advanced?
3. What is the degree of participation in culture formation of the social groups primarily affected by the cultural practices in question?
4. What is culture, anyway? (Rao, 1995, p. 168)

practices whose meanings are influenced by the power and status of their interpreters and participants" (Rao, 1995, p. 173). Mayer (1995) responds to the charge that feminist views are compatible with Western ideology but alien to Eastern and Middle Eastern cultures by arguing that feminism was also "alien" to Western countries and required long periods of struggle and cultural change to gain acceptance. Thus, cultures evolve and receive new ideas—a process that can have positive and negative consequences. It is also true that cultures may defend negative values such as racism or ethnic hatred. Few would argue for preservation of these "values."

The Concept of Harm and Cultural Relativism

Donaldson (1996), speaking from an international business perspective, warns that one cannot act from a "when in Rome" position without the danger of committing serious violations of fundamental values. He implies that the question of doing harm should be used as a criterion to evaluate whether practices encountered when crossing cultural boundaries can be accepted. Although his advice is targeted at those with multinational business ventures, it is applicable to social work.

Those who live and work abroad will need to "grapple with moral ambiguity" because practice considered ethical in one country or cultural setting may be unethical in others (Donaldson, 1996, p. 56). According to Donaldson, the important question for social workers is to "learn to distinguish a value in tension with their own from one that is intolerable" (p. 58). In international work, social workers will encounter some value differences that can be accommodated but others that must be rejected because they stray too far from respect for human dignity, and they do harm. Donaldson cites the example of nepotism in corporations in India and gift-giving in Japan as examples of the first, and forced labor, physical abuse of employees, and toxic waste dumping as examples of practices that stray too far from essential values and cannot be condoned. The first instances are practices that would be unacceptable in U.S. business and would cause discomfort when encountered; however, nepotism and gift-giving probably do not violate core human values. Again, respect for cultural differences is encouraged *unless* the practice causes significant harm. Thus opposition to female circumcision may be more easily justified by the practice's record of causing serious physical harm to many who undergo it rather than attacking the practice's roots in denial of female sexual pleasure. Using the material above, judgments would also be influenced by the fact that the victims of female circumcision are children, who are unable to participate in the dialogue about cultural formation and preservation.

Core Social Work Values and Universalism/Relativism

In reviewing the *Statement of Ethical Principles* and the codes of ethics from social work groups from various countries, common or nearly common elements are evident. These include statements of commitment to the inherent worth and dignity of people, commitment to equality and nondiscrimination, the concepts of multiple responsibilities of the professional (to self, profession, clients, society at large, coworkers, and employers), self-determination, and confidentiality. Self-determination, confidentiality, and equality and nondiscrimination will be examined next in more depth to consider how cultural context influences the operationalization of the value in question.

Self-Determination. Self-determination—fostering the ability of the client to make his or her own life choices and decisions—is an important principle in Western social work. The capacity to make one's own decisions is viewed as central to full adult functioning in an individualistic society. Thus social work practice is often oriented toward assisting individuals, groups, and communities to become more self-directed. This applies whether working with a battered woman to help her realize that she has choices and a right to make them or working with a poor community to help it mobilize and set its own priorities. The principle of self-determination is also intended to prevent the social worker from making decisions and choices for the client. The most revered forms of professional intervention facilitate the client's journey to discovery of his or her or their own options and choices with only gentle guidance and support from the social worker.

Yet, even in Western countries, the emphasis on self-determination varies. It is very strong in the United States; according to Geert Hofstede's studies of societal values in 40 nations (1980, 1993), the United States is the most individualistic society. Denmark is characterized by a strong tradition of communitarianism, "which stresses responsibility of the society for the welfare of all" (Lane, 1998, p. 7). Fitting into the group is more important than standing out as an individual. According to Lane (1998) the value of self-determination is present in Danish social work, however, it is not emphasized: "Deference to decisions by experts, such as medical personnel and social workers, is more acceptable to both Danish citizens and to Danish professionals. The ideal of the individual's rights to self determination, self empowerment and self actualization are not as strong" (p. 10). Protective payments—direct payment of a client's bills by welfare authorities to prevent money mismanagement—are commonly used by welfare offices, a practice often rejected in the United States as a violation of client rights to self-determination.

Social workers in Asia and Africa view self-determination as a particularly problematic ethical principle, advocating actions ranging from discarding it as irrelevant in a communalist society to modifying it to permit more worker-directed interventions in highly role-stratified cultures.

In her study of casework in India, Ejaz (1989) found that caseworkers tended to be directive and to give advice and suggestions to their clients. Almost all workers thought that their clients expected the social worker to make decisions for them (Ejaz, 1991). As one student expressed it: "There is a tendency in me to guide too much. If I don't give suggestions or show ways out, they [clients] gape at me. They tend to lean on us and the easy way out is to provide solutions" (Ejaz, 1991, p. 134). In so doing, however, the social workers reported feeling conflicted about their practice because they saw their approach as violating the concept of self-determination. The Declaration of Ethics for Professional Social Workers, developed by the Tata Institute Social Work Educators' Forum in Bombay, includes self-determination: "I shall respect people's right for self-determination, and shall ensure that they themselves play an active role in relation to the course of action to be taken about their life situation" ("Declaration of Ethics," 1997, p. 339). Ejaz (1991), however, believes that the more directive approach is consistent with sociocultural and religious traditions. She discusses the *guru–chela* relationship, which is similar to a priest–disciple or teacher–student relationship, as a model for social work. It is customary for Indians to look up to elders and to seek and accept advice from those who are more experienced or schooled. Social workers, on the basis of their education and professional expertise, are in the position of elders (regardless of age) and are seen as givers of advice and guidance. In other societies, for example, Jamaica (as mentioned in Chapter 8), social workers also tend to be more directive and prescriptive in response to cultural expectations that experts are there to solve problems. Thus the limits of self-determination are stretched, but not abandoned, in response to client expectations.

The widespread belief in fate in Hindu societies also affects self-determination. In Hindu philosophy, fate, or karma, explains that a person's status and misfortunes are ways through which they atone for misdeeds committed in a prior life (Ejaz, 1991). Clients may therefore accept their problems with resignation and apathy and be resistant to taking charge of their own futures, that is, being self-determining. Some Indian social workers report using fate as a positive force in encouraging clients to take action, however:

> Yes, karma can be used as a double-edged weapon. Either you fight it or succumb to it. I would empathize [with the client] and say—maybe—I'm here to help you and that's part of fate. Maybe you are suffering now but it's fated you are going to get cured. . . . Your good karma can save you. (quoted in Ejaz, 1991, p. 137)

Thus, again, the social worker is able to adapt the concept of self-determination in culturally acceptable ways.

Silavwe (1995) takes a stronger position, stating that the concept of self-determination is inappropriate in solving personal problems in Africa "because it assumes concepts of individuality which are not applicable in an African culture or society" (p. 71). He explains African communalism as follows:

> African society is characterized by the prevalence of the idea of communalism or community. The individual recedes before the group. The whole of existence from birth to death is organically embodied in a series of associations, and life appears to have its full value only in these close ties. Individual initiative is discouraged. . . . Self-initiative or self-determination in resolving personal problems is collectively sanctioned by the community. (pp. 72–73)

Africans' emphasis on "groupness, sameness, and commonality" leads to values of "cooperation, interdependence and collective responsibility" (Cobbah, 1987, p. 320) rather than individual initiative and self-determination. Silavwe recommends that group determination replace self-determination as the dominant value in African social work.

Case 9.1 demonstrates the complexities of the right to self-determination in the context of cultural relativism. Considerations of "groupness," community, and tradition clash with harm, personal and in the global context. Elements of racism and privilege further complicate the case.

Group determination is embodied in the principles of community development. The values of participation, local leadership, democratic decision making, and self-guidance are evident in the following definition:

> Community development . . . aims to educate and motivate people for self-help; to develop responsible local leadership; to inculcate among the members of rural communities a sense of citizenship and among the residents of urban areas a spirit of civic consciousness; to introduce and strengthen democracy at the grass-roots

---

CASE 9.1: SELF-DETERMINATION, CULTURAL RELATIVISM, AND HARM: THE CASE OF FATIMA

This is the case of Fatima, a 22-year-old woman who was born in Canada and still lives there. Her parents were refugees who escaped from Ethiopia in 1976.

Although her parents came from an ethic group that engaged in female genital circumcision, her own mother suffered greatly from this operation, and her parents decided against circumcising Fatima. In any case, this operation is illegal in Canada.

Fatima has decided to marry Ali, a recent refugee from Ethiopia. Ali thinks that to be a good wife a woman should be circumcised. Fatima thinks that she should be true to her Ethiopian traditions. She has suffered in Canada from being a member of a minority, and, as she grew up, she became more interested in her people's customs and tradition.

Fatima argues that since she is of age, she should be given this operation if she wants it. After all, other women in Canada have operations to enlarge their breasts, or make their faces look younger. She argues that as a Canadian, it is her right to do what she wants with her own body. If the operation is performed in a modern, hygienic hospital in Canada, she lowers the risk of health consequences considerably.

If Fatima approaches a social worker to ask for help in advocating for her right to this operation, how should the social worker respond?

Case from Rhoda E. Howard-Hassmann, 2001, Case 1.

level through the creation and/or revitalization of institutions designed to serve as instruments of local participation; to initiate a self-generative, self-sustaining, and enduring process of growth; to enable people to establish and maintain cooperative and harmonious relationships; and to bring about gradual and self-chosen changes in the community's life with a minimum of stress and disruption. (Khinduka, 1975, p. 175)

In addition to participation in decision making, the community members themselves accomplish the selected projects through their own actions. The role of the social worker in community development is to assist, facilitate the "self-choosing" of goals, promote indigenous leadership, and work with the community to prevent leadership from being authoritarian. Therefore, this is group determination for addressing community problems and aspirations. Its applicability to the problems of individuals remains more unsettled.

The 1994 International Code of Ethics took a moderate relativist stance on self-determination. The term was not used in the document. Instead, the relevant standard read: "Help the client—individual, group, community or society—to achieve self-fulfillment and maximum potential within the limits of the respective rights of others" (IFSW, 1994, Section 3.3.4), a modest attempt to blend individual rights with communalist ideas. The 2004 document, however, specifies "respecting the right to self-determination" as the first ethical principle under human rights and human dignity: "Social workers should respect and promote people's right to make their own choices and decisions, irrespective of their values and life choices, provided this does not threaten the rights and legitimate interests of others" (4.1.1). It is not clear whether this reflects a conscious shift toward self-determination on the part of the ethics committee.

Confidentiality. Silavwe (1995) also challenges the relevance of confidentiality. In traditional Africa, problems are resolved through open discussion, with involvement of extended families and village or tribal elders. The Western notion of confidentiality—that problems of individuals are secret and private matters to be protected, even from the circle of caring others—is harmful in this context. A social worker from Zambia related Case 9.2, an experience with confidentiality upon returning from his studies in the United States.

Case 9.2 does not indicate that confidentiality is a meaningless concept. Silavwe believes that clients must be protected from careless and ill-meaning use of their personal information. In different cultural contexts, however, confidentiality may have different limits. The rules of confidentiality are not meant to cut the client off from support and assistance. The headman's question "How's our boy?" signaled his right to information as part of the boy's circle of caring others, indeed, in Africa, as part of his "extended" family.

To learn from this example, U.S. and other child welfare social workers might want to think about ways to avoid the situations in which confidentiality sometimes "protects" a child's information to the detriment of the child. Potential care-giving relatives have sometimes been kept unaware of family

---

CASE 9.2: VALUES AND CULTURE CONFLICT—A CASE
OF MISPLACED CONFIDENTIALITY

A young social worker returned to Zambia after completing his MSW in
the United States and was assigned by his agency to take an adolescent boy
back to his home village. The boy, a runaway, had committed several
minor thefts and had been arrested by the police in Lusaka. As the social
worker and the boy neared the end of the 10-hour drive into the rural area,
they approached the village. The official car was spotted pulling into the
village, and the village headman and several other elders came rushing
toward the car. As the social worker slowed to a stop the headman cried
out: "How's our boy? What has happened to our boy?"

The social worker answered quickly: "I cannot tell you. It's confidential. I must see his parents and discuss it with them." Looking up, he
saw a look on the older man's face that was at once stunned and bemused.
The young social worker was suddenly overcome with a feeling of es-
trangement. How removed he felt from his culture; his remarks suddenly
seemed foolish in the face of the older man's obvious concern. As the social
worker relayed the story, that moment in the rural village marked the
beginning of his journey to indigenize his practice and to adapt his recently
gained professional knowledge and to search for ways to blend the principles of social work with the strengths of Zambian society.

Personal story told to author, August 27, 1982, anonymous.

---

crises and unnecessary foster placements have resulted. The cases in which
this occurred are examples of values interpretation at the far end of the in-
dividualistically oriented continuum.

Some African social workers discuss traditional networks and methods of
problem solving that require modification of confidentiality. Marriage problems, for example, may be discussed by the elders of the village in an open
forum; Silavwe recommends that social workers endorse and utilize these
methods, giving the example of a "social casework and remedial services
committee" in Zambia in which personal cases are brought to a group where
they are discussed by community members including elders, clergy, doctors,
and social workers. Even research interviews may need to be conducted in the
open, with village members watching, rather than in confidential settings
(Silavwe, 1995). Not all agree. Jacques (1997) argues that some clients may not
wish to have their problems resolved or even discussed by the village elders,
who may be particularly ill equipped to cope with the issues that bring people
into counseling. Individuals struggling with modern issues in Africa, especially conflicts arising between changing roles of women and traditional expectations, such as cases of spouse abuse, and problems related to AIDS, may
not find the advice of village elders adequate. Thus even within the same

cultural context, different cases may require differential use of both confidentiality and self-determination principles.

The 2004 international ethics document says simply, "Social workers should maintain confidentiality regarding information about people who use their services" (IFSW/IASSW, 2004, 5.7).

Equality and Nondiscrimination. Social work codes of ethics contain strong statements of equality and nondiscrimination. The International Code and a number of national codes commit social workers to support equality and oppose discrimination on a variety of grounds, including gender, age, culture, marital status, political opinions, socioeconomic status, spiritual beliefs, color, race, or sexual orientation (IFSW/IASSW, 2004, 4.2.1). The Indian Social Workers' Declaration of Ethics emphasizes the special responsibility of the profession to serve and advocate for oppressed classes, specifying that the profession is "committed to solidarity with the marginalised peoples" ("Declaration of Ethics," 1997, p. 336). It is clear from codes of ethics that social workers must practice equality of treatment and nondiscrimination in their work. In addition, a number of national codes require social workers to take steps to oppose discrimination and promote social justice and equity in the broader society.

These commitments bring the profession into conflict with operative values in many societies. Social workers in the European Union (EU) recognize the trends toward social exclusion, increasingly turning the EU into a fortress denying access to immigrants and socially and economically isolating the minority populations already within their borders. Still other policies may deny rights to cultural integrity. In Denmark, for example, policies aimed at promoting integration of refugees and immigrants into Danish society require dispersed settlement, "without regard to personal preferences about where to live" on the part of the immigrants themselves (Lane, 1998, p. 12). Lane found a surprising absence of concern with community participation, empowerment of immigrant groups, or of their self-determination in debates about work with immigrants. Multiculturalism and respect for diversity were relegated to secondary concerns, with the emphasis on helping people from other countries to become Danish (Lane, 1998). Issues of discrimination were often overlooked and had not been a focus of social work discussions.

Extending equality on the basis of sexual orientation puts social work at odds with their societies in a number of countries and has led to some divisions within the profession along religious lines. Studies in Jamaica, for example, indicate "very strong and deep-rooted local, religious and other socio-cultural prejudices" against homosexuals (Carr, 2003, p. 76). Reflecting majority views in many Caribbean nations, the director of the Caribbean Council for Europe blasted pressure on Caribbean countries to liberalize their laws on homosexuality as a form of human rights imperialism (Jessop, 1998). Religiously affiliated colleges in the United States pressured the Council on Social Work Education (CSWE) to modify the accreditation requirements of nondiscrimination against lesbians and gays. Yet the obligation of the individual social worker to practice nondiscrimination is clear. The Canadian Association of Social Workers' (1994) Code of Ethics specifically states that its requirements exceed those in legislation; thus social workers' professional responsibility for nondiscrimination on sexual orientation is greater than their legal responsibility.

Distributive Justice

Social work's role in distribution of scarce resources is related to the equity value commitment. All social workers are involved in distributive justice as they make decisions about who is to receive what services, material aid, or even professional time. For social service planners and administrators, distributive justice considerations are frequently at the heart of practice actions. Pursuing one program often means not pursuing others; allocating funds or staff resources in one area will mean that other options go underfunded or unstaffed; providing one client or one group of clients with more resources means fewer resources available for other claimants. Whether guided by conscious or unconscious principles, social workers are involved with distributive justice as they make these decisions. There are a variety of approaches to distributive justice, that is, principles by which scare resources can be allocated: merit, productivity, equal distribution to all, utilitarian (benefitting the largest number), need, and Rawlsian principles, which allow inequality in distribution if the most disadvantaged people benefit (Congress, 1996).

Imagine the set of program choices outlined in Case 9.3. In making this decision, principles of distributive justice and equity will be considered. How will one choose between prevention and palliative care or treatment for those who are suffering acutely? Between reaching large numbers of youth, or

---

CASE 9.3: DISTRIBUTIVE JUSTICE—AIDS AWARENESS

An international development agency has funding available for an AIDS program in the target country. The possibilities are:

1. a media campaign to make high-school-age youth aware of the dangers of AIDS and modes of transmission

2. an outreach education and intervention program for prostitutes and long-distance truck drivers who frequent prostitutes, the groups with the country's highest incidence of AIDS and HIV infection

3. a community residential program for persons suffering from AIDS, who are typically shunned by family and society and die homeless

4. providing antiretroviral drugs to AIDS patients; cost means relatively few can be treated.

reaching the groups at highest present risk? Between serving the "innocent" or groups such as prostitutes who are stigmatized by society? Considerations of merit, productivity, justice, benefit to the largest number, or benefit to the most disadvantaged will need to be weighed.

Practice decisions will be shaped by differing cultural views on acceptable principles of distribution. Whereas equal access is an accepted (although not always practiced) value in the United States, in India, taking care of one's own family is the first responsibility; therefore, assisting one's brother-in-law in getting a job is quite acceptable. Status considerations may also enter the equation. Deference to an applicant's high status may lead a social worker to give him or her a position at the top of the waiting list. Whatever the cultural context, awareness of the principles underlying distributive justice is important for social workers, especially those in administrative, policy, and planning roles.

VALUES AND ETHICS FOR INTERNATIONAL PROFESSIONAL ACTION

One dimension of preparing for practice in today's interdependent world is clearly that social workers need to address and wrestle with the universalism–cultural relativism issue. However, this alone is only a piece of international social work values. The various codes of ethics for social workers need improvement in order to serve as effective guides for international professional action.

As mentioned earlier in this text, the Joint Working Group on Development Education (1984) called for acceptance of global interdependence "as an irrefutable fact of life on which action must be based" (pp. 3–4). Accomplishing this requires a major shift in attitudes and values. This working group from InterAction, comprising development professionals, identified a set of critical values for the globally conscious practitioner and citizen. As listed in Table 9.1, the relevant values include accepting personal responsibility for global justice and relief of world poverty, and showing respect for differences in culture and beliefs. This list of values could readily be adopted as values for international social work. The inclusion of a value of respect for differing expressed needs is worth underscoring as social workers often play a mediating role between organizational agendas and client wishes.

The 1994 *Human Development Report* (UNDP, 1994) proposed another ethical principle relevant to social work: the universalism of life claims. This principle is defined as the belief that no child "should be doomed to a short life or a miserable one merely because that child happens to be born in the 'wrong class' or in the 'wrong country' or to be of the 'wrong sex'" (p. 13). Universalism of life claims globalizes the value of equity and nondiscrimination and could serve as a starting point for redefining social work values for international professional action. Most social work codes of ethics include

TABLE 9.1 Values for a Globally Interdependent World

- Concern for global justice and equity
- Respect for differing cultures, traditions, beliefs, and expressed needs
- Sense of personal responsibility for promoting development
- Clarification of personal values related to world hunger and poverty
- Acceptance of sharing and cooperation as the means to improved global security

Joint Working Group on Development Education, 1984.

principles of equity. The international ethics document, however, contains no mention of country of origin in its nondiscrimination principle that does include gender and social class, along with other characteristics. In the United States, the National Association of Social Workers (NASW; 1996) Code of Ethics specifies that social workers should not practice or condone discrimination and, in addition, that they should "act to prevent and eliminate domination of, exploitation of, and discrimination against any person, group or class on the basis of race, ethnicity, *national origin*, color, sex, sexual orientation, age, marital status, political belief, religion, or mental or physical disability" (p. 27). Application of this clause, however, has been interpreted to mean that social workers should prevent discrimination against those persons already in the United States regardless of their national origin. The implications for social work practice and advocacy of an ethical obligation to eliminate discrimination on a global scale have not been explored, yet would be considerable. Adopting universalism of life claims as a social work value would require the profession to commit to improving the lives of children living in misery anywhere in the world and to consider the global implications of equity for its practice, knowledge development, and, especially, policy development and advocacy efforts. It is also clear that although adding such a statement to the International Code of Ethics would be a fairly easy task, the challenge would be to make it operational and define the policy, practice, and advocacy responsibilities for social workers in all countries that could emerge from this value commitment. Implications for distribution of resources, immigration and refugee policies, giving aid, trade, and more would be far reaching.

The 1994 International Code contained two references to international responsibilities. The preamble expressed the goals that social workers are dedicated to including "development of resources to meet individual, group, national and international needs and aspirations" (IFSW, 1994, Section 3.1). And one of the general standards of ethical conduct stated was "to identify and interpret the basis and nature of individual, group, community, national and international social problems" (IFSW, 1994, 3.2.8). In moving to a general statement of principles, the 2004 IFSW/IASSW document expresses no global responsibilities for social work—an unfortunate retreat in the era of globalization. The Canadian and U.S. ethical codes do reflect a level of increased global awareness in their most recent editions. Under the section on responsibilities to the broader society, the U.S. code now says that social workers "should promote the general welfare of society from local to global levels, and the development of people, their communities, and their environment" (NASW, 1996, p. 26). The Canadian code says "a social worker shall advocate change for the overall benefit of society, the environment and the global community" (Canadian Association of Social Workers [CASW], 1994, p. 9). What is missing from these codes is interpretation of the implications of these rather ambiguous statements. However, they do provide a starting point by identifying world mindedness as a social work value.

International value commitments also carry with them ethical obligations to be knowledgeable and skillful. In a paper on world hunger, Haru (1984) calls for adding the concept of effectiveness to practitioners' ethical obligations. Morally justified ineffective action on serious global problems, such as hunger, is not truly moral, she argues. This is reflected in the social work codes of ethics as the principle of professional competence. Adding universalism of life claims to social work ethics would require considerable work on new knowledge and skills for social workers around the world in order to ensure effectiveness.

CONCLUSION AND RECOMMENDATIONS

In concluding this discussion of values for international social work, we must return to the question of whether there are universal social work values. There is considerable agreement that some level of universality exists. Indeed, without fundamental value agreements, it is questionable whether international social work is a viable concept. Belief in the inherent worth and dignity of all persons is at the core of social work. Among the brave authors writing on the topic of universal social work values, Gray (1995) identifies the profession's altruistic mission of helping others and responding to human needs and the pursuit of social justice as universals. Taylor-Larsen (1996) agrees and adds "social work's radical respect for the clients themselves as being experts on their own life situations" (p. 2), although this moves into more controversial territory.

Moving away from the polar positions on the universalism–cultural relativism continuum, social workers can find comfort either in Donaldson's (1996) moderately relativist position or Donnelly's (1984) moderately universalist one. According to the former, there are a set of core human values that must be respected "as an absolute moral threshold"; these should be mixed with "respect for local traditions and a belief that context matters when deciding what is right and what is wrong" (Donaldson, 1996, p. 52). Donnelly (1984) recommends a framework within which there would be a form of "weak relativism" that "would recognize a comprehensive set of prima facie universal human rights and allow only relatively rare and strictly limited local variations and exceptions" (p. 401).

It does seem evident that social work must reject a purely relativist stance. Human right abuses cannot be condoned, and cultural change may be called for in some situations. The questions raised by Rao (1995) on participation and representation in culture formation are important considerations for social workers in their assessment of culture-specific values. Answering these questions, however, is very difficult for a "cultural outsider."

Also clear is that the profession must move beyond ethical principles bound up in individualistic values. The cult of individualism, especially in its "rugged" and competitive forms, negates reciprocity, generosity in social relations, cooperation, and other directedness as values. Needed are ethical codes that not only encourage cooperation and generosity but also respect fundamental and equitable human rights. To date, development of codes of ethics based on communalist values has lagged. The following statement from the CASW (1994) code is a beginning: "The social worker will consider the client as an individual, a member of a family unit, a member of a community, a person with a distinct ancestry or culture and will consider those factors in any decision affecting the client" (p. 4). Additional work is needed to infuse communalist perspectives into ethical documents and identify how they can be used to guide ethical decision making.

Identifying practice principles is somewhat easier. Silavwe's (1995) description of African communalism contains important implicit practice principles: "The whole of existence from birth to death is organically embodied in a series of associations, and life appears to have its full value only in these close ties" (pp. 72–73). This statement is instructive for practice in many cross-cultural cases. In work with a refugee woman from Cambodia or from Ethiopia at a battered women's program, the social worker should make a special effort to understand the woman's ties to her family, extended family, and community. Counseling, while still respecting her dignity and right not to be abused, should also involve the client in a search for ways to maintain her connectedness. Otherwise, the outcome of intervention may be to protect her from abuse but also to diminish the value of life itself through severing of crucial close ties.

Link (1999) identified four common principles that she believes apply to social work throughout the world: *(1)* be responsible in professional actions; *(2)* act in a way that enhances peoples' lives (note here that "enhance" will be differentially defined); *(3)* focus on the process as well as the task; and *(4)* act with cultural understanding. Her more detailed set of universal ethical principles instruct the practitioner to focus on self-awareness of cultural bias and "geocentrism." Dialogue is crucial to ethical cross-cultural practice throughout the intervention and in evaluating both the process and outcome of the professional action (see Box).

Finally, new values of world-mindedness and global social work competence must evolve to position the profession for assuming its responsibil-

PRINCIPLES: GLOBAL ETHICS

Widest perspective for assessment

- Before acting, review personal value, history, and cultural bias; ask the question, "How am I influenced personally and professionally by this question or problem?"
- Review the value base, history, and culture of the other(s) concerned with the ethical question.
- Question geocentrism and the impact of the location of people involved; what would be different if this dialogue were happening elsewhere in the world and why?

Inclusion of the service user in dialogue and decisions

- Discuss the "right to reality" of the service user and their family or community; spend time defining this reality.
- Acknowledge the "power" of the professional.
- Attend to the use of clear language.
- Consider the question of "conscientization": To what extent is the immediate ethical tension reflective and part of wider societal and global issues?

Joint evaluation

- Was the outcome lasting in its resolution of the ethical questions in the workers', service users', and community view?
- Which actions by the workers worked best?
- Which actions by the service user(s) worked best?
- Did all members feel included and respected?
- What would be different in a future instance of this ethical decision?

Link, 1999, p. 90.

ities in the global era. In knowledge development, practice, and policy advocacy, nationalistic limits on value commitments must be removed. Concern for equity must extend beyond national boundaries, and this concern should be reflected in the ethical obligations of social workers wherever they practice.

REFERENCES

Annan, K. (1997, October 20). Speech delivered to the Communications Conference, Aspen Institute, Aspen, Colorado. Accessed November 11, 1998, at www .unhchr.ch

Canadian Association of Social Workers. (1994). *Social work code of ethics*. Ottawa, Ontario: Author.

Carr, R. (2003). On "judgements": Poverty, sexually based violence and human rights in 21st century Jamaica. *Caribbean Journal of Social Work, 2*, 71–87.

Cobbah, J. A. M. (1987). African values and the human rights debate: An African perspective, *Human Rights Quarterly, 9*, 309–331.

Congress, E. P. (1996). *Social work values and ethics: Identifying and resolving professional dilemmas*. Chicago: Nelson-Hall.

Declaration of ethics for professional social work. (1997). *The Indian Journal of Social Work, 58* (2), 335–341.

Dolgoff, R., Loewenberg, F. M., & Harrington, D. (2005). *Ethical decisions for social work practice* (7th ed.). Belmont, CA: Brooks Cole.

Donaldson, T. (1996). Values in tension: Ethics away from home. *Harvard Business Review, 74* (5), 48–62.

Donnelly, J. (1984). Cultural relativism and universal human rights. *Human Rights Quarterly, 6*, 400–419.

Ebadi, S. (2004). Human rights embody the fundamental values of human civilizations. In UNDP *Human Development Report 2004: Cultural liberty in today's diverse world*. New York: Oxford University Press.

Ejaz, F. K. (1989). The nature of casework practice in India: A study of social workers' perceptions in Bombay. *International Social Work, 33*, 25–38.

Ejaz, F. K. (1991). Self-determination: Lessons to be learned from social work practice in India. *British Journal of Social Work, 21*, 127–142.

Gould, K. H. (1989). International perspective on women, development and peace. *Swords and Ploughshares* [Bulletin of the program in Arms Control, Disarmament and International Security], *III* (4) 11–13. Available from the University of Illinois at Urbana-Champaign.

Gray, M. (1995). The ethical implications of current theoretical developments in social work. *British Journal of Social Work, 25*, 55–70.

Haru, T. (1984). Moral obligation and the conceptions of world hunger: On the need to justify correct action. *Journal of Applied Behavioral Science, 20*(4), 363–382.

Hofstede, G. (1980). Motivation, leadership and organization: Do American theories apply abroad? *Organizational Dynamics, 9*(1), 42–63.

Hofstede, G. (1993). Cultural constraints in managements theories. *Academy of Management Executive, 7*(1), 81–94.

Howard-Hassmann, R. E. (2001). *Cultural relativism and human rights: Human rights training scenarios*. Hamilton, Ontario: McMaster University.

International Federation of Social Workers. (1994). *International code of ethics for the professional social worker*. Oslo, Norway: Author.

International Federation of Social Workers/International Association of Schools of Social Work. (2004). *Ethics in social work: Statement of principles*. Accessed August 10, 2006, at www.ifsw.org

Jacques, G. (1997, July). *The baby and the bathwater: The dilemma of modern social work in Africa*. Paper presented at the Third Conference of Caribbean and International Social Work Educators, Port of Spain, Trinidad.

Jessop, D. (1998, February 1). Caribbean norms vs. European ethics. *The Sunday Observer* [Jamaica], p. 13.

Joint Working Group on Development Education. (1984). *A framework for development education in the United States.* Westport, CT: Save the Children (for InterAction).

Khinduka, S. (1975). Community development: Potentials and limitations. In R. M. Kramer & H. Specht (Eds.), *Readings in community organization practice* (2nd ed., pp. 175–183). Englewood Cliffs, NJ: Prentice Hall.

Lane, T. S. (1998, March). *Social work values and ethics from an international perspective.* Paper presented at the Annual Program Meeting, Council on Social Work Education, Orlando, Florida.

Link, R. (1999). Infusing global perspectives into social work values and ethics. In C. S. Ramanathan & R. J. Link (Eds.), *All our futures: Principles and resources for social work practice in a global era* (pp. 69–93). Belmont, CA: Brooks Cole/Wadsworth.

Mayer, A. E. (1995). Cultural particularism as a bar to women's rights: Reflections on the Middle Eastern experience. In J. Peters & A. Wolper (Eds.), *Women's rights, human rights: International feminist perspectives* (pp. 176–188). New York: Routledge.

National Association of Social Workers. (1996). *Code of ethics.* Washington, DC: Author.

Rao, A. (1995). The politics of gender and culture in international human rights discourse. In J. Peters & A. Wolper (Eds.), *Women's rights, human rights: International feminist perspectives* (pp. 167–175). New York: Routledge.

Silavwe, G. W. (1995). The need for a new social work perspective in an African setting: The case of social casework in Zambia. *British Journal of Social Work, 25,* 71–84.

Taylor-Larsen, Z. (1996, July). *International social work: Is there a body of values, theories and methods in social work education which is culturally transferable?* Paper presented at the Congress of the International Association of Schools of Social Work, Hong Kong.

UNICEF. (1997). *The progress of nations 1997.* New York: Author.

United Nations. (1979). *Convention on the elimination of all forms of discrimination against women.* Available at www.unhchr.ch

United Nations Development Programme. (1994). *Human development report, 1994.* New York: Oxford University Press.

United Nations Development Programme. (2005). *Human development report 2005.* New York: Oxford University Press.

CHAPTER 10

INTERNATIONAL RELIEF AND DEVELOPMENT PRACTICE

Lara Herscovitch* with Lynne Healy

*Director of Programs, Greater Bridgeport Area Foundation;
Education Specialist, Save the Children/USA

In the world of international relief and development, nongovernmental organizations (NGOs) apply skills and knowledge that are partly drawn from, and are relevant to, the field of social work, yet these organizations do not necessarily consider themselves social work or social welfare institutions. Similarly, as discussed earlier in this book, the social work field in industrialized countries has not traditionally targeted the international domain as central to its mission. However, there is significant crossover between the two, in terms of principles and implementation methodologies. The goal of this chapter is to help readers bridge that gap between international and traditional domestic social work practice. The following topics will be addressed:

- the specific context and content of international relief and development work
- roles that social workers play in international relief and development practice
- key lessons learned from international relief and development practice and the ways these lessons can be applied to social work practice everywhere

THE CONTEXT AND CONTENT OF INTERNATIONAL RELIEF AND DEVELOPMENT PRACTICE

Traditionally, international NGOs focused on either relief or development. Historically, the relief domain is social assistance work that is conducted under emergency circumstances—in a war environment or in response to a natural disaster, such as famine, an epidemic, or an earthquake. Generally, relief work involves a rapid response to basic human needs: shelter, food, water, safety, and family reunification. Relief interventions emphasize immediate responses to immediate needs, and practitioners struggle with the questions about how to serve populations in emergencies without creating a "handout," or dependency, dynamic. This is particularly the case in long-term refugee camp situations in which need for relief is protracted.

Development work, on the other hand, has traditionally been looked at as that which is carried out under normal (that is, nonemergency) circumstances. Applications of development work include such areas as:

- the environment: wildlife, ecology, agriculture, pollution/industrialization, desertification
- human development: education and early childhood development, health, population
- economic development: agriculture, microbusiness development, group loan programs
- democracy building: citizenship, local governance / decentralization
- infrastructure: water systems, wastewater disposal, irrigation systems.

It is important to note that although a program can focus on a single theme, most focus on more than one to respond to real-life situations in communities in which needs are multiple and linked. Furthermore, many development approaches in the past successfully targeted medical interventions and are moving beyond the minimal goals of the Health for All campaign, which aimed at basic health services and communicable disease control. As stated by Ennew and Milne (1990) "If the future is to be viable, today's adults must meet the challenge not only of ensuring their [children's] physical survival but also of preventing that survival being a mockery of human dignity because of exploitation, poverty and violence" (p. 8).

The modern "relief vs. development" landscape has changed. Much of the dialogue among international practitioners is now around the "relief-to-development *continuum*." There is an increasing understanding of the issues that connect relief and development work and how one can pave the way to the other. For example, poorly planned agricultural practices—typical development work—can cause soil erosion or deforestation, which can cause severe landslides during a heavy rainy season or hurricane thus leading to the need for relief work. Similarly, well-executed relief work, conducted through and in full cooperation with community groups, rather than simply handing out goods, can pave the way to solid development work during nonemergency times by building local capacity to identify and create solutions for local problems. The example of relief after Hurricane Gilbert in Chapter 8 demonstrated this principle. Other areas of clear overlap include land mine education and removal of land mines, activities that can be conducted in times of political peace but clearly are connected to war situations—traditionally considered to be the clear territory of relief workers.

International relief and development practice aims to facilitate change on a number of levels—behavioral, cultural, institutional, or political. To achieve these goals, development practitioners employ a range of strategies. Practitioners work at different times with individuals, communities, institutions / organizations, and policy makers in order to leverage change (Midgley, 1995). While some organizations focus more on direct community-based work and others more on policy-level work, most work on a number of different levels simultaneously, and expatriate social workers are expected to be able to interact on most levels. The major strategies for international development are:

IS INTERNATIONAL RELIEF/DEVELOPMENT SOCIAL WORK?

Yes

The process of international development was originally conceived of as largely economic and physical and emphasized large-scale infrastructure projects. Since the 1960s, there has been increasing emphasis on the need to build human capacity as a proactive strategy in facilitating large-scale change (Levinger, 1996). The "social" or human dimension of development has links to social work, which has from its founding emphasized the centrality of positive change on individual and family levels and the importance of holistic approaches. An example of this is the move in development away from a narrow health focus in child survival programming to holistic early childhood development programs that benefit the 12 out of 13 children who do survive (Myers, 1992).

A survey of development agencies found a high degree of fit between social work qualifications and the skills and knowledge sought by the agencies (Healy, 1987). The planning, management, training, and community organization skills often taught in macropractice curricula are highly valued in development work along with interpersonal competence and cultural sensitivity. The success of earlier social workers, from Eglantyne Jebb to the workers in UN Relief and Rehabilitation Administration (UNRRA), suggest that relief and development work are social work.

No

Social work is a "caring" profession that is responsive to human suffering but in a reactive and palliative manner not consistent with the aims of development. The development community perceives social work as preoccupied with individual treatment and ill-prepared or disinterested in addressing problems of mass poverty. The profession usually focuses its attention on those who are the most marginalized—addicts, the mentally

(continued)

ill, offenders, teen mothers—much like Mother Theresa's work in India; although the intentions of social work are good, they have little impact on mainstream social development. Thus a survey of development agencies conducted in 1981 found that "none of the agencies...felt they had any particular need for social workers" (National Association of Social Workers, 1981). Although the respondents may have based their opinions on misconceptions, social work has a lot of work to do before it can define its work as international development.

- *Direct implementation,* also known as a bottom-up or grassroots approach, involves designing and directly delivering community-based programs and services.
- *Community mobilization* stimulates communities to organize, plan, carry out, evaluate, and sustain actions to address the problems that they identify.
- *Partnering and institutional development* are becoming more common in international work (see "Social Work Roles in International Relief and Development" for further details) and involve collaborating with other organizations in pursuit of common goals as well as assisting other organizations in the development of skills that will enable them to better plan, carry out, and sustain their programs.
- *Policy and advocacy* focus on working with governments and donors in order to influence policies and practices to impact more positively on the client(s).

SOCIAL WORK ROLES IN INTERNATIONAL RELIEF AND DEVELOPMENT

Although some may still debate the relevance of the profession in international work, in fact social workers hold many and diverse roles within international NGOs. These include program implementation; casework; program development/technical specialist; program management; program monitoring and evaluation and research; training/training of trainers; disaster response, relief, mitigation, and recovery; organizational development/network building; and advocacy / policy making. Central to each role is the focus on building the capacity of the client—whether an individual, family, community, government, organization, or network. In addition, although many of these roles are distinctive, in many cases there is functional overlap. This is particularly true in the advocacy arena; all social workers serve as advocates on many levels—with families, local leaders, community groups, NGOs, and government officials at local, regional, and/or national levels. There are similarly overlapping responsibilities in the other areas. For example, in many cases a fieldworker will be responsible for collecting data to be used for monitoring and evaluation (M&E) purposes, a program manager may implement or facilitate a field training event, and a technical advisor or specialist may help manage a field program. Because social work is rooted in the *holistic*, or *ecological model*, of human development (Germain & Gitterman, 1996), practice seeks to influence decision making and practice in many arenas. Each particular role is described below.

Program Implementation: Community-Level Work

Staff members who are responsible for program implementation on the community level are based *in the field* (that is, overseas) and work directly with program participants. They may work on a number of levels, depending on the objectives of the program. Typical tasks of a program implementer are organizing after-school activities, teaching literacy classes, building the capacity of a women's microbusiness group, organizing communities around women's rights, forming school management committees, educating youth about reproductive health and HIV/AIDS, or building potable water systems. Usually these positions are held by individuals who are nationals of the country in which the program is located, because they are the ones who understand local culture, language, values, and so on. Sometimes a successful implementer can be an expatriate as well, as in the case of the U.S. Peace Corps' animators, or community organizers.

Educational training of implementers may focus on a number of different areas but normally includes learning about social services or one particular social sector or technical area. It is important to note that educational opportunities can be limited for nationals, either for access or economic reasons, and thus experiential learning is often a meaningful substitute or complement. The role of the community implementer can overlap with that of *institutional development*, in which the focus is on building the capacity of local or national organizations to do their work more effectively. Organizational development is described below.

Casework

The casework function is a subset of the community-level program implementation role, and associated tasks can be viewed on a continuum. Caseworkers respond, as appropriate, to clients' needs for short-term psychological "first aid," long-term therapy or rehabilitation, or psychiatric interventions for individuals suffering from clinically diagnosed post-traumatic stress disorder (Garbarino, Kostelny, & Dubrow, 1991). The role of the caseworker tends to be more prevalent in relief work or in urban programs, for example, dealing with street children. This role is only carried out effectively by those caseworkers or clinicians who have a deep understanding of local and cultural issues—and thus can empathize with needs vis-à-vis the unique ways in which a given population normally copes and "heals." Expatriate clinicians, therefore, need to be fully bilingual and bicultural. In some cases, instead of providing direct service, it is more appropriate for expatriate caseworkers to support national staff in their own delivery of casework/therapy. It is important to note that, especially in emergency and war situations, program *staff* also need psychological support to effectively cope with their roles as helping agents. Educational training for a caseworker often includes groupwork as well as individual casework and may include an area of specialization that targets a particular population. Case 10.1 describes a casework project.

Success of the project was aided by a number of factors, including the social worker's language competence, her openness to receiving new information and redefining the scope of the project, and her embrace of mutuality in the training process. Thus mental health services to Cambodian refugees were improved in the Thailand camp and in the social service agency in Connecticut where the social worker was employed.

CASE 10.1: IMPROVING CASEWORK THROUGH NATURAL HELPERS IN A REFUGEE CAMP
Vichhyka Ngy, MSW, Director, Asian Family Services

A social worker, herself a Cambodian refugee, received a small grant to improve mental health service in Site II, a large refugee camp in Thailand. The social worker did not intend to do counseling herself, as seeking counseling for personal problems from a professional is unknown and culturally inappropriate to most Cambodians. Therefore, the initial goal of the project was to improve casework services by training Buddhist monks on mental health assessment and referral, assuming that they were a main source of help to camp residents. During the study phase of the project, the social worker discovered in her interviews of Buddhist monks that women in the camps were more likely to go to Buddhist nuns for help with personal and relationship crises and that the nuns had longer relationships with people in need. Cultural taboos prevented the refugees, especially women, from discussing sexuality or relationship problems with the monks. The monks' role was primarily to perform rituals to deal with the spirits causing the illness or depression. Support and "counseling" were done by the nuns.

The second phase of the project, the training of natural helpers, therefore shifted to a different target group—the Buddhist nuns. The social worker reported that the training was actually mutual training. She provided the nuns with knowledge on the causes and symptoms of depression, on mind/body links, on assessment techniques, and on when and how to refer (after discovering that there were few links between the temples and the formal mental health service in the camp). The nuns taught her meditation techniques and their role in alleviating stress and Buddhist concepts of health and illness. She was able to apply these in her work in the United States with Cambodian refugees, especially older and more traditionally religious refugees.

Program Development/Technical Specialist

The role of program development or technical specialist is focused on the programmatic *content* of projects as contrasted with administration or management, to be discussed next. It can be based in the field where actual program implementation is taking place or in a headquarters office. Program development focuses on strategizing and designing program approaches either in a single sector, such as education or health, or in multiple sectors that are integrated in their implementation, such as in a project for life skills development for youth. Specific tasks associated with program development include conducting needs assessments or a careful situation analysis and designing projects, developing and writing program or project proposals, representing the program in technical forums and with donors, providing technical assistance and guidance, documenting program progress, and designing and writing technical publications. Case 10.2 demonstrates the importance of a thorough situation analysis to effective programming. The educational training for a technical specialist normally includes an advanced degree in a particular program area, complemented by in-depth experience implementing or managing programs in the same sector. Case 10.3, while lengthy, illustrates both the tasks of a program developer and the content of the work.

CASE 10.2: GETTING GIRLS TO SCHOOL IN MOZAMBIQUE—A SITUATION ANALYSIS

Save the Children initiated a project in one region of Mozambique to increase primary school enrollment and retention. The usual program consists of classroom construction, teacher training, and community mobilization to encourage parents to send their children, especially girls, to school. Getting girls to school proved particularly challenging in this region. Girls had very low enrollment, and those that enrolled tended to drop out after a few years. A situation analysis was conducted to identify barriers to school attendance. The analysis identified the usual barriers of attitudes about gender roles, early marriage, chores at home, and care for HIV-infected parents. The analysis also revealed that this area suffered from severe water shortage. Girls were spending hours each day gathering water for their families, having to walk long distances or to line up and wait hours to fill their containers. The demands of water gathering kept many girls from school. The existing school had no water facilities and also no latrines. Lack of latrines meant that the children simply had to go outside and use the grass. Boys and girls used the same area of the grass surrounding the school. As girls became older, they were not comfortable

(continued)

using the same "toilet" area on the grass as the boys, so they dropped out of school. This was discovered only because the Save the Children staff held meetings with the children themselves as part of the analysis.

When a water component—drilling of bore holes for the community—and a latrine were added to the usual school program, girls' enrollment increased.

In many communities in Mozambique, AIDS orphans are another group with low school participation. Girls are often kept out of school to care for their ill parents and, after their parents die, to care for siblings. Attitudes about the relative importance of educating boys versus girls means that even if the brother is older, the oldest girl will become the caretaker of the siblings while the older brother continues in school. Another innovative program response is the OVC program—Orphans and Vulnerable Children. Save the Children works with a group of parents in the community as a committee to plan for and oversee the orphans; part of their role is to encourage school attendance. As this case shows, through situation analysis, critical barriers to program success can be identified and remedied.

Case contributed by Jose Marin, Save the Children, Mozambique.

Program Management

The role of the program manager is more administrative in function than that of program development/technical specialist. This role can also be field-based or headquarters-based but tends to be field-based to effectively oversee day-to-day operations. Specific tasks associated with program management include representation of the program with partner agencies and donors; oversight of program budget and personnel; oversight of implementation, including monitoring and evaluation, as well as oversight of technical assistance provided to the program; and assistance with fund raising, including large-scale proposal development. One challenge for program managers is how to balance decentralized, participatory decision making and management with the need for quick decision making and efficiency (Latting & Gummer, 1994). Educational training of program managers often concentrates on general macro-functions such as administration, financial management, program planning and monitoring, and staff supervision.

The social worker who is employed overseas as a program manager will have a broad range of responsibilities and the opportunity to exercise a variety of skills encompassing administrative, program, and community functions. The next case, 10.4, was written by a social worker deployed as a program manager in the Sudan, implementing food security programs

CASE 10.3: DEVELOPING A PROGRAM
FOR REGIONAL APPLICATION IN AFRICA

The Sara Communication Initiative (SCI) was developed by UNICEF (the UN Children's Fund) for application in 15 countries located in the eastern and southern regions of Africa. Ms. Russo de Sa, communication officer for UNICEF/Mozambique, was the point person for developing the Sara program. SCI was being developed in response to assessments of the situations of female children in several countries of the region, which indicated common problems of sexual harassment and abuse as well as inequity in access to education. SCI is a multimedia project with animated film as its core. Complementing the program's animated videos, each episode has one accompanying comic book and a poster to reinforce the positive messages for children and their families. Animation was chosen as a medium because it can illustrate difficult issues in a less threatening way than real-life film.

Sara, the heroine of all the stories, is a 14-year-old schoolgirl living in a peri-urban environment. Her skills include communication, negotiation, critical thinking, and decision making, but she expresses a wide range of human emotions and is resilient in the face of challenge. Sara's stories provoke debate among peers and parents, teachers, and community leaders about the status and rights of adolescent girls in modern African society. Employing the 90% entertainment 10% education formula, SCI promotes the protection, status, and self-esteem of girls in the countries of the eastern and southern regions of Africa. Examples of episodes are:

- Episode 1: "The Special Gift"—on importance of girls' education
- Episode 2: "Sara Saves Her Friend"—on sexual harassment
- Episode 3: "The Daughter of a Lioness"—female genital mutilation
- Episode 4: "The Trap"—on "sugar daddies"

As the point person for the development of the Sara project, de Sa coordinated implementation, including:

- advocating for and promoting the initiative with donors within UNICEF and with partner agencies, including potential implementing agencies
- providing technical and financial support to partners (mainly NGOs and schools), including conducting or coordinating research around adolescence and associated problem areas on which to base new local stories
- providing comprehensive training to partners on the use of the program materials and to writers for the production of local Sara stories

(continued)

- ensuring the production of the core materials in Portuguese (they were also produced in French, English, and Swahili), and ensuring the local production and dissemination of the 13-part radio series, with the support of BBC and Radio Mozambique (the radio series was produced in Portuguese as well as three other local languages by local radio stations with UNICEF support)

A key challenge in developing this kind of regional project is to produce stories that have the same level of interest and acceptance in each individual country. To address this challenge, locally produced materials are developed, after research is conducted to determine which issues are most appropriate and of most interest and concern for country-specific (and in some cases locality-specific) young audiences.

The overall goals of the Sara initiative are first to provoke discussions about challenging issues relating to girls and second to spark changes in behavior around those issues. In an isolated district within Zambezia Province (the highly populated center of Mozambique, with approximately 4 million people), UNICEF staff attended a meeting with members of Community-Schools Linkages Committees, National and Provincial Ministry of Education staff, community mobilizers from the National Institute of Social Communication, and numerous community members. Over the course of two nights, UNICEF projected the Sara video on a large screen for the audience, which numbered in the hundreds. This showing represented the first time in 10 years that many audience members had seen a film, and for most it was the first time they had ever seen an animated film. During the fourth showing, one teacher began interacting with other audience members and through questions and answers made the story clear to the other viewers. After the viewing, UNICEF staff noted that male community members were openly discussing their opinions and regrets about why their girls did not attend school (many were blaming themselves). Current statistics show that the level of girls' schooling in this district has increased. Although evaluations cannot prove whether this change is due solely to the Sara project, most involved believe it played a stimulating role.

Case contributed by Amilia Russo de Sa, Communication Officer, UNICEF/ Mozambique

for war- and drought-affected people; he had overall responsibility for all aspects of program support. He describes his role and experiences in a typical day.

As the case demonstrates, the role of program manager requires multiple skills in planning, negotiation, and fiscal and personnel management; the setting in isolated rural Sudan required additional adaptation and cross-cultural learning.

CASE 10.4: A DAY IN THE LIFE OF A PROGRAM MANAGER
David Bourns, MSW, Save the Children

The Sudan has been torn by civil war for several decades, with the current phase beginning in the mid-1980s. Many people who rely on traditional subsistence farming and herding for their livelihood have been displaced or have been subject to frequent attacks by roving military squads. Food stocks and essential household items have been stolen and destroyed, and traditional planting areas have become inaccessible due to insecurity. Working in this environment requires not only sound program design but also detailed attention to a reliable program support infrastructure, including human, mechanical, and administrative, and to security precautions for staff working in the field. Save the Children sponsored a food program, comprising seed distribution, tools, relief food, and food for work. I was hired to provide overseas on-site management of the project.

A typical day might be as follows: I awaken around dawn to join program staff in visiting several target communities within a few hours drive of the office (over rough or nonexistent roads). The visits will entail observing project implementation and meeting community members to discuss their thoughts and concerns. Such dialogue might take place only with community leaders or might involve a larger group discussion with many residents. Site visits also provide the opportunity to meet with staff members who are based in the field to discuss pending issues related to implementation. In this predominantly Muslim area, the visits are scheduled so as not to conflict with the regular prayers that take place five times a day. Occasionally we may be invited to a breakfast, traditionally at 10:00 a.m. that may include roasted camel meat or boiled camel liver.

On return to the office, a meeting is held with available program staff to discuss the morning's observations and plan follow-up, and to review the status of monitoring and evaluation activities. New program opportunities will also be identified and tasks assigned for data collection and proposal development. It will eventually fall on the program manager to refine and finalize the new proposal, based on discussions with beneficiaries, government counterparts, and staff, for submission to donors. The program manager will participate in meetings with existing and potential donors throughout the year to report on existing projects, to strengthen the case for additional funding, and to pave the way for new proposals.

Once the program meeting has ended, it is time to review and approve administrative documents related to such things as supplies procurement, vehicle repair and maintenance, personnel issues such as evaluation and recruitment, and local legal issues. Some matters will require further discussion with the administrative staff, the review of internal procedures and guidelines, and occasionally the physical monitoring of routine procedures. Vehicles, which take a hard beating in an environment of poor roads

(continued)

and ever-present sand, require particular and constant attention to ensure that they are properly maintained, that parts are procured efficiently, and repairs completed at the lowest possible cost. Time is then required to complete additional paperwork such as the editing of regular project reports written by field staff for donors, the preparation of internal reports to be submitted to the field office director and other senior staff, and correspondence to / from partners and counterparts.

Next, I have scheduled an afternoon meeting with the manager of a program suboffice who is visiting for several days. This manager runs a program office located in a particularly insecure and politically sensitive area, and there are always a number of important issues to review. In this case I am especially concerned with reports that staff from this office are ignoring security guidelines and beginning the day-long drive to this office too late in the day and traveling through insecure areas after dark. For emphasis, I remind him of the two staff from this office that were killed in an ambush 2 years previously and of the vehicle we now have parked in the compound that is full of bullet holes from an attack a number of months ago. In the latter instance, amazingly, no one was injured. The office manager is a dedicated and hardworking staff person whose enthusiasm is the cause of this problem. Although all staff are strongly committed to our mission, we have no wish to compromise their safety while implementing programs. We take this opportunity to review with the senior administrative officer all security guidelines and make sure that preparations for an upcoming visit of USAID personnel, including a visit to a suboffice, are on schedule.

Near the end of the day a meeting is held with the staff finance officer to review monthly budget reports, which must be submitted to headquarters, and to monitor project spending against grant line items. Because there are several grants and other funding sources that make up the entire office budget, monitoring is essential to ensure that costs are being allocated properly and that project spending requirements are being met. Findings from the recent internal audit of the field office conducted by headquarters have just been received and also require written responses. Funding is very difficult to find in northern Sudan, and it is especially important to maintain meticulous financial records and monitor funds closely.

As the office closes for the day, the administrative officer reminds me that government visitors are expected that evening in time for dinner and will be spending the evening in the agency's guest house. (I try to ignore the chicken clucking in the compound that I know will be the evening's meal.) Over dinner I respond to their questions and comments about programs and government regulations, and we plan a joint site visit for the following week. They invite me, and other senior staff, to attend a local football match the following week as their guests (only after we arrived, following a long drive, did they add that they would like us to participate in half-time activities, which revealed to the entire town my complete lack of athletic prowess).

Program Monitoring and Evaluation (M&E) and Research

The program evaluator may be employed by the agency for which the evaluation is being conducted or may work for a research-focused organization that is contracted externally to conduct the work. Program evaluations are often conducted by outside/external evaluators because those individuals do not have a stake in whether the evaluation results are positive or negative and thus are viewed to be more objective; therefore, the evaluation is viewed to be more credible. Normally, staff working on direct implementation of programs collect data on a day-to-day basis, with guidance from an evaluator or technical specialist. The M&E data may be fed into an impact evaluation, but normally individuals assessing program impact will collect data independently as well. Specific tasks can include setting up baseline surveys and training field staff in data collection; analyzing data collected; holding focus groups with program participants and/or program staff; writing evaluation reports for NGOs, governments, or donors. Program evaluation and research have gained much attention in recent years because implementing organizations have realized that while they *want* to focus on "program learning," often there are insufficient resources to support it. As a result, individuals conducting program research are supported, in many cases, by specific grants that are associated with a university. These research studies may use a number of different methods and may occur over different lengths of time; they may include cross-sectional or longitudinal studies, quantitative or qualitative studies, and various methods including sampling, experimental or single-subject designs, or surveys, among others (Rossi & Freeman, 1993; Rubin & Babbie, 1993). Funding for research can be difficult to obtain; additional efforts to study program effectiveness are needed. Case 10.5 tells of an "in-house" effort and the difficulties of obtaining an objective evaluation.

CASE 10.5: EVALUATING CHALLENGE— "A TYPICAL PROGRAM DAY?"

Getting a true sense of the quality of a program can be challenging for a technical specialist who is based in a headquarters office. One such social worker/technical specialist in education was visiting a number of El Salvador schools with colleagues to monitor the implementation of a new primary education program. Generally, these visits unfold as follows: (*a*) before a guest's arrival at a program site, she or he is perceived as important and in a position of authority, with some control over the fate of the program, especially its funding; (*b*) the visit is announced in advance and is planned in detail, including songs, gifts, food, and a formal presentation; (*c*) the program participants (in this case, school administrators, students, teachers, and parents) stop the implementation of the program to tend to (*b*); and (*d*) the visitors are supposed to evaluate how the program looks on a "typical day."

One way to reduce this kind of disruption to a program is to plan a visit on a day when group activities are already taking place. For example, the same social worker mentioned in Case 10.5 visited a Mozambican land mine awareness program on a day when a community theater event was also taking place. The skit performed was intended to raise awareness of community members about the dangers of land mines, as well as educate them about how to spot a land mine and what action steps can be taken after one is spotted. The visitors, in this case, were audience members along with community members; program implementation was not compromised due to the external visit. Another suggestion is for visitors to encourage program activities to continue, to show interest in "regular," day-to-day activities, and, of course, to view them as unobtrusively as possible.

Training/Training of Trainers (TOT)

The trainer's role involves building the capacity of other individuals in order that they conduct their work more effectively. The trainer sometimes targets those individuals who are providing direct service, other times those who are managing or developing programs, and in some cases those who are responsible for training activities. This last category is called training of trainers (TOT). The trainer is responsible for facilitating active learning as well as modeling effective training techniques. For example, during a training for youth workers around reproductive health activities, the trainer not only is teaching the content about reproductive health practice but also is modeling the training techniques that she or he hopes the youth will learn as a result of participating. Some of this training content includes designing and planning training that responds to the needs of multiple stakeholders; group dynamics and learning; stimulating discussion; team building; use of role playing and small groups; feedback and evaluation, including self-assessment; awareness of adult nonformal education theory and techniques to support it (e.g., traditional banking-style education—where learners are seen as passive and empty of knowledge and teachers are seen as the holders of all relevant information who thus "deposit" the knowledge into learners—versus more progressive problem-posing education—where learning takes place as a result of active participation and dialogue by teachers and learners alike). TOT workshops focus on teaching individuals training techniques that can in turn be applied to any sector area (Silberman & Lawson, 1995; Vella, 1989).

Disaster Response, Relief, Mitigation, and Recovery

Individual social workers in many countries have long been involved in responding to natural disasters, and there is a literature on lessons learned. Although probably most disaster response is domestic in nature, large-scale human disasters attract international teams of responders, coordinated (or not) by relief agencies. Social work roles have usually focused on assisting with coordination of relief efforts or in more specialized roles in trauma response. While Chapter 8 contains a sound example of developmental practice by local social workers in Jamaica, Pyles (2007) states that social work has often neglected the need for longer term development programs following disasters. The more devastation that occurs, the more prospects for long-term recovery are imperiled. Survivors, especially those who were poor or vulnerable before the disaster, have usually lost not only their home and possessions, but often their places of employment and prospects for new employment.

Pyles (2007) identifies disaster service coordination, community assessment, and organizing for "community-based participation in disaster management" as important practice roles, in addition to trauma interventions (p. 323). Mathbor (2007) elaborates on social work roles, including, in addition to the above, community education on ways to mitigate the impacts of disasters, "community capacity building at the social, economic and environmental levels," resource mobilization, assisting in reuniting families following disasters, recruitment of local volunteers to assist in response and planning, and, of course, "playing a monumental role in providing psychological support for disaster survivors" (p. 367). He also notes that internationally, the profession should learn from those who have developed a special expertise through regular exposure to natural disasters, citing the example of Bangladesh, where floods and cyclones occur frequently.

Lessons learned from recent large-scale disasters led UNICEF and several major NGOs to develop principles for intervention with tramatized children. The principles call for an emphasis on normalization, rather than psychotherapeutic inventions, and avoidance of unsustainable psychological interventions,. Although recognizing that most children who experience major disasters will show some signs of psychological distress and that some will show longer term effects, the principles state that "'trauma counselling' should *never* be the point of departure for psychosocial programming, because structured, normalizing, empowering activities within a safe environment will help the majority of the children recover over time" (Psychosocial Care, 2005, p. 1) (emphasis in the original). Two additional principles in the document are particularly significant: "trauma counseling should never be provided unless an appropriate and sustained follow-up mechanism is guaranteed"; and "grounding all psychosocial interventions in the culture, unless it is not in the best interests of the child, is both ethical and more likely to produce a sustained recovery" (p. 2). These principles, though perhaps controversial to some social workers, grew out of experiences with mental health professionals who flew into countries for very short-term assignments and implemented short-term therapy with little or no knowledge of the local culture, including people's understanding of the very concept of mental health. Such interventions are often unsettling at best and can delay or damage prospects for recovery.

UNICEF's focus on normalcy is corroborated by the findings from research on the impact of the destruction caused by volcanic eruptions on

Montserrat. Ring and Carmichael (2006) found that resiliency and strength were the dominant themes from their interviews of women who remained on the island. They conclude that "the activities and interventions of social workers based on a resiliency model are essential in providing prevention, crisis, and post-disaster and long-term recovery services to individuals, families, groups, and communities dealing with natural disasters" (p. 13).

Although these cautions are well taken, social workers can make a special contribution in ensuring attention to particularly vulnerable populations in disasters. Hurricane Katrina struck New Orleans and the Gulf Coast of the United States revealing lack of planning for the elderly, patients in hospitals and nursing homes, and the poor. Evacuation orders were issued without regard to access to transportation; shelters were hastily opened without food, water, or essential medicines. Large shelters initially opened with no security or means of identifying unaccompanied children, thus creating additional risks for already-traumatized populations. Social workers have special knowledge of the needs of the elderly, ill, disabled, and children and would be valuable participants in disaster preparation, planning, and response.

Case 10.6 shows how a long-term development effort suddenly turned to relief intervention when disaster struck. Ultimately, disaster mitigation and long-term recovery require a social development approach. The United Nations International Strategy for Disaster Reduction (UN ISDR) aims to build "disaster resilient communities" through sustainable development (Zervaas, 2007). This approach integrates risk awareness, environmentally sound land use planning, and development of early warning systems with community-building strategies that encourage people to work together to address problems. Social workers can play important roles in the strategy by mobilizing communities toward increased preparedness and resiliency.

Organizational Development/Network Building

The role of organizational development/network building is becoming more common although it often is linked to other social worker roles, particularly training. The role of an individual working in organizational development usually focuses on two levels. The first level is working to build the capacity of one client organization: organizing, building, and supporting the development of organizational vision and developing positive organizational values and culture, work processes, and organizational learning. The second level is to build the capacity of local organizations to allow them to more effectively conduct their direct implementation. Most organizations working internationally are moving toward institutional/organizational development to increase the scale of their work, as will be discussed later in the chapter.

CASE 10.6: FROM DEVELOPMENT TO RELIEF: DISASTER IN BANDA ACHE

Save the Children had been running a "classic example" of a good grass-roots development program in Banda Ache, Indonesia. It was led by local staff and focused on capacity building. One component of the program was a midwives' training program to increase the capacity of traditional midwives to improve safe childbirth in the area. A large number of midwives had been successfully trained and continued to meet monthly for additional training.

On the morning of December 26, 2004, 25 midwives were meeting for their monthly training session at their facility on the beach. The huge tsunami hit, and everything was lost in a matter of minutes. Many of the women and their trainers were killed, the equipment, materials, and the building were lost. In just these few minutes, the local capacity to deliver babies was completely wiped out. According to a Save the Children staff member, they had to start over not only to build capacity, but "to begin to build the capacity to build capacity." Suddenly, the agency had to completely change its mode of operations. Although good development programs are built slowly and rely on studies, consultation, analysis, and pilot projects, disasters require immediate response and action without much process.

Case contributed by Elizabeth Daoudi, Save the Children.

When focusing on network building, an individual seeks to link, connect, and facilitate interorganizational collaboration. Network building is becoming a more popular organizational practice due to an increased recognition that organizations can complement each other's work as well as increased pressure from donor agencies to work cooperatively. Often, many NGOs and UN agencies are at work in the same area, and lack of coordination may impede success. One social worker in Somalia achieved results by negotiating a protocol for effective coordination among agencies (D. Bourns, personal communication, December 2005). There remains considerable tension around collaboration though, because funding environments are very competitive and organizations struggle with whether to invest limited resources in developing coalitions or to focus on their own organization solely (Rosenthal, Mizrahi, & Sampson, 1994). For this reason, networks are a popular trend. As part of a network, organizations can jointly plan and advocate, but they do not have to outwardly compete for limited resources. In addition, networks help build the understanding and trust that is helpful for further joint work. The education of those working on organizational development/

network building usually focuses on macropractice, including administration, management, policy/planning, or specifically, in organizational development.

Advocacy/Policy Making

The advocacy/policy-making role seeks to leverage change on a macrolevel and can be viewed as three somewhat different subroles. The *lobbyist* works to influence congressional actions and/or voting behavior of legislators. More often social workers play the role of the *advocate*, working for an organization that seeks to leverage its field practice into larger scale change by demonstrating to other organizations, donors, and governments which types of approaches are most effective and thereby influencing them on what types of activities they should fund or otherwise support. The third role, the *policy maker*, can be broadly defined. Policy makers may lead NGOs but more often hold roles within globally influential institutions, such as the World Bank, a UN agency, or a bilateral donor organization.

Cross-Cutting Practice Skills

In any social work position—in any country—there are skills that are central to the successful execution of the above-described roles. Social workers will be engaged in a number of different tasks with clients—whether individuals, organizations, communities, or nations. These tasks typically include engagement; assessment(s); selection/design of intervention(s), including the formulation of goals and objectives; implementation; M&E; and termination and follow-up. There may be some instances in which one task is completed before the next; however, often the process is not linear. Thus social workers engaged in relief or development work may be focusing on one or more of these practices at any given point. As an illustration of the cycle, a social worker may

- engage a certain population (e.g., impoverished families living in rural West Africa)
- assess what "problem(s)" to target (e.g., girls do not attend or drop out of primary school)
- select and/or design the intervention to be applied, including the formulation of goals and objectives, in relation to local conditions, constraints, and resources (e.g., in partnership with local community members, the creation and sustaining of safe, relevant, high-quality primary schooling opportunities for girls)
- implement the intervention
- monitor and evaluate the effectiveness and quality of the school(s) (e.g., collect data on a day-to-day basis and periodically evaluate program quality)

- terminate the intervention and provide follow-up support as needed (e.g., phase out external support to the schools and support local school management committees to take on more intensive roles; set up systems within the Ministry of Education to continue to support teacher training and local community management) (adapted from Kettner, Moroney, & Martin, 1990; Meyer & Mattaini, 1995; University of Connecticut School of Social Work, 1998)

The skills needed to successfully build the capacity of a client, whether that client is an individual, a community, or an organization, include strong interpersonal and communication skills (including language capability where applicable) and critical thinking and analysis, presentation, organizational, writing, decision making, and collaboration/teamwork skills; knowledge of human behavior and cross-cultural knowledge that allows the worker to adapt his or her general principles of human behavior to local culture(s) are also necessary. Social work training provides a solid foundation in human behavior and interactions, but it is important to recognize that workers need to bring humility and openness to all interactions, particularly with individuals from different cultures, as Case 10.7 illustrates.

This is just one result of social work training that instructs on how to learn to communicate in cross-cultural situations, how to be patient with others and self, and how to adapt knowledge and experience to fit new situations.

CASE 10.7: MEETING THE COMMUNITY

Social workers who are not from the communities where they are working need to be aware of how they may be perceived. One social worker, engaged with a rural Haitian community, was staying in an NGO guest house. During her free time, she left the grounds (which were completely surrounded by a tall fence and gated door) to sit and read in a gazebotype structure in the community's central area. Although she was eager to interact with community members, she was approached very cautiously at first, usually by children. Over time, she built relationships with parents and children alike. She discovered that most expatriates never left the guest house grounds except to go to work—usually in an expensive four-wheel-drive vehicle. Thus the community members had not experienced an expatriate who spent time sitting and getting to know them on their terms. Although cautious, the community members were happily surprised when the social worker made attempts to interact with them. The informal conversations turned into a giving and receiving of informal Kreyol/English language lessons, and lasting friendships were built.

LESSONS LEARNED FROM INTERNATIONAL RELIEF
AND DEVELOPMENT: PROGRAM PRINCIPLES

All effective international work, whether relief or development, seeks to create sustainable solutions. To do this, certain principles may be applied that are based on key lessons that have been learned by both domains. Whereas many organizations working in international relief and development share program principles and strategies, each has its own particular goals and objectives and, thus, strategies to accomplish its mission. Similarly, different international organizations target their interventions on different levels and with different emphases—whether with policy-making institutions, national governments, local or national NGOs, directly with communities, or others (as discussed above). Although institutional practices are becoming more similar as organizations learn what is effective, there remain some significant differences between organizations.

While program principles and strategies are distinct among international NGOs, there are some similarities. Following is a description of broad principles and strategies that are employed by international NGOs, based on significant lessons that have been learned over decades of international relief and development work. The principles have considerable applicability to social work in developing and industrialized countries.

Focus on a Disadvantaged Population Within a Holistic, Multisector Approach

Most NGOs have a primary area of activity such as the environment/natural resources, education, health, or economic development. Because real-life issues are connected, most NGOs working through direct service strategies ultimately focus on numerous cross-cutting issues. A multisector approach is increasingly required. One illustration of this dynamic is in the area of basic education. Many children do not attend school because their families need their labor to earn income. Even though their long-term earning potential would be higher if they attended and stayed in school, many families cannot afford to do without children's short-term assistance in harvesting crops or performing other work tasks. Other families have enough resources to send only one child to school (because of costs associated with school uniforms, basic supplies, etc.), and parents choose to send sons instead of daughters because sons stay with the immediate family while daughters are "married off" to other families. In addition, research has proven that healthy children in school learn more than sick or hungry children. Thus education programs focus not only on quality issues within a school, such as curriculum development and teacher training, but also on health, gender, and economic issues. Indeed, one can argue that on a national or international level, "sustainable development requires economic growth" and all development issues are linked (Stoesz, Guzzetta, & Lusk, 1999, p. 157). Families therefore have more children to work in fields, but the increase in workers further degrades the soil, which requires more workers to reap the same yields, and so on. Applying the lessons from development, social work can learn to simultaneously focus on oppressed or marginalized populations while looking holistically at needs and problems.

Capacity Building and Empowerment

Capacity building as a social work task, built on the core principles of enabling and facilitating self-help, can take many forms at different levels in varying international relief or development situations. Building the capacity of the client is central to creating approaches that will last over time. What this means in practice is that all work done *for* a client, should be done *in collaboration with* the client. In many situations it is easier to focus on capacity building in a development setting in which the luxury of time and peace allows for participatory planning. In some emergency circumstances, especially when health needs are at stake or clients are traumatized, it is much more difficult to engage clients substantively in planning and implementation. To the extent possible, however, it is critical that all interventions be planned, implemented, and evaluated in partnership with the client, whether an individual, family, community, or organization. This ensures program relevance as well as program sustainability. Capacity building approaches develop the human and social capital that is critical for further progress.

Impact, Sustainability, Cultural Relevance, and Scale

Programs are designed to achieve maximum positive impact on the group or issue of concern. Because all social programs are difficult to implement successfully due to the large number of factors that are outside the control of the program, many programs adopt Freire's concept of praxis, that is, implementing, reflecting, and adapting the program (or activity) based on lessons learned regarding what went well and what did not (Freire, 1992). One challenge with using this approach is that most major fund providers, particularly bilateral donor agencies, require a project to predetermine program outcomes. There is greater flexibility today in *how* to reach the outcomes, however, which allows a project to adapt its implementation to meet any unforeseen circumstances. Nevertheless, "NGOs who wish to remain effective and accountable . . . should diversify their funding sources and pursue strategies to raise funds locally—the only way to promote sustainability (and associated legitimacy) in the long term" (Edwards & Hulme, 1996).

Organizations working in development and relief have learned that for programs to be successful, they must first create positive change, and then positive change must continue to be made in the absence of the external support. In addition, the positive outcomes must affect many people. Need is too great to allow the luxury of programs that only serve a small number of beneficiaries. For this reason, achieving large scale is widely perceived as central to having a maximum impact. Beginning at the design stage, plans must be made for "scaling up" or bringing the program to scale. That is, programs must seek to reach the maximum number of beneficiaries, or clients, with vital benefits while also retaining the highest quality. A major challenge facing relief and development work is that of maintaining high quality as a program becomes larger (Herscovitch, 1997).

Programs also need to be culturally relevant if they are to succeed and continue. As discussed above, if programs are designed and implemented in partnership with the client(s) (including men and women, youth, teachers, community leaders, etc.), they will be culturally relevant. Partnerships with communities provide insight into relevant local needs—ensuring program relevance and cultural sensitivity. UNICEF's 1989 State of the World's Children report summarizes the issue as follows: "One of development's 'Seven Sins' is Development without participation: Sustained development ultimately depends on enhancing people's own capacities to improve their own lives and to take more control over their own destinies" (in Myers, 1992, p. 309). Sustainability of projects requires that external agents must plan their exit strategies at the outset and maintain focus on ways to make projects self-sustaining. Although it is difficult to plan relief activities to be sustainable (i.e., the hope is that refugees living in camp situations will eventually return home), this goal is furthered when activities in emergency circumstances are planned and implemented in partnership with the affected population(s).

Flexibility is an important element of practice. Case 10.8 illustrates the need for flexibility when the unexpected happens—as it almost always does in international projects.

Gender Equity

Most programs that are focused on human development seek to promote increased equality, opportunity, and leadership of women and men to ensure maximum benefits for all. As discussed above, programs that seek empowerment and sustainability work to increase the capacity of disadvantaged individuals and groups to make choices and take actions *on their own behalf* from a position of strength. This can be particularly challenging in cultures where men and women are not seen as equals. For example, in Afghanistan under the Taliban, women were ordered to leave their jobs and return to their homes. NGOs working during this situation were forced to choose whether to continue to help the disadvantaged in, arguably, greater need, or whether to evacuate their staff in the hopes of putting more macro-political pressure on leaders who are viewed as oppressing the population. As discussed in Chapter 9, tensions between gender equity and culture raise numerous ethical dilemmas.

Costs

One issue central to the sustainability of programs is that they be low cost. If local communities and national/local governments are to sustain program

CASE 10.8: FLEXIBILITY AND CULTURAL SENSTIVITY ARE ESSENTIAL

Farhan has worked as a relief and development staff member in emergencies in Iraq, Afghanistan, Haiti, Darfur, and Indonesia. One of the important lessons learned is the need for high levels of flexibility and cultural sensitivity. Also required is the ability to accept the unusual to accomplish program goals. His experiences in Afghanistan illustrate these points.

Based in Afghanistan for 3 years, Farhan worked on projects in microcredit, health, education, and emergencies related to the ongoing conflict there. Many challenges arose that required considerable flexibility on the part of staff. There was a place near the Turkemenistan border with incredibly high infant mortality. To reach the location of the child survival project, staff had to travel on donkeys for several days—all the while communicating by satellite phone with headquarters to assure the agency they were safe. Among other challenges, they had to negotiate with a local warlord to get him to allow delivery of food to the project.

A microcredit project was also sponsored in the area and was very successful. Islam does not permit charging interest, an obstacle to sustaining the loan program. The group instead instituted an application fee to take care of overhead expenses, satisfying local cultural restrictions, but permitting the program to move forward. After 7 years, the program was taken over by locals and is now self-sustaining with only a little technical assistance.

Development workers are not likely to learn donkey riding or essentials of negotiating with warlords in degree or training programs. These examples underscore the critical importance of flexibility, adaptability, and cultural sensitivity to success and, indeed, survival as a development worker in emergency situations.

Case by Farhan bin Irshad, Save the Children USA.

---

activities, these activities need to be affordable. One way of achieving this is to draw on locally available materials and resources. For example, in building schools, local materials such as wood, straw, bamboo, tin, and so on may be used rather than importing foreign materials. Where a community has no hard resources to contribute, in-kind contributions such as labor can be an effective substitute. Thus in some cases, external materials may be given as part of a larger cost-sharing strategy. For example, one national NGO, in its reconstruction efforts after Hurricane Mitch devastated parts of Central America, provided the raw materials needed to rebuild housing, schools, water systems, and other structures. The communities receiving the goods took the lead in planning and implementing all rebuilding efforts, with technical support provided (as needed) by NGO staff.

CONCLUSION: WHAT INTERNATIONAL PRACTICE MEANS FOR SOCIAL WORK DOMESTICALLY

There is some difficulty in transferring particular program models between social work in industrialized and developing nations because the specific contexts—needs and resources—between the two can be radically different. However, many, if not all, of the principles and strategies are effectively used across and between borders. The lessons learned in relief and development are equally applied to Western social work settings: focus on a disadvantaged population or issue of concern; a holistic approach to capacity building, empowerment, and gender equity; achievement of impact and sustainability; and keeping costs as low as possible.

The roles that social workers play in international relief and development work are the same ones they play in industrialized countries. These include casework, program implementation, program development/technical specialist, management, monitoring and evaluation/research, training, organizational development/network building, and advocacy/policy making. Just as in developing countries, the central focus of fulfilling any role successfully is focusing on the self-help philosophy of capacity building so that clients, including communities, are able to create positive change(s) on their own behalf. Within the roles played by social workers internationally, the same tasks are undertaken: engagement, assessment, selection, and design of an intervention, implementation, M&E, and termination and follow-up. Although the content or focus of the tasks will differ from country to country and community to community, the skills required to successfully complete them are the same.

Thus the work that social workers are conducting internationally, in relief or development settings, is applicable to the work that social workers are conducting everywhere. This trend is increasing in this age of rapid globalization and industrialization, with populations more mobile than ever before (Valle, 1994). Children growing up in urban environments in developing countries are facing the same challenges as children in more industrialized settings. As more children are left on their own because both parents have to work, they become more susceptible to violence and other negative influences, or what has been called a "socially toxic environment" (Garbarino, 1995, p. 115; Kotlowitz, 1991). Social workers in all settings, working within the ecological framework of human development, have the opportunity to counteract some of these trends through the positive and sustainable approaches learned through relief and development practice. And social workers who devote their careers to international work will find ample relevance from their professional training. Thus it is quite appropriate to state that international relief and development work is social work.

REFERENCES

Edwards, M., & Hulme, D. (1996). Too close for comfort? The impact of official aid on nongovernmental organizations. *World Development, 24*(6), 961–973.

Ennew, J., & Milne, B. (1990). *The next generation: Lives of third world children.* Philadelphia, PA: New Society.

Freire, P. (1992). *Pedagogy of hope: Reliving pedagogy of the oppressed.* New York: Continuum.

Garbarino, J. (1995). *Raising children in a socially toxic environment.* San Francisco: Jossey-Bass.

Garbarino, J., Kostelny, K., & Dubrow, N. (1991). *No place to be a child: Growing up in a war zone.* Lexington, MA: Lexington Books.

Germain, C. B., & Gitterman, A. (1996). *The life model of social work practice* (2nd ed.). New York: Columbia University Press.

Healy, L. M. (1987). International agencies as social work settings: Opportunity, capability, and commitment. *Social Work, 32*(5), 405–409.

Herscovitch, L. (1997, April). *Moving child and family programs to scale in Thailand: Integrated program for child and family development* [Program Review]. Bangkok: UNICEF.

Kettner, P. M., Moroney, R. M., & Martin, L. L. (1990). *Designing and managing programs: An effectiveness-based approach.* Newbury Park, CA: Sage.

Kotlowitz, A. (1991). *There are no children here.* New York: Doubleday.

Latting, J. K., & Gummer, B. (1994). Can administrative controls and pressure for efficiency and effectiveness be balanced with the staff's demand for decentralization and participation? In M. J. Austin & J. I. Lowe (Eds.), *Controversial issues in communities and organizations* (pp. 251–266). Needham Heights, MA: Allyn and Bacon.

Levinger, B. (1996). *Critical transitions: Human capacity development across the lifespan.* Newton MA: Education Development Center.

Mathbor, G. (2007) Enhancement of community preparedness for natural disasters: the role of social work in building social capital for sustainable disaster relief and management. *International Social Work, 50*(3), 357–369.

Meyer, C. H., & Mattaini, M. A. (Eds.). (1995). *The foundations of social work practice: A graduate text.* Washington, DC: NASW Press.

Midgley, J. (1995). *Social development: The developmental perspective in social welfare.* London: Sage.

Myers, R. (1992). *The twelve who survive: Strengthening programmes of early childhood development in the third world* (Rev. ed.). Ypsilanti, MI: High/Scope Press.

National Association of Social Workers. (1981). *International social work program plan.* Washington, DC: Author.

Psychosocial care and protection of tsunami affected children: Guiding principles. (2005). Statement adopted by the International Rescue Committee, Save the Children UK, UNICEF, and UNHCR.

Pyles, L. (2007). Community organizing for post-disaster social development: Locating social work. *International Social Work, 50*(3), 321–333.

Ring, K., & Carmichael, S. (2006). Montserrat: A study of Caribbean resilience (1999–2005). *Caribbean Journal of Social Work, 5*, 9–28.

Rosenthal, B., Mizrahi, T., & Sampson T. (1994). Should community-based organizations give priority to building coalitions rather than building their own membership? In M. J. Austin & J. I. Lowe (Eds.), *Controversial issues in communities and organizations* (pp. 9–22). Needham Heights, MA: Allyn and Bacon.

Rossi, P. H., & Freeman, H. E. (1993). *Evaluation: A systematic approach* (5th ed.). Newbury Park, CA: Sage.

Rubin, A., & Babbie, E. (1993). *Research methods for social work* (2nd ed.). Pacific Grove, CA: Brooks/Cole.

Silberman, M., & Lawson, K. (1995). *101 ways to make training active.* San Francisco: Pfeiffer.

Stoesz, D., Guzzetta, C., & Lusk, M. (1999). *International development.* Needham Heights, MA: Allyn and Bacon.

University of Connecticut School of Social Work. (1998). *Foundations of social work practice* [Unpublished Course Outline] West Hartford, CT.

Valle, I. (1994). *Fields of toil: A migrant family's journey.* Pullman: Washington State University Press.

Vella, J. (1989). *Learning to teach: Training of trainers for community and institutional development.* Westport, CT: Save the Children.

Zervaas, D. P. (2007, January 10). *United Nations International Strategy for Disaster Reduction (UN/ISDR).* Presentation at Disaster Planning, Management and Relief: New Responsibilities for Social Work Education. A Seminar sponsored by CSWE with IASSW and NACASSW, Barbados.

CHAPTER 11

INTERNATIONAL/DOMESTIC PRACTICE INTERFACE

> The complex problems that social workers are confronted with on the home ground often have their origins in forces at work beyond its borders.
>
> Suen Hessle, 2007, p. 231

Globalization has increased the number and variety of internationally related aspects of domestic social work practice in most countries. Although relatively few social workers will have the opportunity to engage in the full-time development practice discussed in the previous chapter, all are likely to engage in internationally related social work within their usual jobs. For some this will occur frequently, while for others it will involve only an occasional case or administrative challenge. This chapter will discuss social work practice with refugees, immigrants, and other international populations; international adoption; intercountry casework; social work in border areas; and administrative and community organizing issues. Practice principles will be emphasized and illustrative case used. The growing phenomenon of transnationalism will be highlighted.

TRANSNATIONALISM AND SOCIAL WORK WITH INTERNATIONAL POPULATIONS

The Migration Process and Its Impact

As migration continues to bring large numbers of refugees and immigrants to new countries, social workers encounter them in schools, hospitals, child welfare agencies, and community organizations. Many professionals are unprepared to provide informed and skilled assistance to individuals and families from other countries and cultures. Faced with cultural and language gulfs between them and their prospective clients, workers may retreat in fear and avoid providing needed services or may deliver inappropriate services.

The amount of knowledge required for cross-cultural competence in the era of globalization may seem overwhelming. It is well accepted that social workers should have knowledge about the cultures of those they serve, but gaining and utilizing such knowledge about multiple cultures is a large task. Matthews (1994) found that even social workers who have specialized knowledge about an immigrant population may not always apply this knowledge in practice. Drachman (1992) suggests using a stages-of-migration framework to aid in assessment and intervention planning with immigrant populations. The framework specifies that the knowledge and information needed to effectively assist a foreign-born individual or family must address the three stages of their journey—premigration and departure; transit; and resettlement—and may include many dimensions, as outlined in Table 11.1 (Drachman, 1992, p. 69).

In applying the framework to an individual case, the worker seeks information about critical history that has shaped the individual's current reality, cultural influences, and particularly traumatic events that may have occurred. Experiences in each of the stages will vary considerably between groups and individuals. A young refugee from the Southern Sudan may have fled attacks on his village as his home was being torched and endured a dangerous trek to Kenya, surviving while fellow travelers died from exhaustion, hunger, or attack. His transit phase likely included several years of deprivation in a refugee camp. For a Jamaican immigrant, the transit phase in

TABLE 11.1 Stages of Migration Framework

Stage of Migration	Critical Variables
Premigration and departure	Social, political, and economic factors
	Separation from family and friends
	Decisions regarding who leaves and who is left behind
	Act of leaving a familiar environment
	Life-threatening circumstances
	Experiences of violence
	Loss of significant others
Transit	Perilous or safe journey of short or long duration
	Refugee camp or detention center stay of short or long duration
	Act of awaiting a foreign country's decision regarding final relocation
	Immediate and final relocation or long wait before final relocation
	Loss of significant others
Resettlement	Cultural issues
	Reception from host country
	Opportunity structure of host country
	Discrepancy between expectations and reality
	Degree of cumulative stress throughout migration process

Drachman, 1992, p. 69.

contrast was probably a 4-hour flight to New York or a slightly longer one to London. But the Jamaican is likely to endure a lengthy period of family separation during resettlement because children are often left behind until the parent(s) is economically established and can secure visas for his or her children. A social worker who attempts to treat either client for depression without understanding his or her experiences in premigration, transit, and resettlement is unlikely to provide effective intervention.

Transnationalism

The traditional static view of migration as movements of people from one country to another for permanent settlement is being challenged by growing transnationalism and by the often-circular patterns of migration that include secondary migration to a third country and/or eventual return migration to the country of origin. Drachman has revised her original three-stage model to include additional phases of temporary or permanent return to country of origin and possible migration for settlement to a second or third country. Increasingly, migrants see themselves as transnational, meaning that they live "at one and the same time in two different countries" (Martin, 2001, p.2). Transnational populations are those "whose networks, activities, and patterns of life encompass both home and host countries"; their "lives and networks cut across national boundaries" and their "social fields exist in two countries" (Drachman & Paulino, 2004, p. 3). Transnational families may span more than two countries, as family members settle in different countries for work or family reasons. The case of a migrant as recorded in his newspaper obituary in the United States is not unusual. The subject was born in rural Jamaica and immigrated to the United States, where he had lived in several states. Of his five siblings, two were living in England, two in Jamaica, and one in the United States. His own children continued the pattern; some had settled in Canada, some in Jamaica, and others in the United States (April 26, 2001). Thus, this family—disbursed across at least four nations—illustrates the growing phenomenon of transnationalism and challenges the home country/ host country focus of traditional migration practice.

Transnational Family and Economic Relationships. Transnational families maintain relationships although members may be separated for long periods of time. Relationships are maintained through telephone calls, e-mail messages, and, if immigration regulations permit, visitation. Many immigrants leave home with the idea of eventual return: "every departing Jamaican is a potential returnee" (Small, 2007, p. 249). Relatively small percentages do return home, but the hope or dream of return is an element of transnationalism.

The strength of transnational family relationships is underscored by the flow of money and goods sent by immigrants to their family members in the home country. Remittances—money sent back to family members in the home country by immigrants—are significant at the family and the macro-economic levels. As Small (2007) notes, "remittances are unplanned mechanisms for transferring capital and redistributing wealth across a wide cross-section of families, primarily poor families" (p. 252). The volume of remittances is enormous; the World Bank estimates that remittances are more than twice the total amount of foreign aid disbursed. Globally, as noted in Chapter 2, $126 billion was estimated to have been remitted in 2004 (Moreno, 2006). The impact of remittance receiving at the family level has been documented in numerous countries. A study of survival strategies of low-wage earners in Jamaica, for example, found that remittances were often a life line. Finding that 47% of domestic workers, 78% of free zone workers, and 64% of security guards received money from relatives abroad, the authors concluded that "the main support for all groups came from relatives and friends living overseas" (Henry-Lee, Chevannes, Clarke, & Ricketts, 2000, p. 26).

Less well-studied is the impact of remittance sending on migrant individuals and families. Social workers are often unaware that their clients are fulfilling obligations to family members beyond those listed on the intake form or in the case record. Often relatively poor immigrants and even refugees struggling to meet self-sufficiency requirements are sending money and goods to family, without their social worker's knowledge. When discovered, there is a danger that the immigrant's understanding of family and family obligations will conflict with those of the host-country social worker or social welfare institutions, suggesting another area for cross-cultural understanding. Ultimately, transnationalism may ameliorate the trauma of family separation and reunification as family members maintain closer contact with their relatives abroad.

Yet separation and loss are important themes in working with immigrant children. One social worker from the Caribbean, reflecting on his own migration experience, tells of being flown to England at the age of 11 to join his mother, who had left him with his grandparents at the age of 3 months. "When I finally arrived at Victoria Train station, in central London, any person could have claimed me because I had no idea what my parents looked like. I have never been sure if my mother recognized me or read the sign around my neck" (Williams, 2007, p. 263). Often, such children join not only their mother, but a stepfather they have never met and new siblings. If reunification occurs in the early teen years, severe family tensions are likely as in Case 11.1. Social workers may be called on to assist children in adjusting to new families and new and different educational systems. Parents expect their children to be grateful for the sacrifices made and are often still working long hours to support their families, leaving little time or emotional energy to devote to the reunification process.

There are also challenges for social workers in countries of emigration, where children left behind suffer from levels of abandonment and may exhibit problems in school or community as they await reunification. In other cases, children may be left in inadequate care situations; in some cases, teenagers have been left to fend for themselves, relying on barrels of goods sent to them by their mothers in the United States (Crawford-Brown & Rattray, 2001). A study of children in Jamaica found that children left behind by migrating parents did more poorly in school and suffered from a variety of psychological problems, suggesting that migratory separation is similar in its impact on children to separations caused by other factors such as death or divorce (Pottinger, 2005).

Social workers need to understand the changing nature of migration and family relationships. They must also gain knowledge of immigration laws and statuses, appropriate cultural knowledge, and skill in working through interpreters. Each area will be discussed below.

CASE 11.1: ISSUES IN FAMILY REUNIFICATION

Internationally related cases may occur in any social worker's caseload. The following example case is based on comments shared in group sessions by adolescents in the Toronto, Canada, school system. The teenagers involved had recently migrated to Canada from Jamaica after years of separation from their mothers, who had migrated earlier. The comments suggest the adjustment difficulties faced by these teens and their parents and the special challenges for their social workers who are attempting to help them.

Teen 1 recounts: "My mom told me that I messed up her whole life since I came to Canada—that her husband left her, that she never has money anymore and that I eat out all her food. She went so far as to call me a fat, black, lazy-ass, good for nothing kid and threatened to send me back home" (Glasgow & Gouse-Sheese, 1995, p. 14).

Another student relayed:

> The first day after arriving in Canada I got into a big fight with my mother. I left all my clothes back home. I pictured things were cheap in Canada and my room was full of new clothes, the kind I really wanted. But, I was wrong! My mother got mad at me. She cuss and swore at me. She asked if I think money grew on trees. I wanted to say "yes" but I did not. I wondered what happened to the nice mother I met back home. From since then things got bad between us. (Glasgow & Gouse-Sheese, 1995, p. 10)

Other teens in the group told of conflicts with new step-parents and siblings they had never met, of feeling strange around their mothers because they had spent very little time with them, and of missing their caretakers in Jamaica. The social workers decided to involve these teens in a support and discussion group. The choice of intervention was important for several reasons. First, West Indians tend to be suspicious of therapeutic

(continued)

services and would not be likely to use individual counseling. More important, each of the teens felt isolated. Each entered the group feeling that he or she was the only one experiencing these problems. Thus, the groupwork approach reduced the teens' isolation, provided a safe place for them to vent—a behavior not condoned at home—and provided an avenue for facilitated problem solving through the group and its leaders.

Immigration Statuses

The immigration status of foreign-born individuals affects their rights and access to social and health services and may restrict other rights, such as the right to travel out of the country of current residence. Professionals who interact with international populations need information about the various immigration statuses that apply and the rights and duties associated with each. To advise without proper information could jeopardize a family's status and even lead to deportation. Immigration restrictions may restrict optimal social work practice, preventing or delaying family reunification, for example. In Case 11.2, an undocumented client's fear of deportation was misinterpreted as child neglect and resistance to help.

CASE 11.2: IMMIGRATION STATUS MISUNDERSTOOD
Ada Sanchez, Department of Children and Families

A child welfare supervisor, herself an immigrant from Peru, relates this case. A 6-year-old Hispanic girl was referred by her school to our child protection agency as at risk of medical neglect. The child had a rash; although the mother had been advised by the school nurse to take the child to a doctor, she had not. The social worker tried to interview the child, but the child seemed afraid and would not answer questions. The social worker then visited the mother with an interpreter and provided a list of doctors. The mother promised to take the child the next day; however, when the social worker visited the mother a week later, she had not followed through. The social worker told me that she was planning to recommend a protective services follow-up for medical and emotional neglect. During her visits, she had become concerned that the mother was always sleeping, could never find her medical or Social Security cards, and provided very little information. In addition, the worker suspected that the child could be developmentally delayed because she would not engage with the worker. I decided to accompany the social worker on a home visit.

(continued)

As soon as the mother opened the door, and her mouth, I realized she was from South America. Everything suddenly made sense to me. The mother and father were illegal residents. Mother worked third shift so that she could be home with her child and the father could work during the day. They had no insurance and no money to pay for medical care. The mother was putting money aside so that she could take the child to a private doctor. The child was quite intelligent but knew she was forbidden to talk about her family situation. I was able to offer some services, including a local pediatrician who was willing to see the child without charging. I also put the mother in touch with local churches who could be of assistance. I took this opportunity to train my social work supervisees about illegal immigration and ways to help. The case was closed.

Work with the undocumented must be done carefully to balance social work ethical obligations for safeguarding self-determination and confidentiality, legal and agency obligations, and client safety and well-being. In the United States, all government-supported services except public education and emergency medical care are unavailable to the undocumented. Support services will need to be secured from informal and nontraditional sources, as suggested in the case above. Fearfulness and reluctance to share information with professionals are normal protective behaviors in such circumstances and should not be interpreted as pathological. Social workers need to take care not to be perceived as taking actions that put the client's status in jeopardy, or they may contribute to decisions that worsen the client's well-being, such as precipitous moves. The first step to effective service is awareness of immigration status and sensitivity to the possibility that the family being served may be undocumented.

Refugees are a special group of immigrants, defined as persons who are persecuted on the basis of race, religion, nationality, social group, or political opinion (Drachman, 1995). Those accepted into a country as refugees are usually given at least time-limited eligibility for special resettlement services. In Denmark, for example, priority is put on language training and family reunification. Families are supported by public assistance while adults are given intensive Danish lessons to facilitate their integration into the new society. Resettlement assistance in the United States has become more focused on employment. Length of eligibility for resettlement benefits has been reduced and language training, while offered, is secondary to preparation for employment and self-sufficiency.

It is easy to underestimate the difficulties refugees face in resettlement and adaptation. Almost all face what one Vietnamese scholar called "seven main agonies" of resettlement: culture shock; a language barrier; collapse of their support systems, including family; loss of status, loneliness, and cultural disorientation; lifestyle differences and value differences; unemployment or underemployment; and often, resulting emotional and mental health problems (Thuy, 1986, p. 7). Social workers encountering refugees during resettlement or in the years following the official resettlement period will need to assist them in coping with these multiple cultural and emotional challenges, as well as their needs for help with housing, job searching, and other basics.

Welfare reform in the 1990s has created special problems for legal refugees and immigrants in the United States. In one state, a particularly stringent set of regulations sanctions clients who fail to conform with job preparation and job search requirements, reducing their benefits with each sanction and permanently banning benefits to any family with three sanctions. The rules are implemented with little regard for language competence or cultural barriers to work and service, as Cases 11.3 and 11.4 illustrate.

In Case 11.3, 5 years after arrival, the Tran family is unprepared for self-sufficiency or employment. The many problems of resettlement, including language barriers, limited support system, unemployment, and disorientation have been complicated by the husband's illness and death and by welfare regulations that do not consider these to be reasons for continued support.

In another state, researchers found numerous barriers to adequate work for Sumali, Hmong, and Latino immigrants (Hollister, Martin, Toft, & Yeo, 2005).

CASE 11.3: RESETTLEMENT AND SELF-SUFFICIENCY
Vichhyka Ngy, Asian Family Services

Mrs. Tran (not her real name), a Vietnamese mother of three teenagers, was referred to Asian Family Services after receiving a sanction from the TANF (Temporary Assistance to Needy Families) program. She had not attended a required job-training session being held at a community agency. Mrs. Tran and her family had been receiving benefits for the past 2 years after her husband died of cancer. The family had come from Vietnam about 3 years prior to his death during the Orderly Departure Program. The family had suffered considerable trauma prior to departure, as the husband had been an official in the South Vietnamese government and was imprisoned and tortured after the war. The father was diagnosed with cancer soon after arriving in the United States, and his wife devoted herself to caring for him. Mrs. Tran spoke and understood almost no English, had no working experience in the United States, and no vocational skills. The social worker at Asian Family Services explained to her that she had to attend the training course or she could lose her welfare benefits. After sitting through several all-day sessions entirely in English, she understood nothing and dropped out. She was given her second sanction by the welfare department. Asian Family Services had obtained a small grant for day-care training, delivered

(continued)

in the Asian languages. The social worker was able to intervene with the welfare department and enroll Mrs. Tran in the training. She completed the course and received a positive evaluation. However, her English ability was so limited that she was not able to get a job. Her welfare benefits were terminated, leaving the family without income. Subsequently, repeated calls to her home went unanswered, and the social worker from Asian Family Services has not been able to contact Mrs. Tran. A neighbor reported that the family moved to another state to be with relatives.

Cultural Knowledge

Lack of knowledge of culture can easily lead to misdiagnosis and labeling of clients as resistant. Case 11.4 was referred by the welfare department after a Vietnamese family was sanctioned when the mother failed to comply with a

---

CASE 11.4: RESISTANCE OR ABUSE—MISDIAGNOSIS
Vichhyka Ngy, Asian Family Services

At the request of the welfare department, the social worker from Asian Family Services went to the home to explain the job readiness requirements to Mr. and Mrs. Nguyen and their three adolescent children. The husband had come to the United States from Vietnam first, later sponsoring his wife and children. When the social worker explained the requirements of the welfare department that Mrs. Nguyen attend a job readiness program, the family agreed to comply. The social worker arranged to pick the client up and drive her to the training. On the arranged day, however, the client was not waiting and no one answered the door. Several days later, Mrs. Nguyen appeared at the Asian Family Services office in great distress and very fearful that her husband would find out that she had come for help. The story she told to the worker was that she had not answered the door or complied with the welfare department regulations because her husband would not let her leave the house. He was extremely controlling and abusive. He destroys everything she enjoys to punish her; he chopped off the plants she was growing, destroyed the fish tank she enjoyed, and threw away the radio that her children had bought for her. He threatens her with deportation. Tensions in the home continued to escalate, and one of the children shared some of this with the school psychologist, resulting in a referral to the child welfare agency. Mr. Nguyen responded by moving to an adjacent town. His wife was forced to join him after the welfare department cut off all benefits for her noncompliance with the job readiness requirements. The loss of benefits has escalated family violence and increased Mrs. Nguyen's dependence on her abusive husband.

directive to attend a job readiness program. The Asian Family Services agency was asked to intervene to work on the family's resistance.

It is clear that social workers in the mainstream welfare departments and child welfare agencies are unable to effectively serve the population of Southeast Asians if they communicate in English-language directives, order clients to attend trainings they cannot comprehend, and apply unrealistic job expectations. Failure to communicate with clients and to understand family dynamics and cultural expectations exacerbate negative case results, as in missing or ignoring family violence.

Cultural knowledge is necessary for competent social work. Workers should refrain from quick judgments or labeling of families until cultural practices are understood. For example, in many cultures, it is usual for parents and very young children to share bedrooms or even beds. In the West, this may be considered abnormal. Certain traditional healing practices, such as coining or cupping, may leave marks that can be confused with marks of child abuse. As noted earlier, many immigrants, no matter how limited their incomes, send money to family members in the home country. In other circumstances, they may pass up important opportunities for self-advancement to help a family member in a small business or to care for relatives. Understanding the importance of the extended family and the extent and intensity of family obligations is needed for social workers to properly interpret client behavior. Because "family" has different definitions in different cultures, social work methods must be adapted. A Canadian social worker told of her difficulties in working with a woman around placement of her child, as the woman was receiving intense pressure from relatives about the proper course of action and felt compelled to follow their advice (Legault, 1996). In other cases, the family that comes to meet with the social worker may include parents, children, grandparents, and an uncle. Clashes between the worker's and client's concepts of family may make case progress difficult. Gender roles are another common area of misunderstanding and culture clash between social workers and immigrant families. If a woman is passive and submissive during a family interview, she may be acting in a culturally appropriate manner, not exhibiting low self-esteem. To resolve problems, it is important that the social worker understand who makes family decisions and who listens to whom within the family if interventions are to be successful. Social workers in such cases may struggle to find new and more subtle ways of satisfying the goal of self-determination.

In Asian cultures, it is not typical to discuss relationship problems outside the family or to identify problems as emotional or mental in nature. Thus a client may present with a physical compliant or with a financial problem. If the social worker refers the case too quickly, the underlying relationship and/or emotional problems will be missed. In such cases, the worker must first work on concrete needs to build trust. Many immigrants also experience huge barriers in accessing normal social and health services, especially problems of transportation and language. Advising a client to "have your family take you to the clinic" will not be effective if the family fears going to the clinic or if the only family members who can drive are in factory jobs in which they cannot get time off. Social work with immigrants may require the worker to do more for the clients in the beginning to prepare the clients for the long term by teaching them how to be more independent. Thus instead of telling a client to take the bus to the health clinic, the worker may need to give detailed instructions about how to take the bus or find an escort for the first trip, and to write out the English request to the clinic staff for the client to present on arrival.

Immigrants may expect the social worker to be directive and often will not respond well to "talk therapy" or to facilitative approaches that work to get the client to arrive at the solution to the problem. An educational approach to treatment is often useful. Educational efforts should be attempted in child neglect and abuse cases if the child is not in imminent danger of serious harm. It is usual in West Indian, African, and Southeast Asian families to use physical punishment. Indeed, West Indian families may assert that spanking or beating children is necessary if children are to grow up to be disciplined and responsible. These families may exhibit no other characteristics of dysfunctional families; rather, they may be loving and strongly dedicated to their children's education and future. Precipitous child removal in such cases will likely cause more harm to the children than leaving them in the family home. An approach of education and partnership with the parents should be attempted. The child welfare worker can support the parents' desire to raise well-disciplined children and acknowledge the parents' wish to be seen as responsible and law-abiding residents of their current community. Thus careful explanation of legal requirements combined with teaching of alternative means of child discipline may prove successful and should be attempted unless the child is at serious risk of injury.

It is also important not to apply cultural information rigidly and to all members of a group without individualization. Cultural knowledge applied indiscriminantly is as damaging as no cultural information. Utilization of the stage-of-migration framework on a case-by-case basis will help ensure that social workers do not assume that all Afghan refugees or immigrants from Guyana had a similar experience.

Working Through Interpreters

Ideally, interventions are provided by professionally trained personnel who speak the same language as the person being served. In many cases, this is not possible, especially in areas with diverse populations but without large concentrations of any single linguistic group. Social workers therefore need to learn to work through interpreters to provide adequate service. The first imperative is to secure an interpreter. In several of the cases presented above, agencies attempted to interact in English with families who spoke no English. It is also important to use a professional interpreter, not a family member. In many instances, family members will not translate correctly because they will want to protect each other or safeguard certain information. They may also be unable to interpret accurately due to lack of familiarity with the concepts, terminology, or laws being discussed by the social worker. The potential for miscommunication is considerable. It is especially important not to use children to interpret for their parents, as this exacerbates already problematic generational conflicts in role and respect. Child welfare agencies have sometimes made the mistake of using a child as interpreter during investigation of his or her own case. In one case, a refugee mother was being investigated for child neglect after neighbors reported that she was leaving her 10-year-old daughter home alone to care for younger siblings. The child welfare worker used the 10-year-old child to tell the mother that she must never put a child as young as 10 in charge as it was against the law. The mother must have found the message very confusing, because the social worker had just put the child in charge by using her as the mother's translator (Barbour & Buch, 1986).

Whenever feasible, the agency should employ translators. This permits adequate training and supervision and can minimize problems of translation. Unless the translator fully understands the purpose of the interviewing process and has linguistic skill and appropriate empathy, he or she may translate verbatim even when this masks the meaning of the communication. Baker (1981) cites a case in which verbatim translation of a judge's question about agency custody led three unaccompanied minors to believe they were being put into slavery. Even more problematic is when a translator takes such liberties that he or she provides "independent intervention," usually without the social worker's knowledge, by telling the worker what he or she thinks is the correct case decision rather than repeating the client's expressed wishes.

Social workers and other mental health professionals rely on subtle cues of body language, and the way the client expresses his or her concerns, not just on words. This is the most difficult challenge to overcome in the use of translators as only the best trained and empathetic will be able to interpret these cues and feed them back to the professional without intervening. It should be emphasized that without cultural knowledge of the meanings of gestures or postures in the culture of the client, it is dangerous for a therapist or other professional to interpret these. Those who work with immigrants who cannot communicate in the professional's language need to secure training in working with interpreters so that difficulties can be minimized. They will also have to advocate to ensure that adequate translation services are provided. Social work administrators have the responsibility to ensure that translation services are adequately and fairly arranged, which will be discussed further below.

A final point in this overview of practice challenges with international populations is use of cultural consultation. In working with clients from a different culture, the worker will encounter "gray" areas in assessment in which there is uncertainty as to whether a behavior is culturally appropriate or is pathological. Before proceeding to attach labels to the behavior or to design an intervention, it is wise to seek consultation from someone with the specific knowledge of the culture.

INTERNATIONAL ADOPTION

Worldwide, there are an estimated 40,000 adoptions per year in which families from one country, usually an industrialized country, adopt children from another, usually developing, country (Barry, 2006). In the United States, the number of international adoptions was in the range of 7,000–10,000 per year from 1986 through 1995, accounting for 10% to 15% of all adoptions. Since 1996, the number has grown and is now over 20,000 per year (U.S. Department of State, 2007). In FY 2006, the largest number of adoptees came to the U.S. from China, Guatemala, Russia, and South Korea, in that order. Among other countries with significant international adoptions are France with 4,136 in 2005 and Canada at 1,871 in 2005 (Adoption Council of Canada, 2007; Joint Council on International Children's Services [JCICS] 2007). In Norway, Denmark, Holland, and Israel, there are so few native infants available for adoption that most adoptions are international (Simon, Altstein, & Melli, 1994).

Interest in international adoption has roots in humanitarian concerns about war orphans after World War II and the abandoned children, including those fathered by foreign servicemen, of the Korean War. The practice has expanded as the availability of infants for in-country adoption has decreased dramatically in Western Europe and North America as a result of birth control, abortion, and lifestyle changes that have made single motherhood more acceptable. More infants are without homes in countries with high rates of poverty, high birth rates, and the enduring stigma for bearing an out-of-wedlock child. Countries may also become sources for adoption due to special circumstances. Romania had large numbers of young children abandoned in institutions as a result of the policies of the Ceausescu regime. After the fall of that regime, revelation of conditions in the institutions fueled concern and considerable interest in adopting Romanian children; in the period from January 1990 to April 1991, for example, Canada admitted more than 1,000 Romanian adoptees (Marcovitch, Cesaroni, Roberts, & Swanson, 1995). China's one-child policy coupled with traditional preferences for male children has led to availability of Chinese baby girls for adoption.

At the policy level, international adoption is controversial. The debates center around two issues. The first is whether it is good for a child to be raised by parents of a different culture, and often a different race, and therefore to lose their cultural identity. Children adopted by people from a foreign country leads to "the separation of children not only from their birth parents, but from their racial, cultural and national communities as well" (Bartholet, 1993, p. 90). The second is a macrolevel critique that views adoption as another case in which poor countries are asked to provide resources (children) to wealthier countries, a practice some believe ultimately exploits women and children (Herrmann & Kasper, 1992). Complicating these debates are cases of baby-selling and of agents who place children for adoption against the wishes of their birth parents. Although all experts agree that the procedures for good adoption must include adequate prerelease counseling and a freely chosen decision to relinquish a child, not pressured by either coercion or the offer of money, the complexities of international adoption have allowed some unscrupulous practices to occur. Opinions in developing countries are influenced by rumors that children are adopted by foreigners for use as slaves, for sexual abuse, or even for sale of vital organs. Debates over what is best for the child and the macrolevel symbolism of international adoption remain active.

Overview of the Basic Facts

"International adoption is a three way intersection between social work, law, and international relations" (Kendrick, 1998). All three dimensions are important to its practice, and social work professionals involved in international adoption must have knowledge of the law and knowledge of and skill in international relations to fortify their social work expertise. Through a complex process and the efforts of social workers or other professionals in at least two countries, "a child without parents in one country is united with parents in another country" (Kendrick, 1998).

International adoption practice first requires sound adoption practices. Families applying to adopt need to be carefully screened; home studies are required to ensure that the family is willing and capable of providing a good home and parenting for an adopted child. Second, children approved for international placement must be legally free for adoption, with informed and uncoerced consent of their parent or parents. Once these two conditions have been met, the third element of good adoption practice usually requires a period of supervision before the adoption is legally finalized. All steps of the process take on new complexities in international adoption in which laws and regulations of two countries must be satisfied.

Some countries forbid international adoption while others heavily regulate the practice. Countries allowing children to be placed for out-of-country adoption may set standards for approval of adoptive parents. Some do not allow single-parent adoptions; others have minimum or maximum age restrictions. Social agencies working with adoptions in these countries must comply with these guidelines in addition to applying their own criteria for acceptable families.

International adoption is often an expensive process. In addition to the fees paid to adoption agencies to cover the cost of the process, a number of countries require that the parents travel to the country for the adoption placement. At times, lengthy and uncertain stays are required. A family expecting a 3-week stay in Bolivia may be required to stay for 6 or more weeks before a placement is approved. Costs in travel, living expenses, and lost wages can be considerable; social workers need to provide families with

accurate information about fees and travel requirements while also preparing them for the need to remain flexible to on-site changes. During the
time of the country visit, families must also live with uncertainty about the
outcome of their efforts. Although agencies try to protect families from
unscrupulous agents and highly unstable local conditions, some families
have paid large fees to reputable agencies and traveled to distant sites only
to have to return without the promised child. Increased international policy
setting and regulation are intended to prevent these unfortunate occur-
rences.

Many of the children placed for foreign adoptions are cared for in institutions prior to their placement. The quality of caregiving varies, but often
staff–children ratios are high, resources are limited, and children suffer various types of physical and emotional deprivation. Adoptees from institutions,
especially if the stay was prolonged, will be more likely to have developmental delays and disabilities (Groza, 1997). Parents who travel to the child's
country may see firsthand the institutional conditions and have an idea of
what the child has experienced. Others may have very limited information
about the child's preplacement experience or background. Adoption practice now emphasizes providing parents with detailed information on the
child's background and heritage. This is not always possible in international
adoption.

Follow-up studies of international adoptees have generally shown positive adoption and adjustment outcomes. While initially many children, especially those adopted at an older age or from very deprived institutional
settings, exhibit a number of physical, medical, and behavioral problems,
these usually decrease over time. Reports in the tale 1990s suggested that
adoptions of children from orphanages in Russia and Romania were dis-
rupting at a much higher-than-normal rate, raising concerns over the impact
of severe early deprivation (Holtan, 1999). However, long-range studies have
shown that by young adulthood most foreign adoptees differ little on adjustment measures from their nonadopted peers, and most report positive
relationships with their adoptive families.

In spite of positive findings, some researchers, especially in Europe, have
concerns over international adoption. Simon et al. (1994) report on several
such studies from Scandinavia. Although finding overall success, adopted
adolescents in Norway exhibited traits that suggested they may become
marginalized as adults in Norwegian society; and in Denmark, 90% of international adoptees surveyed "reported feeling 'mostly Danish' " (Simon et
al., p. 65); however, about 20% had limited education and faced dim employment prospects. Acknowledging successful family integration in most
cases, the researchers question whether the almost homogeneous societies of
Scandinavia can provide suitable environments for foreign adoptees of different races. Overall, however, follow-up studies of adult and adolescent
international adoptees discovered adjustment similar to in-country same-race
adoptees and quite similar to nonadopted persons (Bartholet, 1993; Groza,

1997; Simon et al., 1994). The growing multicultural makeup of nations may also assist the process of adjustment.

Social Work Roles in International Adoption

Although other professions are involved in international adoption work, social workers play the full range of roles in adoption practice: home study and preparation of families; cultural plans; follow-up services, interaction with foreign orphanages and agencies; and adoption policy influencing.

Home Study and Preparation of Families. Follow-up studies conducted with adopting families have shown that good preparation contributes to adoption success. Furthermore, most families indicate that they would have liked more preparation than what was received and expressed an interest in continuing support services. Groza (1997) recommends a thorough educational preparation for families.

Early in the preparation process, social workers guide families in examining their reasons for considering international adoption and exploring the ramifications of adopting a child from a different culture and race. Some couples may not have thought through these issues beyond early childhood. Or they may not have considered the support that will be given or withheld by extended family members. It is crucial that adopting couples recognize and accept that by adopting a foreign child, they are becoming a multicultural and usually multiracial family forever. The social worker plays an important role in facilitating this exploration.

IMPORTANT ELEMENTS IN EDUCATING FAMILIES ABOUT INTERNATIONAL ADOPTION

- details on the legal and social process of adoption in both the United States and abroad
- issues of abandonment, separation, grief, loss, and mourning for adoptees that are evident throughout the life cycle
- issues of separation, grief, loss, and mourning for infertile couples that are evident throughout the life cycle
- the adoptive family's life cycle and unique issues in family formation
- individual and family identity development in adoption
- unique issues of attachment in adoption
- outcomes and risks in international adoptions

Groza, *Encyclopedia of Social Work*, 1997, p. 4.

Social workers also help families to consider the possibility that the child they adopt may have medical or developmental problems that are not evident in the initial medical screenings and to decide whether they can parent a child with disabilities. A Canadian study of parents of Romanian adoptees showed that more than 88% had considered the risks of such problems before adopting, suggesting good preparation (Marcovitch et al., 1995).

In assessing suitability for adoption, maturity and flexibility are important family characteristics. These will be tested early as the couple negotiates the often-tortuous path to a finalized adoption, and tested often throughout parenting a child who may have developmental delays, medical problems, attachment difficulties, and adolescent identity concerns complicated by his or her status as a foreign-born adoptee. Care in the assessment phase is particularly important. After being helped by social workers to explore motivation, implications, and their own readiness, some families will decide not to proceed.

Assisting With a Cultural Plan. One of the objections to international adoption is that it deprives a child of his or her culture. It is therefore important that the adoptive family "have positive feelings about the child's country, racial and cultural heritage" and that they take purposeful steps to maintain the heritage in some ways (Kendrick, 1998). Groza (1997) recommends that social workers help each adopting family to develop a "cultural plan that will help the child build an identity as a cultural and ethnic person" (p. 4). He suggests adapting the life book idea (a type of scrapbook to help children placed in out-of-home care to remember their earlier life) to prepare a cultural life book. The period of in-country time required for child placement and approval can be productively used by the parents to familiarize themselves with the culture and begin a collection of photographs and other items. One mother told of purchasing a small emerald in Bogata that she planned to present to her Colombian adopted daughter when she was old enough to appreciate not only the gem but its origins. Another family has made an album documenting the entire adoption process, with ample photographs of the child's town of origin in Bolivia. The initial journey should be only a foundation for continued efforts to ensure that the child has opportunities to learn about his or her culture and country of origin.

Social workers also need to prepare families for legal hurdles and for complications that can arise in negotiating between two legal systems. A thorough knowledge of laws and procedures in all "sending" countries, as well as of U.S. adoption and adoption-related immigration laws, is essential.

Follow-up Services. After the finalization of an adoption, some families will need continuing services for special medical problems or for emotional problems of their children. Many families welcome continued or intermittent support in coping with the "normal" issues of parenting a child from another culture. Holtan (1999) recommends "ongoing post-finalization services as needed over time over the life of the family" in order to address special needs of international adopting families (p. 4). For those families who need mental health intervention, adoption agencies should be ready to make appropriate referrals. Other families seek only support and some may take a role in developing their own services. Adoptive parents in some locales have developed groups; some of the more successful ones hold periodic cultural events, support group meetings, and events for the adoptees, including teen activities and support groups. Social workers can assist families by suggesting involvement in such activities or by organizing a group in areas where none exist.

Relationships With Source Country Agencies. In some agencies, social workers travel periodically to the sending (birth) countries and help build and maintain positive and trusting relationships between adoption agencies, orphanages, and local legal authorities. Their practices may also have positive effects on child welfare practices in the source countries (Stiles, de la Rosa, Dharmaraksa, Goldner, & Kalyanvala, 2001). One agency, for example, uses videotapes of children in orphanages to introduce them to prospective parents. The orphanage staff in Russia was shown how to take a video that would show a child's gross motor skills and whether the child follows voices. Through this activity, the importance of attention from adults and the importance of developmental activities were communicated; in small ways, this subtle education may improve institutional practices. Other contributions by adoption social workers have been more direct. Adoption social workers helped develop a foster care system in Romania and developed a training curriculum on child development for institutions in Bulgaria. Some direct financial assistance to improve care for children remaining in their countries has also been provided (E. Kendrick, personal communication, July 15, 1999). With additional attention to these roles, international adoption might be one "spur" to improve services to children worldwide.

Social Work's Influence on International Adoption Policy. In spite of the research showing positive outcomes for children, international adoption remains controversial. The Convention on the Rights of the Child clearly states a preference for in-country placement but does approve of intercountry placement when that is not feasible: "Recognize that inter-country adoption may be considered as an alternative means of child's care, if the child cannot be placed in a foster or an adoptive family or cannot in any suitable manner be cared for in the child's country of origin" (United Nations, 1989, article 21(b)). The reporting requirements under the convention underscore this hierarchy of options by asking countries allowing international adoptions to report on the extent to which "due regard is paid to the desirability of continuity in the child's upbringing and to the child's ethnic, religious, cultural and linguistic background" in considering alternative placements (Rios-Kohn, 1998, p. 22). Article 21 of the convention further calls for safeguards to ensure that inter-country adoptions maintain good standards, are carried out by competent authorities, are not done for financial gain, and are contingent on informed consent following counseling of parents, relatives, and guardians.

The Hague Convention on Protection of Children and Cooperation in Respect of Intercountry Adoption, approved in 1993, reflects a more favorable view of international adoption, indicating it is a legitimate option for children who cannot be raised by their own parents and probably better for the child than in-country foster care or institutionalization (Groza, 1997; Rios-Kohn, 1998). The conference that drafted the convention also developed standards for adoption that could improve the process and reduce child trafficking if implemented by a majority of countries. The convention became effective in 1995 in ratifying countries.

The United States has been working to come into compliance with the requirements of Hague Convention. The Department of State has been designated as the Central Authority and processes for accreditation of adoption agencies are being developed. At the time of writing, it was expected that the United States would submit its "instrument of ratification" of the treaty by late 2007 and the Convention would enter into force 3 months following the submission, or some time early in 2008 (JCICS, 2007). This very significant piece of international law will regulate the practice of intercountry adoption and reduce abuses.

Social workers in sending and receiving countries can contribute to informed discussions on the topic. They can ensure that agency practices are ethical, taking care that payment of fees is not allowed to influence judgments about adoption suitability, and can advocate for adequate preparation, screening and, follow-up services. Social workers in sending countries can also be vigilant about not allowing fee payments to influence practice. They can also work to ensure that informed consent is secured and that birth parents have access to counseling. Dialogue between social workers from sending and receiving countries would be useful in resolving challenging issues—such as what happens to the child when an overseas adoption fails—and in cultural maintenance for adopted children.

INTERCOUNTRY CASEWORK

"Intercountry casework is a method of extending individualized social services to persons whose problems require study or action in another country [and] a method of interagency co-operation designed to bring together on behalf of a client social services in more than one country" (cited in Cox, 1984, p. 44). In certain respects, refugee resettlement and international adoption require elements of intercountry casework. As migration and other forms of international contact have increased, there are many additional situations that require intercountry work. Among these are cross-national marriages and divorces, child abductions, repatriation or return migration, claims for retirement or disability benefits earned in another country, medical crises that occur in another country, crimes committed by noncitizens, and a host of other family relationship problems when family members live in different countries, or, as noted above, when migrants live in more than one country at

---

CASE 11.5: SIMPLE INTERCOUNTRY CASEWORK CAN BE COMPLEX

As one social worker related:

Although I did not identify it as such at the time, I tried to engage in inter-country casework on one occasion and experienced tremendous obstacles. I advocated for a client's spouse, who was trying to obtain a copy of his birth certificate from his country of origin, Guatemala. My client's spouse was from a small village and informed me that he was not familiar with the larger institutions of the country. The obstacles I faced included: not knowing where to begin, not being able to get any guidance from my co-workers or supervisors who were equally uninformed, not knowing Guatemala's political structure or government institutions, not knowing the Guatemalan culture or customs, and not knowing Spanish. Needless to say, I proved to be an ineffective advocate in this case. (Carroll, 1997)

---

the same time (Cox, 1986). Indeed, resolving even simple client requests may present overwhelming difficulties to the untrained social worker.

Marriage, Divorce, and Child Custody

Marriages between partners from different countries can pose special challenges. Marriage does not bring the partner rights of citizenship, and procedures must be followed to gain proper visas and entry permits. Children born in mixed-country marriages often have automatic dual nationality. This grants the children a number of rights and privileges, but it may also involve unforeseen duties. Boys, for example, may be subject to military service requirements in both countries. And whichever country the child is physically in will treat the child as their own national, not as a foreign citizen. This has important implications in cases of parental child abduction, which will be discussed next. Social workers may be most likely to encounter the partners of these mixed marriages when they experience marital discord; the special challenges of cross-cultural marriage often contributes to the couple's difficulties. In other cases, social workers will be called on to assist with inter-country work to resolve problems of child support, custody, and visitation, especially in families in which the parents are divorced.

International Child Abduction

In working with divorced or separated families in which parents are from different countries, social workers should be aware of the possibility of international child abduction. This is not a common phenomenon, however, between 1973 and 1986, at least 2,700 children were kidnapped by one of their parents and taken from the United States to another country (Hegar & Greif, 1991). Recovering a child taken to another part of one's own country can be difficult, but recovering a child taken out of the country is much more complicated, especially in those countries that have not signed the Hague Convention on the Civil Aspects of International Child Abduction.

In many international marriages, stresses arise due to cultural differences. These also exist during separation and after divorce. Hegar and Greif (1991) suggest that abduction may occur due to the stress on the noncustodial parent in seeing their children brought up largely outside of their culture. Custody guidelines may also highlight cultural conflict. Whereas custody decisions in the United States have tended to favor mothers, Islamic law favors fathers in custody disputes. In other countries, such as Kenya, the children traditionally belong to the father, although young children are customarily left in the mother's care. Older children, however, will usually be given to the father or even to the father's relatives over the claims of the mother. These differences in traditional expectations will exacerbate emotional stress during initial custody procedures and, if an abduction occurs, will make recovery of the child less likely.

Hegar and Greif (1991) suggest preventive steps in working with parents whose international marriages are breaking up. In addition to the usual efforts to work out custody and visitation arrangements, workers may advise parents to learn about requirements for exiting the country and to see if they can block having a passport issued for a child. Other precautions such as frequent photographs and fingerprinting may also be advised. Social workers also need to learn about the risks of international abduction and familiarize themselves with the custody expectations of the cultures represented in their caseload. Cases may pose practice and ethical dilemmas. For example, how should the social worker advise a divorced mother as to whether to allow her ex-husband to take or send the children to visit grandparents in Africa? How can the value of extended family contact and cultural maintenance be weighed against the risk of the children's not returning from the visit? These are not easily resolved issues. What is clear is that the social worker should not give any advice without adequate legal and cultural knowledge.

The Hague Convention may offer some protection, yet additional work on international standards and agreements appears necessary. A study by the International Social Service (ISS; 1979) found that even involvement of social workers in investigating the best interests of the child often did not resolve the situation. Rather, they found that social workers tended to "identify with the parent of his own nationality and language" (p. 114). Nonetheless, their recommendation at the time was that professional investigation by internationally experienced social workers be used to determine the best course of action. Cooperation between nations in honoring such judgments should also be required by international law. Until that time, the experience of ISS suggests that successful return is most often accomplished when the parents are helped to come to an agreement on which country is best for raising the child (Cox, 1984).

Family Reunion

Work with international populations often involves assisting with attempts at family reunion. Immigrants and refugees, once established in their new environment, often wish to bring additional members of their immediate or extended family to join them and may turn to social workers for assistance. Depending on the national policies and the relationship of the parties, the ease with which families reunite will differ. In other cases, the immigrant may be considering return to his or her own country and may need assistance in making plans for the return. This is frequently contemplated at the time of retirement.

Social Security and Other Benefits Casework

In an example cited earlier in the chapter, a social worker related how difficult it was to attempt to obtain a birth certificate from another country. Securing entitlements earned in another country for clients is another challenge of international casework. Adults who have worked in various countries may have earned pensions, accident coverage, or family allowances in a country other than the one of their current residence. Returning migrants often can claim pensions earned in the country in which they spent their adult lives. Liaison work with the appropriate offices in the other country is often needed. Benefit eligibility should not be neglected even if the social worker's primary role with the family is to assist with the emotional impact of a death or accident. Workers should explore with international families whether they may be eligible for benefits from either or both countries of parents' origin and current residence (or perhaps even additional countries in which part of their work life was spent).

Deportation

Other types of cases may include work with persons who commit crimes in a country other than the country of their nationality and potential deportation cases. These require professionals to be knowledgeable about criminal or civil law where the crime was committed plus relevant immigration law. Regulations in the United States, for example, make persons subject to deportation for even relatively minor criminal convictions that occurred years earlier. Sample cases include a Jamaican deported at age 40 when he applied for citizenship because of a conviction for jumping over a subway turnstile when he was 19. Or, a 12-year U.S. Army veteran from Jamaica who was jailed and threatened with deportation for involvement in a minor skirmish during his military service in Japan more than 15 years earlier. The incident was judged so minor by the army that he had still received an honorable discharge (Caribnet, personal communication, February 17, 1998). Unless well informed about the laws and regulations, social workers may take such threats too lightly and misadvise clients on necessary actions.

SOCIAL WORK IN BORDER AREAS

A special case of intercountry work involves work in border areas. In these regions, social workers will encounter some families who are actively transnational in that they move back and forth over borders, legally or illegally. Sometimes, a move is precipitated by a social welfare investigation, such as suspected child abuse; in other instances, it may be involuntary, as when a juvenile offender is sent back to Mexico by authorities in Texas. In child welfare, there are many cases with overlapping jurisdiction: American children with relatives in Mexico, Mexican children in Mexico with relatives in the United States, Mexican children in the United States with relatives in Mexico, and so on (Daigle, 1994). Women migrate from interior regions of Mexico to the Mexico–U.S. border to work in the *maquiladoras*, factories often owned by foreign companies. Poverty and lack of opportunity lead them to move back and forth across the border in search of work. Lack of adequate services and persistent poverty plague many migrants and their families in border regions (Marquez & Padilla, 2004). In all cases, continuity of service is compromised. An important strategy for service improvement is the development of interagency collaboration agreements between agencies on both sides of the border. These are enhanced when social workers in both locales exchange information and develop personal working relationships.

Padilla and Daigle have discussed international social work collaboration at the U.S.–Mexico border in several articles. Their research shows the importance of international work because problems of child welfare, health care, and youth services deteriorate unless flexible and coordinated service can be developed on both sides of the border. They cite a case example of effective collaboration in which a child under protective custody of the state of Texas was placed in a relative's home in Mexico; there the placement was assisted by a Mexican social worker who conducted home visits for the Texas agency (Padilla & Daigle, 1998). The Los Angeles Department of Children Services has set up an international placement office as an extension of provisions of the Interstate Compact. The caseload is sizable; estimates are that 50 to 70 cases involving overlapping jurisdiction with Mexico or Asian countries are usually open and that three to four children per month are placed from Los Angeles into Mexico (Daigle, 1994).

Cooperation between agencies in different countries usually begins with informal contacts, often one social worker to another, and is later formalized in agreements. Agreements call for such activities as assisting each other in obtaining key documents, conducting home studies or other investigations, assisting with information and referral to service resources in each community, exchanging literature and information, and other activities necessary to ensure that child protection is not compromised by the border location (Padilla & Daigle, 1998, citing an agreement between agencies in El Paso and Juárez). The researchers found that immigration status—whether or not clients were legal or illegal—was seldom a focus in the agencies' collaborative activities. This is facilitated by the local nature of the agreements for cooperation. The authors fear, however, that mandatory reporting requirements, if enforced in the future, could jeopardize many current arrangements.

Effective international border practice requires the following elements: "forming working relationships, structuring formal agreements, ensuring reciprocity, and establishing effective systems of information exchange" (Padilla & Daigle, 1998, p. 66). Ability to communicate is key, of course, and some collaborations have been disrupted by the loss of bilingual workers. Thus careful attention to bilingual communication is needed on both sides of the border. The model used in one agency was to appoint bilingual social workers to official positions as international liaisons. Formal agreements are important to ensure that collaboration continues when personal relationships are disrupted by personnel changes.

Effective collaboration builds on an understanding of the differences between social welfare systems and philosophies of social work in both countries. As explained in Chapter 8, social work roles and priorities may vary by country and these differences need to be understood for coordinated practice. Daigle (1994) found that cooperative efforts had to recognize that definitions of child abuse and philosophies about caring for children differed between Mexican and U.S. social workers. These differences had to be accommodated in working agreements. Regular communication was helpful in addressing these differences; one Texas agency held joint staff meetings with Mexico's Desarrollo Integral de la Familia every few months (Daigle, 1994).

Padilla and Daigle (1998) found that working agreements are most feasible if done at the local and the agency level rather than systemwide or national. These are, therefore, agreements that can be developed through the efforts of individual social workers and social work administrators. Achieving agreement at higher levels of government involves complications with laws and international relations. Daigle (1994) recommends that states as well as cities develop policies on areas of overlapping jurisdiction in child welfare, for example, policies that would detail legal procedures and set "case philosophy" (p. 42). Ultimately, it is important that national governments recognize the binational nature of child protection and set appropriate guidelines. Binational issues are not confined to border areas. Many immigrants settle far from borders, in areas less able to handle relationships with home countries. Nappa County, California, for example, has a large foreign-born population, but no social work contacts in Mexico. Therefore, a number of undocumented children are in long-term foster care, even children who have relatives in Mexico willing and able to provide care (Daigle, 1994).

As movement of people and sensitivity to internationalization of social problems increase, efforts to manage services in border regions and in binational cases are likely to grow and improve through binational collaboration.

INTERNATIONAL PRACTICE ISSUES FOR SOCIAL WORK PLANNERS, ADMINISTRATORS, AND COMMUNITY ORGANIZERS

Social work planners, administrators, and community organizers also face challenges of internationally related practice in their daily functions. For example:

- A community organizer is upset that so few of the black parents in the school district turned out to vote on the school funding referendum. She is unaware that the majority of them are West Indian immigrants and few are citizens; therefore, although they pay property taxes, they are not eligible to vote.

- The administrator of a mental health clinic serving a diverse clientele, including Asians, is interviewing a Vietnamese man for a position as program director. The man is very quiet during the interview, looks down frequently, and downplays many of the accomplishments his reference letters extolled. The administrator is puzzled and does not know how to assess the man's competence for the position.

- The program planner for a community youth center notices that the number of teenage girls utilizing the drop-in center has declined gradually. The neighborhood has experienced an influx of immigrant families from Colombia.

- Staff relations at a health clinic serving a diverse community have deteriorated. The receptionist has resigned, and the only Khmer-speaking clinician has indicated that she is unhappy. Both have frequently been asked to serve as interpreters, which is outside of their job descriptions and duties.

- The campaign director for the local United Way is preparing her approach to a corporation that historically has been a major donor. Within the past year, the corporation has been acquired by a Japanese corporation and this will be the first campaign approach to the new team.

- An executive director must guide a board of directors through a contentious decision to divest the agency portfolio of investments in companies using child labor in Asia.

In carrying out interventions to address these six scenarios and others like them, social work planners, administrators, and organizers will need their macro-practice skills and knowledge about cross-cultural communication and international policy.

As community demographics change and international populations grow, social agencies need to change in several areas. First, they must reexamine their services to ensure they are needed by area residents. New services may be needed, or current ones may need to be redesigned. The agency may also need to revise its marketing strategies to reach new residents, who will not respond to traditional means of marketing such as flyers or radio advertising. Staff composition and staff cultural competence will also need to be addressed; these issues are part of the broader issue of service accessibility, which includes cultural relevance, language, and service design.

Good social service planning requires good data, beginning with basic demographic data. This may be difficult to obtain. Racial and linguistic group statistics may not reveal nationality, cultural group, or immigrant status. Thus West Indian immigrants may be counted as African Americans and Colombian immigrants as Hispanics. In areas of changing demographics, agencies may need to conduct their own population surveys—ideally in collaboration with other agencies and organizations.

Client groups are more likely to use services or to participate in organizations whose staff and leadership include members of their group. An important administrative role is recruitment and maintenance of a diverse staff, which is as representative as possible of the service area. This will require new types of outreach and employment advertising to attract candidates from a wider pool. Administrators will need skill in cross-cultural interviewing to accurately assess potential candidates from diverse ethnic backgrounds (Thiederman, 1988). In interviewing a Vietnamese candidate, for example, the culturally competent administrator would not expect a lot of eye contact; to elicit information about how the candidate might perform on the job, the administrator would frame questions more as discussions of problem-solving methods than as invitations for the candidate to boast about past accomplishments.

Similar types of cultural knowledge will also assist in designing services and marketing. A mixed-gender teen drop-in center that was freely used by African-American girls may not be used by immigrant girls from South America, as their families may not allow them the freedom of attending activities in the evening unescorted by family chaperones. Service planners could redesign the service, or use personal outreach to families in their homes and through the local churches attended by the families to explain the services and reassure the families of their children's safety. Thus culture and tradition must be considered in designing and marketing social services just as it is used in one-to-one delivery of service.

Providing translators and interpreters is crucial to adequate social services for non-English-speaking clients. The optimal solution is to hire multilingual staff; however, this is difficult, especially when there are many linguistic groups in one service area. Typically, social workers or other professionals are "borrowed" from their normal work to serve as translators or paraprofessionals and clerical staff are asked to take on translation tasks. These strategies often create job dissatisfaction. Staff asked to take on extra duties may become overburdened, and professionals may resent being used in what they consider paraprofessional tasks. Social work administrators must address staff workload fairness issues while working to ensure adequate interpreter services. Potential solutions include providing extra pay for

---

CASE 11.6: KNOWING LEGAL AND ETHICAL RESPONSIBILITIES

The administrator of a nonprofit shelter for battered women received a request from a shelter in a neighboring area to accept a transfer client. The woman's husband had discovered the location of the shelter, and it was believed that her life was at risk. Agency policy permitted accepting clients from other shelters in such circumstances; in fact, the agency's mission identifies ensuring safety for women without regard to their race, religion, national origin, sexual orientation, or political beliefs as its number one priority. The woman in question, however, was an undocumented immigrant from Central America; she spoke only Spanish and had no relatives in the host country. The shelter had Spanish-speaking staff. However, the director feared that accepting such a client might break a law or violate funding arrangements. The administrator refused the request.

Anonymous personal communication.

---

translation services by professionals and paraprofessionals or creating a new classification of support staff, such as combining usual clerical or aide duties with translation responsibilities, possibly at better pay and, at least, with a specific title. Plans should be made with consent and participation of all staff involved (Healy, 1996).

Lack of knowledge can cause serious errors in service judgment in internationally related matters. Case 11.6 illustrates an administrative decision made without adequate knowledge of relevant law and agency responsibility.

Knowledge gaps and fear of the unknown interfere with rational approaches to decision making. Sound administrative practice requires clear definition of problems and the gathering—sometimes very quickly—of enough information for action. The director in this case needed basic information on the legal rights and obligations of nonprofit agencies and their staffs under immigration laws. Optimally, a discussion of this issue among leadership staff and members of the board of directors would have occurred prior to a crisis, and as in the direct service case (Case 11.2), the director would have trained the staff in identifying and utilizing alternative support sources to assist the undocumented client in making plans for the future.

Policy Issues and Agency Boards

Some social service agencies, through their boards of directors, have a public policy component through which they speak out directly on issues or participate in coalition efforts. Administrators need to be sure that relevant internationally related policies in areas such as immigration, adoption, and family reunification are included in agency's policies. In addition, agencies may express their policy agenda in other ways, such as through socially

CASE 11.7: HELPING A BOARD GAIN
INTERNATIONAL KNOWLEDGE

In 1987, the board of directors of a large YWCA spent almost a year to reach a decision whether to divest its $10 million portfolio from companies doing business in apartheid South Africa. Antiracism had been identified as the agency's most important goal: "to eliminate racism wherever it is found and by any means necessary." Thus the decision initially seemed clear-cut. The group soon discovered that there were areas of conflict—What about the financial stewardship responsibilities of the board? Were some board members more concerned with racism in South Africa than at home? Members also discovered gaps in their knowledge—would divesting truly aid in eliminating apartheid? With the executive director's guidance, the board began an educational process: experts from nearby universities were invited in to talk with the board, written materials were collected for board use, and input was solicited from the YWCA of South Africa. Eventually, the board resolved its conflicts and voted to divest the portfolio of South African holdings.

responsible investment of the agency's assets. The area of investing has led agencies into some limited discussion of international issues and has often exposed gaps in board knowledge. Case 11.7 tells the story of a board of directors and an executive wrestling with divestiture during the antiapartheid movement. More recently, divestiture is again on agency agendas as divesting from holdings doing business with Sudan is used to protest government involvement in the ongoing genocide in Darfur. State governments in the United States and universities are among entities that have divested holdings in Sudan ("Divestment from Sudan: A Moral Sense," 2007).

The process of educational strategies and utilization of worldwide networks in human services can be used by administrators to resolve similar policy-level dilemmas. Expansion of the international component of public policy work is important for agencies who are active in the domestic–international interface of social work. Additional information about the policy role of the profession, including its agencies, will be covered in Chapter 12.

CONCLUSION

This chapter has briefly discussed many areas of practice that may involve social workers in international work. It is hard to imagine a social work career in the twenty-first century that will not bring the practitioner into periodic contact with situations that require knowledge beyond the borders of one's own country. Even if migration were to end today, the current numbers of binational and even multinational families would generate a substantial caseload of internationally related practice problems in many countries. Undoubtedly, migration will continue and the demand for international knowledge and intercultural sensitivity will grow. Transnational migration profoundly affects sending and receiving countries and the lives of individuals and families, creating the need for new types of social services and humane and rational social policies. In addition to internationally related practice, social work will be asked to respond to the challenges of global policy formulation. This will be examined in the next chapter.

REFERENCES

Adoption Council of Canada. (2007). *Adoption statistics.* Accessed June 24, 2007, at www.adoption.ca/news/050527stats04.htm

Baker, N. G. (1981). Social work through an interpreter *Social Work, 26*(5), 291–297.

Barbour, J., & Buch, T. (1986). Child welfare. In L. M. Healy (Ed.), *Toward improving service to Southeast Asian refugees.* West Hartford: University of Connecticut School of Social Work.

Barry, C. M. (2006). Testimony of Acting Assistant Secretary for Consular Affairs Catherine M. Barry Regarding Asian Adoptions to the United States. U.S. Senate Committee on Foreign Relations, Subcommittee on East Asian and Pacific Affairs, June 8, 2006. Accessed December 27, 2007, at www.senate.gov/~foreign/testimony/2006/BarryTestimony060608.pdf

Bartholet, E. (1993). International adoption: Current status and future prospects. *The Future of Children: Adoption, 3*(1), 89–103.

Carrol, S. (1997). *Unpublished student paper,* University of Connecticut School of Social Work, West Hartford.

Cox, D. (Ed.). (1984). *Intercountry casework: Some reflections on sixty years experience of international social service, 1924–1984.* Geneva, Switzerland: International Social Service.

Cox, D. (1986). Intercountry casework, *International Social Work, 29,* 247–256.

Crawford-Brown, C. P. J., & Rattray, J. M. (2001). Parent child relationships in Caribbean families. In N. Boyd Webb (Ed.), *Culturally diverse parent-child and family relationships* (pp. 107–132). New York: Columbia University Press.

Daigle, L. (1994). *Child welfare services along the U.S.-Mexico border: Efforts in binational cooperation* (Working Paper No. 74). Austin: University of Texas at Austin.

Divestment from Sudan: A moral sense. (2007 May 12). *The Economist, 383,* p. 31.

Drachman, D. (1992). A stage-of-migration framework for service to immigrant populations. *Social Work, 37*(1), 68–72.

Drachman, D. (1995). Immigration statuses and their influence on service provision access, and use. *Social Work, 40*(2), 188–197.

Drachman, D., & Paulino, A. (Eds.). (2004). *Immigrants and social work: Thinking beyond the borders of the United States.* Binghamton, NY: Haworth Social Work Practice Press.

Glasgow, G. F., & Gouse-Sheese, J. (1995). Themes of rejection and abandonment in group work with Caribbean adolescents. *Social Work With Groups, 17*(4), 3–27.

Groza, V. (1997). Adoption: International. In R. L. Edwards (Ed.), *Encyclopedia of social work* (19th ed.), (1997 suppl., 1–14). Washington, DC: NASW Press.

Healy, L. M. (1996). International dimensions of diversity: Issues for the social agency workplace. *Journal of Multicultural Social Work, 4*(4), 97–116.

Hegar, R. L., & Greif, G. L. (1991). Parental kidnapping across international borders. *International Social Work, 34*, 353–363.

Henry-Lee, A., Chevannes, B., Clarke, M., & Ricketts, S. (2000). *An assessment of the standard of living and copies strategies of workers in selected occupations who earn a minimum wage.* Kingston, Jamaica: Planning Institute of Jamaica, Policy Development Unit.

Herrmann, K. J., Jr., & Kasper, B., (1992). International adoption: The exploitation of women and children. *Affilia, 7*(1), 45–58.

Hessle, S. (2007). Globalisation: Implications for international development work, social work and the integration of immigrants in Sweden. In L. Dominelli (Ed.), *Revitalising communities in a globalizing world* (pp. 231–241). Aldershot: Ashgate Publishing Limited.

Hollister, C. D., Martin, M., Toft, J., & Yeo, J. (2005). Obstacles to welfare-to-work transitions for Somali, Hmong, and Latino immigrants in the United States. *Social Development Issues, 27*(2), 59–69.

Holtan, B. (1999, March/April), "From the director...Barb Holtan." *Tressler Family Connections*, 2–4.

International Social Service. (1979). International child abduction. In D. R. Cox, (Ed.), *Intercountry casework: Some reflections on sixty years experience of international social service 1924–1984* (pp. 113–115). Geneva, Switzerland: Author.

Joint Council on International Children's Services. (2007). Hague Adoption Convention. Accessed June 14, 2007, at http://jcics.org/Hague.htm

Kendrick, E. (1998). *International adoptions.* Paper prepared for the Lutheran Social Services, New England. (Rocky Hill, CT office).

Legault, G. (1996). Social work practice in situations of intercultural misunderstandings. *Journal of Multicultural Social Work, 4*(4), 49–66.

Marcovitch, S., Cesaroni, L., Roberts, W., & Swanson, C. (1995). Romanian adoption: Parents' dreams, nightmares, and realities, *Child Welfare, 74*(5), 993–1017.

Marquez, R. R., & Padilla, Y. C. (2004). Immigration in the life histories of women living in the United States-Mexico border region. In D. Drachman & A. Paulino (Eds.), *Immigrants and social work: Thinking beyond the borders of the United States* (pp. 11–30). Binghamton, NY: Haworth Social Work Practice Press.

Martin, S. F. (2001). *Remittance flows and impact.* Paper prepared for the Remittances as a Development Tool Regional Conference, Inter-American Development Bank, Institute for the Study of International Migration, Georgetown University. Accessed January 3, 2002, at www.iadb.org

Matthews, L. (1994). *Social workers' knowledge of client-culture and its use in mental health care of English-speaking Caribbean immigrants.* Unpublished doctoral dissertation, Hunter College of the City University of New York.

Moreno, C. (2006 February 28). *Gender and remittances.* Panel presentation at the UN Commission on Women, New York.

Padilla, Y. C. & Daigle, L. E. (1998). Inter-agency collaboration in an international setting. *Administration in Social Work, 22*(1), 65–81.

Pottinger, A. M. (2005). Children's experience of loss by parental migration in inner-city Jamaica. *American Journal of Orthopsychiatry, 75*(4) 485–496.

Rios-Kohn, R. (1998). Intercountry adoption: An international perspective on the practice and standards. *Adoption Quarterly, 1*(4), 3–32.

Simon, R. J., Altstein, H., & Melli, M. S. (1994). *The case for transracial adoption.* Washington, DC: The American University Press.

Small, J. (2007). Rethinking and unravelling the interlocking dynamics of Caribbean emigration and return. In L. Dominelli (Ed.), *Revitalising communities in a globalizing world* (pp. 243–254). Aldershot, UK: Ashgate Publishing Limited.

Stiles, C. F., de la Rosa, R., Dharmaraksa, D., Goldner, T., & Kalyanvala, R. (2001). Famlies for children: International strategies to build in-country capacity in the Philippines, Thailand, Romania, and India. *Child Welfare, 53*(5), 645–655.

Thiederman, S. (1988). Overcoming cultural and language barriers. *Personnel Journal, 67*(12), 34–40.

Thuy, V. (1986). The psychosocial needs of Southeast Asian refugees: Principles for understanding. In L. M. Healy (Ed.), *Toward improving service to Southeast Asian refugees.* West Hartford, CT: University of Connecticut School of Social Work.

United Nations (1989). *Convention on the Rights of the Child.* Accessed August 23, 2000, at www.unhchr.ch

United States Department of State. (2007). Immigrant visas issued to orphans coming to the U.S. Accessed June 9, 2007, at http://travel.state.gov/family/adoption/stats/stats_451.html

Williams, L. (2007). Home alone. In L. Dominelli (Ed.), *Revitalising communities in a globalizing world* (pp. 255–269). Aldershot, UK: Ashgate Publishing Limited.

CHAPTER 12

UNDERSTANDING AND INFLUENCING GLOBAL POLICY

There are numerous, often untapped, opportunities for social workers to influence global social policy. These range from local or national lobbying and educational campaigns to collaborative ventures on a global scale. Three dimensions of international social work action, as defined in Chapter 1, relate to global social policy. The first is the capacity of social workers to develop and promulgate positions on social aspects of their own country's foreign policy and other policies that affect people in other countries. The second is social work's competence to work as a worldwide movement to develop positions on important global social issues, to contribute to the resolution of global problems related to the profession's sphere of expertise, and to influence global social policies of world bodies. Comparative policy analysis, undertaken to gain a better understanding of social policy or to identify potential innovations that can be borrowed from other systems, is the third aspect of international social work action. It will be discussed briefly in this chapter and more fully in Chapter 13.

This chapter emphasizes the what, why, when, and how of policy action in the international social work arena. Following a brief definition of social policy and social welfare, the focus will be on international policy and the emerging field of global policy. A rationale for social work action will be discussed, including consideration of policy content and values. The stages of international/global policy processes will be described in the context of opportunities for influence. Influence strategies will be briefly outlined before turning to case examples that illustrate the policy arenas, stages, and strategies discussed.

INTERNATIONAL AND GLOBAL SOCIAL POLICY DEFINED

Social policy shapes social work interventions defining what can be done, for whom, and toward what goals (Karger & Stoesz, 2006). Policy, therefore, has a profound impact on clients' well-being. *Social policy* usually refers to "those principles, procedures, and courses of action established in statute, administrative code and agency regulation that affect people's social well-being" (Dear, 1995, p. 2227). More simply, social policy is "social action sanctioned by society" (Epstein cited in Karger & Stoesz, 2006, p. 3). The scope is potentially broad, including social services, health, education, housing, and the social impacts of economic and environmental policies. The goal of social policy is enhanced *social welfare*, defined by Midgley (1997) as "a condition of human well-being that exists when social problems are managed, when human needs are met, and when social opportunities are maximised" (p. 5). Midgley's broad definition is useful in examining global social policies because the concept of maximizing social opportunities fits with the human rights emphasis of many such policies.

Although an earlier emphasis in international social work was on comparative social policy analysis, an action-oriented policy-influencing approach is more in keeping with the definition of international social work used in this book. This approach also fits with general trends in the field of social policy:

> The social policy context of social work practice is being transformed from strictly descriptive, historical and conceptual orientations that exclude practice realities to a prescriptive, problem-solving, action- and practice-oriented interventive method for social policy reform. Helping people by formulating and implementing social policy is the core of this development. (Iatridis, 1995, pp. 1855–1856)

Types of Policy or Policy Arenas

In Chapter 1, the increasing impact that the policies of one nation are having on the people and policies of other nations was described as a facet of global interdependence. Each country has social welfare policies that identify social entitlements, benefits, and social protections and address social rights and their limits. These are usually labeled domestic policy; however, in the global perspective, policies are rarely purely domestic in impact. The policies of one nation may influence the development and content of policies of other nations, discussed in Chapter 2 as social policy emulation. Some policy actions at the national level have a direct cross-national impact and affect people from other countries or the general state of well-being in other countries. Immigration laws stand out as particularly cogent examples. It is also at the national level that social aspects of foreign policy should be considered, including foreign assistance programs and issues dealing with social questions at the UN and other intergovernmental bodies. Although international in impact, the targets of influence for such policies are individual national governments; therefore, they may be referred to as international aspects of national policy.

For social workers in the industrialized countries, influencing internationally related national policies is a particularly important role. This was underscored at a 1986 gathering of African nongovernmental organizations (NGOs); these organizations issued a declaration calling on "Northern NGOs to 'reorient their activities' towards development education, advocacy and information flows, and in particular to attack 'policies of their governments, corporations and multilateral institutions...which adversely affect the quality of life and political and economic independence of African countries' " (Clark, 1992, p. 195). European educators who were asked to suggest international roles for American social workers expressed the same sentiment, indicating that an important international role for social workers is to monitor the international actions of their own governments and to seek to influence these toward social justice (Healy, 1985).

Other policies are more truly global in content and impact and by nature of the processes through which they are adopted. Global social policies are those formulated by international intergovernmental bodies either with or without the force of sanctions to encourage compliance. The targets for influence efforts are therefore international organizations.

Deacon, Hulse, and Stubbs (1997) argue that globalization will transform traditional social policy analysis and lead to more emphasis on global social policy. They predict the increasing "supranationalization or globalization of social policy instruments, policy and provision" (p. 2). The three essential purposes of social policy—regulation, redistribution, and social provision—are at least weakly present in some global policies. Current evidence of these, although somewhat minimal to date, exists most clearly in the European Union (EU), and in policies from the UN and World Bank. There are international organizations that raise money from nations and spend it on the basis of social needs, thus engaging in redistribution. UNICEF (the UN Children's Fund), UN Development Programme (UNDP), and the World Food Program are all examples of this. The World Bank raises money from member states and lends it to others at nonmarket terms, also a form of redistribution. Recent pressure on the International Monetary Fund (IMF) and the World Bank to soften loan conditions and preserve a broader social safety net in developing countries is the result of a global social reformist effort aimed at redistribution of resources.

These international bodies—the UN, World Bank, IMF, the Organization for Economic Co-operation and Development (OECD), the International Labour Organization (ILO), and the EU—also have the "capacity to influence national social policy" (Deacon, et al., 1997, p. 24). The role of the IMF in regulating the policies of debtor nations was explained in Chapter 2. The UN human rights conventions, such as on women and on children, include compliance provisions that require changes in national policy in many nations. Thus there is considerable regulation in the human rights area. Whereas direct provision by international organizations is less frequent, Deacon et al., (1997) cite the UN High Commission for Refugees as an example of an agency involved in considerable international social provision. Using Midgley's (1997) definition of social welfare, expansion and guarantees of human rights are also social provisions. Therefore, "global standards and agenda setting play roles in the rapid expansion of programs of some states" (Deacon et al., p. 6). In addition, there are a growing number of instances in which supranational agencies are undertaking efforts "to secure poverty programmes, to secure human and political rights, and to protect minorities" (Deacon et al., p. 26).

Each of the areas discussed above is a potential arena for social work policy practice and action.

RATIONALE FOR SOCIAL WORK INVOLVEMENT: POLICY AGENDA AND PROFESSIONAL VALUES

Strong arguments for the necessity of social work involvement in global policy are the nature of the policy agenda and the ethical commitments of the profession.

Policy Agenda

Global policy agenda is dominated by issues that are within the expertise and concern of professional social work. As discussed in Chapter 3, most of these fall within the two overarching themes of development and human rights. In the discussion of globalization and global social problems, numerous issues were presented, including migration, HIV/AIDS, poverty, the status of women, aging, street children, and more. Each is part of the policy agenda at both the national and global level. And there are many more issues on the global agenda that are of concern to social work, including drug abuse and other addictions; interethnic violence and conflict; child abuse and neglect, and other child welfare issues; mental health; and the rights of minority groups and indigenous peoples. All of these are appropriately within the domain of social work expertise, which supports the claim that the profession has a role in policy formulation and implementation. The cases later in this chapter will

Figure 12.1 Social workers gather at Social Work Day at the United Nations to learn about the UN policy agenda.

focus on immigration, violence against women, and child welfare as policy issues.

Values and Ethical Commitments

Social workers are bound by ethical codes at the international level and the national level, as explained in Chapter 9. Many of these codes define all social workers' responsibilities as including social reform or social change, in addition to their everyday practice duties. As stated in the International Federation of Social Workers (IFSW) Code of Ethics (1994), social workers should "contribute professional expertise to the development of policies and programs which improve the quality of life in society" (Section 3.2.6). Although the current global ethics document is less specific, it still includes responsibilities for promoting just social conditions and policies. Principle 4.2.4 addresses the responsibility to challenge unjust policies and practices: "social workers have a duty to bring to the attention of their employers, policy makers, politicians and the general public situations where resources are inadequate or where distribution of resources, policies and practices are oppressive, unfair or harmful" (IFSW, 2004). The principles also call on social workers to "promote social justice" and to "work towards an inclusive society." Many national codes express similar values. There are a number of points addressing social responsibility in the National Association of Social Workers (NASW; 1996) Code of Ethics, but one provision explicitly states: "The social worker should advocate changes in policy and legislation to improve social conditions and to promote social justice" (VI.F.6).

The involvement of the social work profession in social policy varies from country to country. In the United Kingdom, *social policy* is defined as a separate profession, and in the U.S. tradition, both areas are part of social work. In spite of this difference, the IFSW Statement of Ethical Principles suggests that social workers must accept the responsibility for social change in the interdependent world.

SOCIAL POLICY ACTIONS IN PRACTICE

Comparative and Global Policy Analysis

Policy analysis is an important skill for international policy action because social workers must know how to analyze domestic policies for their international impact and global policies in order to determine appropriate action. Einbinder (1995) describes *policy analysis* as "a set of technical skills used to describe, assess and influence social policies and a perspective about what government should do that is based on an assessment of the circumstances and potential for interventions to make things better" (p. 1850). Comparative social policy involves analysis of other countries' social welfare policies to learn different ways of addressing social problems and to gain a better understanding of the policies of nations in relation to each other. Cross-national analysis is concerned with understanding why services and benefits are provided in "a particular way at a specific point in history given all possible options and alternatives" (Tracy, 1992, p. 344). It is a focus on the reasons that explain policy and program service delivery choices that differentiates analysis from description.

There are considerable methodological challenges involved in comparative policy analysis. Among the most common problems are accuracy and comparability of data across nations; variations in definitions of terms and concepts; and the need to explore cultural differences in policy environment, content, and process to make appropriate interpretations (Midgley, 1997).

In keeping with their assessment of policy as increasingly global, Deacon and colleagues advocate a shift in the locus of analysis from comparative to global. They recommend a process for global policy analysis that includes an analysis of pressures for globalization versus national sovereignty in the policy being considered and recasting such traditional analytical concepts as social justice, rights and entitlements, universality and diversity, and public versus private provision as global phenomena. The analyst would also examine global goals, obstacles, and strategies for policy improvement (Deacon et al., 1997). An understanding of comparative policy and the skill of analysis at the comparative and global level are important foundations for global policy influencing efforts.

Stages of the Policy-Making Process: When to Influence Policy

The making of policy is a continuous process that begins with agenda setting and continues throughout the implementation of a regulation or program. Thus policy can be influenced during three stages of this process: agenda setting, policy formulation, and implementation (Willetts, 1996).

Agenda Setting. Agenda setting is a critical stage of the policy-making process. It is during this phase that what will be discussed or worked on is decided. According to DiNitto and Dye (1983), "Deciding what is to be decided is the most important stage of the policy-making process. . . . Societal conditions not defined as problems never become policy issues" (p. 14).

Through data gathering, educational campaigns, and other public activities, new social problems are defined and recognized and become part of the policy agenda. The example of violence against women demonstrates the emergence of a new social problem. Thirty years ago, in almost every country in the world, domestic violence was regarded as a private issue. Today, it is widely recognized as a social problem requiring intervention. As a result of information and publicity campaigns, the problem of violence against women was placed prominently on the agenda of the 1993 World Conference on Human Rights in Vienna; the Vienna Declaration and Programme of Action (United Nations, 1993) specifically called for establishing a Special Rapporteur on Violence Against Women. Two years later, the Beijing Platform for Action

(United Nations, 1995), emanating from the Women's Conference, identified violence against women as one of 12 areas of critical concern. More recently, the Secretary-General's Report on Violence Against Women and Security Council Resolution #1325 called more attention to the issue. Case 12.2 below demonstrates the use of international machinery to influence a national policy agenda on violence against women.

Policy Formulation. The policy formulation phase is, of course, the core phase when policy intent and content are specified and agreement is secured. The target for influence at this stage is a national legislature, a national delegation to the UN, a UN committee, the UN General Assembly, or, perhaps, a world conference. To influence this phase, social workers and the NGOs through which they work need to have a vision of desired policy directions; these become the ingredients for efforts to influence policy makers to include particular elements in a policy. Sharing research and documentation with policy makers can be useful at this stage, especially if the authors have credibility. The UN NGO Committee on Social Development, for example, shapes its agenda to influence the outcomes of the Commission for Social Development. The Commission identified the theme "decent work for all" for its 2-year cycle in 2007 and 2008. The NGO Committee designed a survey to gather data on successful employment initiatives in diverse countries. The survey was disseminated through the network of member NGOs. Case 12.3 below demonstrates social work involvement in a global policy formulation effort.

Policy Implementation. During the implementation phase, policy can become operational, be neglected, or as often happens, redefined. Influencing implementation is essential to reshape policy, to ensure that directives are carried out, and to influence interpretations and regulations (Willetts, 1996). In the past, social workers (and others) often assumed that the need for influencing was complete when a policy was adopted or a law was passed. Implementation analysis has shown that there is a continuing need for oversight and advocacy by interested parties to ensure that policies are implemented as designed, with appropriate resources and attention to policy intent. This requires focus on new targets of influence, usually multiple ones, including funders, administrative bodies, and sometimes, courts and the original legislative body.

Strategies: How to Influence Policy

There are many strategies available to social workers for influencing international and global policy. As explained above, many policies with international impact are made at the national level. In large part, skills used by social workers to influence local or national policy can also be adapted to the global policy arena. It is important, however, that social workers understand how policy is developed at the global level to identify differences in the process; these include the nature of representation and special provisions—reporting

requirements, complaint procedures, rapporteurs—that create opportunities
for influencing policy making and implementation. In the process of policy
influencing, social workers may take on roles as researchers, community educators, lobbyists, coalition builders, advocates, and even diplomats. Radda
Barnen, the Save the Children organization in Sweden, identified these roles
for NGO action on human rights policy, as illustrated in the box below.

These multiple roles are more broadly relevant for social work action in
the global policy arena. Each will be discussed briefly.

Social workers have opportunities through their practice to collect data on
social problems. These data can make important contributions to shaping the
policy agenda and to policy formulation, especially because social workers
have access to information about how people experience social conditions.
Quantitative data are enlivened by selective use of case examples from social
work practice; such cases certainly capture public attention but are also effective in helping legislators and diplomats understand the human face of
social problems. The NGO Social Development Committee survey yielded a
number of relevant case examples of decent work projects and policies. Thus
gathering data, developing case studies, and other research on social conditions are useful influence strategies.

Lobbying is well understood as a strategy for policy influence. Letter
writing and calling legislators to support or oppose policy initiatives or to
suggest new laws or revisions to proposed laws are important actions when the
target for influence is a national legislature. Offering to share data and technical
expertise with legislators who are drafting or supporting legislation may be
useful. Lobbying is more effective if coordinated through professional organizations or other NGOs in order to mobilize many constituents to contact
legislators on the same issues. Ensuring that policies with international social
impact are added to the legislative action agendas of such organizations is
an important step. Thus an important role is to influence the lobbying agenda
of social work professional groups. Direct lobbying of representatives at

---

ROLES FOR NGOS IN POLICY INFLUENCING

- monitoring and fact finding in their own or other countries;
- investigating and reporting on violations;
- informing and educating about human rights matters and the work of
  international organisations;
- mobilising interest groups and lobbying national governments and international bodies;
- advising on or directly contributing to the implementation of human
  rights standards.

Radda Barnen, 1993, quoted in Longford, 1996, pp. 234–235.

intergovernmental bodies is less often used. Instead, influencing is done by lobbying at the national level to affect the votes of country representatives or by using consultative status through NGOs to influence policy development. Some direct contact with delegates may also be useful. Using preliminary results from the survey mentioned earlier, small groups of NGO committee members visited delegations of member countries on the Commission for Social Development. These strategies are illustrated in Case 12.3 later in the chapter.

Electronic lobbying is an important supplement to traditional letter writing, telephoning, and radio or television advertising. The power of international communications technologies was demonstrated in 1989 when student activists and their supporters were able to use fax machines to notify the world of the democratization movement in China and of the crushing of student dissent in Tienanmen Square. E-mail is now used to share information, issue calls for action, generate and circulate petitions around the globe, and directly lobby policy makers. Dedicated Web sites can be developed; they are useful in educating the public on policy issues. Fitzgerald and McNutt (1999) argue that electronic advocacy, "the use of technologically intensive media to influence stakeholders to effect policy change," is replacing older techniques that have been rendered less effective by changes in the policy environment (p. 334). On a similar note, Ife predicted that more widespread use of the Internet would "allow links to be developed between people working on a social justice agenda in different countries, so that they can learn from each others' experiences and develop common action strategies" (quoted in Johnson, 1999, p. 378).

Public education is particularly important in shaping international policy. Effective public education campaigns require skill in developing educational messages and in use of the media to get wide distribution of information. Public opinion is an important element in global policy. Olsen (1996) suggests that the public is more internationally minded than official government representatives and may be an important force for global humanitarianism in the future. Public opinion, shaped by media attention, has been important in mobilizing action on a number of global issues. When the devastating tsunami hit the Indian Ocean region at the end of 2004, extensive television coverage resulted in unprecedented private giving and demands for government action. The successful action campaign against marketing baby formula to poor countries in the 1980s was due in part to public outcry, stimulated by an effective media public education campaign. These cases and many others demonstrate the effectiveness of educational campaigns and media attention in influencing action on global problems. Public education, then, is likely to grow in importance as a strategy for global social change.

Education combined with community organization can be useful in empowering affected communities to advocate for themselves. Direct work with the poor, usually through NGOs, leads to raised consciousness and concerted action (Clark, 1992). In this way, social work contributes to the building of small and large social movements that will have an impact on policy. Grassroots movements have been important in formulation of environmental and development policies, drawing on the direct experience of those affected.

To make an impact in the global arena, interdisciplinary efforts are almost always necessary. Development and human rights, the major policy foci, are multidisciplinary fields. Social workers must form coalitions with persons from law, agriculture, public health, education, child development, and other fields to influence the interdisciplinary bureaucracies of the UN. The NGO committees on which social workers serve comprise diverse interests from the voluntary sector including religious, environmental, educational, and social service groups. Links to economists may be useful in pressuring the World Bank about policy issues. Although important in domestic work, interdisciplinary efforts are essential internationally. Readers will recall that in Chapter 7 lack of skill and effort in interdisciplinary work were suggested as causes of social work's diminished influence in the UN system as development became the focus.

Diplomacy, including an understanding of the politics of compromise, is also essential in most policy work, especially in the international arena. When they approach country representatives, policy influencers must be sensitive to cultural differences in communication and to the impact of national interests and international politics. In designating members to visit delegations, the Committee on Social Development took language facility and experience in the delegation's country into account whenever possible. As Case 12.3 will illustrate, knowing how and when to compromise is an essential part of international diplomacy. In the case of the Convention on the Rights of the Child, the right to freedom of religion and the issue of abortion were left vague to secure agreement to the treaty as a whole. At times, to press for specificity could unravel months of hard work.

Another aspect of diplomacy in work with the UN is to make connections with staff. The Committee on Social Development annually invites Bureau staff to brief the Committee and collaborates in planning a companion NGO Forum in advance of the official Social Development Commission meeting.

The international policy-making and implementation processes have special provisions that create opportunities for influence. For the social rights protected by human rights treaties, advocates can utilize the international complaint-recourse procedures and complaint-information procedures provided under the treaties to draw attention to policy implementation problems and violations (Byrnes, 1993). The treaties also require reporting by states parties on their compliance with treaty provisions. The UN committees designated to deal with human rights reports accept input from NGOs and use such information as part of the review of a country's progress. When the United States submitted its first report on compliance with the Convention on the Elimination of all Forms of Racial Discrimination in 2000, the World Organization Against Torture USA (WOATUSA, 2000, 2007) submitted an alternate report calling attention to racial profiling, police brutality, and the number of racial minorities in prisons. Similarly, the NGO Coalition on the Rights of the Child in Jamaica submitted an alternate report on Jamaica's compliance with the Convention on the Rights of the Child (CRC). Some of the points raised were addressed by the Treaty Committee during review of Jamaica's progress in complying with the Convention. Social workers can work through NGOs to submit relevant data on policy noncompliance or implementation problems in areas such as children's services, rights of women, and treatment of minorities. If the UN body finds areas of concern, this criticism becomes pressure for policy change if it is publicized widely. Social workers and NGOs can utilize these as opportunities for effecting change.

Shaming may be an unusual term for social work practice, but shaming can be another tool for policy influence by using the global standards in conventions to cajole or embarrass countries into policy improvements or better implementation of international agreements. Byrnes (1993) refers to this strategy as "bringing the international back home" to influence the national context (p. 58). Another way of expressing this role is that social workers will act as what Sankey (1996) referred to as "the conscience of the world" (p. 273), a label he gave to human rights NGOs.

TYPES OF POLICIES AND STRATEGIES FOR INFLUENCE

Three cases have been selected to illustrate aspects of international and global policy. Case 12.1 discusses a domestic policy that is having significant impact on international populations and affects other countries—an example of internationally related domestic policy. Case 12.2 is an example of utilization of international human rights machinery to influence national policy development, and Case 12.3 demonstrates a long-term policy formulation effort in global social policy. Each of the cases will illustrate use of various influence strategies and aspects of the phases of the policy process.

The laws and proposed legislation presented in Case 12.1 are examples of domestic policies that are having an impact on international populations and on the countries from which they come—policies at the domestic–international interface. The targets for change efforts in such cases are at the national level; in this case, legislative changes and court challenges are being pursued.

Social work involvement has included legislative lobbying, public education, coalition building, and public policy development. To lobby for legislative change, social workers had to determine what policy is desirable yet achievable and what elements are negotiable—policy formulation. Efforts are strengthened by coalition building, especially collaboration with immigrant groups and human rights advocacy groups. Participation in public education with other like-minded groups is an important function for social workers working to create the climate for policy change; it has particular urgency in this case. Public opinion is of critical importance in swaying legislators' votes. U.S. immigration policy has always included elements of humanitarianism and exclusion; at various times public attitudes favor exclusion and at others, the public is welcoming toward immigrants. Social workers can contribute

CASE 12.1: DOMESTIC POLICY WITH
INTERNATIONAL IMPACT

Reacting to growing concern about the size of the undocumented immigrant population in the United States, now estimated at about 12 million,
several policies have been adopted by Congress and other proposals for
further immigration reform are being considered. In 1996, a series of laws
were passed that affect legal as well as illegal immigrants: the Illegal Immigration Reform and Immigrant Responsibility Act; the Anti-Terrorism
and Effective Death Penalty Act; and Personal Responsibility and Work
Opportunity Reconciliation Act (welfare reform). These laws resulted in
deportations of legal immigrants who had committed relatively minor
offenses in the past and severely restricted eligibility of legal immigrants
for various public benefits. Just as public attitudes began to soften and
liberalization proposals were being considered in 2001, the terrorist attacks
on New York and Washington, D.C., occurred. Since that time, border
security has been a prominent feature of immigration reform proposals
and legislation. Perhaps because the presence of 12 million illegal immigrants is a reminder of the porous nature of U.S. borders, public and
legislative antipathy to the undocumented has grown. Many of the new
legislative proposals to address illegal immigration are a serious threat to
social work values and practice.

In 2005, the U.S. House of Representatives passed the Border Protection Antiterrorism and Illegal Immigration Control Act of 2005 (HR 4437).
This proposed legislation was particularly "draconian" and contained
numerous punitive measures that targeted not only illegal immigrants but
also personnel in the helping professions. The bill would have made un-
lawful presence in the United States an aggravated felony. In addition, it
extended the definition of "alien smuggling" so broadly that "anyone who
assists an undocumented person to live or remain in the U.S. could be
charged with a criminal (felony) offense" (NASW, 2007, p. 17). With many
other harsh provisions, this bill would have driven illegal immigrants
further into the shadows and posed a significant danger to social workers
who would have had to choose between ethical practice and committing a
felony. Fortunately, this bill did not pass in the Senate and did not become
law. Still other proposals have required reporting of immigration status
as a condition for receiving any services, including police protection or
emergency medical care. At the time of writing, several additional major
immigration policies were under debate.

The NASW (US) has made immigration policy a priority for 2006–2008
but has a much longer history of policy-influencing efforts on immigration.
The Association adopted a new public policy statement on Immigrants
and Refugees in 2006. The statements commits NASW to support immi-

(continued)

gration policies that "uphold and support equity and human rigl protecting national security" (NASW, 2006). Among other provis policy opposes mandatory reporting of immigration status by "health, mental health, social service, education, police, and other public service providers." The policy calls for continued access to emergency services and public education for the undocumented, elimination of provisions that target immigrants based on race or religion, protections from family violence without fear of deportation, and a number of provisions to ensure children's rights.

Social workers have promulgated this policy statement in a number of ways. The president of NASW held a press conference to speak out against the HR 4437. One speaker at the press conference declared that the bill "would make it a crime to do our jobs" (NASW, 2007, p. 16). An opinion column from the NASW president was published in the organization newsletter *NASW News* in February 2006. Members were encouraged to write similar columns to their local newspapers to influence public opinion as well as legislators at state and national levels. Through its "Action Alert" legislative network, NASW has kept members apprised of legislative proposals and asked members of the association to contact their elected representatives in Congress to lobby for fair immigration reform. Local chapters of NASW have also joined the efforts to influence immigration policy. In Connecticut, social workers have lobbied for a bill that would permit noncitizen children of undocumented immigrants to attend higher education as state residents—an important step toward decriminalizing children who are brought into the country through no fault of their own. Connecticut social workers have joined in a coalition of organizations working on immigration issues: the Connecticut Immigrant and Refugee Advocacy Coalition. In Massachusetts, the NASW chapter issued a press release and joined in protest against raids that resulted in the detention of 350 alleged illegal immigrants in that state in the spring of 2007. This one event dramatically showed the impact of immigration policy and enforcement on social workers and those they serve. As parents were rounded up at their workplace and flown to distant detention centers, local authorities were not given notice. "This raid left hundreds of children abandoned at their schools, day care centers and other child care placements...the well-being of children was callously overlooked" (Gewirtz & Scannell, 2007, p. 26).

real-life stories from their case experiences that can engender public sympathy and build support for fair and just laws. Thus appropriate social work policy actions would include education of the public and members of the profession, legislative lobbying, and coalition building. Policy development would be guided by the values of "social justice, equality, democratic processes and

330 VALUES, PRACTICE, AND POLICY

empowerment of disadvantaged and powerless people" (Iatridis, 1995, p. 1856).

Immigration policies in receiving countries create the need for policy actions in sending countries. In cases of increased deportations, for example, social workers might help in ensuring that deportees are assisted in resettlement or, in the case of dangerous offenders, that mechanisms are developed for follow-up monitoring. Together, social workers and migration advocates might join to initiate cross-national discussions on new migration issues.

Of course, the laws and issues outlined in Case 12.1 have also heightened the need for social work knowledge. Misinformed advice to a client could result in deportation and permanent barring from the United States. Thus any social worker working with immigrants should be informed of the risks. Another practice challenge is the interaction of the immigration provisions with domestic violence laws and guidelines for "good practice." Should a social worker encourage a battered woman to call the police on her immigrant partner and father of her children if the result may be his deportation and therefore loss of all support? What impact might these provisions have on child protective services practice? As noted above, the NASW (2006) policy statement on immigrants and refugees opposes laws that make domestic violence crimes by immigrants deportable offenses. The current reality, however, is that deportation may result from convictions for family assault. And although it would seem clear that social work confidentiality ethics would prevent social workers from complying with any mandatory reporting of illegal immigrants to authorities, clearer guidelines may be needed. At a minimum, social workers have an obligation to learn all that they can about reporting requirements in immigration cases and the ethical implication of compliance. In these areas, social work policy development is needed to guide professional action.

Among the useful policy influence strategies are using international human rights machinery to promote change and bringing international standards into domestic policy discussions to encourage change at home. Case 12.2 demonstrates these with emphasis on the successful efforts of a research and action group in Japan in using international human rights hearings and conferences to promote change in Japanese government policy.

Case 12.2 demonstrates the effective use of international human rights machinery to lobby for policy changes at the national level. Although this strategy may not work in all countries, many nations are influenced either by the "pull" of participating in international movements or by the "push" of negative international publicity showing them to be out of compliance with world standards. Sometimes, merely using international standards to encourage change at home will be effective; this strategy can be enhanced by research on programs and policy changes that have been enacted elsewhere (Byrnes, 1993). In other cases, such as the Japanese example in Case 12.2, "shaming" is needed through drawing international attention to lack of compliance with standards. Thus as one observer noted, human rights treaties are

---

CASE 12.2: USING INTERNATIONAL MACHINERY
TO INFLUENCE DOMESTIC POLICY

Movements to address violence against women began in Japan in the 1980s. Perhaps the greatest obstacle was the prevailing official attitude in Japan that domestic violence is "a personal, private and infrequent problem, as opposed to a prevalent, serious social problem" (Yoshihama, 1996, p. 1). Groups conducted research studies, documenting considerable incidence of violence against women and showing that a serious problem existed. Still, the national government was slow to acknowledge the issue.

A working group, the Domestic Violence Action and Research Group (DVARG), decided to take their advocacy efforts to the international level. Members of the group included social workers and colleagues from other disciplines, including law and education. In 1993, DVARG participated in the NGO forum at the UN World Conference on Human Rights in Vienna. Through a workshop on Violence Against Asian Pacific Women and distribution of results of the research conducted in Japan to conference participants, delegates from other governments, and UN staff, the group was able to "let the rest of the world know of the virtual lack of responses by the Japanese government to the problem of domestic violence" (Yoshihama, 1996, p. 3). The group continued with the international strategy, presenting workshops at an Economic and Social Council (ECOSOC)-sponsored Asian Pacific Symposium on Women in Development in Manila in late 1993 and at the World Conference on Women in Beijing in 1995. The Japanese study results were included in several global reports on domestic violence, including the final report of the Special Rapporteur on Violence Against Women appointed by the UN.

Through these activities and the global publicity that accompanied them, the DVARG succeeded in getting the attention of the Japanese government. Responding to this combination of internal and external pressure, the Japanese government proposed creation of a UN fund to combat violence against women in 1995. At home, a plan to develop antiviolence legislation was announced in 1996.

Case developed from Yoshihama, 1996, 1998.

---

both "a tool and a stick to use in lobbying government" (cited in vander Straeten, 1990, p. 31).

As noted earlier, a number of international mechanisms exist through which human rights–related policies can be influenced. In Jamaica, the NGO Jamaica Coalition on the Rights of the Child filed an alternative NGO report that supplemented and challenged the official report by the Jamaican government on compliance with the CRC. The information provided was used by a UN committee in its recommendations to the government for needed changes in policy and services for children. This example also demonstrates successful influencing of the implementation phase of policy. The CRC, in particular, includes basic standards for certain social services. The process that led to the convention is discussed in Case 12.3

The 10-year period of the drafting of the CRC provided numerous opportunities for social work participation in the shaping of global policy. An excellent example of global social policy, the Convention recognizes a wide array of children's rights. "To recognize in a legally binding document that children are members of the international community and have specific rights as individuals, separate from the government, separate from the family, is remarkable—and I think revolutionary is a fair word to use for that" (cited in vander Straeten, 1990, p. 27). First proposed in February 1978 by the government of Poland, the CRC was unanimously adopted by the UN General Assembly in 1989 and has been ratified by all but two UN member nations as of 1999.

Case 12.3 illustrates that social workers can have an important influence on the formulation of global policy. Through activities that have followed the adoption and ratification of the CRC, social workers have also influenced the implementation process in many countries. The importance of this role is underscored by the fact that the convention is the only human rights treaty that gives NGOs a role in monitoring compliance (Longford, 1996). In this case, social workers were able to capitalize on an opportunity to work on an issue raised by UN delegates.

CASE 12.3: SHAPING GLOBAL POLICY— THE CONVENTION ON THE RIGHTS OF THE CHILD

Social work involvement in the convention's drafting process was channeled through various NGOs with consultative status to the UN, including the International Council on Social Welfare (ICSW) and Defense for Children International (DCI). The CRC was drafted by a working group comprised of member states of the Commission on Human Rights but open to all governments and to NGOs with consultative status. More than 40 NGOs participated. "There seems to be general recognition within the UN, among governments, and in the NGO community itself, that their impact on the Convention on the Rights of the Child was both quite unprecedented in degree and particularly useful and constructive" (Longford, 1996, p. 222). Although the outcome is an important international policy affecting social work, the process is instructive to those who wish to influence policy on the global level in the future.

NGO influence did not get off to a good start. As described by Longford (1996), who represented Britain on the working group, "The NGO contribution at the 1983 meeting was not particularly impressive. . . .

(continued)

Some of the NGO speakers were inexperienced and put forward in an unconvincing way points of view that were either irrelevant or impracticable" (p. 221). Nigel Cantwell, from the lead NGO, DCI, put it this way:

> There was a feeling of great frustration among NGO representatives, however; they knew that they had a potentially major contribution to make and that they—and children—were somehow losing out because of an inability to "get the message" over in the right way and at the right time. Very few had had previous experience of working within this kind of context. Individual NGOs were certainly given the floor almost every time they requested it, but all too often they wasted these valuable opportunities by labouring a viewpoint that was clearly not viable or even arguing a point among themselves, rather than putting a reasoned proposal to the government delegates. (cited in Longford, 1996, p. 223)

The NGOs took action and reorganized themselves to improve their impact. They formed a group to address two major problems: lack of preparedness and the need to develop a more unified NGO position. Over the next 5 years, about 20 NGOs cooperated through the group, with DCI assuming the role of secretariat. The group met regularly and developed cogent proposals for submission to the working group. Patience and willingness to stick with the process over many years were important to a successful strategy. Cairnes, a representative of the UN Office of the Presbyterian Church, described the efforts of the core group who monitored the ways issues were being shaped during the drafting process: "If there were concerns about certain elements, they might publicize that and say 'we need to get a rush on and put some heat on governments to see if we can get this turned around.' It's that kind of back and forth—revision, revision, revision—process until you get to the point where you've got the best available" (cited in vander Straeten, 1990, p. 11).

The NGOs also developed strategies for formal and informal influence of working group members, holding annual "briefings" for country delegates prior to the official meetings and taking advantage of opportunities to interact informally with the country representatives:

> As the NGO representatives became more familiar with the procedures within the U.N., they became more skilled negotiators, and they organised themselves to become an effective lobby....Members of the NGO group made the most of the opportunities provided by social events to develop informal contacts with governmental delegates and the Working Group Chairman. The friendship which built up during our weeks in Geneva were certainly an important ingredient in the teamwork which developed in the whole Working Group as drafting progressed. (Longford, 1996, pp. 224–225).

(continued)

At the end of the process, the NGO group believed it had had substantial influence on the substance of about 15 of the articles, had some impact on almost that many, and had, in fact, proposed the language adopted for 2 (Longford, 1996). This impact was achieved by adding organization and coordination to the already substantial NGO advantage of expertise in children's issues. In addition, increased knowledge of UN procedures and sensitivity to the demands of international policy formulation and adoption proved critical. International policy making, especially in declarations and conventions, is a process of working for achievable concensus, not securing a majority of votes. "NGO delegates showed great wisdom in not pressing too hard for the inclusion of over-ambitious provisions which could have created problems for many countries" (Longford, 1996, p. 227).

CONCLUSION

The cases and other examples discussed in this chapter demonstrate that social work has considerable potential to influence international and global policy and has had some modest success in past efforts. The agenda is large, perhaps daunting. Deacon et al. (1997) argue that the major challenge in global policy in the future will be to determine how to balance human needs with global capitalism. Lorenz (1997) argues that the social work profession should make this its priority in global policy; because of the extensive contact social workers have with those who "lose" in the global economy, the profession is well positioned to call attention to the negative effects of market principles dominating the social domain. Thus he calls for social work to play a role in educating the public on "the distinction between what the market can achieve and what it cannot achieve" (p. 9). Another emerging policy priority is climate change and its potential impact on vulnerable populations.

Such a macrolevel agenda will seem beyond the reach of many social workers, but there are opportunities for much more modest action. The greatest barrier to international or global action, however, is failure to consider global responsibilities as part of professional commitment. Educational efforts to help social workers remove "borders" from their thinking about social policy and action are needed. The impact of globalization on professional roles and responsibilities needs much greater attention.

As suggested in Chapter 9, attention to values will assist in this redefinition of role. It is useful to draw on the values that Iatridis (1995) suggests for policy practice because they are highly relevant in developing policy positions at the global level; global policy practice should be shaped by commitments to "social justice, equality, democratic processes, and empowerment of disadvantaged and powerless people" (p. 1856). These values provide a link to social work's mission, and they can be useful to individual social workers, to NGOs, and to organized professional bodies in selecting a policy agenda and in guiding policy content and strategy formulation.

Nonetheless, the challenge to address global capitalism and climate change and to engage in policy analysis and influence at the global level will seem overwhelming to many social workers. There are shorter term policy actions that may help social workers who wonder where to start. Examples of realistic shorter-term actions are:

1. Encourage and develop cross-border agreements on social service practice, such as those discussed in Chapter 11.
2. Encourage the signing, ratification, and implementation of global treaties related to social work, such as the Hague Convention on Intercountry Adoption and the new Convention on the Rights of Persons with Disabilities. Social workers in the United States can lobby and conduct public education campaigns to urge ratification of the CRC and Convention on the Elimination of all Forms of Discrimination Against Women (CEDAW) while those in countries that have registered official reservations to provisions in CEDAW can work to overcome these.
3. Engage in public education campaigns on global policy issues, including human rights issues and treaty obligations. This will require increased knowledge of the global policies and treaties and their potential to influence national policies and services.
4. Learn as much as possible about how immigration policy affects families in countries with significant levels of immigration or emigration, and work to influence policies to keep immigration processes as "family friendly" as possible. Included in this is the responsibility to be fully informed of reporting requirements and their legal and ethical ramifications.

Social service agencies have a role in international policy. Beyond specific services offered, agencies express their commitments through public policy activities and through use of agency resources. Agency public policy agendas should include related international issues, especially immigration policies that affect agencies' clients. Agencies can also include international issues within their sphere of interest—for example, a family-planning agency might advocate world population assistance, a YWCA could lobby on global women's issues, and international adoption agencies could address child welfare improvements for children in other countries. Some international advocacy can be done at very local levels by bringing case experience to policy makers.

Public policy can also be influenced using agency resources. Socially responsible investing is one such strategy for influencing international policy. Widespread in the 1980s around the issue of apartheid in South Africa, more recent programs of socially responsible investing have avoided investments in companies involved in gun sales, in sales of products produced with exploitive child labor, in companies engaged in environmental degradation, and in companies doing business with the Sudan government while genocide goes on in the Darfur region.

Finally, the international professional organizations could expand their efforts in policy influencing. The process would be more dynamic and involve more social workers if part of the agendas of international social work meetings were devoted to policy and issue discussions. The purposes of such discussions would include member education but would emphasize development of a policy agenda and action plans. Issues for international attention could be identified and priorities agreed on. The meetings could facilitate the formation of international coalitions to work on social work's positions on issues, with lobbying conducted electronically between meetings. Some of this is currently done by IFSW and IASSW, but it could be expanded within these organizations and in regional groups. A strong global policy presence will be essential for the profession to maintain its viability in the twenty-first century.

REFERENCES

Byrnes, A. (1993). Some strategies for using international human rights law and procedures to advance women's human rights. In M. Schuler (Ed.), *Claiming our place: Working the human rights system to women's advantage* (pp. 51–64). Washington, DC: Institute for Women, Law and Development.

Clark, J. (1992). Policy influence, lobbying and advocacy. In M. Edwards & D. Hulme (Eds.), *Making a difference: NGOs and development in a changing world* (pp. 191–202). London: Earthscan Publications.

Deacon, B., Hulse, M., & Stubbs, P. (1997). *Global social policy: International organizations and the future of welfare.* London: Sage.

Dear, R. (1995). Social welfare policy. In R. Edwards (Ed.), *Encyclopedia of social work* (19th ed., pp. 2226–2237). Washington, DC: NASW Press.

DiNitto, D. M., & Dye, T. R. (1983). *Social welfare politics and public policy.* Englewood Cliffs, NJ: Prentice Hall.

Einbinder, S. D. (1995). Policy analysis. In R. Edwards (Ed.), *Encyclopedia of social work* (19th ed., pp. 1849–1855). Washington, DC: NASW Press.

Fitzgerald, E., & McNutt, J. (1999). Electronic advocacy in policy practice: A framework for teaching technologically based practice. *Journal of Social Work Education, 35*(3), 331–341.

Gewirtz, R., & Scannell, N. Statement of immigration raid. (Originally in *Focus: The newsletter of the NASW Massachusetts Chapter, 34*[4].) In National Association of Social Workers. (2007). *Immigration Policy Toolkit.* Washington, DC: Author, p. 26.

Healy, L. M. (1985). *The role of the international dimension in graduate social work education in the United States.* Unpublished doctoral dissertation, Rutgers University, New Brunswick, NJ.

Iatridis, D. (1995). Policy practice. In R. Edwards (Ed.), *Encyclopedia of social work* (19th ed., pp. 1855–1866). Washington, DC: NASW Press.

International Federation of Social Workers. (1994). *International code of ethics for the professional social worker.* Oslo, Norway: Author.

International Federation of Social Workers. (2004). *Ethics in social work: Statement of principles.* Accessed May 18, 2007, at www.ifsw.org

Johnson, A. (1999). Globalization from below: Using the internet to internationalize social work education. *Journal of Social Work Education, 35*(3), 377–393.

Karger, H. J., & Stoesz, D. (2006). *American social welfare policy: A pluralistic approach.* Boston: Pearson Education Inc.

Longford, M. (1996). NGOs and the rights of the child. In P. Willetts (Ed.), *The conscience of the world* (pp. 214–240). Washington, DC: Brookings Institution.

Lorenz, W. (1997, August 24). *Social work in a changing Europe.* Paper presented to the Joint European Regional Seminar of IFSW and EASSW on Culture and Identity, Dublin, Ireland.

Midgley, J. (1997). *Social welfare in global context.* Thousand Oaks, CA: Sage.

National Association of Social Workers. (1996). *Code of ethics.* Washington, DC: Author.

National Association of Social Workers. (2007). *Immigration policy toolkit.* Washington, DC: Author.

National Association of Social Workers. (2006). Immigrants and refugees. In *Social Work Speaks 2006–2009.* Washington, DC: Author.

Olsen, G. R. (1996). Public opinion, international civil society, and North-South policy since the cold war. In O. Stokke (Ed.), *Foreign aid towards the year 2000: Experience and challenges.* London: Frank Cass & Co.

Sankey, J. (1996). Conclusions. In P. Willetts (Ed.), *The conscience of the world.* Washington, DC: Brookings Institution.

Tracy, M. (1992). Cross-national social welfare policy analysis in the graduate curriculum: A comparative process model. *Journal of Social Work Education, 28*(3), 341–352.

United Nations. (1995). *Platform for action and the Beijing Declaration.* New York: Author.

United Nations. (1993). *The Vienna Declaration and Programme of Action.* New York: Author.

vander Straeten, S. (1990). *The United Nations Convention on the Rights of the Child: An interviewing and oral history project of social work in the international community* [Interview with Jim Cairnes]. Unpublished transcript. Warren Wilson College. Asheville, NC.

Willetts, P. (1996). Consultative status for NGOs at the United Nations. In P. Willetts (Ed.), *The conscience of the world* (pp. 31–62). Washington, DC: Brookings Institution.

World Organization Against Torture USA. (2000). *Alternate report. United States compliance with the International Convention on the Elimination of All Forms of Racial Discrimination.* Accessed January 6, 2002, at www.woatusa.org/cerd/toc/html

Yoshihama, M. (1996, November). *Anti-domestic violence movements in Japan: A nationwide action-oriented research project and advocacy through international mechanisms.* Paper presented at the International Social Work Conference, School of Social Work, University of Michigan, Ann Arbor, MI.

Yoshihama, M. (1998). Domestic violence in Japan: Research, program developments, and emerging movements. In A.R. Roberts (Ed.), *Battered women and their families* (2nd ed.). New York: Springer.

PART IV

STRENGTHENING INTERNATIONAL SOCIAL WORK: STRATEGIES AND CHALLENGES

CHAPTER 13

INTERNATIONAL EXCHANGE

An Essential Mechanism for International Social Work

International exchange exists on many levels and is an important mechanism for the development and expansion of international social work. International exchange projects and programs have been prominent in the development of social work as a global profession. As explained in the earlier chapters on history, there was extensive exchange of ideas, information, and personnel in social work's early decades. The founders were strong advocates for international exchange and active participants in it. A paper at the First International Conference called for "constant contact between social workers on an international intellectual basis" (Jebb, 1929, p. 651). The cross-fertilization and inspiration that resulted led to the founding of schools of social work throughout the world. Direct service programs were also initiated as social workers transplanted and adapted ideas they learned through foreign travel or through exchanges of ideas with colleagues at international meetings. The desire for sustained exchange led to the creation of the various international professional organizations, organizations that through regular conferences, newsletters, an international journal, and other projects continue to encourage intercountry contact and sharing. According to Hokenstad (2003), "international collaboration is one potentially effective method for preparing social workers to function in the context of global realities" (p. 133). It is also a potential means for influencing these realities.

IMPORTANCE OF INTERNATIONAL EXCHANGE RELATIONSHIPS IN HIGHER EDUCATION

A substantial literature on exchange exists within the field of education and educational institutions have led the way on international exchange. UN Education, Scientific, and Cultural Organization (UNESCO; 1998), in the *World Declaration on Higher Education* asserted that "international cooperation and exchange are major avenues for advancing higher education throughout the world" (preamble). Further, "quality ... requires that higher education should be characterized by its international dimension: exchange of knowledge, interactive networking, mobility of teachers and students, and international research projects" (Article 11b). The U.S. Department of Education and Department of State have long histories of supporting international exchange. The Bureau of Educational and Cultural Affairs of the Department of State (2002) recently identified the following benefits of international linkages between academic institutions:

1. strengthened teaching, research, administrative, and public service capacity for all partner institutions
2. establishment, expansion, or reform of educational programs
3. new pedagogical models and educational materials
4. collaborative research
5. outreach to local communities and relevant professional, nongovernmental, and government entities.

Many studies have shown that exchange experiences have long-lasting positive effects on students and teachers. One example is a study by Sandgren and colleagues reported in the *Journal of Studies in International Education.* Their research showed that study abroad experiences for educators—even short-term ones—had important and multidimensional impacts on teaching. According to the findings, such experiences are "likely to produce dramatic and enduring transformative change in participants and their teaching" (Sandgren, Ellig, Hovde, Krejci, & Rice, 1999, p. 55). Beyond the finding that the instructors were more likely to add international content to their courses, they reported "increased self and social awareness, new consciousness of the teacher-student relations, and changes in teaching style" (Asamoah, 2003, p. 4).

There are many types and levels of international exchange. Broadly defined, exchange goes beyond the face-to-face exchange accomplished through travel, although that is an important category of exchange efforts. Exchange also occurs through books, media, and increasingly through the use of communications technology to facilitate cross-border sharing of ideas, experiences, and resources. A range of exchange models will be explored below.

LEARNING FROM ABROAD: COMPARATIVE POLICY ANALYSIS AND TECHNOLOGY TRANSFER

International social work encourages many forms of international learning and sharing, beginning with the traditional activity of comparative social policy analysis. There are two major benefits to be derived from comparative policy analysis in social work and social welfare. The first is enhanced knowledge of one's own system through assessment of its place in the global system. The other is technology transfer—the identification of innovations in other countries that can be adapted and adopted at home.

It is only possible to fully understand a social welfare system by comparing it with other systems and by assessing a system's place in the worldwide network. Such study may expose widely accepted truisms as mere opinions. Politicians and corporate leaders in the United States, for example, have resisted the idea of paid maternity and paternity leaves, claiming that to grant such leave would destroy American business competitiveness in the world economy. The argument sounds less convincing when compared to the policy and business practices of America's competitors in Western Europe, where almost all countries offer leave with pay to new parents and employees with ill family members. Thus, the comparative view shows that to claim that such a policy is impossible is clearly invalid; more accurately, it can be asserted that parental leave is not a policy priority in the United States.

Through comparative study, policy analysts may discover programs or policies that have potential to enhance domestic social welfare. The process of borrowing an innovation from abroad is called *technology transfer*. The adaptation of microloans and self-employment ventures described in Case 1.3 in Chapter 1 is one example of technology transfer, in this case from Bangladesh to the United States. The literature has sometimes labeled this "reverse technology transfer," assuming that most transfer is from industrialized to developing nations. The process of international sharing, exchange, and borrowing, however, need not be tied to preconceived ideas of the origins of the donor and recipient. These ideas are explored further below.

Although exchange is an important mechanism, there have been some barriers, especially the reality and the legacy of what is called the export model.

Legacy of the Export Model

At times in the history of social work, inequality of opportunity and inequality in access to resources among the countries of the world have led to negative patterns in professional communication and exchange. In the export model, social welfare theories, practice models, and curricula have been inappropriately and uncritically exported or borrowed. Exchange relationships under these conditions were largely one-way relationships between an expert or donor and a recipient. Although the situation has improved, unequal exchange still occurs; some of the recent consultation projects to former Soviet bloc countries appear dangerously close to earlier models of large-scale transplantation of models of social work education or professional organization developed for industrialized countries with very different socioeconomic and cultural environments. It is questionable whether one-way or unequal exchange relationships deserve the label "exchange." Models based on export and imposition do little to contribute to international social work and may do damage to the programs they affect.

Many authors have been harshly critical of these export efforts (see, for example, Khinduka, 1971; Midgley, 1981). Wagner (1992) interprets the issue more gently, labeling the one-way transfer of benefits "gift-giving." Exchange is an economic concept, using market terminology to apply to ideas and information in the profession; exchange is likely to occur only when each party to the transaction has something of value to transmit to the other. Thus, "it is unlikely that in an early phase of contact between unequal partners, transactions will be exchange-dominated" (Wagner, p. 125). Instead, one-way transfer of resources is likely to characterize the relationship between social workers in industrialized and developing nations, or between those in countries with long-established social work institutions and those exploring the field. Wagner suggests that social workers may feel particularly comfortable with this approach: "social workers and social work educators probably have more affinity with the concept of unilateral transfer than with the concept of exchange, because it is based on altruism, rather than economic utility and self-interest" (p. 126). Unfortunately, the altruistic intent has led to transplantation of social welfare models ill suited to some of their recipients and impeded the development of local variety in social work. It may have also impeded the development of international social work by stalling true exchange relationships in the field. Some in the profession may avoid international exchange out of fear of entering into unequal or exploitive relationships. Noble (2004), however, indicates that increasing global dialogue has actually diminished western dominance:

> the opening up of local-global discourse has contributed to the fracturing of the predominantly Anglo-Western pedagogical hegemony by including different cultural perspectives, beliefs, practices and historical intergroup connections, thus making a significant contribution to multicultural awareness in social work curricula at national and international levels. (p. 528)

In pursuing exchange, she cautions that "awareness about the tension between core universalistic characteristics and the resurrection of indigenous voices and the postmodern challenge must also be present" (p. 534).

MUTUAL EXCHANGE IN SOCIAL WORK

In spite of past difficulties, international exchange must be embraced as a mechanism to move social work forward. International dialogue is essential for the growth and development of social work theory and methods and to foster collaborative work on the social problems that have been discussed in previous chapters. The most important dimension of exchange is mutuality. Indeed, true exchange requires mutuality. According to theories of exchange, exchange only exists when all partners benefit from a relationship or transaction. Optimally, the benefits received are equal or equally valued, although partners may receive different "commodities" from the exchange. Highest levels of satisfaction with exchanges are found when there is symmetrical and substantial interdependence between the participants (Schmidt & Kochan, 1977). Mericourt (2001) notes that mutuality in an exchange relationship in which all parties benefit can override obvious inequalities in resources between partners. Exchange is a broad concept and does not only apply to personnel. Exchange can involve physical resources—money, equipment, books—information, ideas, access, referrals, or even reputation/legitimation. Thus, benefits are not always easily measured.

The literature on exchange and interorganizational relations suggests that the following factors are related to success: goal interdependence—the identification of common interests; mutuality in resource exchange—each partner contributes resources valued by the receiving partner (Schmidt & Kochan, 1977); frequent contact and communication between the partners (Morris, 1962); and the attitudes and behaviors of the personnel involved. Participants in successful exchanges tend to have high levels of interpersonal trust; open-mindedness; a willingness to take risks and try new approaches; and sensitivity to organizational and cultural differences (Healy, Maxwell, & Pine, 1999; Maxwell, 1994). International exchange also requires a "cosmopolitan ethic" among participants, defined as a world-minded openness that allows learning from others (Healy, 2003; Maxwell, 1994). Recent interorganizational literature defines *collaboration* as a higher order form of exchange relationship. A collaboration is "a mutually beneficial and well-defined relationship entered into by two or more organizations to achieve common goals" (Mattessich & Monsey, 1992, p. 39).

Social workers will find exchange projects particularly useful if they focus on mutual problems or issues. Global migration patterns provide opportunities for linkages between source and receiving areas of migration. For example, a multiyear project developed between the University of Connecticut in the United States and the University of the West Indies in Jamaica to work on issues related to large-scale Jamaican migration to the Hartford, Connecticut, area. Linkage activities included training of service providers in Connecticut on West Indian family issues, joint faculty scholarly work on issues of migration, student exchange, and two-way curriculum consultation and exchanges of materials (Healy et al., 1999; Maxwell & Healy, 2003). Emphasis on a social issue or problem of mutual interest is another mechanism for fruitful exchange. The School of Social Work in Esbjerg, Denmark, is part of a multicountry linkage focused around issues of aging and social work. Activities include annual conferences, curriculum exchange, and development of materials for teaching (I. Hjerrild, personal communication, June 1998).

Exchanges in social work occur at many levels. Some are episodic in nature; these include the exchanges of information at professional conferences and relatively short-term dialogue between social workers by mail or computer, often to address a particular issue or research question. Organized programs or projects of exchange may develop between educational programs, between social work professional organizations, or between agencies. Many educational programs promote student exchanges through international field placement or service learning programs. The European Union (EU) efforts to encourage exchange through funded projects of Erasmus,

Tempus, and Socrates are particularly notable. Schools of social work have set up bilateral exchange projects; some have been relatively short in duration, whereas others have extended over many years. The interorganizational efforts of child welfare agencies in Texas, California, and Mexico described in Chapter 11 provide examples of agency-based exchange programs. Types of exchanges will be discussed below, after considering the impact of technology on exchange.

TECHNOLOGY AND EXCHANGE

Advances in technology are making exchange far easier. It is interesting to note, however, that prior generations have observed the same. At the 1928 First International Conference of Social Work, a delegate from Budapest remarked in a speech:

> The world of today is smaller than it has ever been before. New methods of communication and transport facilities and the new techniques of production, link nations, classes together. Goods, thoughts, ideas and knowledge circulate through the countries and the masses in one continuous stream and prepare the minds of people for a broader and deeper understanding of life. (Rajniss, 1929, pp. 441–442)

A very optimistic statement for the era of steamships and telegraph! With jet travel, satellite television, and international phone and fax service a given, exchange possibilities are being revolutionized by computer communication. From low-tech e-mail, bulletin boards, or chat groups to online video conferencing, international exchange is within reach of many. Although low-income countries have less access to computer technology and others are hampered by the barriers of English-dominated software and Internet Web sites, computer and Internet access are comparatively inexpensive as contrasted to other technologies. Thus, Internet access is common enough to have caused the Peace Corps to worry about whether e-mail would corrupt the tradition of volunteer immersion and relative isolation in their local placements (although it is now welcomed as a tool to improve safety).

Practitioners and researchers are able to exchange files, papers, or research results electronically, easing the processes of intercountry casework or cross-national research. Estes reported that as of 1999, there were more than 2,000 scholarly journals published exclusively on the Internet. The number has grown since that time. The availability of various types of publications online and often free of charge stimulates international social work in a number of ways and make transnationalism more feasible as migrants can keep up with their home countries by reading newspapers online.

Listservs and computer bulletin or message boards offer possibilities for global dialogue. A problem or question posed on a message board or to a listserv is likely to generate helpful (and perhaps some not so helpful) responses from all over the world. Questions such as "I am developing a peer-support and counseling program in Tanzania aimed at adolescents at risk of HIV—any ideas for what works?" might be posed. The questioner is put in touch with "experts"—admittedly self-appointed ones—from many parts of the world. The contribution of such technologies to technology transfer in social work is considerable (P. Petrella, personal communication, May 18, 2000).

Chong (1998), a social work educator in Malaysia, found listservs useful in teaching and socializing students to the profession.

> When I first started teaching, I discovered the NISW (National Institute of Social Work, U.K.) listgroup and got answers to every question I sent out. I also used the NISW listserv to get comments and statements from social workers all over the world about what social work meant to them or what they did as a social worker in their country. These statements were then used as part of an exhibition to expose students to the breadth and depth of social work. (p. 179)

Chong concluded that "information technology and the borderless world provide students with a potential arena to discover the ethos of the profession" (p. 179). Chong's observations about what he labeled "telesocial work" have relevance for exchange among all countries. The telesocial work concept means that social workers in one country can access appropriate expertise from around the world, adapt the knowledge to the local context, and then, through ongoing exchange, broaden the knowledge base of others.

The use of technology in educational programs is considerable and includes Web-based and Web-enhanced courses. Teaching over the World Wide Web removes geography as a limitation to education. Students from various countries can be enrolled in the same course, or "guest speakers" can be brought into classes from diverse countries. Although fewer in number, multicountry workshops for practitioners have also been delivered by distance education. In one modest venture, a professor from Connecticut delivered a workshop to social work practitioners in four Caribbean locations by conference call.

Social work can mine these new tools to improve and expand exchange among colleagues around the world. Coalitions of nongovernmental organizations (NGOs) developed online are now playing major roles in political activism on the global scene. "New coalitions can be built online.... More important, the Internet allows new partnerships between groups in rich and poor countries" ("The Non-Governmental Order," 1999, p. 21). Local activists collect data on local conditions and feed these by e-mail into global NGOs; the information becomes a powerful tool to address issues such as debt reduction, world trade agreements, or exploitive labor practices. Through computer technologies and more traditional means, exchange can assist social work to develop a global social movement, capable of contributing to solutions to social problems and issues of the present and future.

Although the inequities of the "digital divide" should not be ignored, computer technologies often do benefit developing countries. Costs of development and testing are borne in richer nations, and developing countries often purchase equipment after it has been mass produced at lower costs. On balance, the Internet is a significant resource and is a benefit to scholars and some practitioners in developing countries where books and professional journals are scarce and prohibitively expensive. The English language dominance of software and search engines remains problematic.

INTERNATIONAL FIELD PLACEMENTS AND EDUCATIONAL EXCHANGES

International learning and exchange in social work can also be facilitated through field practicum opportunities. Many schools of social work have arranged international field placements for students. A surprising 44% of responding schools in a global survey reported having had students complete field placements in other countries; Europe accounted for nearly one-half of these (Healy, 1990). Although 44% of schools is an impressive total, closer examination revealed that most of these schools had placed relatively few students in such placements and that international placements were handled on an episodic basis rather than as planned components of regular programs. Recently, another study yielded similar results among schools in the United States. The researchers found that U.S. schools are still placing relatively few students internationally, and most schools are doing so inconsistently, usually only one student per year (Pettys, Panos, Cox, & Oosthuysen, 2005).

There are some examples of organized approaches to international field education. One was a program between Denmark and Great Britain in which students completed their practicum in the country other than their own. For several years during the 1980s, Fordham University (New York City) had a fieldwork unit in a refugee camp in Thailand. The program was funded by Catholic Relief Services and included an instructor from Fordham who traveled with the students and assisted them in integrating their practical experience in Thailand with the rest of their education. And, as mentioned earlier in the book, the Social Welfare Training Centre course in Jamaica had an established program for Jamaican participants to complete an internship in Puerto Rico while those from other Caribbean islands did internships in Jamaica. Each of these organized programs was undergirded by a philosophy of the value of cross-national experiential learning.

It is important to consider international field placements, as they are potentially powerful tools for international learning in social work and particularly important preparation for international practice. Through such placements, students become immersed in a cross-cultural learning experience and must confront different views of human behavior and perspectives about how things should operate. They learn within different systems of social welfare and address problems that may exist in their home communities, but that are viewed and remedied in very different ways. In addition to the learning, completing an international field placement can prepare interested students for future international work by providing them with the valuable prerequisite of previous overseas experience. Students often return from international placements and report that these were life-altering experiences.

There are many difficulties in arranging such experiences, and these have prevented full development of international placements as usual or accepted parts of social work education. The educational barriers can be inferred from the earlier chapters. Social work is defined differently in different countries. Educational standards and content vary considerably between countries. Because the functions of social workers vary, the tasks expected of practicum students will not be a perfect fit with those expected by the sending educational program. For example, Danish students who completed a practicum in the United States resisted working with children, as the major work with children in Denmark is done by social pedagogues; the U.S. agencies that were most eager to take on the Danish students were child-serving agencies. Arrangements for appropriate experiences and supervision require considerable preparatory work and must be built on linkages between sending and host programs or between faculty members in those programs. Programs subject to strict accreditation standards worry about comparability issues. And all educators are concerned that the experiences students have are applicable to their future careers and consistent with the goals of the schools.

In addition to linkages between sending and host programs, good international field experiences require a sound philosophy and adequate preparation and debriefing. Unless the educational program and the student place high value on cross-cultural learning, international placements should not be attempted. The student is most likely to find a field experience that provides exactly what the school requires if he or she stays home. Interpreted more broadly, however, an international field placement can provide a professional development experience that is profound in its impact. Students— and their supporting faculty members—must be prepared for difference. They must be prepared to tolerate ambiguity and struggle to learn cultural meanings throughout their experience—facets of all international exchange experiences. A student who returned from a 4-month internship in India related that he found it difficult to know whether he was performing well in the eyes of his supervisor. At times, he was asked to take on tasks that made no sense to him: for example, to attend a meeting conducted entirely in Hindi, although he understood no Hindi. Yet his field instructor wrote very glowing evaluations and requested that the student return to India to assist the agency further. It took several months after return to the United States to fully integrate the experience; eventually, the integration was successful, and the student did return to India for another short work experience (anonymous, personal communication, October 1994). The process of adaptation and learning can be assisted by offering preplacement preparation seminars and ensuring that there are opportunities to discuss and integrate the experiences upon return. Communications technology has also made contact between host and sending programs much easier. In most places, students can keep in regular e-mail contact with faculty in their home program; voice or video contact may be possible, allowing for supplementary advising and support.

Lyons and Ramanathan (1999) offer a classification of models for international placements that is useful more broadly in considering the purposes and potential outcomes of international exchange in social work. The first model is observational/educational; within this model, a student's primary assignments would be to make a variety of field visits or to shadow one or more local practitioners. This may be combined with attendance at classes or seminars. Students would record their observations and impressions for discussion during the placement and on return to their home institution. At the other end of the continuum are placements aimed at professional skill development in the student's area of social work specialty, such as administration, casework, community organization, or medical social work, child and family, etc. Assignments would emphasize actual practice—doing—while also including cross-national and cross-cultural analyses. A third model, perhaps the least often used, includes some practice opportunities but would emphasize "the students' ability to organize themselves and to adapt and learn effectively, under probably very different circumstances" (Lyons & Ramanthan, p. 185). A fourth model, which can either stand alone or be used in combination with one of the others, is described as a "project approach" (p. 185). The student plans and carries out a study on an area or topic of interest, permitting comparative analysis with work the student has done in his or her home country.

Discussion of these alternative models and agreement among the student, the home institution, and the host institution and agency as to which model will best fit the placement would avoid problems of conflicting and often-unstated expectations. The process may also assist the student and participating institutions to identify the important components of the international exchange to ensure that goals are met. International placements for master's level students have usually expected the second model mentioned above: skill development. This is the most demanding to arrange and complete in terms of language and cultural competence. Replacing or blending this with Model 3 may offer more realistic and useful learning opportunities.

THE EUROPEAN EXAMPLE: EXCHANGE AS A TOOL TO PROMOTE EUROPEANIZATION

Within the EU, provisions for professional mobility mean that social workers educated in one member-country can freely travel to other member-countries to work as social workers, as long as the training received meets agreed-on Union standards. The EU has sponsored a number of initiatives to provide funding for professional exchanges to facilitate mobility and to encourage development of European perspectives. Under the ERASMUS program in effect from 1987–1997, social work exchanges among EU countries grew. ERASMUS provided funds for curriculum development, faculty exchange, and multicountry seminars, as well as for student exchange programs, in an effort to facilitate "Europeanization at social as well as economic levels," and "development of a European consciousness and identity" (Lyons & Ramanathan, 1999, p. 177). Additional exchanges with former Eastern bloc nations were funded through another EU initiative, Tempus. Out of these funding schemes, several intensive exchange experiences in European social work have emerged. Lyons (1996) described two: a collaborative program between Britain and Denmark, and a Cooperative European Social Studies program in the Netherlands. In the first, 12 Danish and 12 U.K. students study together for one term in Copenhagen and another in Portsmouth, England. In between the academic semesters, students complete a field internship experience in the "other" country (Horncastle, 1994; Lyons, 1996). In 1994, a master's degree in comparative European social studies was established at the school of social work in Maastricht, The Netherlands, with an emphasis on comparative European welfare; drawing students from various European countries, a potential outcome is development of a European social welfare perspective (Lyons, 1996).

Lyons critiqued the developments for focusing too narrowly on European comparative social policy. This approach ignores larger global issues and fails to provide "opportunities for students to participate and give meaning to their own aspirations to work cross-culturally and internationally" (Lyons, 1996, p. 190). Nagy and Falk (1996), who surveyed international curriculum efforts in Europe, as well as Australia, Canada, and the United States, also found international content in European schools to be "Eurocentric." Nonetheless, the funding provided through these EU programs has enabled many professionals in social work and other fields to have useful exchange experiences in other countries and has moved social work closer to at least a regional, if not global, perspective.

REGULATION AND LABOR MOBILITY FOR THE PROFESSION

Labor mobility has been an issue in some countries for many years. Many educated professionals from developing countries emigrate to practice elsewhere, leaving their own countries short of trained professionals. The Caribbean area, for example, loses the majority of its personnel; for Guyana, over 80% of educated persons emigrate. There is concern that some countries, notably the United Kingdom, recruit for social workers and nurses from abroad as a way of keeping their own higher education costs low at other countries' expense (Firth, 2007).

More recently, labor mobility has taken on wider relevance. The General Agreement on Tariffs and Trade (GATT) includes provisions on fair and open trade in services. To what extent will this open social work to imposed standards? One of the arguments for the development of the Global Standards in Social Work Education and Training (IASSW, 2004) was to ensure that the profession could point to accepted standards for social work education to ward off attempts by international trade bodies to permit other types of standards setting. In Europe, the Bologna agreement has brought increased "harmonization" of requirements for higher education (Lyons, 2005). This strengthens the provisions to allow labor mobility within the EU. Thus, at least in principle, a social worker trained in one country should be prepared to practice in other countries in the EU and has the right to seek such employment. All of these developments make international exchange even more important.

PARADIGM SHIFT IN INTERNATIONAL EXCHANGE

In spite of the research showing the value of cross-cultural experiences, experts in international education report that a paradigm shift is taking place in the arena of international collaboration and exchange. This shift is from an emphasis on experiences to an emphasis on competencies. Rather than valuing exchange itself, the new emphasis is to look for more measurable outcomes. "The traditional ideal of a cultural experience has been superceded by the goal of obtaining knowledge useful for the new internationalized professions of the postindustrial era" (Albach & Teichler, 2001, p. 17). This shift may be good and bad news for international connections in social work. The positive is that the social work profession is beginning to recognize that international exchange does build competencies for practice in the era of globalization. The negative side of the shift is the devaluation of cross-cultural understanding and personal transformation as sufficient benefits from international connections.

THE PROMISE OF INTERNATIONAL CONNECTIONS FOR DEVELOPING THE PROFESSION

It is fair to say that educational programs have led the way in exchange in social work through field placements and service learning projects for students and, especially, through international exchanges of faculty members. In the field of social work, there is important untapped potential in practice collaborations and exchanges, regionally and globally, as well as room for strengthening exchanges among students and teachers. International practice and educational exchanges can result in important outcomes for the profession. Exchanges can contribute to

• leadership development
• new ideas for social work practice and education

- more successful adaptation among the increasingly globally mobile social work workforce
- increased cultural competence of participating practitioners, faculty, and students
- skills development as well as concrete products (such as those from cross-national research)
- expanded international knowledge among participants
- exposure to different value orientations—that may lead to rethinking of service and educational models
- increased collaborative international advocacy on regional and international policy issues.

Indeed, an examination of collaborations among local social agencies found that collaborations build social capital. According to the study author, "continued interaction and discourse translated into shared understandings and mutual trust which created relational resources that could be called upon at future times. This building of relationships created social capital" (Reilly, 2001, p. 70). International exchange, built on mutuality, may build human and social capital for international social work. Or, as expressed by Noble (2004), "improving international communication and exchange between and across social work programmes as each country grapples with the forces of globalization will be the key to developing models of practice that are able to address emerging social issues" (p. 533).

PREPARATION FOR INTERNATIONAL SOCIAL WORK: BEYOND EXCHANGE PROGRAMS

Beyond international exchange, social workers need preparation for international action. Many authors have written about the need for increased international content in social work education. Proposals for learning objectives, content, and educational structures and strategies have been suggested in some detail. There have also been recent positive developments to expand international learning for social work students. In the United States, for example, the body that accredits social work programs, the Council on Social Work Education, changed its curriculum policy in 2002 to include requirements for international content in the teaching of social policy and human oppression. The Council also launched the Katherine A. Kendall Institute on International Education to encourage further initiatives in this area. In Norway and Denmark, several schools of social work have begun specialized tracks in international and cross-cultural social work. These and other innovations are important steps forward; however, there is much more to be done in the area of global education for social workers.

In a work now considered a classic, Hanvey described the outcome of global education as consisting of the following five elements: "perspective consciousness, 'state of the planet' awareness, cross-cultural awareness, knowledge of global dynamics, and awareness of human choices" (as cited in Hughes-Wiener, 1988, p. 140). More recently, Tye (1999) described global education as

> learning about those problems and issues which cut across national boundaries and about the interconnectedness of systems—cultural, ecological, economic, political, and technological. Global education also involves learning to understand and appreciate our neighbors who have different cultural backgrounds from ours; to see the world through the eyes and minds of others; and to realize that other people of the world need and want much the same things.

The profession and its organizations, especially the International Federation of Social Workers (IFSW) and International Association of Schools of Social Work (IASSW), need to consider ways to ensure that practicing social workers have opportunities to increase their knowledge of international issues and practice-relevant knowledge through exchange and other types of global education. Cox and Pawar (2006) called for changes in social work practice including the need to "develop a global orientation and an understanding of the dominant pressing needs that are global in nature" (p. 367). Their recommendations for education of international practitioners resonate as reasonable goals for all social workers in the increasingly globalized world. They urge social workers to develop an "enhanced ability to think globally both at the situation analysis level and in the devising of intervention programs" (p. 368). They further recommend that social workers have strong cross-cultural practice skills, be able to work in interdisciplinary efforts, be able to work at multiple levels from the grassroots community to local and global NGOs and governments, and "have a high degree of commitment to the social justice and human rights dimensions of practice" (p. 368). To do so, social workers must gain knowledge about international social problems, diversity in a global context, and the globally relevant concepts that will be reviewed in the final chapter.

CONCLUSION AND RECOMMENDATIONS

The discussion of international exchange began by noting that the history of international exchange within the profession is as old as the profession itself. Exchange and international collaborations are important tools and strategies for international social work development and action. To improve and expand international exchange, professionals must first of all ensure that mutuality is indeed the cornerstone of all cross-national exchange efforts within social work. Mutuality is central to the ethical underpinnings of exchange and also to successful and sustainable partnerships. The profession should also consider new types of international linkages to promote exchange among practitioners. Finally, perhaps with leadership from IASSW and IFSW, the profession should initiate cross-national or global policy advocacy networks through which social work students, educators, and practitioners can work together for change on issues of poverty, development, and human rights.

REFERENCES

Altbach, P. G., & Teichler, U. (2001). Internationalization and exchanges in a global-ized university. *Journal of Studies in International Education, 5*(1), 5–25.

Asamoah, Y. (2003). International collaboration in social work education: Overview. In L. M. Healy, Y. Asamoah, & M. C. Hokenstad (Eds.), *Models of international collaboration in social work education* (pp. 1–14). Alexandria, VA: CSWE.

Chong, G. (1998). Information technology and social work education in Malaysia: Challenges and prospects. *Computers in Human Services, 15*(2/3), 171–184.

Cox, D., & Pawar, M. (2006). *International social work: Issues, strategies, and programs.* Thousand Oaks, CA: Sage Publications.

Estes, R. (1999). Informational tools for social workers: Research in the global age. In C. Ramanathan & R. Link (Eds.), *All our futures: Principles and resources for social work practice in a global era* (pp. 121–137). Belmont, CA: Brooks-Cole.

Firth, R. (2007, January 9). *Mobility and experiences of overseas social workers in England.* Paper presented to the Public Panel Discussion on International Social Work, sponsored by the Department of Government, Sociology and Social Work, University of the West Indies, Cave Hill Campus, Barbados.

Healy, L. M. (1990). [International content in social work educational programs worldwide]. Unpublished raw data.

Healy, L. M. (2003). A theory of international collaboration: Lessons for social work education. In L. M. Healy, Y. Asamoah, & M. C. Hokenstad (Eds.), *Models of international collaboration in social work education* (pp. 15–22). Alexandria, VA: CSWE.

Healy, L. M., Maxwell, J. A., & Pine, B. A. (1999). Exchanges that work: Mutuality and sustainability in a Caribbean/USA academic partnership. *Social Development Issues, 21*(3), 14–21.

Hokenstad, M. C. (2003). Global interdependence and international exchange: Lessons for the future. In L. M. Healy, Y. Asamoah, & M. C. Hokenstad (Eds.), *Models of international collaboration in social work education* (pp. 133–141). Alexandria, VA: CSWE.

Horncastle, J. (1994). Training for international social work: Initial experiences. *International Social Work, 37*(4), 309–318.

Hughes-Wiener, G. (1988). An overview of international education in the schools. *Education and Urban Society, 20*(2), 139–158.

IASSW. (2004). *Global standards for social work education and training.* Accessed December 27, 2007, at www.iassw-aiets.org

Jebb, E. (1929). International social service. In First International Conference of Social Work, *Proceedings of the Conference, July 8–13, 1928* (pp. 637–655). Paris: International Conference of Social Work.

Khinduka, S. (1971). Social work in the third world. *Social Service Review, 45*(1), 62–73.

Lyons, K. (1996). Education for international social work. In IFSW, IASSW, & HKSWA, *Proceedings: Joint World Congress July 24–27, 1996* (pp. 189–191). Hong Kong: Authors.

Lyons, K. (2005). *Internationalising social work education: Considerations and developments.* Birmingham: British Association of Social Workers.

Lyons, K., & Ramanathan, C. S. (1999). Models of field practice in global settings. In C. Ramanathan & R. Link (Eds.), *All our futures: Principles and responses for social work practice in a global era* (pp. 175–192). Belmont, CA: Brooks/Cole.

Mattessich, P. W., & Monsey, B. R. (1992). *Collaboration: What makes it work? A review of research literature on factors influencing successful collaboration.* St. Paul, MN: Amherst H. Wilder Foundation.

Maxwell, J. A. (1994, July). *Educating social workers for interorganizational coordination.* Paper presented at the 27th Congress of the International Association of Social Workers, Amsterdam, The Netherlands.

Maxwell, J. A., & Healy, L. M. (2008). Mutual assistance through an ongoing United States-Caribbean partnership. In L. M. Healy, Y. Asamoah, & M. C. Hokenstad (Eds.), *Models of international collaboration in social work education.* Alexandria, VA: Council on Social Work Education.

Mericourt, B. (2001). Unequal but mutually beneficial partnerships in social development: A case example. *Social Development Issues, 23*(3), 43–49.

Midgley, J. (1981). *Professional imperialism: Social work in the third world.* London: Heinemann.

Morris, R. (1962). New concepts in community organization. In *The social welfare forum* (pp. 238–245). New York: Columbia University Press.

Nagy, G., & Falk, D. (1996, July). *Teaching international and cross-cultural social work.* Paper presented at the Joint World Congress of the International Federation of Social Workers and the International Association of Schools of Social Work, Hong Kong.

Noble, C. (2004). Social work education, training and standards in the Asia-Pacific region. *Social Work Education, 23*(5), 517–536.

The nongovernmental order. (1999, December 11). *The Economist,* 20–21.

Pettys, G. L., Panos, P. T., Cox, S. E., & Oosthuysen, K. (2005). Four models of international field placement. *International Social Work, 48*(3), 277–288.

Rajniss, F. F. (1929). The contribution of social casework to other fields of social endeavor. In First International Conference of Social Work, *Proceedings of the Conference, July 8–13, 1928* (Vol. 2, pp. 441–461). Paris: International Conference of Social Work.

Reilly, T. (2001). Collaboration in action: An uncertain process. *Administration in Social Work, 25*(1), 53–74.

Sandgren, D., Ellig, N., Hovde, P., Krejci, M., & Rice, M. (1999). How international experience affects teaching: Understanding the impact of faculty study abroad. *Journal of Studies in International Education, 3*(1), 33–56.

Schmidt, S. M., & Kochan, T. A. (1977). Interorganizational relationships: Patterns and motivations. *Administrative Science Quarterly, 22,* 220–234.

Tye, K. A. (1999). Global education: A worldwide movement. *Issues in Global Education. Newsletter of the American Forum for Global Education,* Issue No. 150. Available at www.globaled.org/issues/150/a.html

United Nations Educational, Scientific and Cultural Organization. (1998). *World declaration on higher education.* Accessed November 10, 2002, at www.unesco .orgeducationeducprogwche/declaration_eng.htm

U.S. Department of State, Bureau of Education and Cultural Affairs. (2002). *Educational partnership programs.* Accessed August 2, 2002, at http://exchanges/state/gov/education/partnership

Wagner, A. (1992). Social work education in an integrated Europe: Plea for a global perspective. *Journal of Teaching in Social Work, 6*(2), 115–130.

CHAPTER 14

SOCIAL WORK AS A FORCE FOR HUMANE GLOBAL CHANGE AND DEVELOPMENT

Now that the world has entered the twenty-first century and social work its second century, major global challenges abound. The need for international social work action is as great or greater than ever in the face of a widening rich–poor gap within and between nations. Social exclusion, exacerbated by globalization, has widened the gap between those who benefit from economic progress and those left outside or cast aside by global processes. Human security, long a centerpiece of international relations, has taken on added meaning as even those not affected by war risk insecurity caused by long-term unemployment, poverty, and personal violence. Although progress continues to be made in setting global standards for human rights, there has been a failure to realize the promises made in the twentieth century to guarantee implementation of human rights for all. Indeed, new threats to civil liberties have emerged as a result of the "war on terrorism." Peace and intergroup harmony remain elusive in the face of ongoing war and sustained or perhaps growing interethnic, racial, and religious conflict in many parts of the world. Lack of political will and resource shortages, especially resources devoted to human service needs, make it unlikely that the targets set in the Millennium Development Goals (MDGs) will be reached and create an urgent need for sustainable, resource-efficient social interventions.

Social work is positioned to address these global challenges better than ever before. The profession can now rightly claim to be a global profession. Not only has the organized profession entered its second century but also social work exists in most countries of the world and has been present in all regions of the world for more than 60 years. The international professional organizations have joined to adopt a revised Global Definition of Social Work, a set of ethical principles, and, for the first time, *Global Standards for Social Work Education and Training.* The profession's attention can now turn to efforts to strengthen its role in international action as a force for humane social change and development. In this final chapter, globally relevant concepts for social work dialogue and theory development will be discussed. Brief comments on preparation for professionals in the global era will be made prior to concluding with discussion of opportunities and threats to social work's participation in global civil society and the prospects for international social work.

GLOBALLY RELEVANT CONCEPTUAL FRAMEWORKS

Early in this volume, the important concepts of *globalization, development, human rights,* and *transnationalism* and their relevance to international social work were emphasized. These and other universally relevant concepts can serve as what my coauthors and I labeled in an earlier article "conceptual channels" for meaningful global communication in social work (Asamoah, Healy, & Mayadas, 1997). Additional salient concepts are *multiculturalism/ global cultural competence, social exclusion/inclusion, human security,* and *sustainability.* These concepts are salient because they are current issues of focus in the international arena and because they are within social work's domain. After expanded comments on development and human rights, these four additional concepts will be discussed.

Development

As discussed earlier, development is optimally understood as a continuum without an endpoint. There is no point at which a country can be labeled "developed" nor one at which a country is "undeveloped." Thus the concept of *development* understood as a continuing process to improve human well-being is a universally relevant concept. Modern approaches to development emphasize a holistic view of human well-being, equity, and participation.

Midgley (1999) recommends three sets of intervention strategies to operationalize the social development approach: human capital development, social capital development, and encouragement of self-employment or other productive employment projects. Human capital development involves investments in people that increase productivity, including enhancements to education, health, and nutrition. Social capital is enhanced through capacity building in communities and other social units, often through mobilizing groups to engage in self-help and infrastructure-creating efforts. Social capital development embodies much of traditional community organizing and community development methods. Self-employment projects provide assistance, often in the form of microloans and technical assistance, to help individuals begin small income-generating ventures. These three approaches are illustrated in the case examples; the emergency education program for young children in war-torn Bosnia described in Case 1.4 is an example of human capital development; the program used a development model for enhancing the capacity of the children to move forward after their traumatic war experiences. The community shelter clinics project implemented in Jamaica following Hurricane Gilbert (in Case 8.1) is an example of social capital development; the project met the dual goals of infrastructure development through improved housing, and community capacity building, in its impact on strengthening or initiating community organizations. The Grameen bank microloan and microenterprise efforts in Case 1.3 illustrate the development approach of productive employment and self-employment. The case also illustrates the universal relevance of development concepts and strategies in demonstrating the transfer of the microenterprise approach to industrialized countries.

Given the persistence of severe poverty and slow progress on the MDGs, development remains a particularly important topic for international exchange and dialogue within the social work community.

Human Rights

Human rights has been addressed several times in the preceding chapters. As stated in Chapter 7, the International Federation of Social Workers (IFSW) has asserted that social work is a human rights profession. Human rights can serve as a statement of social work values, a source of guidelines for adopting policy positions, and a framework for professional practice. As such, it is a core concept for global dialogue and action.

The practice dimension of social work as human rights is particularly interesting. Direct social work practice with individuals and groups, as well as community and policy work, can be defined as human rights practice. The human rights orientation helps social workers focus on social justice rather than individual pathology. "Their [social workers] work puts them in a particularly sensitive position in society, where their way of intervening in situations deemed 'problematic' can either reduce these problems to the level of individual pathology or help to articulate them as issues of social injustice" (Lorenz, 1994, p. 167). Lorenz urges social workers to base their practice on the promotion of rights. Using a human rights model in work with a woman abused by her spouse, for example, the social worker considers the woman to be a victim of human rights violations. This definition expands the role of case documentation, as information about human rights violations are used not only to assist the victim through individual interventions, but also as public documentation for use in working to end domestic violence. In some settings, defining a client as a victim is seen in a negative light. In human rights work, however, the impact of this label is different, and the client and the social worker are empowered by seeing themselves as part of a broad struggle for global human rights. The human rights model bridges the gulf between individual interventions and advocacy/social change; through assessment, service, and case documentation, both purposes are served. The social worker—quite possibly with the client—uses the documentation to influence legislatures, funders, and/or public opinion. An example of the power of this approach is that in several cases in Canada women have been given refugee status based on their history and continuing fear of domestic violence.

There are many challenges for social work in the arena of human rights. One has been discussed in some depth in Chapter 9—the dilemmas that arise in balancing cultural rights with universal human rights. A second is the profession's focus on economic and social rights. In contrast to the first-generation civil and political rights, economic and social rights are not spelled out in detailed standards. It is difficult to assess when rights are being met, and therefore advocacy is more complicated than for the political prisoner. Economic and social rights are also dependent, of necessity, on the resources available in the country in question. In an interesting article on the topic, Mishra (2005) states that "Social rights are not about reducing inequality per se but rather about ensuring that a minimum of basic resources and opportunities are available to all to ensure a life of human dignity and social inclusion" (p. 17). The notion of "progressive realization" of economic and social rights—that countries will implement these rights according to their capacity to do so—guarantees that inequities will persist. Thus, two dilemmas result for a profession devoted to economic and social equity: that standards for achieving these rights at present are vague at best, and any practical standards developed will in effect implement a variable standard in which people in poor countries are deemed entitled, at least in the short run, to a lower level of social rights than those in richer countries (Mishra, 2005).

Since 2001, however, there have also been new threats to first-generation rights that should concern social work domestically and internationally. The "war on terrorism" and the public fear of terrorism have led in some countries to new violations and restrictions on basic civil and political rights. It is becoming evident in the United States that the response to terrorism may well be far more damaging to the institutions and principles of the country than the terrorist attacks themselves. "Executive orders have been signed to 'impose guilt by association on immigrants; authorize the indefinite lock up of aliens on mere suspicion . . . allow the use of secret evidence in immigration proceedings that aliens cannot confront or rebut'" (Bello, cited in Matthews, 2002). The USA PATRIOT Act (Uniting and Strengthening America by Providing Appropriate Tools Required to Intercept and Obstruct Terrorism) legitimized secret searches and "ensures the deportation of immigrants who support organizations that, known or unknown to them, fund terrorism" (Matthews, 2002, p. 105). Thus, rules are suddenly being applied retroactively.

Although the impact on immigrants has been particularly severe, citizens, too, have lost important civil rights. Abridging basic civil rights by permitting unreasonable searches or detention without charges changes the social compact to such a degree that far-reaching impact is likely. The long struggle for racial and social justice in the United States has been built on the rule of law and on civil liberties, and it is these assumptions that underlie the teaching of social justice in schools of social work. There is a danger of policy emulation by other countries, as explained in Chapter 2. The United States has a history of a narrow but fairly well-developed approach to human rights. Although the U.S. government has steadfastly opposed notions of social and economic rights, the United States has been a champion (even if an imperfect champion) of civil and political rights. A weakening of adherence to basic civil and political rights in the United States and Britain is likely to spread internationally. These new threats to the rule of law are another challenge to social work.

Finally, though social work's commitment to human rights ideals is embedded in its international documents and many national ones, the profession has not been a highly visible force in the international human rights area. Much more could be done to strengthen the social work voice on human rights advocacy.

Multiculturalism and Cultural Competence

Cross-cultural understanding and sensitivity are essential to all aspects of international social work wherever it is practiced. Yet these are daunting goals. Two trends are giving added importance to social work emphasis on cultural competence and multiculturalism. The first trend is continued large migrations that have and are turning formerly homogeneous populations into diverse ones, and increasing the cultural, racial, and ethnic diversity of most nations. Migration and its impacts have been discussed in several of the preceding chapters. The second trend is the growing incidence of ethnic conflicts. Some of the conflicts are instigated by direct appeals to racism or by politicians who use ethnicity to mobilize discontent or, if in power, who overtly pursue policies that favor their own ethnic group. Too often, "the escalation from ethnic superiority to 'ethnic cleansing' and then subsequently to genocide can become an irresistible process" (Mehta, 1997, p. 96). The horrific violence of Serbs against Moslems in Bosnia, of Hutus against Tutsis and moderate Hutus in Rwanda, the conflict between ethnic Albanians and Serbia in Kosovo province, and the violence between Sunni and Shia in Iraq are recent examples of severe ethnic conflict. Added to these are many more minor or less publicized conflicts and the long-term struggles such as those between Catholics and Protestants in Northern Ireland and between Palestinians and Israelis in the Middle East.

The profession has long recognized the influence of culture on human behavior, and social workers are probably ahead of many other professions in their knowledge and competence in this area. Much more, however, remains to be done, in reexamining and refining the utility of relevant concepts and in improving knowledge and skills for conflict avoidance and resolution. Expressions of the tensions between immigrant and long-term resident populations in many countries call attention to the need for ongoing attention to cultural competence. In France for example, 3 weeks of violence and rioting among immigrants resulted in attacks on public buildings and burning of hundreds of vehicles. The riots were attributed to "a crying lack of integration" of immigrants, especially marked by high unemployment among youth ("After the Riots," 2005).

Approaches to study, practice, and policy in the area of cultural diversity are varied. The assimilationist model is largely discarded, although it still has adherents. As discussed in Chapter 11, the immigrant resettlement policies in Denmark emphasize assimilation into Danish culture. Although some countries, among them the United States and South Africa, have used affirmative action policies to ensure some level of inclusion of formerly excluded groups,

France refuses to recognize or track racial categories, seeing this as a divisive policy. The two more dominant approaches to diversity (although there is far from terminological agreement on these labels) are cultural pluralism and multiculturalism, both of which reject a "Eurocentric" view of the world. As defined by Manning (1995), *cultural pluralism* "emphasizes the unique attributes/experiences of 'distinct' social groups in isolation of each other" with the aim of creating mutual understanding among groups (p. 150). This contrasts with *multiculturalism*, which "explicitly recognizes the interrelationships between various racial/ethnic/national and cultural groups along the multiple dimensions that define social life" (p. 150). Multiculturalism as so defined examines issues of structural inequality and power relationships, whereas cultural pluralism focuses on learning about others to improve intergroup understanding.

These divergent approaches pose challenges for social work, where use of the terms has been less clear than the definitions given above. Within what is broadly labeled multicultural practice, the emphasis may be on ethnic sensitivity and cultural competence, or it may be on oppression of diverse populations (Gutierrez, Fredricksen, & Soifer, 1999). The goal of preparation for cultural competence is to improve the capacity of social workers to serve diverse cultures through learning about cultures and cultural differences; when the emphasis is on racism, sexism, and other oppressions, the aim is to prepare social workers to work for social justice and empowerment of oppressed groups (Gutierrez et al., 1999). Professional debates have taken place as to whether antiracist practice should supplant culturally competent practice. The historic dual commitment of the social work profession mandates attention to both approaches to cultural diversity. Learning about cultures to improve services and to address intergroup conflict is essential, but not sufficient. The social justice mission of the profession requires an anti-oppression framework and action agenda. Thus, cultural competence and antiracist practice, for example, are important, and the profession's attention to further development of these ideas should intensify. As discussed in depth in Chapter 9, multicultural social work must maintain a delicate balance in respecting culture without treating it as sacrosanct when human rights are being violated, and strive to simultaneously promote human rights and cultural pluralism (Ayton-Shenker, 1995).

Within these areas, there is a need for increased attention to the process and impact of migration. Here, too, knowledge about the cultures of international populations within nations and knowledge of the oppressive forces that force migrants to flee and that continue to impede justice in their places of resettlement need to be addressed. Social workers through linkages and exchanges or through the international organizations could be more effectively engaged in working at systems level to address migration and multicultural issues.

The profession also needs to work on conflict avoidance and conflict resolution strategies that can be applied at micro- and macrolevels. Social work has developed some expertise in this on microlevels; however, there is a need to work collaboratively across nations and with other disciplines to develop and apply macro-strategies for encouraging ethnic harmony and ethnic justice. The scale of the challenge and urgency ranges from the everyday social relations in a highly diverse society such as Mauritius to the reconstructive efforts needed to build human relations in places such as Bosnia and Iraq that have seen ethnic tension turn to widespread ethnic slaughter among former neighbors. Mehta (1997) encourages social work to become involved in preventive diplomacy, efforts to "discourage hostilities, reduce tensions, address differences, create channels for resolution and alleviate insecurities and material conditions that tempt violence" (p. 101). Reconciliation and reconstruction are also important; these phases of intervention involve "monitoring violations of human rights; mediating; fostering interethnic dialogue; institution building; strengthening government infrastructure; national capacity building in all spheres; and promoting education for peace and nonviolent conflict resolution" (p. 103).

Social Exclusion/Inclusion

Led by social science scholars in Europe, including social workers, social exclusion has become an important theme in social planning, policy analysis, and practice. Definitions of social exclusion range from relatively narrow ones focusing on the market to broad "inclusive" definitions. A simple definition is offered by the Commission of the European Communities (CEC): *social exclusion* is exclusion of "part of the population from economic and social life and from their share of the general prosperity" (as quoted in Rodgers, Gore, & Figueiredo, 1995, p. 43). The term *social exclusion* originated in France in the 1970s and was originally applied to disadvantaged or marginalized social groups, such as the mentally ill, substance abusers, or multiproblem families. It was in the 1980s that the term evolved to refer to "the nature of the 'new poverty' associated with technological change and economic restructuring" and characterized by "a progressive rupture of the relationship between the individual and society" (Gore, 1995, pp. 1–2). Important elements of the concept are French ideas about citizenship and social integration; social exclusion expresses the loss of social solidarity as part of the population no longer participates in significant opportunities available in the society (Gore, 1995).

As a method, the concept provides "a way of analysing how and why individuals and groups fail to have access to or benefit from the possibilities offered by societies and economies" (Rodgers, 1995, p. 44). Many groups can be covered by this concept, including refugees, street children, ex-offenders, the long-term unemployed, the never employed, the minimally educated, the mentally and physically disabled. The relevance of the concept to social work should be evident. As Lorenz (1994) explained, "Social workers deal with people who potentially do not belong: homeless people, people excluded from mainstream life because of their poverty, their physical or mental difficulties in coping with social demands, people who have become victims of power inequalities within the family" (p. 136). Poverty is a major factor and/or outcome of social exclusion, and social workers may be particularly interested in the way that poverty is defined within social exclusion. *Poverty* is defined in social terms and as relative deprivation, rather than as falling below a particular income level or lacking a set of commodities or expenditures. Rather than using "the Anglo-Saxon notion of poverty as distributional, social exclusion focuses on relational issues—inadequate social participation" (Gore, 1995, p. 9).

Social exclusion can be applied nationally or globally. The growing gap in wealth between the richest and poorest nations and between the richest and poorest segments of the population within nations is a major indicator of social exclusion. Refugees, migrants, and the displaced are often excluded from all benefits of citizenship—sometimes for their lifetimes and even those of their children. This is especially true of the undocumented. Within the globalization of economies and other institutions, social exclusion can be applied to analysis of trade, aid, migration, debt policies, etc. The concept also links to other critical concepts: the socially excluded include those who are excluded from human rights, and those who are excluded from security. An example of the latter will be given in the next section.

The social work profession needs to work cross-nationally to determine if the concept of *social exclusion* adds important insight to existing concepts such as poverty and marginality, and to further specify its social work applications. The concept needs additional work to broaden its Eurocentric focus. As an applied profession, social work will be particularly interested in development of effective strategies for social inclusion. Research indicates that expanding rights of disadvantaged ethnic, racial, and caste groups and women will be important, as these have surfaced as factors in exclusion in countries at all levels of development (Rodgers et al., 1995). Participatory strategies are also key, as social and civic participation are forms of inclusion. Bringing marginalized groups into active participation in global civil society would be an appropriate goal for social work.

Security

Human security has not been a significant concept in social work; however, it may increase in relevance due to new global understandings of the term. No longer confined to security from crime or war, although these certainly remain major issues, *security* now refers to prospects for a peaceful existence, without threats of violence, or present or future hunger, or lack of income. Insecurity has increased in the industrialized nations, as fewer can count on long-term employment and as the benefits of the welfare state are reduced or restricted to those who are "socially included." Low-skilled workers are most at risk, and globalization has perhaps worsened their plight. "Globalization thus simultaneously increases the demand for social insurance while decreasing the capacity to provide it" (Sutherland, 1998). In the United States, insecurity has increased considerably due to job instability, layoffs, and cutbacks; decreases in the proportion of jobs that provide health and retirement benefits; and abolition of the government's obligation to provide public assistance to those without income (under the label of welfare reform).

Refugees and other immigrants experience lack of security in many aspects of their lives, whereas those who are illegal live in continual insecurity in every aspect of daily living. The threats to security are obvious in the transit and refugee camp stages of migration. However, insecurity continues in places where immigrants may face expulsion or unexpected deportation. Gore (1995) cites the example of migrant workers from Yemen who were working in the Gulf States until they were expelled after the outbreak of the Persian Gulf War in 1991. Insecurity in the Gulf region resulted following the invasion of Kuwait by Iraq and the subsequent U.S. and allied military response; one result was disruption in production and reduced need for guest workers. One million workers were returned to Yemen; two-thirds of them had been out of Yeman for more than 10 years, and an even higher number had no housing or land in Yemen (Gore, 1995). The 1996 changes to U.S. welfare and immigration laws increased the insecurity faced by even long-term legal resident immigrants in the United States; under these laws, they are denied provisions for security in the face of old age and illness that are provided to citizens and may be denied security of country of residence if found to have committed offenses in the distant past. These are just two examples of the large numbers of people around the world who live without security. The linkages among the concepts of *security, social exclusion*, and *human rights* should be apparent. The challenge for social work is to design interventions and policies that improve client security.

It is also undeniable that terrorism, fear of terrorism, and, in many cases, the official response to terrorism have added to personal insecurity. Immigrants and immigration policy have been targeted for intense scrutiny. As Lear Matthews (2002) explained: "immigrants from all levels of the social stratum, who share the pain of Americans (due to September 11th) have been further victimized by attitudes of intolerance, stereotyping, ethnic profiling and stricter immigration policies" (p. 105). There has been selective detention of thousands of immigrants, including foreign students deemed to be a risk. In one of the worst examples, this insecurity cost an immigrant in Britain his life, as police shot and killed an unarmed immigrant from Brazil, thinking he was a terrorist, when he was actually running to catch a train.

Sustainability

The importance of sustainability in interventions is one of the lessons learned from development experience, as discussed in Chapter 3; understanding of its importance has been heightened by increased awareness of environmental limits and resource scarcity. The concept fits well with the ecological perspective in social work, as sustainability requires practice that is sensitive to the interactions among ecosystems, economics, and social and human factors, and a goal of progress that preserves future capacity. Defined by the Sustainability Education Center (1999) as an "evolving paradigm for planning and decision making," sustainability is a useful concept in social work practice at both macro- and microlevels (p. 1).

At the microlevel of practice with individuals and families, attention might focus on ways to ensure that social work interventions can be sustained by the client in terms of the client's capacity to make continuing use of lessons learned through treatment. In family preservation and interventions to improve parenting, for example, the social worker needs to examine whether skills taught are likely to be sustained in terms of their demands on the parent's time, financial resources, energy, literacy, and cultural acceptability. A program for teen mothers in May Pen, Jamaica, teaches the mothers how to use educational toys with their children and how to make the toys from scraps—milk carton blocks decorated with cut-outs from old magazines, for example; these homemade and resource-efficient toys are used in the program, although its grant would pay for expensive developmental toys from abroad. Through this simple strategy, the likelihood of sustainability is increased. Some of the child survival strategies initially favored by development agencies were found to be unsustainable because of the demands on the time of already greatly overworked and undernourished women in Africa. Interventions must match clients' resources—including their literacy, energy, and available time. This is as true in Boston, Massachusetts, and Esbjerg, Denmark, as in Kingston, Jamaica, or Addis Ababa, Ethiopia.

In planning and administering social programs, social workers can also use the concept of sustainability to assess program dependence on material and human resources, including available leadership talent and human energy. Many programs do not survive past the term of outside grants, as they fail to consider availability of ongoing resources. Sustainability, then, is an additional concept that is universal in social work and likely to grow in significance in the face of dwindling funding for human services.

The six concepts introduced above are particularly relevant for linking social work to global action in the twenty-first century. The goal of international social work is to work toward a global society that is just, inclusive, and sustainable (borrowing from Korten & Klauss, 1984). There are many opportunities to do this on a microlevel through individual practice. There are also ways to work together as part of global civil society to create larger scale change.

GLOBAL CIVIL SOCIETY AND HUMAN SOCIAL CHANGE

An often-positive force in the context of globalization is international or transnational civil society—the activities of nongovernmental bodies and of the citizenry of the world as independent of their governments. *International civil society* is defined as "all the complex relationships and political processes that lie outside national territory and the control of national states" (Olsen, 1996, p. 335). *International civil society* refers to those nongovernmental/

nonprofit organizations or coalitions that have cross-border linkages (Florini, 2000). The development of international civil society has been fueled by globalization and by advancements in communication technology that facilitate planning, negotiating, and lobbying without face-to-face contact. As one author put it, "the global social exclusion it (globalization) generates has deleterious social effects but also tends to create a range of countermovements within society" (Munck, 2005, pp. 164–165). Using the tools of "credible information and moral authority" civil society organizations and movements have been important in focusing public attention on global issues and in getting issues on the agendas of the international intergovernmental organizations (Florini, 2000).

Not all civil society efforts have been positive, as there are also global hate networks, and there are some concerns about lack of transparency and accountability. In general, however, "transnational civil society can serve humanity well" (Florini, 2000, p. 236). Indeed, the very existence of many global organizations suggests more attention to the global dimension for the future and encourages more global mindedness.

> The main forms of genuinely transformative social action derive from the range of social movements seeking to counter the hegemony of neo-liberal globalization and to gain social control over the free market.... They are all based on democratic empowerment and point in the direction of social and political transformation of the dominant order. (Munck, 2005, p. 165)

The concept of *global responsibility* is at the core of international civil society (Olsen, 1996). In an international civil society, *citizenship* takes on new meaning and has global dimensions. Lorenz applies the term *committed citizenship* to the role that social workers can play globally in integrating rights and humanitarian obligations through action. This is related to the ethic of "humane internationalism," defined as "an acceptance by the citizens of the industrialized states that they have ethical obligations towards those beyond their borders and that these in turn impose obligations upon their governments" (Pratt, as quoted in Olsen, 1996, p. 336). What these ideas suggest is growing strength of public opinion and nongovernmental forces in international policy and action. This in turn suggests increased avenues for social work impact, first as citizens, but more important, as professionals acting through nongovernmental organizations (NGOs) and civil society movements, including the international professional organizations, to channel this humane internationalism into action on world problems.

Humane internationalism would influence how social workers think about a broad range of policies, from immigration policies and intercountry adoption to more macro-issues of trade and aid relationships. An important focus for international social work professional action is to bear witness to the failures of the market and to work to improve the well-being and inclusion of those who are at risk of being left behind by globalization. UN Development Programme (UNDP) reports since the early 1990s have underscored that global interdependence demands action to address equity issues and have warned of overemphasis on global economic efficiency (as discussed in Olsen, 1996). NGOs and citizens may serve as important counterweights to the forces of global capitalism; social workers who "see and work with the consequences of these processes" can assist by encouraging political and economic behaviors that are sensitive to the global village (IFSW, 2004). In discussing growing international links within social work, Noble (2004) noted that these provide an important "link into activist work at the local, national and international level by providing educators and practitioners across the globe with an international mandate to help moderate the impact of international economic expansion" (p. 528). The linkages discussed in Chapter 13 are important within the profession and in multidisciplinary civil society movements.

Threat of New Isolationism?

There is much to celebrate in terms of the social work profession's renewed interest and activity on the international scene over the past decade. After a period of neglect of international concerns, the profession is now engaged in globally focused scholarship, education, and action. Renewed isolationism within nations and within the profession are possible threats to this progress. In the post–September 11, 2001, environment, there is a danger that fear of terrorism will generalize into fear of the foreign, making international connections more difficult. A newspaper article reported that the U.S. government may now view international contact as suspect (D'Arcy, 2003). The investigation cited cases of scientists/researchers who were denied security clearances because of their international ties. In some cases, these are family ties; in others, the ties are professional, such as those encouraged to promote international social work. One citizen was denied a security clearance when "an investigation showed that she had relatives in Iran with whom she maintained regular contact." In a second case, an American researcher who had studied and worked abroad "remained friendly with his former colleagues." "Though his correspondence 'may be relatively infrequent, the totality of the applicant's contacts with various foreign citizens are not minor or trivial' the decision read" (D'Arcy, 2003, p. A5). In this case, the scholar's period of study and friends were at a Swedish university, and he had helped organize a scholarly conference in Brazil. Although the cases cited affected scientists, social work may ultimately be affected in multiple ways. The implication for transnational families, either clients or professionals, that maintaining family contact makes one suspect is a highly dangerous assumption. And the suggestion that maintaining contact with colleagues across national boundaries reflects negatively on a professional threatens to undermine the international connections that are essential for international social work. Although the cases cited occurred in the United States, the growing "fortress Europe," the rise of fundamentalism and xenophobia in many areas are other manifestations of fear of the foreign. It is easy for social work to turn inward, as each nation has more than enough social problems to occupy its professionals. As I have emphasized in this book, it is important not to succumb to this temptation in the era of globalization.

CONCLUSION: REVISITING INTERNATIONAL SOCIAL WORK

Since the publication of the first edition of this book in 2001, interest in international social work has grown. More and more scholars are contributing to the knowledge base and to the ongoing debates about the definition and goals of international social work. I have retained my original definition of *international social work* as emphasizing professional international action in a globalized world. The challenges posed by globalization and the ongoing struggles to achieve social inclusion and human rights also require that a direction or purpose be added to the definition, so that international social work is action directed toward a more just, peaceful, human rights–oriented and sustainable social and economic order.

As noted in Chapter 8 and in discussion of the global policies and standards recently emanating from the international professional organizations, there is evidence of what Gray and Fook (2004) called a "quest for universalism in social work" (p. 625). They defined *universal social work* as "a form of social work that transcends national boundaries and which gives social work a global face such that there are commonalities in theory and practice across widely divergent contexts" (p. 628). Yet international social work is not the same as universal social work. International social work indeed transcends national boundaries and gives social work a global face, but more so in terms of actions and presence on the international scene than in terms of sameness or uniformity. While universalism may contest indigenization or multiculturalism, internationalism does not necessarily do so. In fact, successful international social work must embrace multiculturalism, while it struggles with tensions between localism and standards of human rights and well-being, as explored in Chapter 9. Through dialogue and exchange, international social work may well reduce the Western dominance that has long been expressed in social work theory and practice models, as suggested by Noble (2004).

In returning to the deceptively simple question raised by Akimoto (1995) many years ago—whether a practice is considered international social work if done by a social worker from the United States in Japan but domestic practice if done by a Japanese social worker—we realize that the answer is: It depends. It is possible that the practice is simply social work practice in Japan. The practice is international social work if it involves bilateral, multilateral, or global relationships, social policies, or problems. Using the definition in this book, social work done in Japan by a Japanese social worker can also be international social work if it focuses on internationally related issues. And, in the case of our fictitious social worker from the United States, his or her practice may take on international dimensions after the fact if, on returning home, he or she introduces innovations learned during the stay in Japan.

Some have also argued that all social work in the twenty-first century is international social work. Looking forward to the next 5–10 years of theory and practice development, I concur with Lyons, Manion, and Carlsen (2006) that there is value in recognizing international social work as a specialization, while continuing to emphasize the critical impact of globalization on local social work practice:

> There is scope for some development of specialist knowledge and personnel, and that those engaged in social work education and research, and in national and professional associations, bear some responsibility for developing this area, as well as identifying the implications of globalization for local practice. (p. 204)

As another scholar put it, "the trend towards globalization is forcing social work to theorise its position as an internationalizing discipline outside its localized borders" (Noble, 2004, p. 529). Thus, theory and practice development in international social work is essential while exploring and highlighting the universal relevance of global awareness and knowledge to the profession.

Social work has been involved in global movements to improve human well-being and social conditions almost since its inception. In its second century, the profession must exert expanded leadership for humane global change, human rights, and development. The agenda of global social issues needing social work attention is long and challenging; the viability and standing of the profession in the globalized world require bold and vigorous pursuit of opportunities for international professional action.

REFERENCES

After the riots. (2005, December 17). *The Economist*, pp. 47–48.

Akimoto, I. (1995). *Towards the establishment of an international social work/social welfare concept*. Unpublished paper. Japan Women's University, Kanagawa, Japan.

Asamoah, Y., Healy, L. M., & Mayadas, N. (1997). Ending the international-domestic dichotomy: New approaches to a global curriculum for the millennium. *Journal of Social Work Education, 33*(2), 389–401.

Ayton-Shenker, D. (1995). The challenge of human rights and cultural diversity. In *Human rights: United Nations background note*. New York: United Nations Department of Public Information.

D'Arcy, J. (2003, July 14). New hurdles for security clearance. *The Hartford Courant*, p. A1, A5.

Florini, A. M. (Ed.). (2000). *The third force: The rise of transnational civil society*. Washington, DC: Japan Center for International Exchange (Tokyo) and the Carnegie Endowment for International Peace.

Gore, C. (1995). Introduction: Markets, citizenship and social exclusion. In G. Rodgers, C. Gore, & J. B. Figueiredo (Eds.), *Social exclusion: Rhetoric, reality, responses* (pp. 1–40). Geneva, Switzerland: International Labour Organization (International Institute for Labour Studies).

Gray, M., & Fook, J. (2004). The quest for a universal social work: Some issues and implications. *Social Work Education, 23*(5), 625–644.

Gutierrez, L., Fredricksen, K., & Soifer, S. (1999). Perspectives of social work faculty on diversity and societal oppression content: Results from a national survey. *Journal of Social Work Education, 35*(3), 409–419.

International Federation of Social Workers. (2004). Globalization and the environment. *Policy Papers.* Accessed June 24, 2007, at www.ifsw.org.

Korten, D. C., & Klauss, R. (1984). *People centered development: Contributions toward theory and planning frameworks.* West Hartford, CT: Kumarian Press.

Lorenz, W. (1994). *Social work in a changing Europe.* London: Routledge.

Lyons, K., Manion, K., & Carlsen, M. (2006). *International perspectives on social work: Global conditions and local practice.* Houndsmills, UK: Palgrave MacMillan.

Manning, R. D. (1995). Multiculturalism in the United States: Clashing concepts, changing demographics and competing cultures. *International Journal of Group Tensions, 25*(2), 117–168.

Matthews, L. (2002). Coping in the aftermath of the World Trade Center tragedy: An immigrant perspective. *Journal of Immigrant and Refugee Services, 1*(2), 101–108.

Mehta, V. (1997). Ethnic conflict and violence in the modern world: Social work's role in building peace. In M. C. Hokenstad & J. Midgley (Eds.), *Issues in international social work* (pp. 92–109). Washington, DC: NASW Press.

Midgley, J. (1999). Social development in social work: Learning from global dialogue. In C. S. Ramanathan & R. J. Link (Eds.), *All our futures: Principles and resources for social work practice in a global era* (pp. 193–205). Belmont, CA: Brooks-Cole.

Mishra, R. (2005). Social rights as human rights: Globalizing social protection. *International Social Work, 48*(1), 9–20.

Munck, R. (2005). *Globalization and social exclusion: A transformationalist perspective.* Bloomfield, CT: Kumarian Press.

Noble, C. (2004). Social work education, training and standards in the Asia-Pacific region. *Social Work Education, 23*(5), 517–536.

Olsen, G. R. (1996). Public opinion, international civil society and North-South policy since the cold war. In O. Stokke (Ed.), *Foreign aid towards the year 2000: Experience and challenges* (pp. 333–354). London: Frank Cass Co., Ltd.

Rodgers, G. (1995). What is special about a social exclusion approach? In G. Rodgers, C. Gore, & J. B. Figueiredo (Eds.), *Social exclusion: Rhetoric, reality, responses* (pp. 43–55). Geneva, Switzerland: International Labour Organization (International Institute for Labour Studies).

Rodgers, G., Gore, C., & Figueiredo, J. B. (Eds.). (1995). *Social exclusion: Rhetoric, reality, responses.* Geneva, Switzerland: International Labour Organization (International Institute for Labor Studies).

Sustainability Education Center. (1999). The SEC goals. New York: American Forum for Global Education. Accessed January 7, 2000, at www.globaled.org/sustain/sustain.html

Sutherland, P. D. (1998). Answering globalization's challenges. Overseas Development Council Commentary. Accessed January 6, 2000, at www.odc.org/commentarypdsview.html

Ethics in Social Work: Statement of Principles

International Federation of Social Workers and International Association of Schools of Social Work (2000)

1. PREFACE

Ethical awareness is a fundamental part of the professional practice of social workers. Their ability and commitment to act ethically is an essential aspect of the quality of the service offered to those who use social work services. The purpose of the work of IASSW and IFSW on ethics is to promote ethical debate and reflection in the member organizations, among the providers of social work in member countries, as well as in the schools of social work and among social work students. Some ethical challenges and problems facing social workers are specific to particular countries; others are common. By staying at the level of general principles, the joint IASSW and IFSW statement aims to encourage social workers across the world to reflect on the challenges and dilemmas that face them and make ethically informed decisions about how to act in each particular case. Some of these problem areas include:

The fact that the loyalty of social workers is often in the middle of conflicting interests.

The fact that social workers function as helpers and controllers.

The conflicts between the duty of social workers to protect the interests of the people with whom they work and societal demands for efficiency and utility.

The fact that resources in society are limited.

This document takes as its starting place the definition of social work adopted separately by the IFSW and IASSW at their respective General Meetings in Montreal, Canada, in July 2000, and then agreed jointly in Copenhagen in May 2001 (Section 2). This definition stresses principles of human rights and social justice. The next section (3) makes reference to the various declarations and conventions on human rights that are relevant to social work, followed by a statement of general ethical principles under the two broad headings of human rights and dignity and social justice (Section 4). The final section introduces some basic guidance on ethical conduct in social work, which it is expected will be elaborated by the ethical guidance and in various codes and guidelines of the member organisations of IFSW and IASSW.

2. DEFINITION OF SOCIAL WORK

The social work profession promotes social change, problem solving in human relationships, and the empowerment and liberation of people to enhance well-being. Utilising theories of human behaviour and social systems, social work intervenes at the points where people interact with their environments. Principles of human rights and social justice are fundamental to social work.

3. INTERNATIONAL CONVENTIONS

International human rights declarations and conventions form common standards of achievement, and recognize rights that are accepted by the global community. Documents particularly relevant to social work practice and action are:

Universal Declaration of Human Rights

The International Covenant on Civil and Political Rights

The International Covenant on Economic Social and Cultural Rights

The Convention on the Elimination of All Forms of Racial Discrimination

The Convention on the Elimination of All Forms of Discrimination against Women

The Convention on the Rights of the Child

Indigenous and Tribal Peoples Convention (ILO Convention 169)

4. PRINCIPLES

4.1 Human Rights and Human Dignity

Social work is based on respect for the inherent worth and dignity of all people, and the rights that follow from this. Social workers should uphold and defend each person's physical, psychological, emotional, and spiritual integrity and well-being. This means:

1. Respecting the right to self-determination—Social workers should respect and promote people's right to make their own choices and decisions, irrespective of their values and life choices, provided this does not threaten the rights and legitimate interests of others.

2. Promoting the right to participation—Social workers should promote the full involvement and participation of people using their services in ways that enable them to be empowered in all aspects of decisions and actions affecting their lives.

3. Treating each person as a whole—Social workers should be concerned with the whole person, within the family, community, societal and natural environments and should seek to recognize all aspects of a person's life.

4. Identifying and developing strengths—Social workers should focus on the strengths of all individuals, groups, and communities and thus promote their empowerment.

4.2 Social Justice

Social workers have a responsibility to promote social justice, in relation to society generally, and in relation to the people with whom they work. This means

1. Challenging negative discrimination*—Social workers have a responsibility to challenge negative discrimination on the basis of characteristics such as ability, age, culture, gender or sex, marital status, socioeconomic status, political opinions, skin color, racial or other physical characteristics, sexual orientation, or spiritual beliefs.

   In some countries the term "discrimination" would be used instead of "negative discrimination." The word negative is used here because in some countries the term "positive discrimination" is also used. Positive discrimination is also known as "affirmative action." Positive discrimination or affirmative action means positive steps taken to redress the effects of historical discrimination against the groups named in 4.2.1 above.

2. Recognising diversity—Social workers should recognise and respect the ethnic and cultural diversity of the societies in which they practice, taking account of individual, family, group and community differences.

3. Distributing resources equitably—Social workers should ensure that resources at their disposal are distributed fairly, according to need.

4. Challenging unjust policies and practices—Social workers have a duty to bring to the attention of their employers, policy makers, politicians and the general public situations where resources are inadequate or where distribution of resources, policies and practices are oppressive, unfair or harmful.

5. Working in solidarity—Social workers have an obligation to challenge social conditions that contribute to social exclusion, stigmatization or subjugation, and to work towards an inclusive society.

5. PROFESSIONAL CONDUCT

It is the responsibility of the national organizations in membership of IFSW and IASSW to develop and regularly update their own codes of ethics or ethical guidelines, to be consistent with the IFSW/IASSW statement. It is also the responsibility of national organizations to inform social workers and schools of social work about these codes or guidelines. Social workers should act in accordance with the ethical code or guidelines current in their country. These will generally include more detailed guidance in ethical practice specific to the national context. The following general guidelines on professional conduct apply.

1. Social workers are expected to develop and maintain the required skills and competence to do their job.

2. Social workers should not allow their skills to be used for inhumane purposes, such as torture or terrorism.

3. Social workers should act with integrity. This includes not abusing the relationship of trust with the people using their services, recognising the boundaries between personal and professional life, and not abusing their position for personal benefit or gain.

4. Social workers should act in relation to the people using their services with compassion, empathy and care.

5. Social workers should not subordinate the needs or interests of people who use their services to their own needs or interests.

6. Social workers have a duty to take necessary steps to care for themselves professionally and personally in the workplace and in society, in order to ensure that they are able to provide appropriate services.

7. Social workers should maintain confidentiality regarding information about people who use their services. Exceptions to this may only be justified on the basis of a greater ethical requirement (such as the preservation of life).

8. Social workers need to acknowledge that they are accountable for their actions to the users of their services, the people they work with, their colleagues, their employers, the professional association, and to the law, and that these accountabilities may conflict.

9. Social workers should be willing to collaborate with the schools of social work in order to support social work students to get practical training of good quality and up to date practical knowledge.

10. Social workers should foster and engage in ethical debate with their colleagues and employers and take responsibility for making ethically informed decisions.

11. Social workers should be prepared to state the reasons for their decisions based on ethical considerations, and be accountable for their choices and actions.

12. Social workers should work to create conditions in employing agencies and in their countries where the principles of this statement and those of their own national code (if applicable) are discussed, evaluated and upheld.

Approved by the General Meeting of the International Federation of Social Workers and the General Assembly of the International Association of Schools of Social Work in October 2004 in Adelaide, Australia.

For more information, see www.ifsw.org or www.iassw-aiets.org

APPENDIX B

United Nations Millennium Development Goals and Targets

Adopted in 2000 by the United Nations

INTRODUCTION

The Millennium Development Goals, or MDGs, emanate from the Millennium Declaration, a resolution adopted by the General Assembly of the United Nations at the close of the Millennium Summit held from September 6–8, 2000. The MDGs express a set of goals and targets (some more measurable than others) to reduce human misery and preserve the environment for a sustainable future. The goals and the Millennium Declaration state the need for partnership among all countries, regardless of their economic status. In general, however, Goals 1–7 relate to the situation in developing countries, while Goal 8 identifies the agenda for a fairer world system of trade and resource allocation. The MDGs have been published in many formats; the following was taken from the *Human Development Report 2003* published by the United Nations Development Program.

"Goal 1: Eradicate extreme poverty and hunger
  Target 1: Halve between 1990 and 2015, the proportion of people whose income is less than $1 per day.
  Target 2: Halve, between 1990 and 2015, the proportion of people who suffer from hunger.
  Goal 2: Achieve universal primary education.
  Target 3: Ensure that by 2015, children everywhere, boys and girls alike, will be able to complete a full course of primary schooling.
  Goal 3: Promote gender equality and empower women.
  Target 4: Eliminate gender disparity in primary and secondary education, preferably by 2005 and in all levels of education no later than 2015.
  Goal 4: Reduce child mortality.
  Target 5: Reduce by two-thirds, between 1990 and 2015, the under-five mortality rate.
  Goal 5: Improve maternal health.
  Target 6: Reduce by three-quarters, between 1990 and 2015, the maternal mortality ratio.
  Goal 6: Combat HIV/AIDS, malaria and other diseases.
  Target 7: Have halted by 2015 and begin to reserve the spread of HIV/AIDS.
  Target 8: Have halted by 2015 and begun to reserve the incidence of malaria and other major diseases.

Goal 7: Ensure environmental sustainability.

Target 9: Integrate the principles of sustainable development into country policies and programmes and reserve the loss of environmental resources.

Target 10: Halve by 2015 the proportion of people without sustainable access to safe drinking water.

Target 11: Have achieved by 2020 a significant improvement in the lives of at least 100 million slum dwellers.

Goal 8: Develop a global partnership for development.

Target 12: Develop further an open, rule-based, predictable, non-discriminatory trading and financial system (includes a commitment to good governance, development and poverty reduction—both nationally and internationally).

Target 13: Address the special needs of the least developed countries (includes tariff and quota-free access for exports, enhanced program of debt relief for and cancellation of official bilateral debt, and more generous official development assistance for countries committed to poverty reduction).

Target 14: Address the special needs of land-locked countries and small island developing states (through the Program of Action for the Sustainable Development of Small Island Development States and 22nd General Assembly provisions).

Target 15: Deal comprehensively with the debt problems of developing countries through national and international measures in order to make debt sustainable in the long term.

Target 16: In cooperation with developing countries, develop and implement strategies for decent and productive work for youth.

Target 17: In cooperation with pharmaceutical companies, provide access to affordable essential drugs in developing countries.

Target 18: In cooperation with the private sector, make available the benefits of new technologies, especially information and communications technologies."

Source: United Nations Development Programme. (2003). *Human development report 2003.* New York: Oxford University Press for UNDP, pp. 1–3.

APPENDIX C

United Nations Summit for Social Development—Ten Commitments

1. We commit ourselves to creating an economic, political, social, cultural and legal environment that will enable people to achieve social development.

2. We commit ourselves to the goal of eradicating poverty in the world, through decisive national actions and international cooperation, as an ethical, social, political and economic imperative of humankind.

3. We commit ourselves to promoting the goal of full employment as a basic priority of our economic and social policies, and to enabling all men and women to attain secure and sustainable livelihoods through freely chosen productive employment and work.

4. We commit ourselves to promoting social integration by fostering societies that are stable, safe and just and that are based on the promotion and protection of all human rights, as well as on non-discrimination, tolerance, respect for diversity, equality of opportunity, solidarity, security and participation of all people, including disadvantaged and vulnerable groups and persons.

5. We commit ourselves to promoting full respect for human dignity and to achieving equality and equity between women and men, and to recognizing and enhancing the participation and leadership roles of women in political, civil, economic, social and cultural life and in development.

6. We commit ourselves to promoting and attaining the goals of universal and equitable access to quality education, the highest attainable standard of physical and mental health and the access of all to primary health care, making particular efforts to rectify inequalities relating to social conditions and without distinction as to race, national origin, gender, age or disability, respecting and promoting our common and particular cultures; striving to strengthen the role of culture in development; preserving the essential bases of people-centered sustainable development; and contributing to the full development of human resources and to social development. The purpose of these activities is to eradicate poverty, promote full and productive employment and foster social integration.

7. We commit ourselves to accelerating the economic, social and human resource development of Africa and the least developed countries.

8. We commit ourselves to ensuring that when structural adjustment programmes are agreed to they include social development goals, in particular eradicating poverty, promoting full and productive employment and enhancing social integration.

9. We commit ourselves to increasing significantly and/or utilizing more efficiently the resources allocated to social development in order to achieve the goals of the Summit through national action and regional and international cooperation.

10. We commit ourselves to an improved and strengthened framework for international, regional and subregional cooperation for social development, in a spirit of partnership, through the United Nations and other multilateral institutions.

United Nations (1995). *The Copenhagen Declaration and Programme of Action.* World Summit for Social Development. 6–12 March 1995. New York: Author.

Human Development Index Rankings for Countries

The Human Development Index (HDI) is a widely accepted measure of countries' achievements as measured by selected basic development indicators: gross domestic product (GDP) per capita, life expectancy, and literacy/school enrollment. HDI rankings are more commonly cited, indicating countries' relative standings. The indices and rankings are updated yearly by the United Nations Development Programme (UNDP). Below are the most recent HDI rankings for the 177 countries with sufficient data to generate indices.

RANK	COUNTRY
High Human Development	
1	Norway
2	Iceland
3	Australia
4	Ireland
5	Sweden
6	Canada
7	Japan
8	United States
9	Switzerland
10	Netherlands
11	Finland
12	Luxembourg
13	Belgium
14	Austria
15	Denmark
16	France
17	Italy
18	United Kingdom
19	Spain
20	New Zealand
21	Germany
22	Hong Kong

(continued)

RANK	COUNTRY
	High Human Development
23	Israel
24	Greece
25	Singapore
26	Korea, Republic of
27	Slovenia
28	Portugal
29	Cyprus
30	Czech Republic
31	Barbados
32	Malta
33	Kuwait
34	Brunei Darussalam
35	Hungary
36	Argentina
37	Poland
38	Chile
39	Bahrain
40	Estonia
41	Lithuania
42	Slovakia
43	Uruguay
44	Croatia
45	Latvia
46	Qatar
47	Seychelles
48	Costa Rica
49	United Arab Emirates
50	Cuba
51	Saint Kitts and Nevis
52	Bahamas
53	Mexico
54	Bulgaria
55	Tonga
56	Oman
57	Trinidad and Tobago
58	Panama
59	Antigua and Arbuda
60	Romania
61	Malaysia
62	Bosnia and Herzegovina
63	Mauritius

(*continued*)

RANK	COUNTRY
Medium Human Development	
64	Libyan Arab Jamahriya
65	Russian Federation
66	Macedonia, the former Yugoslav Republic of
67	Belarus
68	Dominica
69	Brazil
70	Colombia
71	Saint Lucia
72	Venezuela, Bolivian Republic of
73	Albania
74	Thailand
75	Samoa (Western)
76	Saudi Arabia
77	Ukraine
78	Lebanon
79	Kazakhstan
80	Armenia
81	China
82	Peru
83	Ecuador
84	Philippines
85	Grenada
86	Jordan
87	Tunisia
88	Saint Vincent and the Grenadines
89	Suriname
90	Fiji
91	Paraguay
92	Turkey
93	Sri Lanka
94	Dominican Republic
95	Belize
96	Iran, Islamic Republic of
97	Georgia
98	Maldives
99	Azerbaijan
100	Occupied Palestinian Territories
101	El Salvador
102	Algeria
103	Guyana

(*continued*)

RANK	COUNTRY
	Medium Human Development
104	Jamaica
105	Turkmenistan
106	Cape Verde
107	Syrian Arab Republic
108	Indonesia
109	Viet Nam
110	Krgyzstan
111	Egypt
112	Nicaragua
113	Uzbekistan
114	Moldova, Republic of
115	Bolivia
116	Mongolia
117	Honduras
118	Guatemala
119	Vanatu
120	Equatorial Guinea
121	South Africa
122	Tajikistan
123	Morocco
124	Gabon
125	Namibia
126	India
127	Sao Tome and Principe
128	Solomon Islands
129	Cambodia
130	Myanmar
131	Botswana
132	Comoros
133	Lao People's Democratic Republlic
134	Pakistan
135	Bhutan
136	Ghana
137	Bangladesh
138	Nepal
139	Papua New Guinea
140	Congo
141	Sudan
142	Timor-Leste
143	Madagascar
144	Cameroon
145	Uganda

(*continued*)

RANK	COUNTRY
	Medium Human Development
146	Swaziland
147	Togo
148	Djibouti
149	Lesotho
150	Yemen
151	Zimbabwe
152	Kenya
153	Mauritania
154	Haiti
155	Gambia
156	Senegal
157	Eritrea
158	Rwanda
159	Nigeria
160	Guinea
161	Angola
162	Tanzania, United Republic of
163	Benin
164	Cote d'Ivoire
165	Zambia
166	Malawi
167	Congo, Democratic Republic of the
168	Mozambique
169	Burundi
170	Ethiopia
171	Chad
172	Central Africa Republic
173	Guinea-Bissau
174	Burkina Faso
175	Mali
176	Sierra Leone
177	Niger

Source: United Nations Development Programme. (2006). *Human Development Report 2006.* New York: Palgrave-Macmillan for UNDP.

(Insufficient data did not allow for computation of an HDI for the following UN member countries: Afghanistan, Andorra, Iraq, Kiribati, Democratic Republic of Korea, Liberia, Liechtenstein, Marshall Islands, Federated States of Micronesia, Monaco, Montenegro, Nauru, Palau, San Marino, Serbia, Somalia, and Tuvalu.)

Milestones in the International History of Social Work Around the World

1856	European International Conference on Charity and Welfare initiated.
1861	International Red Cross founded in Switzerland.
1869	Charity Organization Society founded in London.
1873	Octavia Hill conducts first training programs for social workers in England.
1877	Charity Organization Society begins in Buffalo, New York.
1884	Toynbee Hall opens in London.
1889	Hull House opens in Chicago.
1895	First paid employed social worker, Mary Stewart, is hired by the Royal Free Hospital in London.
1898	A 6-week summer training course for social workers in held in New York.
1899	The first school of social work in the world is opened in Amsterdam. The Institute for Social Work Training offered a full 2-year course, including fieldwork.
	A training course for young women interested in social work is organized in Germany by Alice Salomon.
1903	The School of Sociology, a 2-year social work course, grows out of the London Charity Organization Society trainings.
1904	The New York School of Philanthropy is founded (later to become the Columbia University School of Social Work).
1908	First school of social work in Germany is founded by Alice Salomon.
1909	Social workers from several countries meet at the International Congress of Women in Canada.
1915	Jane Addams attends the Women's Peace Conference at The Hague and then travels to Berlin to meet with the German chancellor in an attempt to convince him to end World War I hostilities. Other delegates travel to other capitals involved in the war of nations.
1917	*Social Diagnosis* by Mary Richmond is published. The book has a significant impact on the professionalization of social work in Europe as well as the United States.
1919	Save the Children Fund is founded by Eglantyne Jebb in England.
	The International Labour Organization (ILO) is founded under the auspices of the League of Nations. It is the oldest of the UN specialized agencies.

1921	International Migration Service is founded with headquarters in Geneva and New York. It is later renamed International Social Service.
	Ida Pruitt begins medical social work services in a hospital in Beijing, China.
1922	Social work training is started in a new sociology department at Yanjing University in Beijing, with the assistance of Princeton University.
1924	The Declaration on the Rights of the Child, authored by Eglantyne Jebb, is adopted by the League of Nations.
	The first school of social work in Africa is opened at the University of Cape Town in South Africa.
1925	The first school of social work in Latin America is opened in Santiago, Chile.
	The Training School for Social Work is founded at the Free University of Poland in Warsaw by Madame Helene Radlinska.
1926	Nagpada Neighborhood House, a settlement house, is opened in Bombay, India, by Dr. Clifford Manshardt.
1928	The First International Conference of Social Work is held in Paris.
	The International Conference of Social Work (ICSW) and the International Permanent Secretariat of Social Workers, predecessor to the International Federation of Social Workers (IFSW), are founded.
1928	First world definition of social work.
1929	The International Association of Schools of Social Work (IASSW) is formed with 46 member schools in 10 countries (although it originated through the 1928 conference).
1931	Jane Addams is awarded the Nobel Peace Prize.
1932	Alice Salomon is awarded the Silver Medal for Merit to the State by the Prussian Cabinet, and the School she founded is named the Alice Salomon School of Social Work.
1936	The Tata Institute of Social Sciences is founded in Bombay, the first school of social work in India.
	Egypt opens its first school of social work in Cairo.
1937	The first International Survey of Social Work Education is published. The survey is conducted by Alice Salomon and funded by the Russell Sage Foundation.
	Alice Salomon, stripped of all honors and her name removed from the school of social work, is expelled from Germany by the Gestapo and begins life in exile in New York.
1938	The Moyne Commission, set up as a result of unrest in Jamaica, leads to expansion of social welfare and community development in the then British West Indies.
1939	The first technical assistance program of the U.S. government brings social work educators from Latin America to the United States for training.
1939–46	All international meetings of social workers are suspended, including the 4th International Conference planned for 1940.

1941	The Jan H. Hofmeyr School of Social Work is established in South Africa, the first school of social work for South African nonwhites.
1943	United Nations Relief and Rehabilitation Administration (UNRRA) is founded by 44 nations to solve the relief needs of the 35 countries invaded by Axis powers in World War II.
1944–47	Many social workers contribute to relief efforts in Europe and China through the UNRRA.
1945	The United Nations is founded with 51 nations as members of the General Assembly.
	The World Health Organization (WHO) is established at the request of Brazil at the founding convention of the UN.
1946	UNICEF (UN Children's Fund) is founded.
1948	The UN adopts the Universal Declaration of Human Rights.
1950	First United Nations Survey of Social Work Education is published, authored by Katherine Kendall.
1952	Social work and other social sciences are abolished as fields of study in the People's Republic of China.
1955	Second UN Survey of Social Work Education is published.
1956	International Federation of Social Workers is founded.
1958	*Training for Social Work: Third International Survey* is published by the UN. A landmark study, it explored the nature of social work and was authored by Eileen Younghusband.
1958	The journal *International Social Work* is launched by IASSW and ICSW (joined by IFSW in 1959).
1962	U.S. Council on Social Work Education adopts a curriculum policy statement requiring students to gain knowledge of international issues.
1963–68	U.S. Department of State appoints social welfare attachés to the U.S. embassies in Brazil (Mary Catherine Jennings) and India (Ruby Pernell).
1968	The United Nations International Conference of Ministers Responsible for Social Welfare is held.
1969	The UN adopts the Convention on the Elimination of All Forms of Racial Discrimination.
1971	The Fifth Survey of Social Work Education is published by the UN.
1976	The International Code of Ethics is adopted by the International Federation of Social Workers at its meeting in Puerto Rico.
1977–78	The Inter-University Consortium for International Social Development is founded (date uncertain) (now the ICSD).
1979	The UN adopts the Convention on the Elimination of All Forms of Discrimination Against Women.
1980s	Social Work reestablished in China and parts of Eastern Europe.
1987	The UN Interregional Consultation on Developmental Social Welfare Policy and Programmes is held in Vienna, Austria.
1988	IFSW publishes a set of policy papers for social work on global issues.

1989   The UN adopts the Convention on the Rights of the Child.

1994   *Human Rights and Social Work: A Manual for Schools of Social Work and the Social Work Profession* is published by the United Nations. It is the result of an IFSW/IASSW/UN project.

          A Revised Code of Ethical Principles is adopted by IFSW at its meeting in Sri Lanka.

1995   The World Summit for Social Development is held in Copenhagen, Denmark.

1996   IFSW issues a policy statement on Human Rights.

2000   IFSW adopts a new definition of social work.

2000   World leaders adopt the United Nations Millennium Declaration and the Millennium Development Goals.

2004   IFSW and IASSW adopt *Ethics in Social Work: Statement of Principles*, a revised global ethics document.

2004   IASSW and IFSW adopt *Global Standards for Social Work Education and Training*.

2006   UN General Assembly adopts the *Convention on the Rights of Persons with Disabilities*, the first major human rights convention of the twenty-first century.

2007   IFSW declares March 27, 2007, the First World Social Work Day.

Glossary of Terms and Abbreviations

AASW American Association of Social Workers; one of the predecessor organizations to NASW

ACF Administration for Children and Families (within DHHS)

AFSC American Friends Service Committee

AID Agency for International Development; the foreign assistance agency of the US government

Bilateral aid aid given from a donor country directly to a recipient country

CARE Cooperative for American Relief Everywhere; a U.S.-based relief and development NGO, now known only by its acronym

CASW Canadian Association of Social Workers

CEDAW Convention on the Elimination of All Forms of Discrimination Against Women

CIDA Canadian International Development Agency; the foreign assistance agency of the Canadian government

CIP Council of International Programs

COS Charity Organization Society

CRC Convention on the Rights of the Child

CSWE Council on Social Work Education; professional association for social work education in the United States

DAWN Development Alternatives With Women for a New Era (based in Barbados)

DCF Department of Children and Families (an agency of the State of Connecticut, USA)

Debt service interest and principal due on a loan

Devaluation lowering the value of a country's currency relative to other world currencies

DHEW Department of Health, Education and Welfare; former agency of the U.S. government, it has been divided into DHHS and the Department of Education

DHHS Department of Health and Human Services, U.S. government agency

DHR Division for Humanitarian Response (Save the Children's relief division)

ECOSOC Economic and Social Council (UN)

Erasmus a program initiated by the EU in 1987 that funded faculty and student exchanges and other activities among educational institutions in the EU countries; the program was in effect for a decade and was intended to contribute to professional mobility and to development of a European perspective

EU European Union

FAO Food and Agriculture Organization (UN)

FGM Female genital mutilation; term for female circumcision used by those opposed to the practice

GDP gross domestic product

GGLS Group Guaranteed Lending and Savings

GNI gross national income

GNP gross national product

Grameen Bank an NGO based in Bangladesh well known for its microcredit programs

HDI Human Development Index; UNDP's index of progress on human well-being

IASSW International Association of Schools of Social Work

IBRD International Bank for Reconstruction; part of the World Bank Group

ICSD International Consortium for Social Development (formerly IUCISD)

ICSW International Council on Social Welfare

ICVA International Council of Voluntary Agencies

IDA International Development Association; part of the World Bank Group

IFSW International Federation of Social Workers

ILO International Labour Organization

IMF International Monetary Fund

Indigenization the process of adapting ideas, materials, or innovations to make them culturally relevant or of creating indigenous forms that address needs, resources, and culture of a specific country or people

Infant mortality rate annual number of deaths of infants under the age of 1 year per 1,000 live births

InterAction a coalition of more than 150 U.S.-based relief and development NGOs

ISS International Social Service

IUCISD Inter-University Consortium for International Social Development (now ICSD)

Maternal mortality rate annual number of deaths due to pregnancy or childbirth per 100,000 live births

MDG Millennium Development Goal

M&E monitoring and evaluation

Multilateral aid aid provided by contributions of multiple donor countries through an international organization to various recipient countries

NASW National Association of Social Workers; the largest professional association for social workers in the United States

NGO nongovernmental organization

NIC newly industrialized country

Nonaligned a term from the cold war era to refer to countries that were not strongly allied to either the United States, Britain, or their allies or to the Soviet bloc

North roughly geographical, but, more relevantly, a political term referring to industrialized or developed countries (*see* South)

ODA official development assistance

OECD Organization for Economic Co-operation and Development; comprised of the world's most industrialized/developed countries, its aim is to encourage economic cooperation

OPEC Organization of Petroleum Exporting Countries

ORR Office of Refugee Resettlement; part of DHHS

PLAN an NGO focusing on programs for children; formerly known as Foster Parents Plan International

PVO private voluntary organization; a term largely interchangeable with NGO

Rapporteur An official appointed to gather information on a specific topic, usually for limited period of time. The Special Rapporteur on Violence Against Women, for example, was appointed by the UN Commission on Human Rights to report on cases of violence against women

Remittances funds sent by migrants back to family or others in their countries of origin

Repatriation sending refugees back to their countries of origin

SC Save the Children; an international NGO focusing on programs for children

SCI Sara Communication Initiative

SILIC Severely indebted low-income country

Social exclusion a condition of economic and social marginality

Socrates funding program of the EU that replaced Erasmus in 1997; it also funds exchange but places more emphasis on institutional relationships and less on student mobility

South roughly geographical, but, more relevantly, a political term referring to developing countries (*see* North)

Structural adjustment a set of policies imposed as conditions of international loans that require a country to restructure its economy (policies usually include privatization, lower government spending, reduction or elimination of subsidies, and, sometimes, currency devaluation)

Sustainability the preservation of future capacity for development

Tempus similar to the Erasmus program; Tempus funded exchanges between institutions in the EU and those in the countries of the former Soviet Union and Eastern Europe

TOT training of trainers

U-5 mortality rate deaths between birth and exactly 5 years of age per 1,000 live births

UN United Nations

UNAIDS joint UN program on HIV/AIDS; comprised of six UN agencies: UNICEF, UNDP, UNFPA, UNESCO, WHO, and the World Bank Group

UNCTAD UN Conference on Trade and Development

UNDP UN Development Programme

UNESCO UN Educational, Scientific and Cultural Organization

UNFPA UN Fund for Population Activities

UNHCR UN High Commission for Refugees

UNICEF UN Children's Fund

UNIFEM UN Development Fund for Women; has a relationship termed *autonomous association* with UNDP

UNOHCHR United Nations Office of the High Commission for Human Rights

UNRRA UN Relief and Rehabilitation Administration

USAID U.S. Agency for International Development—*see* AID

USIA U.S. Information Agency

WCI Woman/Child Impact

WHO World Health Organization

WTO World Trade Organization

YMCA Young Men's Christian Association

YWCA Young Women's Christian Association

Index